Created and Directed by Hans Höfer

INSIGHT GUIDES

GReece

Edited by Karen Van Dyck
This edition revised by Elizabeth Boleman-Herring

HOUGHTON MIFFLIN COMPANY

APA PUBLICATIONS

Greece

Second Edition (3rd Reprint)
© 1993 APA PUBLICATIONS (HK) LTD
All Rights Reserved
Printed in Singapore by Höfer Press Pte. Ltd

Distributed in the United States by:	Distributed in Canada by:	Distributed in the UK & Ireland by:	Worldwide distribution enquiries:
Houghton Mifflin Company	**Thomas Allen & Son**	**GeoCenter International UK Ltd**	**Höfer Communications Pte Ltd**
2 Park Street	390 Steelcase Road East	The Viables Center, Harrow Way	38 Joo Koon Road
Boston, Massachusetts 02108	Markham, Ontario L3R 1G2	Basingstoke, Hampshire RG22 4BJ	Singapore 2262
ISBN: 0-395-66256-7	ISBN: 0-395-66256-7	ISBN: 9-62421-055-1	ISBN: 9-62421-055-1

ABOUT THIS BOOK

Greece is one of those countries that we all know, or think we know. For centuries, travellers have covered its rocky mountains, ancient cities and myth-laden islands. The cradle of Western culture and Western democracy, it attracts travellers seeking the roots of modern civilization. It is a land that is both hard and soft, with contrasts as sharp as its white-washed houses set against an intense blue sea.

This is an ideal subject for *Insight Guides*, combining into a single volume warm writing, superb photography and sound journalism to prepare, inform and excite the international traveller. This formula for travel journalism is the creation of Hans Höfer, founder of Singapore-based Apa Publications. Höfer, born and raised in Germany, first combined his Bauhaus training in photography, printing and production in the prize-winning volume *Insight Guide: Bali*. That book, published in 1970, was the precursor of the *Insight* and *City Guides* that now cover the world.

Project Editor **Karen Van Dyck** has studied and travelled in Greece since 1977. She translated poetry as part of her doctoral studies at Oxford University. From her many contacts in Greece, she assembled the team for this book, who now take their bow in alphabetical order.

Katerina Anghelaki-Rooke has published seven collections of poems and a number of translations from English and Russian into Greek. She has taught modern Greek poetry at Harvard, the University of Utah and San Francisco State. She received the Greek State prize for poetry in 1986.

David Beatty worked as a researcher on documentaries before becoming a freelance photographer travelling widely in Africa and Asia. His work has appeared in many publications, including *Illustrated London News* and *Time-Life Books*. He has recently photographed *Insight: Tunisia*.

John Chioles's fiction has appeared with the PEN/NEA Syndicated Fiction Project; his version of *Antigone* was produced by Joseph Papp at the New York Shakespeare Festival. He teaches at the

University of Athens and at New York University.

Kay Cicellis is the author of *The Easy Way, Death of a Town* and *No Name in the Street* and the translator of Stratis Tsirkas's *Drifting Cities*.

David Constantine teaches German at Queen's College, Oxford. He has published academic books on Hülderlin and on early travellers to Greece, as well as books of fiction and poetry.

Jane Cowan's work on contemporary Greece began during an undergraduate year abroad in 1975. She continued her studies in sociocultural anthropology and ethnomusicology at Indiana University and returned to Greece for more than two years of fieldwork teaching and to do research for her doctoral dissertation on dance in a Macedonian town.

Sean Damer, a sociologist by training, has done stints as a waiter, trawlerman and mountain guide. His book *The White Mountains: Travels in Western Crete* takes advantage of his mountaineering as well as his sociological skills. He has published numerous articles and has helped prepare television and radio shows.

Markos Dragoumis studied Byzantine Music at Oxford with Egon Wellesz. He is supervisor of the Melpo Merlier Center for Greek Folk Music Studies and heads the Music Department at Athens College. He teaches at the Athens Conservatory and lectures on folk music and *rembetika*.

Dimitri Gondicas lectures in Modern Greek and is assistant chairman of the Committee on Hellenic Studies at Princeton University. An avid hiker, he has climbed most major mountains in Greece.

Kerin Hope, a former archaeologist, is Athens correspondent for London's *Financial Times*.

Nikos Kasdaglis was born on Kos and lives on Rhodes. He has published many well-loved novels and a collection of short stories.

Richard Kindersley went to Oxford in 1967 as a lecturer in Soviet Politics and Eurocommunism at St Antony's College. He is the editor of *In Search of Eurocommunism* and the author of *The First Russian Revisionists*.

Julia Loomis, although trained as a classicist,

| *Van Dyck* | *Anghelaki-Rooke* | *Cicellis* | *Cowan* | *Dragoumis* |

started the Modern Greek programme at Queen's College, CUNY. She was a Fulbright professor at the University of Thessaloniki and is now a freelance writer and travel agent.

Michèle Macrakis spent more than 10 years photographing Greece. In 1981 she was awarded a Fulbright Fellowship to continue her work in Crete documenting the "works and days" of the grape growers. She has contributed her photographic skills to the *New York Times*, UPI, Reuters, *Newsweek International*, *ENA* magazine and to Apa's guides on *Greek Islands* and *Athens*.

Peter Mackridge is a university lecturer in Modern Greek and a Fellow of St Cross College, an Oxford theological school. He is also the author of *The Modern Greek Language*, published by Oxford University Press in 1985. Mackridge has spent much time travelling in Greece and Turkey transcribing disappearing dialects.

Mark Mazower, who read Classics and Philosophy at Oxford, has also studied in Bologna and Athens. He is a research lecturer at Christ Church, Oxford, where he teaches 20th-century Balkan History.

Nelson Moe went to Greece to teach English for a year before embarking on his study of Southern Italy on a Watson fellowship. Although he now teaches English Literature at Naples University, his interest in Greece continues to entangle him in projects such as this guide, for which he was Assistant Project Editor.

David Ricks studied Classics at Oxford and then wrote a doctoral thesis on Modern Greek literature. He is now a research fellow at the University of Birmingham, where he works on medieval and modern Greek literature.

Katy Ricks studied English at Oxford, then taught English at a school in Birmingham.

Anastasia Rubis spent two semesters with College Year in Athens during her undergraduate years at Brown University, and is now advertising manager of the National Tourist Organization of Greece (NTOG).

Lucy Rushton did research in northern Greece for her PhD thesis on religion and identity. Thanks to a post-doctoral grant from Oxford, she was able to continue her work in Greece.

Samantha Stenzel is the cinema editor and a feature writer for *The Athenian*, Greece's English-language monthly magazine. She contributes regularly to a number of American and European publications including *The International Film Guide*, and teaches at the Hellenic-American Union in Athens.

Haris Vlavianos studied Economics and Philosophy at Bristol University and Politics at Oxford. His PhD thesis covered the policy of the Greek Communist Party during the Civil War. He has published three volumes of poetry and two books of translations.

Amanda Weil graduated from Harvard and then worked at the Whitney Museum of Art. She now divides her time between travel photography and her own studio work.

Fay Zika studied Politics, Philosophy and Economics at Oxford, and earned a PhD in Philosophy at the Aristotelian University of Thessaloniki.

Sofka Zinovieff was born in London. She studied social anthropology at Cambridge University, combining work on her PhD with frequent fieldwork visits to Greece.

This latest edition of *Insight: Greece* has been revised and updated by **Elizabeth Boleman-Herring**, publishing editor of the Athens-based *Southeastern Review*. A contributor to several Insight Guides, she has also written Apa's *Pocket Guide to Athens*.

The poem incorporated into "Welcome to Greece" (page 15) is from Olga Broumas's collection *Beginning with O* (Yale University Press).

The publisher and the editor are grateful to the many other individuals and institutions whose assistance and cooperation were invaluable.

We are also grateful to the New York and the London offices of the NTOG and to Olympic Airlines for their generous assistance. And we would like to thank the Athens office of the NTOG for granting permission to reproduce their detailed and useful maps in this volume.

Loomis *Macrakis* *Moe* *Rushton* *Stenzel*

Historical Heritage

Places

Cultural ABCs

Maps

TRAVEL TIPS

**For detailed Information
See Page 317**

WELCOME TO GREECE

Whether you arrive in Greece by boat, train or plane, your first impression as you stretch your legs and climb down the stairs is sure to be of the sun. Glimmering on the water, reflecting off metal and glass, casting shadows, the Mediterranean sun is omnipresent. Like the flash of a hidden camera, the brilliant light catches you unaware and transfixes you.

From the minute you set foot in Greece, you are a part of the Greek landscape – blue sky above, white sand below, the Párthenon, olive groves, a collapsing mosque, a wine festival; whatever the scene, you are in the picture as well. There is a sense that, no matter how many holiday snapshots you may take, Greece will already have taken as many of you.

This country is not merely a holiday resort, ready to satisfy your every desire – it is a population of 10 million people working, eating, arguing, dancing, who will initiate you into the bustle of their everyday life, into the splendour of their mountains, ancient temples and white pebbled shores and into the fellowship of their company. When an older woman offers you a sprig of basil, the traditional gesture of hospitality, she simultaneously introduces you into her world and enters yours. This country is no escape from the everyday; it is an invitation to participate with all your senses, to dive in. A Greek poet remembered it this way:

When the Greek sea
was exceptionally calm
the sun not so much a pinnacle
as a perspiration of light, your brow and the sky
meeting on the horizon, sometimes

you'd dive
from the float, the pier, the stone
promontory, through water so startled
it held the shape of your plunge...

This country is no escape from the everyday, but an excuse to see it, smell it, hear it, feel it, taste it, consider it from another perspective, to roll the basil between your fingers, breathing in its fragrant greeting, and to exchange a smile with this generous woman who has invited you into her world. Just as Greece over the centuries has shaped Western civilization, so it holds the shape of your plunge. Greece's history would be incomplete without you and all the other travellers who have come before you. Welcome to Greece. You are a part of the story that is about to be told.

Preceding pages: basil, a symbol of hospitality; approaching Amorgós; a rural retreat; the Kastellórizo harbour; windmills; a Cretan; the bell towers of the Monastery of St John the Theologian on Patmos. **Left,** passengers descending the gangway of an Aegean ferry.

In Greece the classical past overwhelms you. The visitor's first glimpse of Pláka seems to dissolve the intervening centuries. In a country whose inhabitants proudly remind you of their ancient heritage, it is easy for the newcomer to assume that a simple thread of continuity runs from the ancient world to modern Athens.

But closer acquaintance throws up new historical and linguistic surprises: a crumbling 15th-century house in Pláka offering a reminder of Ottoman Athens, communities to the south of the city where the old people, refugees from Asia Minor, still speak Turkish; suburbs to the north where you can hear Albanian. Or further afield, the roadside tents of a group of nomadic Sarakatsáni shepherds, a Roman Catholic church on a Cycládic island, a Jewish cemetery in Thessaloníki.

Migrations and invasions: The history of Greece is the story of endless movements of people: invasions, migrations, depopulation, resettlement. Sometimes, invasions were brief, like the Saracen attacks by sea in the 8th to 10th centuries. At other times they were gradual, bringing new settlers, like the Dórian tribes three millennia ago, or more recently the Slavs, both entering Greece through Épirus and then moving down the west of the country into the Peloponnése (Pelopónisos).

The other side of the coin was depopulation. In the face of invasion whole populations would leave their towns and villages. The Slav invasions wiped out urban life in southern Greece. Similarly, pirate raids led to the wholesale evacuation of Aégina in AD 896 and the abandonment of Sámos late in the 15th century. Even later, in 1821, the inhabitants of Chíos (Híos) fled from Turkish savagery to Syros.

Depopulation was often a major economic headache: the strain of maintaining Alexánder's empire weakened Macedónia for generations. Byzantine and Ottoman rulers both tried to improve matters by mass transfers of settlers. Alternatively they welcomed

newcomers, like the Albanians, who were admitted to the Peloponnése in 1338 on condition they fought for the local ruler and cultivated the land he gave them.

Albanian tribes were often ready to move; their livelihood involved shifting their sheep between mountain pastures in the summer and lowland grazing in winter. Such communities covered vast distances each year. Two other nomadic groups, the Vláchoi and the Sarakatsánides, also moved into Greece in large numbers. The Vláchoi in particular

prospered in the 18th century, and produced a number of Greece's most famous poets and politicians.

In more recent times these large movements of population have continued. At the turn of the century there was an enormous wave of emigration from the Peloponnése to the United States caused by over-population and economic distress. And in 1923 a compulsory exchange between Greece and Turkey led to the departure of half a million Muslims from Greece and the arrival of well over 1 million Orthodox Greeks from Asia Minor.

Continuities in daily life: In the long run

Left, a Syros kisok owner with a picture of himself as a boy. **Right,** the picture in close-up.

people change, the endless cycle of invasion and assimilation introduces new inhabitants with new customs. But equally in the long run, daily life may change very little, especially in the Mediterranean. Take security, for example: for most of recorded history social life in Greece has been precarious and insecure. Only our own times provide a clear exception.

The pirates who lurked in coves in the Máni in the 18th century – taking prisoners everywhere, as a French traveller reported, "selling the Christians to the Turks and the Turks to the Christians" – were merely following in the steps of their Homeric predecessors who had infested just the same area.

land, there was also the perennial problem of highway robbery.

An English traveller in the 17th century noted that "in order to insure the safety of Travellers, drummers are appointed in dangerous passages; and in Macedónia, in a narrow passe, I saw an old Man beating a drum upon the ridge of a Hill; whereby we had noticed that the passage was clear and free from theeves." In those short periods when an effective central authority held sway, it generally had such limited resources that it could do little to enforce the law. At the end of the last century the Ottoman authorities refused to permit trains to run through Macedónia at night since they could not

When no naval power was strong enough to control their activities, the pirates operated on a large scale. The Genoese were obliged to move the inhabitants of Sámos *en masse* to Chíos when pirate raids made life impossible for them. And in the 8th century, Saracen raiders from North Africa left Páros such a wilderness that hunters used to sail over from Eúboea (Évia) after the deer and wild goats which had become plentiful on the island.

Highway robbery: Life on the mainland was no easier. Pirate bands were likely to raid villages inshore, particularly in daylight when the menfolk of the village would be away working in the fields. For travellers by

guard them against armed attack. The Germans faced a similar problem when they occupied Greece in World War II.

Local communities were left to their own devices. The cheapest security device, if not the most convenient, was a pack of dogs. More solid was a good set of walls and a defensible location. Travelling around Greece today, the visitor still notices how many towns and villages lie off the main road in foothills. Coastal settlements were often set on high ground at some distance from the shore.

Though life was insecure, frightening and violent, it embraced rigidly-observed codes of courtesy and honour. Today the blend is difficult to recapture, except in the Máni, and on Crete, where blood feuds still thrive. Vendettas, for example, which were common in parts of Greece, were conducted according to strict rules which changed little over the centuries. In 18th-century Épirus, as in Homeric Greece, an intended victim was immune from attack while he was farming, but was fair game the moment he picked up his weapon.

Pirates, too, observed rigid codes. When a European aristocrat was ransomed by his friends in the early 19th century his captors were hospitality itself: "Baron Stackelberg was then shaved by one of the gang, a cere-

Greece was told, "in your petty Kingdoms and States men are tryed and convicted, but our great Empire cannot be so maintained, and if the Sultan should now send for my head, I must be content to lay it down patiently, not asking wherefore…in this country we must have…patience even to the losse of our heads and patience after that."

Rulers might come and go, but to the poor such patience remained a necessity for centuries. Their very existence depended upon factors beyond their control. Even when their villages escaped the attention of armies, bandits or the tax-man, a poor harvest raised the spectre of starvation.

The past has never offered these people a

mony which they never omit on these occasions, and handed over to his friends. They were all pressed to stay and partake of a roasted lamb and an entertainment about to be prepared…The robbers then wished them a good journey and expressed their hopes of capturing them again at some future time…"

No doubt such accounts are highly romanticised. Certainly, even if pirates kept to their word, statesmen and those in power often failed to keep theirs. A traveller in Ottoman

Left, etching of Ermoúpolis on Syros, built on a hill as protection against piracy. **Above**, the famous Dillesi brigands before and after capture.

"Golden Age", but always threatened starvation – for the hungry citizens of Athens in the harsh winter of 1941 right back to their exhausted ancestors at the end of the Peloponnésian wars, and back further still. The account that follows describes the changing fortunes of dynasties and kingdoms. However the history of a country involves more than a succession of names and dates. The essential backdrop is provided by the generations of nameless inhabitants whose lives involved those countless imperceptible changes which may escape our gaze but which provide the real origins of modern Greece.

The basis for the modern way of life in Greece was laid around 3000 BC, when settlers moved down from the northeast plains onto rockier land in the Peloponnése (Pelopónisos) and islands, and began to cultivate olives and vines, as well as the cereals they had originally grown. At about the same time a prosperous civilization arose on Crete (Kríti) and spread its influence throughout the Aegéan.

The Minóans, whose rituals have filtered down to us through the legend of Théseus and his labyrinthine struggle with the Minotaur, left proof of their architectural genius in the ruined palaces of Knossós and Festós. Daring sailors, they appear to have preferred commerce to agriculture. They established outposts in the Peloponnése and made contact with the Egyptians.

By 1500 BC their civilization had reached its zenith. Yet barely a century later, for reasons which remain unexplained, most centres of their power were destroyed by fire and abandoned. The settlement on Thíra (Santoríni), at Akrotíri, was annihilated by a volcanic eruption. But the causes of the wider disintegration of Minóan control remain a mystery. Only Knossós continued to be inhabited as Crétan dominance in the Aegéan came to an end.

Its place was taken by Mycénae (Mikínes) the bleak citadel in the Peloponnése. We do not know whether the rulers of Mycénae exerted direct power over the rest of the mainland. But in the *Iliad* Hómer portrays their king, Agamémnon, as the most powerful figure in the Greek forces, and this suggests that Mycénae had achieved some sort of overall authority. In its heyday the Mycenaéan world contained men rich enough to commission massive stone tombs and delicate gold work. Rulers were served by an array of palace administrators and scribes who controlled the economic life of the state, exacting tribute, collecting taxes, allocating rations of scarce metals.

The "Dark Ages": In the 13th century BC

The law code of Gortyn on Crete must be read one line from left to right, and the next from right to left, and so on, "as a field is ploughed".

this civilization, like the Crétan before it, came to a violent end. Classical myth connects the end of the Mycenaéan age with the arrival of the Dórian tribes.

In fact there was no clear connection between the two events. Mycenaéan power had broken down irreversibly by the time the Dórian settlers entered Greece. These invaders, like later ones, entered Greece from the northwest, down over the Píndos mountains into the Peloponnése. Probably they were nomads, which would explain their willingness to travel and their lower level of culture. They also brought their own form of Greek. Where they settled heavily we find West Greek dialects, whilst Áttica, the Aegéan islands and the Iónian colonies continued to use East Greek forms. The hostility – at a later date – between Athens and Spárta (Spárti) was based in part on this division between Iónian and Dórian peoples.

The Dórian invasion coincided with the onset of the "Dark Ages." Historical evidence for the period between the 11th and 8th centuries is patchy; but it is clear that civilized life suffered. The art of writing was forgotten. Trade dwindled and communities became isolated from one another. Building in stone seems to have been too great an effort for the small pastoral settlements that had replaced the centres of Mycenaéan power. Hómer's *Odyssey* is set in a simple society where even the rulers busy themselves with menial tasks; where wealth is measured in flocks and herds.

Writing revives: In the 8th century there were signs of revival: trade spread further afield. There were contacts with civilized peoples such as the Etruscans in the west, and the Phoenicians and Egyptians in the east. Artistic influence from the east was increasingly evident in metalwork and pottery. With the adoption of the Phoenician alphabet, writing revived amongst a much larger circle than before.

Another Greek concept which was borrowed from the Phoenicians was equally important; this was the notion of the *pólis* (city-state). In the "Dark Ages" small, isolated settlements loosely grouped together into large kingdoms. This system survived in western and northern Greece into classical times when Thucydides described how "the Aetolian nation, although numerous and warlike, yet dwell in unwalled villages scattered far apart."

Elsewhere, however, a network of small independent states grew up. These were initially based around clusters of villages rather than one large urban centre. With the population explosion of the 8th century, however, large conurbations evolved and expanded as surplus population moved from the country to the town. Land became more intensively cultivated and highly priced. In the "Dark Ages" the slump in population had caused arable land to fall into disuse.

and Théssaly, an *éthnos*. On the other hand, there were states with a more broadly based citizen body, such as Athens.

From kings to aristocrats: In general the kings mentioned in Hómer must have surrendered power towards the end of the "Dark Ages" to an aristocratic form of rule. But the aristocracy too became entrenched in power and increasingly resistant to change. As commoners settled on land and amassed wealth, pressure grew for constitutional reform. Aristotle seems to have been right in tying the demand for such reform to changes in military techniques. He noted that "when states began to increase in size, and infantry forces acquired a greater degree of strength,

Farmers turned from sowing cereals to stock-breeding; now the process was thrown into reverse. The available land could not support such a rapidly-growing population. There is a clear parallel with the Peloponnése in the 19th century, and in both cases the outcome was the same: emigration on a massive scale.

Together with the division between the new *pólis* and the older *éthnos* (kingdom), a further distinction cuts across the first one. On the one hand, there were states, generally in the Dórian-speaking parts of the country, with a serf population, permanently excluded from power like Spárta, a major *pólis,*

more persons were admitted to the enjoyment of political rights." Just as the shift from monarchy to aristocracy had been reflected in the move from chariots to horseback fighting, so too the emphasis switched from cavalry to infantry; aristocracy lost ground to democratic pressure. Men would only fight in the new larger armies if the aristocrats granted them political rights.

Military power swung away from the traditional horse-breeding aristocracies of Chálkis, Erétria and Théssaly to new powers: Córinth (Kórinthos), Árgos, and above all Spárta, where the state was protected by a hoplite army whose core was a body of citizens who were trained as infantry soldiers from birth.

Often the demand for radical reform met with resistance. The lament of the poet Theogénis typified the aristocrats' response: "Those who previously did not know justice or laws, but wore goatskins on their sides, and had their pasture outside this city like deer they have become respectable men; those who formerly were of high estate have now fallen low. Who can bear such a spectacle?" But other aristocrats, more far-sighted, often recognised the need for change. One such was Sólon, elected in early 6th century Athens to introduce sweeping constitutional changes. Realising that the city's strength

Greeks the word "tyrant" was not pejorative; it simply referred to a ruler who had usurped power instead of inheriting it. In the 6th century, tyrants seized power in a number of states. Usually they were dissident aristocrats, gaining support from the lower classes with promises of radical change – promises which were often kept, as it was in the new ruler's interest to weaken the power of his peers. In the mid-7th century, Kipselis of Córinth was supposed to have redistributed land belonging to fellow-aristocrats.

But it would be wrong to regard the tyrants as great innovators. They were symptoms of social change rather than causes of it. Conscious of their own vulnerability, they re-

would depend upon the organisation of the citizen body, he opened up the Assembly to the poorest citizens and in other ways loosened the grip of the upper class. Inevitably these changes were attacked from both sides, as Solon himself complains in a number of his poems. However they laid the foundations for the expansion of Athenian power in the next century.

Tyrants: Another symptom of these political tensions was tyranny. To the ancient

Left, vase painting of Theseus and the Minotaur, and an earlier octopus painting. Above, a real octopus in the Iráklion fish market, Crete.

sorted to propaganda expedients to stay in power. The most potent of these was the religious cult and it is from the time of the tyrants that religion came to serve the purposes of the state. This was seen at its most cynical in late 6th-century Athens where the tyrant Peisistrátos, making a second bid for power, tried to impress the inhabitants by entering the city on a chariot accompanied by a tall blonde dressed as the goddess Athéna.

Religion was not only important to the state as propaganda; it was also a major economic factor. While religious festivals and games earned revenues, enormous in some cases, for their city, temples, sacrifices and other rituals were very costly. Apart from wars, temple building was probably the greatest drain on a community's resources. Thus the scale of its religious activities provided some measure of the wealth of a community.

The developing arts: Artistic developments too were pushed forward in the archaic period. Though it is the 5th century which received the most attention, the crucial innovations in pottery and sculpture had been made earlier.

Monumental sculpture in stone was at first derived from Egypt, but by the end of the 6th century Greek sculptors had successfully

process of political unification. People in different cities became aware of a common Hellenic culture. The historian Heródotus was a keen promoter of the idea of one Greece, and asserted that the Greeks are "a single race because of common blood, common customs, common language and common religion." The increasing prominence of interstate religious games and festivals spread this view.

But the sharpest spur to unity was a threat from outside: the rise of the Persian empire. Cyrus, halfway through the 6th century, had conquered the Greek cities on the Asia Minor coast, and Persian aspirations were further encouraged by his son Darius (521–486

broken away from the stiff poses of the pioneers towards a more expressive and naturalistic style. On vases black-figure painting gave way to red-figure in the second half of the 6th century and the greater flexibility of the technique began to open up new artistic possibilities. By the end of the 6th century the scale of public building and artistic projects in numerous city-states reflected the resources which these communities had acquired over the previous three centuries.

Greeks and outsiders: The rise of an artistic culture shared across state boundaries seems at one point to have been paralleled by a

BC) who conquered Thrace, subdued Macedónia and, after quashing an Iónian revolt in Asia Minor, sent a massive expeditionary force southwards into Greece. Athens appealed for help from Spárta, the strongest Greek city, but succeeded in defeating the Persians at Márathon before the Spártan forces arrived. This victory did more than save Áttica; it also confirmed Athens as the standard-bearer for the Greek military effort against the Persians. This explains why a frieze displaying the warriors killed at Márathon (situated just over 20 miles from Athens) was placed in a prominent and highly unusual position around the

Párthenon in the 440s BC. Only now was Athens becoming a power to be reckoned with. The silver mines at Lávrion only began producing enough ore to finance a major shipbuilding program from early in the 5th century. For two generations after that, Aégina remained superior to Athens as a trading force in the Sarónic Gulf.

Athens and Spárta: Ten years after Mára-thon, when Darius' son Xerxes organised a second attack on Greece, the city-states rallied around Spárta. For while Athens had the largest navy, the Spártans controlled the Peloponnésian League, with its considerable combined land forces. Both the crucial naval victory at Salamís in 480 BC and the military

trol over the Aegéan. It did so through the Confederation of Délos, formed in 478 BC with the professed aim of liberating the East Greeks and continuing the struggle against the Persians. In fact, a good deal of anti-Spártan sentiment underlay it. The alliance was a primarily naval one, which brought out a crucial distinction between it and the Spártans' alliance, the Peloponnésian League; for whereas the latter consisted of land forces, requiring minimal financing, the creation of a navy required long-term planning and central coordination. Gradually, the smaller allies found it difficult to equip their own ships for allied use, and turned instead to sending money for the Athenians

victory on land at Plataéa the following year, were won under Spártan leadership. But no sooner had the Persian menace been banished then the Greek alliance broke up. There was intense suspicion, especially between Spárta and Athens. Thucydides described how as soon as the Persians withdrew, the Athenians quickly rebuilt their city-walls for fear that the Spártans would try to stop them.

The development of a classical "cold war" became obvious as Athens extended its con-

Left, the ancient stadium at Delphi. Above, a red-figure vase painting of dancing.

to use. Athens grew in strength as its allies became impoverished.

The Persian threat had receded long before peace was officially declared in 449 BC. By that time the Confederacy had become an Athenian empire whose resources were used to serve Athenian interests. Between 460 BC and 446 BC Athens fought a series of wars with her neighbours in an effort to assert her supremacy. Naval rivals such as Aégina were singled out for attack.

In 430 BC war erupted again when Córinth appealed to the Peloponnésian League for help against Athenian attack. This, the Second Peloponnésian War, dragged on for years since neither side was able to deal the deathblow to the other; Athens lacked the infantry to mount an attack on Spárta, whilst the League fielded conventional hoplite forces, unprepared for siege warfare and unable to stop food supplies reaching the city by sea. The war was conducted for the most part in the countryside around Athens on a seasonal basis.

The Peace of Nikias in 421 BC gave both sides a breathing space, but lasted only six years. Only when the Spártans got financial support from the Persians and managed to inflict a catastrophic defeat on the Athenian navy was Athens forced to surrender.

Civic breakdown: Literature and art both

example, could never keep pace with its imperial commitments. This explains the permanent cycle of conquest and revolt. The Spártans had the additional headache of a large serf population, the helots, often prone to revolt in their own province.

The first half of the 4th century seems to continue the pattern. On the one hand, there were long wars between cities, and on the other, evidence of prolonged economic difficulties as Córinth fell into irreversible decline and Athens struggled to recapture its previous prominence. This it failed to do. Spártan power remained supreme until 371 BC when Thebes defeated the Spártan army at Léfktra.

flourished even during these incessant periods of fighting, but economic activity did not. In a world where each tiny *pólis* was determined to safeguard its independence at any cost, war was endemic. Such a world carried the seeds of its own destruction.

The paradox was that city-states with imperial pretensions chose not to take the steps that might have brought success. Unlike Rome, Greek city-states did not extend citizenship to their subject territories. The Emperor Claudius rightly observed that the Greek states failed as imperial powers because they "treated their subjects as foreigners." The military strength of Athens, for

The city-state system was gradually falling apart. The old form of citizen army was superseded by a more professional force, relying on trained mercenaries. Aristotle noted that "when the Spártans were alone in their strenuous military discipline they were superior to everybody, but now they are beaten by everybody; the reason is that in former times they trained and others did not." Now things had changed.

The spread of mercenaries, in fact, reflects the economic problems of the 4th century. Mercenary service, like emigration or piracy, was a demographic safety-valve, and whereas in archaic Greece mercenaries had only come from a few backward areas, in the 4th century they were increasingly drawn from the major cities as well. This points to economic difficulties over an increasingly wide area.

As at earlier times, military changes linked up with political ones. The decline of the citizen armies coincided with a trend away from democracy in favour of more autocratic government. Power shifted from the city-states towards Théssaly, an *éthnos* state, and later still, towards Macedónia, another old-fashioned kingdom.

Both regions had the advantage over Áttica in that they were fertile and not short of land. More rural than the city-states to

their south, they managed to avoid the domestic political turmoil that periodically erupted in the latter. The military successes of the Thessalían tyrant, Jason of Pherae, in the early 4th century, indicated the growing confidence of these newcomers.

A little later Philip of Macedónia moved southwards, secured the vital Thermópylae (Thermopíles) Pass, and after gaining control of Théssaly, defeated an alliance of

Left, scene from a mosaic floor in a Roman house: a man from Kos welcomes the healer Asclepius while Hippocrates sits thinking on the steps. **Above**, an "early owl" Attic drachma.

Thebes and Athens at Haronia in 338 BC. Banded together in the League of Córinth, the Creek city-states were compelled to recognise a new centre of power, Macedónia.

Alexander's Greece: In the *Republic*, Sócrates asserts: "we shall speak of war when Greeks fight with barbarians, whom we may call their natural enemies. But Greeks are by nature friends of Greeks, and when they fight, it means that Héllas is afflicted by dissension which ought to be called civil strife."

This passage reflects three sentiments that were becoming widespread in the 4th century: first, that the Greeks were all of one race; second, that warfare between city-states was undesirable; third, that it was natural for the Greeks to fight their enemies in the East. It is ironic that a successful concerted effort against the Persians was only made under the leadership of Macedónia, traditionally a border power in the Greek world.

The rapid growth of Alexander the Great's Asian empire drastically altered the boundaries of the Greek world. The city-states of mainland Greece no longer occupied centre stage. The mainland was drained of manpower as soldiers, settlers and administrators moved eastwards to consolidate Greek rule. At the same time, the intellectual and religious world of the Greeks was opened up to new influences.

The Greek-speaking world was not only expanding, it was also coming together: "common" Greek replaced local dialects in most areas. In 3rd-century Macedónia, for example, local culture was "hellenised," and the native gods were replaced by Olympian deities.

For the first time coins became widely used in trade – something which had been impossible so long as each city had its own currency. Now the Attic drachma became acceptable in an area ranging from Athens to the Black Sea, from Cappadocía to Italy.

But there were limits to this process, for although the city-states gave up their political freedom, they clung to self-determination in other spheres. Local taxation and customs duties offer examples of this passion for independence. Likewise the calendar: In Athens the year began in July, in Spárta October, on Délos January!

Philosophers were debating ideas of communal loyalties which transcended the old civic boundaries. Perhaps this reflected the way in which these boundaries were being absorbed within larger units like the Hellenistic kingdoms, the Greek federal leagues and, eventually, the Roman Empire.

Whatever the cause, the most influential philosophical school, Stoicism, emphasised the concept of universal brotherhood and talked of a world state ruled by one supreme power. Elements of such ideas could be found in earlier Greek thought, but in its moral fervour, Stoicism was very much a product of the Hellenistic age, and it brought Greek philosophy closer to Jewish and Babylonian religious doctrines.

Roman expansion: The expansion of Macedónia curtailed the political autonomy of the city-states. The process was gradual but inexorable. In the 3rd century they formed federations, and tried to exploit disputes between the generals who had inherited Alexander's empire. The policy had only limited success, mainly because of the paltry military resources available to the Greek leagues.

Early in the 2nd century, disputes among the city-states brought Rome in to intervene for the first time in Greek history. Within 20 years Rome had defeated first Macedónia, and then the Acháean League which had organised a desperate Greek resistance to Roman rule. The Roman consul Memmius marked his victory by devastating Córinth, killing its male population, and selling its women and children into slavery. As a deterrent to further resistance this was brutal but effective. Conservative factions were confirmed in power in the cities and Greece became a Roman protectorate. In 27 BC, when the Roman Empire was proclaimed, the protectorate became the province of Acháea.

Greece – a Roman backwater: Among the educated classes it became commonplace to lament the decay of Greek civilization. Seneca, in the 1st century wrote: "Do you not see how in Achaía (Acháea) the foundations of the most famous cities have already crumbled to nothing, so that no trace is left to show that they ever existed?" But this is misleading. True, Greece was no longer the centre of the civilized world Athens and Córinth could not rival Alexandria or Antioch, let alone Rome. The main routes to the east went overland through Macedónia, by sea to Egypt. Thus Greece was a commercial backwater. But its decline was only relative: along the coast, cities flourished. The *pólis* remained much as it had been in Hellenistic times and the Roman authorities permitted a degree of political self-rule. Philhellene emperors like Hadrian even encouraged groups of cities to federate in an effort to encourage a panhellenic spirit.

But the *pólis* was no longer a political force. Hellenistic rulers had feared the Greek cities' power, the Roman, and later the Byzantine emperors feared their weakness and did what they could to keep them alive. After all, the cities were vital administrative cogs in the imperial machine.

They continued to provide a social ideal for educated Greeks. Pausánias wrote of a town in central Greece "if one may call it a *pólis*, when it has no government offices and no gymnasium; they have no theatre, no market, no piped water supply, but live in hovels, rather like the huts up in the mountains, on the brink of a ravine…"

This was the age of the great benefactors, like Hadrian himself, and Hérod Átticus, both of whom lavished fine buildings on Roman Athens. Since the poorer classes were permanently excluded from power, the rich were obliged to guarantee social stability by making donations – both for emergency items, like imports of food when a harvest failed, and for public buildings and facilities.

Two centuries of relative tranquillity were shattered by the Gothic invasions in the 3rd century. The invasions were successfully repelled, but the shock led to a loss of confidence and economic deterioration. Civic building programs continued on a much reduced scale. The wealthy classes became increasingly reluctant benefactors, and two centuries passed before imperial authorities and the church revived the demand for architectural skills.

By that time much had changed. The emperor Constantine had moved his capital from Rome to Constantinople. Christianity had been made the official religion of the empire. The transition had begun from Rome to Byzantium.

A Coptic angel reminiscent of St George the dragon slayer – but here she's a woman.

A revealing incident occurred in the Byzantine capital, Constantinople, in AD 968. Legates from the Holy Roman Empire in the west brought a letter for Nicephorus, the Byzantine Emperor, in which Nicephorus was simply styled "Emperor of the Greeks" while the Holy Roman Emperor, Otto, was termed "august Emperor of the Romans." The Byzantine courtiers were scandalised. "The audacity of it," they cried, "to call the universal emperor of the Romans, the one and only Nicephorus, the great, the august, 'emperor of the Greeks' and to style a poor barbaric creature 'emperor of the Romans'! O sky! O earth! O sea! What shall we do with these scoundrels and criminals?"

Behind this contemptuous outburst at "Frankish" presumption lies the curious fusion of cultures which made up the Byzantine tradition. From the Hellenistic world came the belief in the superiority of the Greek world, the summary dismissal of outsiders as barbarians. From Rome came a strong sense of loyalty to empire and emperor. And in the fervour which marked their belief in the moral superiority of *their* empire – which they regarded not as the "Eastern Roman Empire" but as the only true empire is the stamp of evangelical Christianity. This strength of purpose was not easily repressed.

The inhabitants of this empire did not call themselves either Greeks or Byzantines: They were Romans, "Roméï." But increasingly, the mark of a *Romaiós* was that he spoke Greek and followed the rite of the Orthodox Church. Thus the three elements were intermingled.

The end of antiquity: The real break with antiquity came late in the 6th century when Greece was first attacked and then settled by Slavic-speaking tribes from the north. The invasions marked the end of the classical tradition in Greece, destroying urban civilization and with it Roman and Christian culture. An 8th-century chronicler reported that the Slavs were "subject neither to the emperor of the Romans nor to anyone else." But the empire fought back. Christian missionaries converted the pagan Slavs in the Peloponnése, and at the same time taught them Greek. The language survived but the old urban culture did not. The disappearance of the city-states is shown by the way in which the word *pólis* came to refer exclusively to Constantinople as though there were no other cities. A small urban elite studied and wrote in ancient Greek but had little impact on the mass of the population; their books were probably not read by more than about 300 people at any one time. Monks' chronicles show how muddled people had become about the history of previous centuries. Ancient monuments were left untouched because peasants thought that they were inhabited by demons.

An archbishop, Michael Choniates, arrived in Athens from Constantinople in 1182 with a solid education and high hopes of discovering traces of Athens' former glory. He was soon disappointed. Not only were the inhabitants' knowledge of the classics lamentable, but they lived in such a primitive fashion. The unwalled *pólis* had become a medieval fortress, as at Mistrá (Mistrás) near Spárta, a place of refuge for the outlying district.

The weaknesses of Byzantine rule: The Byzantine Empire lacked the resources to maintain tight control over its territories. It was beset on all sides by the Italian city-states, the Slav kingdoms to the north, the Persians and Turks in the east. The Greek provinces, being less vital than Anatólia, which supplied Constantinople with corn, were ceded more readily to other powers.

Byzantium's period of glory was short-lived, lasting from the mid-9th to mid-11th centuries. The prosperity it experienced under a succession of Macedónian emperors was cut short in 1071 when a new enemy, Turkoman tribes of nomads from central Asia, cut the Byzantine army to pieces at Manzikert in Anatólia. The threat from the west was soon felt too. The possibility of a Norman invasion was realised in the 12th century when the Norman ruler, Roger of Sicily, invaded Greece and sacked Thebes and Córinth.

But this was only a foretaste of still worse misfortune. In 1204 Constantinople itself was sacked by the crusader forces *en route* to the Holy Land for the Fourth Crusade. The empire was fragmented: Successor states arose in Épirus, Nikea and Trebizond. Greece itself was divided into small kingdoms – the Duchy of Athens under the Burgundian de la Roche, the principality of Achaéa under Villehardouin, islands to various Italian adventurers, crucial ports on the west coast retained by Venice.

Over the following 50 years Byzantium reemerged as Nikean rulers, the Paleológoi, fought back into mainland Greece and recaptured Constantinople. But there was considerable confusion in western Greece, which briefly came under Serbian control, and in Théssaly where the Vláchoi established a separate principality. Southern Greece and

tion of Turkish mercenaries. The Byzantine Empire, like the Roman, lacked the men to do its own fighting. Turkish forces were enlisted to act as a buffer against the Serbs and the Bulgars. They were alarmingly successful, crushing the Bulgars on the Maritsa River in 1371 and the Serbs at Kossovo in 1389. The Greeks took little satisfaction from these victories. It was their turn next. The occasional marriages between Ottoman princesses and Greek princes failed to negate the threat posed by this new power.

By 1400 the empire had shrunk to Constantinople, Thessaloníki and the Peloponnése. Mongol attacks on Ottoman territories in the east gave Byzantium some

the islands remained under the control of the crusaders' successors until in the 14th century the Paleológoi reestablished a Byzantine presence at Mistrá. This political confusion gave rise to ethnically mixed populations. The Peloponnése was inhabited, according to a 15th-century author, by "Lacedaemónians, Italians, Peloponnésians, Sclavinians, Illyrians, Egyptians (i.e. Gypsies) and Jews."

Continual fighting between all these parties was notable for one thing: the introduc-

breathing space but no more. In April 1453 Sultan Mehemet II besieged Constantinople and took the city within two months; eight years later the rest of the mainland had succumbed too. The Aegéan islands held out longer – Tínos until 1715 – but mainland Greece was now part of the Ottoman Empire.

The fall of "The City" reverberated throughout Europe: with it had fallen the last descendants of the Roman Empire itself. Although in the West this seemed the inevitable result of Byzantine decline, to the Greeks it was something more traumatic – the moment when they passed from freedom into slavery.

Carved in stone at Mistrá, a more typical version of St George slaying the dragon.

The Ottoman Turks who now controlled the Balkans were the latest in a stream of nomadic tribes to move westwards from central Asia. Highly mobile, they were set on military conquest though few in numbers.

From Constantinople the Sultan strove to maintain control of his far-flung empire with a minimum of expense. He avoided the creation of rivals with local power-bases by shifting regional governors from place to place, and by rewarding Muslim officers with estates which reverted to imperial control on their owners' death.

Special privileges: Religious tolerance was reflected in the "millet" system of government. The Turkish authorities recognised minority religions, and permitted each "millet," or religious community, a measure of self-government. The Greek Orthodox Church was granted special privileges and came to exert both religious and civil powers over Ottoman Greeks.

Under their new masters the Greeks lived in much the same way as they had done earlier. Their houses, like those of the Turks, tended to be miniature fortresses, built on two floors around a central courtyard. The restored merchant's house in Kastoriá gives a good idea of the effect. Most elements of contemporary Greek cuisine were common then – from the *resináto* wine so distasteful to foreign travellers to the strong coffee which Ali Pashá, the "Lion of Ioánnina", found helpful in poisoning his rival, the Pasha of Vallona.

But autonomy did not rule out oppression. When, from the 17th century onwards, central authority weakened, local magnates were free to burden the peasantry with their own impositions. Many revolts in the Ottoman Balkans, notably that in 1805 which revived the state of Serbia, involved appeals to the Sultan for help against corrupt local landowners or bishops.

Powerful enemies continually threatened the Ottoman grip on the country. The Venetians, and later the French, were thorns in the Ottoman flesh. Within the empire the wild Albanians, the backbone of the Ottoman armies, often threatened to break loose and establish claims of their own. The re-

sulting conflicts left Greece much the weaker.

Thus in 1537 a Turkish army carried off half the population of Corfú after an attack on the Venetian colony there, leaving the island with barely one-sixth of the population it had had in antiquity. The Peloponnése was similarly decimated, caught in a bloody tug-of-war between the same two rivals. It was ravaged by Albanian forces fighting for the Ottomans in 1715 and again in the 1770s. Further destruction came in the wake of the 1821 uprising. Greeks slaughtered Turks in Trípolis; the Turks uprooted the Greek inhabitants of Chíos. Finally Egyptian troops, under Ibrahim Ali, laid waste to most of the Peloponnése.

Deadly foes: Brigands and pirates provided a perpetual undercurrent of violence in daily life, while plagues often reduced populations more dramatically than wars and made entire regions – Théssaly was especially notorious – impassable to travellers.

When, during the 17th century, the Ottoman Empire ceased to expand, new strains appeared. In the hills and mountains, where the Ottoman grip had never been sure, groups of brigands, known as *Klephts* (*Kléphtoi*), were formed. They were bandits, as prone to plunder a Greek village as a Muslim estate, nevertheless, in peasant folklore they came to symbolise the spirit of Greek resistance to the Ottoman authorities.

Perhaps more important for the development of Greek nationalism was the growth of a Greek merchant community. Commercial links with Europe introduced wealthy Greeks to European lifestyles, but they also encountered European cultural and political ideas. Late in the 18th century two ideas in particular, philhellenism and nationalism, found a fertile ground among young educated Greeks.

The Turks had favoured certain groups of Greeks in the hope of heading off rebellious inclinations. Senior posts in the Ottoman administration were frequently filled by Greeks, and in Constantinople aristocratic families, known as the Phanáriots, forged close links with the imperial court. The Orthodox Church benefited similarly from this policy. Consequently these two powerful groups in the Greek community were badly placed to head a revolt against Turkish rule.

The French Revolution provided the political stimulus for revolt, but the ground had already been prepared by the spread of nationalist ideas among the Ottoman Empire's Christian inhabitants. In 1814 three Greek merchants in Odessa formed a secret organisation called "The Friendly Society" (*Filikí Etaireía*) devoted to "the betterment of the nation" which rapidly acquired a network of sympathisers throughout the Ottoman lands. A number of vain attempts to secure themselves powerful and decisive backing were finally rewarded when their

the Turks they turned on each other. Ironically, the belief that this was a national struggle was held with greatest conviction by the foreign philhellenes – Byron and others – who came to help the Greeks. These men were influential in getting Western public opinion behind the Greeks. Thus the major powers, initially unsympathetic to the Hellenic dream, came to put military and diplomatic pressure on the Turks to acknowledge Greek independence. The turning point came with the almost accidental destruction of the Ottoman fleet by an allied force at Navaríno in 1827.

Count Ioánnis Kapodístrias, a Greek diplomat formerly in the service of the Russian

members organised an uprising against Turkish rule in 1821.

The struggle for Greek independence, which lasted from 1821 to 1832, was not a straightforward affair. Greek propaganda glossed over the difficulties of a nationalist struggle in a kaleidoscopic society. Fighting the Turks was a motley crew of *Kléphtoi*, merchants, landowners, primates and Phanáriots – all as keen to further their own interests as to advance the cause of Greek nationalism. When they were not fighting

Dinner at a Greek house at Chríssa in 1801, painted by Dodwell, author of *Views of Greece*.

Tsar, was elected president by a National Assembly in the same year. He encouraged Greek forces to push north of the Peloponnése and was rewarded when the 1829 Conference of London fixed the new state's northern boundary on the Árta-Vólos line. But numerous Greeks were dissatisfied with his administration and suspected him of aiming at one-man rule. In 1831 he was shot by two chieftains of Maina as he entered a church at Naúplia (Náfplion). While the powers – Britain, France and Russia – tried to find a suitable candidate for the Greek throne, the country fell into a period of anarchy and civil war.

The new state had a difficult birth and a sickly infancy. It was desperately poor, overrun by armed bands of brigands, beset by quarrelling among various political factions. In 1834 a rebellion in the Máni resulted in government troops being defeated and sent home without their equipment.

There were few good harbours or roads. Athens remained the squalid, provincial town that Byron had visited. Internally, conditions were worse than they had been under Ottoman rule.

Bavarian absolutism was partly to blame. Kapodístrias' death had confirmed the reluctance of Greeks to be ruled by Greeks. The crown of the new kingdom, which had been offered to various candidates, was eventually accepted by Otto, son of Ludwig I of Bavaria, who arrived at Naúplia (Náfplion) in 1833 on a British man-of-war. Since he was under age, a succession of regents ruled in his stead. They ignored widespread calls for a constitution until in 1843 a brief and bloodless uprising in Athens forced Otto to dismiss his Bavarian advisers and accept the idea of constitutional rule and parliamentary government.

Despite a poor and backward economy, the 1844 and later the 1864 constitutions endowed the country with the trappings of an advanced democratic apparatus. But politics does not function in a vacuum and Greek parliamentary politics reflected the country's strange situation. Rather than political parties representing different classes, there were factions grouped around individuals, valued as much for their powers of patronage as for their ideas. In the absence of class distinctions other issues, generally of foreign policy, separated these factions. During Otto's reign the three main parties were named for the foreign powers they supported: Britain, France and Russia.

The "Great Idea": The new kingdom contained less than one-third of the Greeks in the Near East. The prospect of "liberating" Ottoman Greeks, of creating a new Byzantium by recapturing Constantinople and avenging the humiliation of 1453 was the "Great Idea" which aroused enormous enthusiasm.

The Great Idea had roots embedded in the soil of a fervent nationalism. It was rarely a realistic policy since the Greek army was never on its own a match for the Turks; yet it survived repeated humiliations. After the defeats of 1897 and 1922 it continued to rear its head. King George I, who succeeded the ousted and unhappy King Otto in 1863, was titled, according to the new constitution of the following year, not just "King of Greece" like his predecessor, but "King of the Hellenes".

The most prominent populist of the late 19th century, Theodore Deliyiánnis, encouraged several foolhardy expeditions to Théssaly and Crete. His more far-sighted rival, Harílaos Trikoúpis, realised that such a policy was unwise so long as Greece lacked the resources to sustain it. Greece was dependent on foreign loans, which gave its foreign creditors the whiphand over any foreign policy initiatives. Only economic growth would reduce such dependence.

Trikoúpis, therefore, set out to encourage economic activity. Roads were improved, the Córinth Canal constructed. Piraéus expanded rapidly and became one of the busiest ports in the Mediterranean.

But despite the appearance of a few textile and food factories, industrial activity remained minimal right up to World War I. Greece was a rural nation, a country of peasant small-holders. The lack of large estates ironed out social inequalities but it did mean most farmers remained miserably poor, too poor to adopt modern farming methods. The export of currants brought prosperity for a while, but a world slump in 1893 hit the entire economy. Greece became bankrupt and hunger drove peasants to emigrate in large numbers. By 1912 numerous villages lived on remittances sent from the United States by young exiles.

Such domestic problems seemed to increase Greek enthusiasm for the Great Idea. Further territory had been acquired in 1881, without fighting, as a by-product of the Congress of Berlin. When troubles on Ottoman Crete in 1897 provoked a wave of sympathy on the mainland, Greek naval forces were sent to the island while the army marched northwards – only to be checked by the

Turkish forces who pushed back down into Greece. This defeat was humiliating for the Greeks, but it proved only to delay the future enlargement of the kingdom.

On Crete and in Macedónia (Makethonía) Ottoman rule was crumbling. But the rise of the new Balkan nations – Serbia and Bulgaria – added a new complication to Greek ambitions. Macedónia was a melting-pot of different racial groups (which is why the French call a fruit salad a *macedoine*).

Within Greece, political changes had often been forced through by military uprisings. This had happened in 1843 and 1862. In 1909 it occurred again. Junior army officers staged a revolt against the political establish-

Party, which dominated Greek politics for the next 25 years.

A decade of wars: When the Balkan Wars erupted in 1912, Greece was strong enough to wrest southern Macedónia from the Ottoman forces and then to defend its gains, in alliance with Serbia, from a hostile Bulgaria. The full gains from the fighting included – in addition to Macedónia – Épirus, Crete and the east Aegéan islands. Greece's area and population were doubled at a stroke.

There was barely time to consider what burdens the new territories would impose on the Greek state before the country was embroiled in World War I. In fact, the country was almost continuously at war for a decade.

ment. At their invitation a new politician with a radical reputation, Elefthérios Venizélos, came over from Crete to form a government. A consummate diplomat and a man of great personal charm, Venizélos channelled the untapped energies of the Greek middle-class into his own Liberal

Preceding pages: Panagiótis Zogáphou's drawing for Makroyiánnis's book on the Greek War of Independence. <u>Above left</u>, Ioánnis Kapodistrias, a statesman who played a prominent part in the independence struggle; and, <u>right</u>, *A Great Musician*, from the satirical newspaper *New Aristophanes* (Athens, 1888–95).

Financially it was seriously crippled; politically it was hopelessly divided.

Venizélos and King Constantine quarrelled over whether to bring Greece into the war. The prime minister wanted Greece to give the Entente active support, while Constantine insisted on keeping the country neutral. The quarrel raised vital constitutional issues: who had the final say over foreign policy – the king or parliament? The dispute reached the point of open civil war which ended in 1917 with Constantine being forced to leave the country and Greece entering the war.

Venizélos had hoped that the Entente

powers would reward Greece for its support with new territories. Smyrna (Smyrni) and its rich hinterland in Asia Minor had been promised by the British to Greece during the war, and in 1919 Greek troops were invited to occupy the province and place it under Greek control. It began to look as though the Great Idea might at last be realised.

But in Greece in 1920 the Liberal Party was surprisingly voted out of power and succeeded by a royalist government. The fight against the Turks continued, however, invigorated by the myth that Constantine had been divinely named to lead the Greeks into Constantinople. Encouraged by the Allies, Greek forces advanced inland from Smyrna

Dodécanése islands, at that time held by the Italians). In addition, a massive population transfer was agreed upon: half a million Muslim inhabitants of Greece moved to Turkey in exchange for over 1 million Orthodox Greeks. The Greek presence in Asia Minor, which had lasted for 2,000 years, was ended.

The interwar years: Buffetted and impoverished by 10 years of war, the nation now faced the huge problem of absorbing these impoverished newcomers into an already crowded country. The economy benefited from this new source of cheap labour, and it was in the interwar period that Greece began to industrialise. But the arrival of the refugees also increased social tensions. Over

10 SALONIQUE — Quartier Vardar, Groupe de Réfugiés - Vardar district, A groupe of Refugees

against the Turkish Nationalists, led by a rebel general called Mustafa Kemal. Spirits were high, but the long march over hilly, waterless country weakened the Greeks and stretched their lines of communication. In September 1922, only 50 miles (80 km) from Ánkara, the Nationalists finally pushed back the Greeks. Their retreat turned into a rout. As Greek soldiers and civilians fled from the Turkish army, Smyrna was surrendered without a struggle.

The 1923 treaty, which finally ended the war between Greece and Turkey, fixed the boundaries between the countries which hold today (with the exception of the

half a million refugees settled in urban areas, often in squalid shanty towns outside the large cities, searching for poorly-paid jobs. With them they brought their music, and the Smyrna style of singing – a melancholy vocal line over violin and *bouzoúki* swept the Athenian cafés.

After the "Disaster" of 1922, King Constantine was forced to leave Greece a second time, and a parliamentary republic was established. It lasted only 12 years, a succession of short-lived coalitions and mi-

Above, a group of refugees in Thessaloníki after the 1922 Asia Minor disaster.

nority governments, broken up by military dictatorships and abortive coups d'états. Governments regularly altered the electoral system to keep themselves in power. The only period of stability – Venizélos' years in power from 1928 to 1932 – was terminated by the shock of the international economic depression. In 1933 the Liberals were succeeded by the royalist Populist Party, whose timid and uncertain leaders only half-heartedly supported the republic. Apart from the constitutional issue, little separated the two parties. In matters of economic and social policy both were equally unimaginative. Both ignored the signs of growing inequality and class conflict.

Lacking popular support, parliamentary government remained vulnerable to military pressure. In 1935 this led to the monarchy being restored. In 1936 the king dissolved parliament and offered the premiership to an extreme right-wing politician, Ioánnis Metaxás, a former senior army officer and a fervent royalist. Soon afterwards, Metaxás responded to a wave of strikes by calling out the army and declaring martial law.

Metaxás' dictatorship was run along totalitarian lines. But although people had become dissatisfied with parliament's instability, they did not greet the alternative with great enthusiasm. "The First Peasant" (as Metaxás liked to be called) never succeeded in digging solid foundations for his longed-for Third Hellenic Civilization.

World war and resistance: Metaxás had tried to steer a middle course in foreign policy between Britain and Germany. The latter's increasing dominance in the Balkans had to be set against Britain's naval strength in the Mediterranean. But Germany was not the only power with aggressive designs on the Balkans. In April 1939 Mussolini sent Italian troops into Albania. Eighteen months later he tried to emulate Hitler's record of conquest by crossing the Albanian border into Greece. Metaxás could not hope to keep Greece neutral any longer. Receiving the Italian ambassador in his dressing-gown, he listened to a recital of trumped-up charges and responded to the fascist ultimatum with a curt "No!" Or so the story runs – a story commemorated every year on 28 October by "Óhi" (No) Day.

Fighting on their own in the mountains of Épirus, the Greek forces were remarkably successful and pushed the *Makaronádes* (Spaghetti Eaters) – as the Italians became contemptuously known in later folksongs – back deep into Albania. But in the spring of 1941 Hitler sent German troops south to pacify the Balkans in preparation for his invasion of the Soviet Union.

Britain had sent reinforcements to support the Greeks, but poor coordination between the two allies allowed the Germans to advance unchecked as far as Thessaloníki. German victory was swift. Their invasion of Greece began on 5 April; on 30 April they appointed General Tsokáloglu, who had signed an armistice with them, as a quisling prime minister.

Greece was occupied by German and Italian forces until late 1944. Their hold over the countryside was often tenuous, but firm in the towns: It was the towns which suffered most from the shortage of food, notably in the terrible winter of 1941–42. It was also from the towns that the Germans – against Greek and to some extent Italian protests – deported and eventually exterminated Greece's old and varied Jewish communities. King George and his official government had left the country in 1941 and passed the war under British protection. And when an organised resistance movement did eventually emerge in the hills, most pre-war politicians remained in the towns – on the sidelines. The earliest and most important group was known as the National Liberation Front ("EAM" in Greek). This was organised by the Communist Party, but rapidly attracted a broad base of support, including many Greeks for whom patriotism and anti-royalist feeling were alone sufficient motivating forces. Numerous other groups also sprang up. Drawing on the *klepht* tradition of mountain resistance these groups would make occasional forays down into the plains. Clashes between different groups were unfortunately common.

The dominance of EAM meant that when the British began to establish contacts with resistance groups in 1942, they found military considerations colliding with political ones. EAM, with over 1 million supporters, was well placed to pin down German troops. On the other hand, the British suspected that EAM intended to set up a communist state in Greece after the war, and they therefore armed other groups as a counterweight. EAM, for its part, feared that Churchill wished to restore the monarchy in Greece without consulting the Greek people. This fear was amply justified. Churchill had little sympathy for the guerrillas, whom he described as "miserable banditti," and supported the monarchy with fervour.

Into the Cold War: In autumn 1944, the German forces retreated, to be replaced by British troops. First Britain and then, after March 1947, the United States believed themselves responsible for reintroducing civilian rule. The climate of suspicion made this almost impossible. Resistance forces mistrusted the Allies' intentions and refused to lay down their arms. The Allies feared the exaggerating the communist threat as a means of winning further American support. In fact, the official government forces had to abandon control of large parts of the countryside to the rebels.

Greek Government forces, with American provisions and advice, eventually defeated the rebel army in the mountains of northwest Greece in October 1949. But victory was not achieved without the mass detention of suspected left-wing sympathisers and the forced evacuation of entire villages. The violation of civil rights and the emergence of a powerful security service apparatus did not end in 1950. Once more domestic politics were polarised: the old pre-war split between

spectre of a communist rising and tried to find moderate politicians to whom they could hand over power. But these politicians were reliant upon a heavily right-wing militia to keep order. It was in such circumstances that the king returned to Greece in September 1946 after a bitterly disputed plebiscite. Inflation was soaring, the black market flourished and violence spread rapidly through the country as old wartime scores were settled.

As Greece slid into open civil strife, she became a crucial stage in the rapidly evolving Cold War. The government survived on Allied loans and politicians became adept at royalists and republicans gave way to one between Left and Right.

Greece looks West: Democracy had weathered the civil war – but only just. In the following decade a certain stability seemed to have been achieved, with only two prime ministers – both conservatives – in power between 1952 and 1963. Yet this stability was precarious, relying on a policy of outlawing the Communist Party and discouraging opposition to the regime. Anyone with a suspected left-wing past found life difficult, if not dangerous.

Greece had joined NATO in 1951, and the pro-Western orientation of its foreign policy secured financial support from the United States. However, the relationship was not straightforward: When the Cyprus dispute flared up in 1954 Greece refused to take part in NATO manoeuvres. This foreshadowed the problems that later governments would have in defining Greece's role in Europe. The quarrel over Cyprus was resolved – for a time – when the island was created a republic in 1960. And Greek links with the West were strengthened by its entry into the Common Market as an Associate in 1962.

A troublesome "miracle": In the 1950s and 1960s, Greece, like Italy and Spain, experienced an "economic miracle" which transformed the country. Electric power became

War and lacking a vision of Greece as a modern state.

The 1961 elections saw the resurgence of the political centre, under the leadership of a former Liberal, George Papandréou. The contest was bitterly fought. When the results were announced in favour of Karamanlís, Papandréou alleged that police and rural gendarmes had been used to intimidate voters, and that the results were fraudulent.

Public disquiet at possible links between the ruling party and extreme right-wing violence increased in May 1963 when a left-wing deputy, George Lambrákis, was assassinated at a peace rally in Thessaloníki. Shortly afterwards Karamanlís resigned and

widespread, communications improved. As roads opened up new horizons, young Greeks went to meet them. Athens mushroomed outwards, a chaotic sprawl of concrete apartments, until it contained almost one-third of the country's entire population.

The old forms of political control which had operated best in small rural communities began to lose their effectiveness. A new urban middle class arose which regarded the conservative political elite as culturally backward, rooted in the rhetoric of the Cold

Left, women fought with the Resistance during the Civil War. **Above**, anti-dictatorship posters.

in elections held at the end of the year, Papandréou's Centre Union party won power. This was the first centrist ruling party for over a decade.

The way now seemed open for an extended period of centrist rule. But although conservative politicians were prepared to surrender power, right-wing groups in the military regarded the new government as a threat to their own interests.

When Papandréou demanded a reshuffle of senior army officers he found his own defence minister and the young king, Constantine II, opposed to him. The king tried clumsily to bring down the Centre Union Government, but when Papandréou agreed with the main conservative opposition to hold elections in May 1967, Constantine was faced with the prospect of a further Centre Union victory. He held a series of meetings with senior army officers to make contingency plans for military intervention. But these plans were preempted when a group of junior army officers, working according to a NATO contingency plan, executed a swift coup d'etat early on the morning of 21 April, 1967 . Martial law was proclaimed; political parties were dissolved. The Colonels were in power.

The Colonels: The junta was motivated by a mixture of self-interest and hazy national-

least until they realised the implications for Greece's tourist trade. They prevented Greeks from reading such subversive literature as Greco-Bulgarian dictionaries. They wanted the country to "radiate civilization in all directions" by establishing a "Greece of the Christian Greeks" which would make Greece once again "a pole of ideological and spiritual attraction."

This was the old dream once more: an escape from the dilemmas of the modern world in a fantastic fusion of classical Athens and Byzantium. Perhaps because of the harsh censorship of intellectual activity and the suppression of any dissent, there was little active opposition to the regime.

ism. This combination was certainly not new; on a number of occasions in the interwar period army officers had used the rhetoric of national salvation to head off a possible purge in which they feared they might lose their jobs.

In their policies and attitudes, too, the Colonels drew on earlier traditions. With peasant or lower-middle-class backgrounds, they symbolised a provincial reaction to the "miracle's" new world of urban consumers. Thus they laid great stress on the need for a return to traditional morality and religion. They closed the frontiers to bearded, longhaired or mini-skirted foreigners – at

The first signs of widespread discontent coincided with the economic downturn of 1973. The leaders of the protest were students, whose occupations of university buildings in March and November were brutally broken up. Increasingly the regime was proving incapable of dealing with ordinary problems of government. In the bloody aftermath of the November student sit-in at the Athens Polytechnic, Colonel Papadópoulos, the regime's figurehead, was deposed by army units and power switched to a more

A 1985 rally in Thessaloníki supporting the victorious socialist prime minister Papandreou.

sinister figure, Dimítrios Ioanními̱des, commander of the military police.

In the end it was the Cyprus problem which toppled the junta. A foolhardy Greek nationalist coup, supported from Athens, against the Cypriot president Archbishop Makários led the Turks to land troops in northern Cyprus. Ioanními̱des ordered Greek forces to retaliate, but mobilisation had been so chaotic that local commanders refused to obey his orders. Pressure grew for a return to civilian rule. An invitation was extended to the former premier, Karamanlís, to return from his exile in Paris to supervise the restoration of parliamentary democracy. On 24 July 1974 Karamanlís returned to Athens.

A new start for democracy: The transition to democracy proceeded remarkably smoothly considering the enormous problems which Karamanlís faced. Aware of his own vulnerability, he moved slowly in dismissing collaborators of the regime. At elections held in November 1974, Karamanlís' New Democracy (*Néa Demokratía* or "ND") party won an overwhelming victory, though many people seemed to have voted for Karamanlís simply as a guarantor of stability.

Karamanlís himself was well placed to make any necessary political reforms, since a referendum the month after the elections produced a decisive vote for the abolition of the monarchy, which had been compromised by the king's actions before and during the junta. In its place Karamanlís created a presidency with sweeping powers. It was widely believed that in the event of a swing to the Left, Karamanlís would resign his parliamentary seat and become president.

Signs of such a swing were evident after the 1977 elections in which Andréas Papandréou's Panhellenic Socialist Movement (PASOK) made large gains. The younger Papandréou, George's son, represented a new, post-war generation – at home with the "miracle" and its fruits. With his background as a professor of economics in the United States, he was well placed to lead a party of technocrats. At this time he still had a reputation as a radical and he vehemently attacked Karamanlís' policies, taking a more belligerent stand over relations with Turkey, and threatening that a PASOK government would take Greece out of both NATO and the EEC subject to popular referendum. The future was to show that Papandréou's promises were an unreliable guide to his actions in power. Yet support for PASOK was evidently growing and in 1980, a little over a year before the next elections, Karamanlís resigned as prime minister and was voted in as president by parliament.

After PASOK's victory in the October 1981 elections, based on a simple campaign slogan of *Allaghí* ("Change"), Papandréou took office and formed Greece's first ever socialist government. His significance lies not in his socialism, which existed in name only, but in his remarkable success in articulating the attitudes of his generation. In the 1960s he brilliantly blended the rhetoric of the Left with the social optimism of Kennedy's America. Twenty years later, and despite his recent loss to ND, the rhetoric still culls votes on the Left, but it is a middle-aged, middle-class Left seeking economic security, stability, a "better future" for their children.

The PASOK slogan, accompanied by images of a little girl symbolising a vague appeal to classless desires for peace and prosperity, won PASOK the 1985 general election, and even the scandals of the late 1980s failed to tarnish completely the wily Papandréou's image.

Events since 1974 suggest that for the first time in its history Greece may have evolved a stable three-party system: New Democracy (conservative), PASOK (socialist), KKE (communist). Minor parties have come and gone, but these three parties dominate the scene. The crucial question has always been: Can Greek parties outlive their leaders? Until recently the smallest of the three, the KKE, was unique in having done so. Now New Democracy too has weathered several changes of leadership.

In 1989, in the wake of domestic and economic scandal, Papandréou finally succumbed at the polls, after three rounds of voting, and ceded the position of power to Constantine Mitsotákis, leader of ND, and a Cretan. Tenacious to the end, Papandréou is still very much in the public eye, now married to his former mistress, former air hostess, Dímitra Liáni. That PASOK ministers could be deeply implicated in high-level scandals, and the prime minister himself plunging through an expedient divorce during the election period, speaks for the unwillingness of the Greek people to return to right-wing government.

A
JOURNEY
INTO
GREECE,

BY

George Wheler Esq;

In Company of
Dr SPON of LYONS.

𝕴𝖓 𝕾𝖎𝖝 𝕭𝖔𝖔𝖐𝖘.

CONTAINING

I.   A Voyage from *Venice* to *Constantinople*.
II. An Account of *Constantinople* and the Adjacent Places.
III. A Voyage through the *Lesser Asia*.
IV. A Voyage from *Zant* through several Parts of *Greece* to *Athens*.
V.   An Account of *Athens*.
VI. Several Journeys from *Athens*, into *Attica*, *Corinth*, *Bœotia*, &c.

With variety of Sculptures.

LONDON,
Printed for *William Cademan*, *Robert Kettlewell*, and *Awnsham Churchill*,
at the *Popes Head* in the *New-Exchange*, the *Hand* and *Scepter* in
Fleetstreet, and the *Black Swan* near *Amen-Corner*.
MDCLXXXII.

The Ancient Greeks had a strong sense of their own identity. From the Homeric age until at least the disintegration of Alexander's empire, Greeks were conscious of themselves as a people distinct from all others. These others they called barbarians. "Barbarous" first meant only that: non-Greek. The word was probably imitative of unintelligible foreign speech. It was in their common language and in their common culture that the Greeks, however various and however widely distributed, knew themselves to be Greek.

According to myth, the goddess Athéna chose the land of Greece for her favourite people because of its ideal location between the frozen north and the torrid south. Later civilizations, particularly northern ones, have believed that myth wholeheartedly. The Greeks, it was thought, were Nature's favourites.

Brilliant glimpses: We learn a few epithets from Hómer, and we have discovered that they were exact and telling: windy Troy, sandy Pylos, Mycénae rich in gold. And in Píndar, Sóphocles and Eurípides there are brilliant glimpses of places within and around the limits of the Greek world: of Mount Tmolus and the golden Pactolus in the east, of Aétna in the west (where the Titans were confined), and of Kolónos, Thebes, Cithaeron and Délphi at the centre.

There were extraordinary travellers among the heroes of Greek myth and legend: Odysseus, who was 10 years getting home from Troy; Hérakles, whose labours took him north into the land of the Hyperboreans and west to the Garden of the Hesperides; Jason, who sailed to Cólchis on the Black Sea after the fleece.

The Greeks had a strongly mythical and religious sense of the places in their world; and this sense, or something like it in intensity, survived them and has inspired or coloured the vision of travellers in their country ever since. It should excite the traveller to know that places of terrific mythical resonance really exist. They are not *beyond* the zone, in a nebulous otherwhere but actually within it, substantial and real. Hélicon, Parnássus (Parnasós), Olympus (Ólimbos) are real mountains and can be climbed – which affects the imagination very curiously as an excitement but also, almost, as an offence. The Ahéron still flows and meets the Cocitus by the hilltop Nekromantíon of Perséphone and Hádes, just east of Párga. Párga was a fishing village and is now a holiday place. It is one street wide, and on that one street you will have trouble buying anything as necessary as bread. But there are many travel agencies, and they all offer the same thing: day trips by boat to the entrance to Hádes.

The ancients sited many of their myths very precisely indeed. Citizens of Athens, Córinth or Thebes constantly saw with their own eyes places their divinities and heroes had operated in. Travel was difficult, but people *did* travel; they went about their ordinary business in a country the myths had illuminated. The everyday and the mythical seem to coexist very easily in Greece. Judging from the leaden tablets unearthed at Dodóna, they were often very ordinary men and women who made their way to the sanctuary and oracle there. The questions they put to Zeus through his priests who, as Hómer says, slept "on the ground with unwashed feet," were often very mundane ones: "Will it be all right to buy the small lake by the sanctuary of Demeter?" "Is it good and possible to sail for Syracuse at a later date?" "Shall I be successful in my craft if I migrate?" The answers were given in the rustling of the leaves of the sacred oak.

The mythical and religious sense of place coexisted, from quite early on, with a concern for topographical accuracy. Scholars and travellers in the 18th century made the important discovery that Hómer had sited his story precisely. When Lady Montagu sailed through the Dardanelles it gave her great pleasure, so she wrote to Pope, to check Hómer's descriptions for herself and to find them exact. Others actually used the *Iliad* for their archaeological researches on the plain of Troy. Schliemann, in the 1870s, was only

Preceding pages: 17th-century map of Ancient Greece. **Left,** the title page of Wheler's illustrious account of his and Dr Spon's travels.

the most maniacal, credulous and fortunate of a long line. When travellers and critics called Hómer a "truthful" poet, "a painter after Nature," they meant not just his depiction of human passions but also his eye (blind though it was) for the landscapes and topography of the real world.

Travellers were on firmer ground when they took the historian Heródotus, the geographer Strábo and the tourist-cum-topographer Pausánias as their guides. The latter two particularly are frequently referred to at great length in the early modern travel literature of Greece. Quite simply, until the modern tradition itself became established, travellers in Greece seeking to locate places

Greece in modern times began to be explored; and, not making any hard and fast distinction between poets on the one hand and topographers or historians on the other (Hómer was thought to be accurate; Heródotus honours the myths and enhances the glamour of places), let us say that the texts worked in a dual way: they located the sites and aroused what Dr Johnson called "local emotion." The knowledge the travellers had or gained was, in varying proportions and intensity, both factual and imaginative. Most often, of course, the "local emotion" felt by a traveller at some important site in Greece would be very different from what we may suppose an Ancient

famous in antiquity *only* had ancient testimony to go on. Not only particular monuments – the Temple of Olympian Zeus in Athens, for example, or of Ártemis at Éphesus – but even entire sanctuaries and cities of the very greatest importance (Délphi, Miletus, Spárta) had vanished if not from the face of the earth at least out of all local ken, and could only be located and identified by following ancient directions (converting *stádia* into miles, allowing for changes in the landscape) and searching hopefully for telling inscriptions.

The ancients themselves, then, were the best guides available to travellers when

Greek to have felt. The modern response is almost inevitably a sentimental one; its most characteristic colouring is nostalgia.

The "good old days": Nostalgia for Greece increased as the value of ancient Greek civilization increased in the eyes of later nations. Early modern travellers came to Greece from countries – England, France, Italy – whose cultures were deeply indebted to the classical world, and naturally, in varying degrees, they brought that influence with them and it affected their responses.

Statue of Odysseus, the Western world's archetypal traveller, found in a cave in southern Italy.

It is worth noting that nostalgia for Greece, though not to the same degree, already existed in Roman and Alexandrian times. Both those ages were, in some respects, backward-looking to a civilization which they thought superior to their own. European travellers of the 17th and 18th centuries found in Roman and Alexandrian sentiment towards Ancient Greece a precedent and an authority for what they more intensely (the gap having widened) felt themselves. They would quote Cicero's lament for the decline of Athens at the appropriate moment in their own accounts. And Pausánias, though not himself sentimental, provided *material* for sentiment because, when he travelled, in the 2nd century, much had already been lost. Many of the monuments and sanctuaries he described were already in ruins. His whole undertaking, which was to write a travel guide to Greece, may be objectively called a sentimental one, whether he himself felt sentimental towards the sites or not.

Classical influences: Once the tradition of travel in Greece had become established, each new explorer could refer to and perhaps correct his predecessor's works on the spot; but he would not, for that, forget the ancient texts. The classical authors themselves continued to direct and influence travel in Greece throughout the 18th and 19th centuries, and perhaps they do so still. It was *by* the light and *in* the light of classical literature that the travellers saw the famous localities of Greece; and in Roman and Alexandrian works the moderns discovered the beginnings of their own nostalgia.

Serious exploration of Greece did not get underway until the late 17th century. There were many practical deterrents, not the least of which being the fact that nearly the whole of Greece, from about the late 15th century onwards, was Turkish territory; but also, just as important, the cultural incentive was lacking still in those countries from which, later, the travellers would come. Medieval Christian Europe, though it took a great deal of its learning from Pláto and Áristotle, had no wish to visit Greece – unless as crusaders and robber-knights to carve out feudal domains there.

A confidently Christian culture had no reason to turn with any sentimental or nostalgic interest towards the land of Greece. Geography then was more figurative and symbolic than empirical; there was no impulse from that discipline to map Greece or any other remote country accurately.

The *Mappa Mundi* (of about 1290) in England's Hereford Cathedral illustrates this very well. The world is disposed there almost entirely figuratively: Jerusalem at the centre; the River of Death all around the circumference. If you look on that map for information about the classical lands, you find some very strange shapes and locations. Greece itself has no general designation, unless the word ICAYA (Achaéa) is meant as one. Famous ranges and rivers are hopelessly misplaced, and there are some notable confusions: Áthos appears as Átlas; Délphi as Délos. Thásos and Pátmos have drifted north into the Black Sea. The Peloponnése is drawn as a rounded lump and labelled: INSULA. The Chersonese peninsula in Thrace (Thráki) has the shape which clever etymologists deduced for it from the name of its chief city Cardiá: the shape of a heart.

Two-and-a-half centuries later, even among the learned, the degree of knowledge was scarcely higher. Martin Crusius, for example, a German scholar writing in the 1550s, asked a correspondent in Greece whether it was true that Athens no longer existed. The trade-routes passed the city and Piraéus by; ships rounding the Peloponnése crossed to Smyrna through the islands. On the first modern maps Athens occurred as *Stines* – which is what the Franks heard when the Greeks said *stin Athéna* (in Athens) – and by that misnomer all connection with the ancient city was effectively severed.

In Holland and Germany in the 16th and 17th centuries scholars did write geographies of Greece, but bookish ones, entirely on the basis of classical texts. The author of one of them indeed, Christoph Cellarius, was renowned for having taken only one short walk throughout the 14 years of his professorship in Halle. Such works prove the reverence Renaissance learning had for Greece, and at the same time a nearly medieval indifference to empirical knowledge. The shift that then took place is exemplified by Joseph Pitton de Tournefort who set off in 1700, funded by the King's Academy, to see for himself whether what the ancient geographers and botanists had written was true or false. It needed a cultural incentive to send travellers to Greece, and the Renaissance supplied that but also a shift in the manner of apprehending the world, a shift towards belief in the value of empirical enquiry. A lull in the wars of the Turks and Venetians, after the Turkish victory at Cándia (Irákleion) in 1669, made trade and travel easier. Travel for pleasure or for scientific purposes was greatly facilitated when the trade routes and commercial contacts were secure.

The "Hellenic Ideal": Greece is not just any foreign country but the still surviving site of an excellent and – for the West – a supremely influential civilization. True, there is more to Greece than its classical past; and having such a past, and having had so much outside passionate attention directed at it, has not

presuppositions, with a disposition to be affected each according to his bent.

These particular inclinations were contained within a more general attitude: admiration – admiration of the past. Modern Greeks have never had an easy time of it, being expected by Western Hellenists to live up to their glorious past. Admiration has its obverse disappointment, which may turn hysterical and even vengeful.

Opening up: Greece was opened up to the West as scholarly and sentimental interest in its excellent past increased, and what was learned of Greece and brought back by the travellers further fuelled that interest. This is most apparent in the 18th century. Travel

always been an advantage. Greece, so far as the West is concerned, cannot be neutral ground. The first travellers, or those of them at least who set out deliberately to see Athens, Eleúsis or Délos were not impartial. Even the most reasonable and "scientific" among them had ideas and ideals in mind when they set out which coloured their perceptions when they got there. Fortunately, the "Hellenic Ideal" is a many-faceted thing, and the company of travellers who might all be called Hellenists had very various interests and aspirations. We need not enumerate these. The point is that the earliest travellers *were* interested; they came with ideals and

literature altogether was an important and popular genre. Within it, accounts of Greece had a wide circulation, often went through several editions, and were very quickly translated. Furthermore, booksellers, knowing the market, engaged hack writers to plagiarise and excerpt from the best available accounts and to compose compendium volumes out of them. *The Travels of the late Charles Thompson Esq.*, for example, was put together in this way (in 1744), and was very well received.

Engraving of a Turk and a Greek from Tournefort's *A Voyage into the Levant*, published in 1718.

The best among the early books on Greece were written, naturally enough, by men who travelled there and who, back home again, related what they had learned. Spon, Tournefort, Wood, and Chandler were deliberate travellers who made their discoveries known to an interested public. Their undertakings were in that sense purposeful. But, especially at the beginning, much information about Greece and much assistance in the exploration of Greece was supplied by people who happened to be there on other business. Such figures occur *passim* in the published accounts, and travellers were much indebted to them. They were, for example, Capuchin priests who being residents of Athens, accommodated the first European travellers in their own religious house, showed them around the still visible monuments and supplied them surreptitiously with maps.

One of their number, *le père* Jacques Babin, based at Negropont (Eúboea) but visiting Athens, wrote the very first modern account of the city, *Récit de l'état présent de la ville d'Athènes* (1674). This brief but curiously moving work (we witness in it a man opening his eyes to beautiful things around him; we hear the first accents of true admiration) was sent to Jacob Spon in Lyons. He edited it, and in so doing was inspired to make his own journey. An armchair traveller, Guillet de Saint-Georges, with whom the authentic Spon was later in controversy, got most of the material for his immensely successful *Athènes ancienne et nouvelle* (1675) from Capuchin priests in Pátras and Athens.

Some early travellers: All the early travellers were glad to make use of contacts on the spot and even to supplement their own accounts with eyewitness reports of places they were not able to visit themselves. Merchants were particularly useful in this respect, if they were intelligent observers and had some interest in classical things, since their business took them travelling. Consuls even more so, being in one place for a length of time. Consul Giraud, for example, who served first French and then British interests in Athens, for some 30 years, offered hospitality to travellers and showed them around the sights. He also engaged in scholarly researches, which Spon made grateful use of. A most powerful figure at this time was the French Ambassador in Constantinople, the extravagant Marquis de Nointel. He considered it part of his diplomatic duty to travel through Greece, his domain, with a large entourage and much ostentation, collecting and recording curiosities and antiquities as he went. A Flemish painter in his party did drawings of the Párthenon frieze which, though crude, are of great value still, since they were done before the bombardment of 1687 in which much was damaged. When Spon and Wheler arrived in Greece they were entertained by Nointel, who gave them not only inspiration (he showed them the memorials of his own tour) but also protection and practical information for their further journey.

The researches done and passed on by men who were in Greece in some professional capacity – diplomatic, commercial, religious – were important, but it was the travellers, particularly Spon and, later, Chandler, who published them. An exception was Pierre-Augustin Guys of Marseilles, a most engaging man. He was a merchant who spent nearly all his working life in Greece and loved the land and its people and its classical past with passion. He was both a wealthy and a well-read man, a correspondent of Winckelmann and a devoted admirer of his aesthetic works. Indeed, as he travelled throughout Greece, pursuing his commercial interests, he saw its landscapes, people, climate, customs, with a vision as sympathetic and passionate as Winckelmann's, who never went there.

He was unusual in his day, for instead of dislocation and discrepancy he saw continuity, survival and connections wherever he went in Greece. By insisting on continuity, by refusing to think of the modern Greeks as hopelessly cut off from their heroic past, he contributed in a small way to that raising of expectations and of confidence by which, finally, the Turks were driven out.

Spon and Wheler were in Greece in 1675-1676 and their explorations and their separate publications constituted the first coherent survey of the land for modern Europe. Spon especially wrote as a scholar and a Hellenist; Wheler followed him as well as he could. When he entered the church in 1685 he gave his souvenirs, the bits and pieces of marble he had brought back with him, to Oxford's new Ashmolean Museum, which already housed the Arundel collection. Spon, for his part, had copied thousands of inscriptions. It is worth remembering that from the start journeys to Greece were undertaken with the intention of bringing things back – information, of course; copies of inscriptions; but also anything readily movable. The reasoning was simple: the Greeks were perceived as degenerate and the Turks, their masters, as barbarians who would deface as a matter of religious duty whatever statuary they came upon. Therefore, it was the perceived duty of civilized Western travellers to rescue precious relics.

The travellers recorded numerous instances of Greek neglect and Turkish mal-

the very outset of the tradition. Both professed Protestantism (Spon went into exile for it after his return), but Wheler, Church of England, although the younger man, was much more hidebound and hectoring.

Quite simply, he preferred Restoration England to Greece, even to Periclean Athens, as the imagination of a Hellenist might recover it. He was not a very open-minded man. We may recognise his type even today: the man who travels to confirm his prejudices, and who is profoundly relieved to get home again unchanged.

Spon was the better traveller. True, he was disposed to feel in a certain way; but he was alive and awake on the spot to the places

Lib. VI.

The Greek   Bee-hive

treatment of ancient works – an architrave used in a cowshed here, a sculpted head used for target-practice there – and felt wholly justified in removing whatever they could.

Recording the visits: The first journeys to Greece were, in some cases, extensions of the Grand Tour beyond Italy. Spon, who perhaps always intended to go, made up a party with Wheler and two other English gentlemen when they met in Rome. Wheler had been travelling through France to complete his education with his Oxford tutor. He had money; Spon had the scholarship and enthusiasm.

They were an interesting combination at

themselves. He was consequential in his passion for Greece. His travels, despite Wheler's assistance, impoverished him. When he went into exile he was penniless. He died in a pauper's hospital.

That first enterprise was a private one, largely undertaken on Wheler's funds. Tournefort in 1700 and the *abbé* Fourmont in 1728 were sent and financed by the French Crown. For serious exploration some such backing became increasingly necessary, and in France and England at least there were public bodies and a few wealthy private individuals who were willing to provide it. National pride was a factor certainly, but also a sense of social and cultural responsibility, and of *noblesse oblige*. The early exploration of Greece coincided with the opening of the first public museums and galleries.

Tournefort, primarily a botanist, was a man of the broadest learning, an excellent traveller, wide-awake, good-humoured, resilient. He took in classical sites *en route*, so to speak – not incidentally, but as part of a whole interest.

His book *Voyage du Levant* (1717) is perhaps the best of the early accounts for any reader whose interest in Greece is a general one. He gives the ancient and present state of places, what they produce and pay in taxes, how they are administered, how the people

tural demands had altered, and the Society, founded in 1731 chiefly for convivial purposes, was by the middle of the century beginning seriously to respond to them. In 1751 they had taken up two energetic individuals, the architects James Stuart and Nicholas Revett, who had made their own way to Athens and were measuring and drawing the monuments there. The Society financed the gradual publication of their work – as the *Antiquities of Athens* – and conclusively promoted the Greek style of architecture and furnishings by doing so. In 1764, directed by Robert Wood, they sent a party to Greece and Asia Minor specifically to locate and describe the ancient remains.

live, where the best harbours are. He exerts himself, climbs a high hill to have a good vantage-point, enquires diligently of the *papás* (priest) and village elders who might be able to inform him. Later accounts constantly refer to Tournefort as an authority and point of orientation.

Cultural expeditions: When the London Society of Dilettanti sent their expedition to Greece in 1764 it was with a more specific, more particularly Hellenist intention. Cul-

Left, 18th-century travellers' accounts detail local customs, dress and even bee husbandry. **Above**, a woodcut of Greece made in 1545.

Chandler's account of the tour (in two volumes, 1775 and 1776), may be set alongside Tournefort's as the century's best. Its appeal is rather different, just as the journey it describes was different in character and aims. Chandler knew what he had to look for, and what it was his duty to report. Though his tone is throughout reasonable, unenthusiastic, and his prose style deliberately plain, he was nevertheless writing in the service of a love and admiration of ancient Greece so assured in himself and in the Society he represented as to need no special pleading.

By 1764, when Chandler and his party sailed, there was already a tradition of travel in Greece. In his two books he consolidated that tradition. To an extraordinary degree he worked as a compiler, editor and generous critic of other travellers and their accounts.

With Chandler's expedition the archaeological exploration of Greece was put on a professional footing. He consolidated the tradition to date, and his publications, together with others under the auspices of the Society, established a firm scholarly basis for serious-minded successors in the next century to build on.

Travel practicalities: The tradition of Greek travel literature is a very rich one and this is only a cursory survey of it. Spon and Wheler, Tournefort, Chandler, being very distinctive

the status of Greece ascended at the cost of Rome. Rome was full of classical works – of noble buildings and, in galleries accessible to respectable travellers, of statuary. Most of the statues were Roman copies of Hellenistic copies of truly classical originals; but this was not known and could not be known, since the originals themselves had not yet been brought to light. When, finally, the Párthenon marbles were seen close up, connoisseurs used to the Apóllo Belvedere suffered a severe shock. Travel to Greece, even though great works of art there (since few of the travellers were also excavators) were not often to be seen, was part of the process by which, very slowly, Greece, in the modern

figures, will have to serve also a representative function. Their specifically detailed peregrinations give some sense of the real experience, of the practicalities of travel in Greece, in the years before it became an easy matter.

The starting point was very often Rome. The wish to go farther than Rome increased with the sense that the classical world was in fact more purely represented by Athens. Today this may seem self-evident, but the discovery of Greece, the recovery of Greece from concealment under Rome, took a long time. The Society of Dilettanti were themselves great movers of the process by which

culture of western Europe, eventually triumphed over Rome.

In Rome, by the middle of the 18th century, travellers would meet with others who had come from Greece. Winckelmann, who, despite attractive offers, never made the journey himself, was in dealings with men who had been there and in his official capacity as Papal Antiquary he got to see shipments of finds as they arrived from Greece and Asia Minor for restoration, alas, and

In *Antiquities of Athens*, Stuart and Revett meticulously drafted reproductions of classical ruins such as the Pnyx in Athens.

"completion" before going on to the markets of London and Paris. It was in Rome that Spon and Wheler made up their party for Greece. A third member, Francis Vernon, had diplomatic contacts and was able to get them all a passage, from Venice, with the Italian ambassador. Such influence was of crucial importance. Spon and Wheler were fortunate in having Nointel's protection, and both travelled under French passports issued by him in Constantinople.

The Turks, whose territory Greece was, were notoriously difficult to deal with. It happened that in the 1670s Nointel was in high favour with the Porte, and his English counterpart, Sir John Finch, was not. To travel at all, Westerners needed permission, written permits issued by the Sultan himself or by local Agas; but in remoter areas these might be valueless – in parts of the Peloponnése and Asia Minor the word from Constantinople was disregarded and, to make matters difficult for travellers passing through, local potentates were often in conflict with one another.

Misconceptions: Neither the Turks nor the Greeks had any understanding of what the travellers were about. If the travellers' interests were archaeological, they met with great incomprehension and mistrust. One energetic Turk, seeing a party inspecting the drums of a column, set to pulverising the marble with cannon balls in the belief that gold, at least, must be inside. Stuart and Revett, when they needed to erect ladders and scaffolding, met with objections from Turkish pashas who feared that from that height the Westerners would spy into their harems.

It was also frequently the case that places the travellers wished to explore were of military importance to the Turks. The Acrópolis of Athens was a Turkish citadel, the Párthenon was a store for powder and ammunition. It suffered accordingly when Morosini bombarded it. Drawing and measuring, which a traveller would naturally want to do, were extremely suspicious activities in Turkish eyes. Francis Vernon, examining the Theatre of Dionysios under the Acrópolis, was fired on, and only escaped through the intervention of Consul Giraud. The Capuchin maps were drawn surreptitiously, which partly explains their inaccuracy, and circulated likewise.

In time the travellers produced their own maps. We know that Chandler in the Troad in 1764 had with him a map, done by a Frenchman, which Wood had with him in 1726. Their reliance on one another, and on the ancient authors was very great. But how many books could they actually carry with them? Wood tells us that he and his companions took "a library, consisting chiefly of all the Greek historians and poets, some books of antiquities, and the best voyage writers." But they were perhaps unusually well-provided for, since James Dawkins, one of their party, was a very wealthy man. Spon and Wheler received the newly-published *Athènes ancienne et nouvelle* (by the impostor Guillet) just as they were sailing from Venice. They were able then to check its descriptions on the spot, and found them, in Vernon's phrase "wide from Truth."

A party would hire guides and interpreters and enquire locally, once they had-established the area of their interest; whether any ruins were still apparent in it. The same employees would procure them food, and accommodation (often of a very wretched, flea-ridden kind). In many districts the travellers needed more than guides: They needed armed guards. Bocher, travelling alone, was murdered. James Stuart was two or three times set upon and robbed. The roads at the back of Smyrna were infested with bandits, and travellers there did well to join with caravans of merchants who had Janissaries riding with them. These difficulties should be borne in mind when we evaluate the travellers' achievements. Chandler's party were deterred from climbing Parnássus by the menacing behaviour of some Albanian soldiery camped near them at the spring; they kept clear of Rhamnoús because the local Turks there "bore a very bad character."

Other hardships: We should mention the sea's dangers too. Spon and Wheler, crossing from Constantinople, were tossed to and fro for 37 days. Vernon was taken by pirates and stripped of all he possessed (he escaped with his life only to lose it a few months later in Persia, in a quarrel over a penknife). And had Chandler sailed home in the *Seahorse* as he intended, he and his party would very likely all have been drowned off Sicily when that ship went down.

Sir Giles Eastcourt, the fourth member of

Spon's party, died on the road to Délphi near Náfpaktos. Wood's friend James Bouverie died at Magnesia on the Maeander. Plague was endemic still in many areas. It had a high season in the summer months. The Turks with their fatalistic view of things, allowed it to carry them off in great numbers. The Franks were more circumspect and withdrew into isolation if they could. Chandler and his companions spent three months holed up in a village above Smyrna, the town itself being too dangerous to enter.

A certain piety entered the tradition. Earlier fates were remembered and commemorated. Tournefort got the whole story of Vernon's death from the English Consul in Isphaham, and recounted it. Chandler searched for and found the names of Eastcourt and Vernon where they had scratched them on the south wall of the Theseíon (they are still there and can still be read).

The journeys were often dangerous and – what with mosquitoes, heat, dirt and wolfish dogs – must almost always have been uncomfortable. Though some of the travellers were born adventurers, for others it was only an interlude, perhaps the only escapade of their lives, and they returned to Oxford common rooms and quiet country living with a few mementos and a fund of stories. They had many high moments to remember.

The "travel experience": Discovery, that is the essence of the experience of early travel in Greece. For those travellers seeking to identify, after a lapse of nearly 2,000 years, a particular site famous in antiquity, the satisfaction when they were successful must have been very great indeed. They weren't excavators; they didn't dig their way through to treasures like the Mask of Agamémnon or Helen's Gold: but, knowing their texts, they brought to such places as Márathon, Mistrá or Délphi considerable reverence and a willingness to be moved. They were in a landscape such as they had not seen before; not only the botanists among them were excited by the flowers and shrubs, by their vivid colours and rich scents. Again and again they saw scenes that painters in the 18th and 19th centuries loved to depict: ruins among olive trees, broken columns on a headland against the sun, animals grazing in fields littered with marble. And their interest was not always antiquarian. Guys says rather pointedly of Spon that looking for ancient Greece he found only stones; Guys himself then, as a corrective, looked to the people and their present lives. True, he saw them through a veil of Hómer and Theócritus. But perhaps our perceptions are always coloured. The first Western painters in Greece saw the landscape through a haze of Claude Lorraine. Our view is harsher now and more historical, but the 18th-century images are still appealing. Indeed, at times in certain places they are quite compelling.

Enormous changes, some of them irreparably damaging, have occurred in the experience of travel in Greece. Large areas are going to perdition as rapidly as money will permit. We may look even *more* to the past, in horror at what is being done in the present. Out of that past things have been brought to light – out of the earth, out of the sea which the early travellers never saw the like of, though perhaps the poets of their day imagined them: the great bronzes in the National Museum, for example, the gold of Mycénae, the palaces on Crete. Some sites have undergone marvellous resurrections. On Délos, at Délphi, Olympía and in Athens there is now infinitely more to be seen. Chandler discovered Olympía, Spon and Wheler Délphi, but having identified those sites they saw very little. When we see the richness of Délos nowadays we can scarcely believe that by the early 18th century it was thought nothing there merited a visit.

We have more knowledge nowadays, the museums are richer, the sites more extensive. On the other hand, it may not be easy in present-day Greece to get a sense of what early travel was like. Out of season, and out of the way, is best: at Díon, for example, under Olympus, or at Górtyn in the centre of Crete (where the road runs through what was the ancient city). And of course when you least expect it there are places where a few yards of old walling, or the remains of old irrigation channels, or ledges and niches in a goatherd's cave, will suddenly bring the whole experience upon you with a rush.

In Turkey, in old Ionía, there are some potent reminders. Éphesus, for example, ends in a marsh. There you may see fallen pillars, broken architraves and beautiful carvings sinking among the bulrushes. The Temple of Ártemis, one of the Seven Wonders of the ancient world, lies (what little is left of it) on swampy waste land, on a patch that serves as village green, football pitch, grazing ground and rubbish tip. The precinct falls away into a pond that looks malarial, and there blocks and drums of the temple, swarming with terrapins, emerge and sink according to the season. Selçuk was built out of the ruins of Éphesus. Dressed stones, portions of columns and many ornamented blocks bearing inscriptions were quarried from the public buildings and the temples of Éphesus for the castle walls, and even in the poorest houses, in some wretched slums, you may suddenly spot the glimmer of fractured marble. Your guesthouse in Selçuk might well have a Corinthian capital as a seat in the

Pérgamum something barbaric has been done, something at least as shocking as the things the early travellers were affronted by. The approach to the Sanctuary of Asclépeius, God of Healing, takes the visitor through barbed wire, past soldiers with submachine-guns. Photography of the famous view from the theatre is now forbidden because that famous view is now, largely, of a military camp. The Sacred Way, which used to link the Sanctuary with the Acrópolis, is severed by wire now and blocked by a row of neatly parked tanks.

It is impossible not to feel empathy for those first explorers. Their interest was predominantly Hellenist. In what other spirit

shade by the door. The Roman aqueduct still steps through the town and anyone inclined to can copy the inscriptions embedded topsy-turvy in its pillars. Such details are the stuff on which the nostalgic imagination of the early travellers fed.

Téos, among thorns and holm-oaks, entirely deserted, is in that sense a classic site. The fields the peasants plough through are almost choked with sherds. Priene on its hill looks across to Miletus over what was the sea, over what is now a dusty plain. And at

Early travellers seeking classical sites often found little more than piles of rubble.

would they have gone? True, others were in the country for quite different purposes – commercial, diplomatic, military – but they are not the ones who wrote accounts. The documentation of early travel in Greece is very much coloured by the travellers' perception of that land as supremely important for their own and their national culture. It is doubtful that any traveller can be quite rid of that sense even today. There is something compelling about the old images still. Myths are as necessary as they ever were, and some myths are more productive than others. We all know what the worst are: In Greece, still, we can glimpse some of the best.

Imagine that you are a guest in a Greek family house on a Sunday afternoon. You have just finished an immense and leisurely dinner and though your head floats with a pleasantly sleepy *retsína* high, the weight in your stomach keeps you earthbound. Buoyant dinner repartee subsides as appetites are sated, and someone lazily flicks on the television. A low clarinet wails plaintively, and as the picture focuses, you perceive a dozen human forms clasping hands and gravely circling a green hilltop: women shapeless in weighty layers of embroidered frocks with wide bronze belts and men in white skirts and tights and pom-poms on their shoes. "Épirots," your hostess remarks off-handedly. "How do you drink your coffee?"

"Our Greek Folk Songs" is broadcast nationwide every Sunday afternoon on one of the state-run television stations. With the traditional Sunday afternoon dancing now mostly a picturesque memory, the broadcast makes a peculiarly appropriate substitute, but the "Epirotness" which these symbols evoke is oddly tamed.

In the early 1990s, regional consciousness verges dangerously upon a sentimental *folklorismós*. It often seems a parlour game of regional trivia shorn of its divisive power: knowing that Kalymnians wrap *dolmáthes* in cabbage – not grape – leaves, that potatoes in the "village salad" signal a Cycládic chef, that the novelist Kazantzákis hailed from Crete and the popular singer Kazantzídhis, beloved of immigrants and workers, comes from Asia Minor.

But regionalism was in earlier days hardly a matter of songs and salads. Of neighbouring Italy in the early days of its nationhood, D'Azeglio remarked ruefully that "now that Italy had been created, it was necessary to invent the Italians." And was Greece so very different? The travel-writer Patrick Leigh Fermor once described the Greek world as "an inexhaustible Pandora's box of eccentricities," and doubtless an extreme topography has nurtured great variety in a relatively

little land. Vlach-speaking shepherds in the Macedónian mountains had little contact and little enough in common with shipbuilders of Chíos or Jewish merchants of Ioánnina. Though not all communities were equally isolated by terrain they tended to be introverted socially. *Xénos*, the "foreigner-stranger-guest," is in Greece an elastic designation, and brides marrying in from the next village forever remained "strangers" in their husbands' villages.

It was not just the land which came be-

tween them: but differences in language, culture, religion, education, class. At the same time, that Koutsovlach shepherd was typically polyglot, speaking his own Romance language with his kin, Greek with the cheese-merchants, a smattering of Albanian and Macedónian with the villagers he encountered on his treks with the sheep, and enough Turkish to outwit the odd Ottoman official. Under the tolerant Ottomans, a plethora of religious and ethnic communities thrived: Greek-speaking Orthodox, Macedónian-speaking Orthodox, Bulgarian-speaking Muslims, Romaniot and Sephardic Jews, Turkish farmers, Gypsies, Franco-

Preceding pages: orange seller in Piraéus. **Left,** priest wearing *Raybans*. **Right,** dolls in national costume can be found in most kiosks.

levantine Catholics in the Cycládes, Protestants converted by American missionaries in Asia Minor, Orthodox Albanian shepherds, crypto-Jewish Muslims of Thessaloníki and Smyrna... the list goes on. From this multiplicity, the inhabitants of a newly invented, formally secular nation-state of Greece were charged with inventing *themselves* anew.

The cultural homogeneity which undeniably exists today is as much a goal and a consequence as a precondition of this new nationalism. With one eye on the past and the other on the West, official policies of the Greek state have long worked to eradicate – or at the very least, to trivialise – local variations in language, dialect and custom.

cal fiction required by the new nation, which meant (until PASOK reappropriated the word) "everybody except the Athenians," refuse to imagine themselves a lumpish mass, and remain stubbornly sure of essential differences amongst them. Stereotypes of ethnic groups coexist with stereotypes of regions and topographies. In a society fascinated with "appearances" the stereotype of a place becomes part of its reality, and to see the mountains, the plains and the islands as the Greeks do one must set out on the journey across their cultural terrain.

In the mountains: The *Blue Guide* hardly knows the existence of scenery except under the guise of the picturesque. "The pictur-

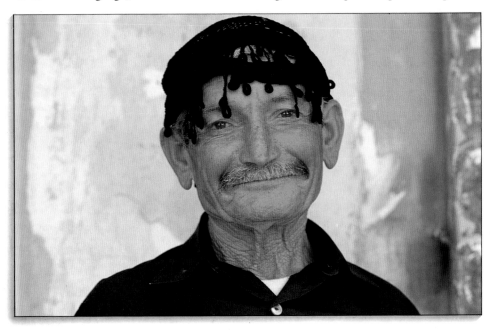

Differences which seemed to threaten the integrity of the state – like the speaking of Slavic-Macedónian – have been systematically suppressed. More insidious, the traditional refusal of both the state and private investors to develop the provinces economically has inflamed a ruinous pattern of poverty, massive emigration to Athens and abroad, and a frequent sense of cultural inferiority by those who have remained in the "backwaters".

Even so, the monolithic vision of the official state, with its images of Péricles and Kolokotrónis, has always been quietly subverted from below. "The people," a categori-

esque is found any time the ground is uneven." If there is any truth to Roland Barthes' wicked verdict, Greece is a veritable paradise of the picturesque. From the scrubby hills of central Greece to the soaring peaks and wide wooded vales of the majestic Píndos, the land seems in continuous undulation, and even from the plains – a "relative" term, so little do they recall the great flats of Nebraska or Hungary – the mountains seldom disappear from view. Romantics who look for the truth in the land often claim that the irregularity of its surfaces has most forcefully shaped "the Greek character".

The settlement of Greeks in mountainous

areas has not been stable and continuous and, for many groups, is "traditional" only if we don't look back too far. Of course, some settlements are of a Byzantine or Frankish vintage. And certain tribal groups of transhumant shepherds – Sarakatsánides, Karagoúnides, Koutsovláchoi, Arvanítovlachoi – who herd their sheep and goats on mountainsides in summer and move them to the plains in winter, have probably always wandered widely across the Balkan territories. Of these, all except the Sarakatsánides built permanent mountain villages where women, elders and young children kept home fires burning when the men descended each winter with the sheep. However, other

when peasants enjoyed a level of justice and prosperity far above that of their counterparts in feudal serfdom in Europe, inaccessible mountaintops held fewer attractions. But as the centralised system – and the safeguards it had ensured – began to break down, Christian and Muslim peasants became increasingly vulnerable to exploitation from all sides: from their Turkish landlord anxious for profits from maize and wheat sold to the west, from local bands of brigands who periodically helped themselves to the peasants' crops and livestock, from unruly Janissaries – the Sultan's professional army extorting tributes for their "protection." By the 17th century, vast stretches of country-

sedentary mountain villages found their *raison d'être* in conditions of Ottoman life.

In island and coastal regions, many towns were (and many still are) situated not at the portside but high on the crest of the mountain, even – indeed, preferably – hidden from view altogether. This town-plan was a response to the threat of pirates. In the late 16th century when the Ottoman State began its long decline the time-honoured random piracy of the Aegéan became systematic.

Pirates did not venture far inland, though, and in the first 100 years of Ottoman rule,

Left, traditional shepherd. **Above**, two sisters.

side began emptying, as disgruntled peasants fled to the cities and upwards to the mountains.

Mountain settlements multiplied, interspersed among already established villages whose inhabitants made a living (sometimes a handsome living) not only by farming and shepherding, but as itinerant stone-masons and charcoal-makers, as wandering merchants and muleteers and mountain guides to Turks and travellers, and as artisans and immigrant labourers to richer regions of the empire. Still required to pay the annual tithe to the Sultan, newly settled peasants terraced the rocky mountainsides, wresting a meagre living from their flocks and gardens and small fruit orchards. Still vulnerable to extortion by brigand and Ottoman official alike, the community drew inward, socially and physically. In this setting developed the ethic and organisation of village life which has come to be regarded – by foreigners, but by Greeks, too – as classically "Greek."

The "traditional" mountain village: Every Easter, Athens spits out its millions toward numberless villages, only to swallow them up again two weeks later, laden with baskets of olive oil, cheese, homemade bread. Every Athenian, every Thessalónikan speaks reverently of "his or her" village, and when was "his or her" village ever *not* a mountain vil-

was – and is – the central unit of Greek society, enormously interdependent economically, socially and emotionally, and whatever the harmony or tumult within its four walls, to the "outside" the "house" stood, stands, united. Indeed, the unconditional loyalty to the family and the demand that each member must help further its collective interests made friendships outside the house inevitably fragile. Tenuously bound by ties of religion and local patriotism, these families competed for scarce resources: for land, water, pasturage, and for that most ephemeral substance: honour.

Anthropologists, who have tended to study small villages, have conventionally

lage? The mountain village is never merely real but partakes of the archetype, the village poor in all but rocks. Ah, but so beautiful…

The mountain village typically comprises a cluster of houses, often with adjoining walls, circling a central church and a square. This physical arrangement reveals a moral geography, for the boundary between the "civilized" human space and an unsanctified wilderness teeming with human and supernatural dangers is marked by a ring of tiny churches and shrines. United by Orthodoxy and a common way of life, villagers were nonetheless divided into separate households. The family, rather than the individual,

identified "honour" and "shame" as key moral values in Greece. According to this moral code, a family could rarely be considered to have honour if its women were seen to be immodest. Since Orthodox teachings and native thought both agreed that woman was by nature sensual and seductive, social chaos was avoided by strictly segregating unrelated men and women, and defining various tasks as "male" or "female". Segregation relaxed only during feast days and weddings.

Recent work suggests that the image of meek womenfolk in household purdah and domineering but protective men is both outdated and overly simplistic. Moreover, what acting "honourably" means varies from one Greek community to the next, and whether one is rich or poor, male or female. Today, to be *filótimos*, to "love honour," can mean something as vague as acting as a "good" person should, though this presupposes no small knowledge of what the community considers good. It differs from the Protestant idea of "conscience" in one crucial way: one must be *seen* to act honourably, for it is a judgement which only others – almost begrudgingly – bestow. In such conditions, reputation becomes all-important, taking on a public "facticity."

A Sarakatsánides' feast: From the grounds

her off to the distant kin camped in these mountains, and she plainly found them both quaint and exotic. "Sarakatsáni women," she insisted as we wended our way through the shadows, "they know nothing about sex. When they have their babies, they are still virgins!"

When we finally emerged from the canopy of trees, we could see a flat and treeless plateau, and upon it three huts constructed on branches, a mud-oven and a cooking fire. Tassoúla shouted a greeting, which set a dog yelping, and a laughing woman in a kerchief invited our little band of four to the campsite.

We stayed the afternoon, squeezed together all eight of us on a cot of branches,

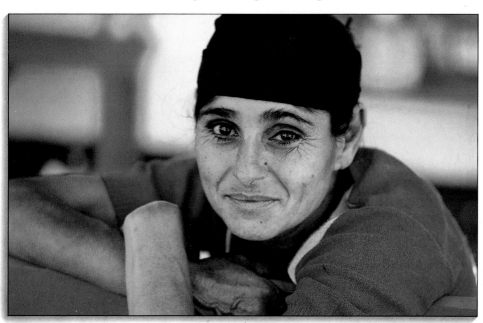

of the monastery, thick with cherry and chestnut, to the encampment of Sarakatsánides it is less than an hour's walk. Yet the land itself never hints at any human presence in this high landscape, and it was on the barest trace of a path that we threaded our way along a mountainside choked with trees and brush one afternoon in August. Only Tassoúla, the daughter of a family which ran a restaurant for the visitors, could read its signs. She was engaged to a Sarakatsáni policeman who had taken her once to show

Gypsies, Greece's migrant farmers, stop for a midday picnic (left) and for the camera (above).

thick with woven blankets and sheep skin *flokátis*, fed on stodgy and slightly sweet cheese-pies warm from the oven, talking with the women and the young girls. Eléni, 15, was on holiday from secondary school in Lárissa, on the plains where she lived in the winter months with relations who had already left the difficult shepherding life. She loved the sheep and the mountains, she confessed, but she wanted to be a secretary.

Because it was a feast day – the Assumption of the Virgin Mary – the three Marias in this encampment of 19 souls were "celebrating," and by late afternoon, the central ground between the thatch houses filled with grimy children and many new adults. The old man, Eléni's grandfather, entered with a sheep's cape around his shoulder and a long carved shepherd's crook.

Three youths soon followed, dusty and smelling of sheep and Turkish tobacco. We discovered then the bittersweet twist to the celebration, for these three cousins were soon to be inducted into their army service. Amidst much giggling, the central ground became a dance floor, but as we had no music, we sang. The youths wrapped their arms across each other's shoulders, and in voices deepened with exaggerated bravado, started the simple tune, "I'll become a swallow, and fly to Arabia..."

An ancient truck lurched up an invisible road and screeched noisily behind the huts and the dance dissolved in excitement. The driver, yet another young man, was greeted with raucous hoots and cheerfully complied with the dancers' now insistent demands to turn on the *kaséta*. He turned the volume up "full." The music, sizzling with static, gashed at the green tranquillity of the hill, but even this frantic distortion could not quite block out the thumping bass which signalled when to move our feet and our bodies.

The myth of the mountain man: The mythology of the mountains is emphatically masculine. Greeks are inclined – like the romantics

among us – to see in the mountain man an embodiment of alpine virtue. In his "craggy" face they discern a "harsh" pride, a "rugged" individualism, a moral "purity" as pristine as the mountain springs. For the ferocious clans of the Máni and Crete which always kept the Turks at bay, and the Soúliot women who danced into the abyss rather than submit to the finally victorious Turks, they reserve their highest praise. In the figure of the *klepht* they celebrate a more pugnacious heroism. Scholars protest that the *klepht* – which means "thief" – was seldom more than a self-serving outlaw, preying on landlord and peasant alike, intent on building a local empire in the time-honoured Balkan style com-

bining coercion of the weak and spoils to his own minions. But in the national mythology, the *Klephts* became symbols of resistance to the "hated Turkish oppressor." If the myth glorifies a selfless klephtic patriotism, surely the Greeks do not fail to relish the cunning which turned patriotism to personal advantage.

On the slopes of Crete's Mount Ída shepherds steal each other's sheep to prove their honour and daring, and insist that their way of life upholds a Greek ideal degraded by

Caught between East and West, young people struggle for a post-dictatorship identity.

morally slack, soft-palmed Athenian bureaucrats. And 40 years ago, during the German occupation, resistance fighters lived like klephtic heroes, in small wandering bands and attacked from the mountains. The great rebel leaders, the *kapetánoi*, absorbed that heroic aura and held control of a newly democratised, mountainous "Free Greece" long after the Germans were ousted. To many, the *kapetánoi* resuscitated a dream of a Greece liberated from foreign domination – not Turks this time, but Germans and British and Americans. The image lives, and the dream won't quite die.

Of Vláchoi and empty mountains: There is an underside to the myth of mountain man. The word *Vláchos* – both the ethnic label of many of Greece's transhumant shepherds, and the simple occupational term for "shepherd" – holds a hint of scorn. It is the Greek equivalent of the term "hill-billy" and draws on the same imagery. Moreover, *vláchos* sounds almost like *vlákos*, "idiot," and though Greek ears keenly distinguish *chi* from *káppa*, the phonic resemblance is gleefully savoured. *Vláchoi* – the lot of them – are the butt of countless jokes, which portray them as brawny but dull and silent.

This underside reveals less about ethnic slurs than about a vaguely guilty disdain for a whole way of life. As people have gradually abandoned the mountains for Athens and Chicago and Vancouver, they have learned to reject that life, even to see that once "heroic" shepherd as uncouth, unlettered, slightly ridiculous.

On the lower slopes, some villages survive by combining small-scale shepherding and livestock raising with the growing of high-quality tobacco and cereals, and by cultivating orchards which thrive in the cooler climate: peaches, apples, pears, cherries, walnuts and chestnuts. If they happen to be beautiful – like old stone-built villages – and not too hard to find, they might attract tourists, and then sweaters and weavings and souvenir hand-carved shepherds' crooks may bring in needed income. All too many villages are hardly more than "old people's homes," with too few children to support a school (to say nothing of a doctor), where the only weddings are those of the children of urban migrants returning for a "traditional" celebration in their parents' beloved village, and where Gypsy musicians complain that celebrations have become "cold" things. At the funerals – far outnumbering weddings – old women lament not only their dead kin but the empty houses of this high place, "forgotten by God."

On the plains: The plains – the *kámboi*, as Greeks call them – hold no hallowed place in the national mythology. Marshy and malarial, muggy in summer and muddy in winter, they have seldom inspired the poets, who find few metaphors in their flatness. So, absent among the rocks and mountains and sea and sun of tourist board posters, we are almost surprised that plains exist here. Redeemed at times by the curiosities of human architecture (the abundance of windmills on Crete's Lassíthi Plain) or by the surprise of mountains (Mount Parnássus rising from the Boeotian plains) the *kámboi* arouse our respectful interest, not our passions.

Yet the plains – flat, rolling, and if we stretch the term, sloping patches of plateau – have been among the most coveted of spaces in Greece. Certainly the Ottomans recognised their value. As their empire expanded in the 15th century, they awarded a parcel (*timar*) of this most fertile of Greek land to each loyal warrior (*spahi*). In return for defending and managing (not owning) this land (since all land belonged to Allah, and was overseen by his earthly representative, the Sultan), he was allowed to collect a set tithe from Muslim and Christian peasants who retained firm rights to cultivate it. It was a system designed to prevent a strong landed aristocracy (of the sort which wrought havoc in a deteriorating Byzantium) and as long as it worked, the peasants fared reasonably well. As it began to break down in the face of pressures from the West as from within the empire, peasants suffered.

Poorer peasants: From the 16th century onward, the *timar* system gradually gave way to that of the infinitely more oppressive *chiflik*. The Ottomans had initially introduced the *chiflik* (a large tract of land under hereditary ownership) as a way of putting previously unused land under cultivation, but this relatively minor form of landholding gradually became dominant, coming to include formerly *timar* lands and expanding to the fertile plains areas of the Peloponnése, Théssaly, Macedónia and Thrace. These *chiflikia*, never recognised as legal by the Ottoman state, enriched the landlord but made the share-cropping peasant poorer and less secure, sometimes ending a harvest season with barely a third of what he and his family had produced.

Those who did not escape endured poverty and upheaval. Many such peasants joined in the early 19th-century struggles for national independence in the hope of acquiring a bit of the ousted Turks' lands. As it happened, some land fell into the hands of equally powerful Greek landlords, while other properties reverted to the state. Many families acquired small pieces by "squatting" while formal redistribution of Turkish *chiflikia* proceeded fitfully. In 1905 and 1910, the government's failure to redistribute *chiflikia*

reform was completed only when Metaxás, a bizarrely populist-fascist dictator, came to power in the 1930s.

A continuity of uncertainty: The major way of making a living on the plains has always been farming. Despite the richness of much of this land, most farmers have remained poor especially in relation to their European counterparts. This is less a consequence of peasant fatalism, familism, and superstition than of a complex combination of factors, including historical patterns of land ownership, Greek state policies, patterns of economic interdependence between Greece and the West, and various commercial priorities and practices over which the farmer has had

of the rich Thessalían plains, annexed to Greece in 1871, resulted in peasant revolts, bloodily repressed. Anxious to stave off a serious social revolution, Venizélos in 1909 launched a programme of radical reform, including land reform; but this faltered in mid-course when Greece became embroiled in the Balkan Wars. The 1923 exchange of populations between Greece and Turkey in the aftermath of the Asia Minor catastrophe forced the government's hand, and thousands of the 1.5 million Greek speaking refugees were resettled in Macedónia and Thrace, on *chiflikia* and in houses and villages abandoned by the Turks. Major land

absolutely no control.

A chronic problem of Greek agriculture has always been too many farmers for the land to support. Small plots and inefficient farming methods made life on the land quite marginal, yet few alternatives outside of emigration to America existed in the 19th and early 20th century.

Historical conditions have also quite literally "shaped" agricultural lands. Large farmsteads are rare; rather, farmers have traditionally clustered their houses in a village and walked out daily (and today, ride out on donkeys or tractors) to scattered fields. Inheritance practices, though varying somewhat among localities, have generally ensured that a father's fields, and those his wife had brought as part of her dowry, would be divided equally among all his children, with daughters awarded their portion – or its equivalent in livestock, a house, or cash – as a dowry at marriage. Since fields varied in fertility, protection from wind and access to water, it has not been uncommon for even small parcels to be subdivided, and then re-subdivided, with each generation.

The system is not as mad as we might think. It is surprising to learn, accustomed as we are to thinking that only massive fields and mono-cropping make sense, that a handful of tiny plots, growing varied produce,

to Athens, others to Australia) to harvest together is a logistical nightmare, and those who could be present are unwilling to risk "misunderstandings," like accusations of filching from those who cannot. On the ground, plots become so small, and so scattered, they cannot support a family.

The large agricultural estate – whether an Ottoman legacy or a more recent conglomeration – can be found, too. From Naúplia's citrus groves to Naoússa's peach orchards and Théssaly's fields of cotton, estate owners search for extra hands at harvest time. Along with impoverished tourists and local day-labourers, Gypsies figure importantly in this migrant labour force. Though wages are

may provide the farmer a real stability in areas where rain is unpredictable and soil fertility marginal. "A little bit of everything" can be better than a big crop that fails.

Yet the land's progressive fragmentation has sometimes reached ludicrous proportions. Tales abound of single trees – an olive tree, say, or walnut tree – in which 15 households of second-and third-cousins own shares. Ironically, such a tree often goes unharvested: trying to gather all 15 representatives (some of whom have now moved

often low, such seasonal work allows them to preserve their independence. While their Romany-speaking compatriots (perhaps 100,000 or more live in Greece) survive as musicians or peddlers, these Gypsies move across the land with the harvests, setting up roadside encampments of trucks and tents.

Like peasants everywhere, Greek farmers were – and are – perpetually vulnerable to all manner of disaster: drought and pestilence, crop failures, fluctuations in the price of agricultural produce internationally and locally, the whims of changing governments. Indebtedness – to the grocer, as to the state controlled Agricultural Bank (established in

Left and **right**, Greek salads mix *féta*, olives and lots of the local baker's bread for dunking.

1929) which they approach for loans – has been the rule. Farmers once dependent on the *chiflik* owner have now become dependent on the state.

Indeed, one of the basic themes in farming life is the confrontation between the farmer and the state bureaucracy. Traditionally, the only place more crowded than the land was the civil service. When the state apparatus was being developed after 1830, politicians and lawyers with "pull" handed out endless minor clerkships to constituents fleeing rural poverty. (By 1880, Greece had seven times as many civil servants per 10,000 as Britain.) Thus was created a bloated bureaucracy of barely literate peasants, mostly from the

dónians, we are the grass she eats and eats. When she is finished, the politicians milk her dry, and she is so happy, she drops a great load of dung on us!"

To farmers, the impersonal bureaucracy was just as arbitrary as any Ottoman official and infinitely less responsive. Its hierarchical character has meant that petty clerks refused to process even the most routine applications without the immediate superior's approval; while he, in turn, checked with *his* superior, and as requests climbed, so did the piles of paper. Moreover, unless the farmer had some moral claim on him – as a relative, godparent or co-villager – the bored civil servant offered him only the most

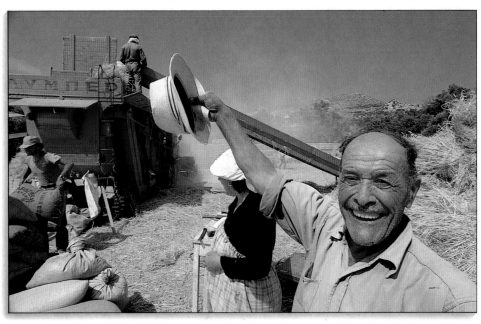

then-politically dominant Peloponnése. Even today, if you talk to plains farmers from the north (and since most such farmland is in Théssaly, Thrace and Macedónia their attitudes reveal a double antagonism: north versus south, farmer versus functionary), they are scornful of the southerners who – until recently – seemed to occupy with all the self-importance they could muster the bulk of the clean and comfortable civil posts: doctors, teachers, lawyers, administrators, policemen. Northerners are fond of saying that the poor but powerful southerners are parasitical on the north's wealth. "The civil service is a big cow," they explain, "and we Mace-

perfunctory assistance. Understandably daunted by this state of affairs, farmers turned to those they considered to have the clout (*méson*) to intervene at higher levels and push through their modest requests. The local politician, the ambitious lawyer, the doctor with connections "helped" the less powerful, obliging them to return the favour (their votes or their custom) afterward. Born of such conditions, patronage became endemic. Providing individualistic solutions to systemic problems (and obstructing the requests of the "uncooperative"), patronage thwarted collective action among farmers, at the same time as it ensured that they remain politically and socially docile. Yet resentment to the system grew as well, and it was in no small part PASOK's pledge to make war on *rousféti*, "string-pulling," that landed its election victory in 1981.

A Macedónian "coffee-bar-disco": In southern Macedónia, in the melodious-sounding region of Roumlouki, a refugee village of 800 – laid out in the typical manner of such "new" villages, with houses plunked onto individual plots in symmetrical rows – sits on the crevice joining mountain to plain. Looking backwards, westwards, that is, you see only green mountain rising. Looking eastward – as all the houses do – to the sea, invisible yet present, you see an endless,

it is ethnically mixed: half "indigenous Macedónians," wiry and taciturn with an accent both thick and abrupt; and half "Póndoi," refugees from the Black Sea. Póndoi are a remarkable people: literate, progressive, solidaristic, they still write plays and TV serials in their distinctive dialect, while their rhythmically subtle, exhilarating dances are popular throughout the northern countryside. Yet they, along with the Chíots, remain the scapegoats of Greek national humour.

The village's Macedónians, though poorer, consider their indigenous status – *dópyi*, "of this place" – a source of an irrefutable moral superiority, and view these inter-

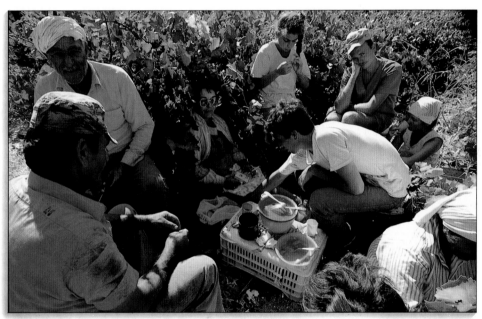

hazy flatness. Once a *chiflik*, cultivated with tobacco, it is now covered with peach orchards and fields of wheat.

The village is described by one travel guide as "insignificant"; presumably it cannot compete with the spectacular ancient ruins found nearby. And although it is in summer deluged by busloads of tourists, in winter it supports only one young archaeologist and one bored archaeological guard. Oblivious to its fame the village carries on in its quite ordinary way. Like many in the area,

Left, a happy farmer during harvest. **Above**, workers break for a mid-morning snack.

lopers with their strange language "Turks." Though their children study and court and sometimes marry each other, those beyond middle-age stick mostly with their "own people," eyeing each other warily from across the coffee-house.

Amalía, namesake of Greece's first Bavarian queen, is 15, chubby, and wants to be an actress, and she is the only girl in the "Paradise," a bleak, chilly coffee-bar in the upstairs of a two-storey concrete cavern. She chatters gaily while her 17-year-old brother, Ioánnis, on whom she dotes, and who is now "chaperoning" her, slouches gloomily at the next table. Since it is winter, the young men aren't sitting on top of tractors or ladders wedged into peach trees, spraying fertilizer and pesticide: Instead they're sitting here, not playing cards, not arguing politics (like their fathers), just sitting, smoking, waiting for something to happen.

Amalía's mother, Stavroúla, grew up here, a child of Póndian refugees, but her father, Yiórgos, was born of refugee parents hailing from Bursa, who were resettled in 1923 in a village near Véria. Yiórgos' father was a cloth merchant before the 1912 catastrophe, and could never accustom himself to the farming life. Yiórgos, on the other hand, loved to make things grow, but with the devastations of the wars and the uncertain-

If it weren't for the "Paradise", Amalía would be miserable. The girls her age never go there – their fathers are too strict, or they're cramming for university entrance exams, so they can escape this place – which just proves her theory that people here are "bad," that they have nothing to do but gossip! Sometimes, Amalía visits her aunt, whose house in the long empty spaces of winter is a gathering place for neighbourhood women, and one of them always reads the residue in her coffee-cup, for a laugh, telling her who she'll marry, while Amalía protests she's not interested in marriage.

She won't have to stay here forever. Her parents have already built her a flat in Véria

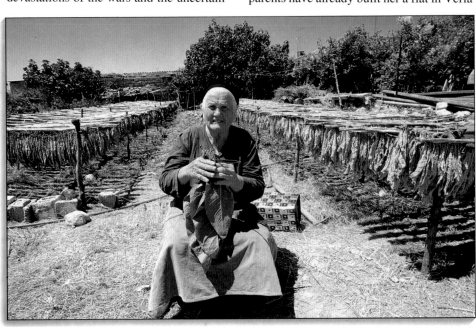

ties of farming, he decided to leave the land in 1953, to work in a German plastics factory. When he came back in 1963, he married, and opened a small café in Véria. But, nostalgic for the "clean air" of the countryside, he made frequent visits to his wife's village, planting peach trees on land she'd inherited from her father, until he decided, in 1982, that they should move there permanently. They opened a small grill on the road at the bottom of town, which a stalwart but always exhausted Stavroúla manages. They began to build a "villa" on the plain. Still in mid-construction, it is a huge damp concrete mansion with marble floors and no toilet.

– her "dowry" house. They don't really want her to marry a farmer; a bank teller would be nice, or some decent fellow with his own shop. Like the one with the record store who makes the "pirated" tape copies for the "Paradise Disco," where every Saturday night, teenagers from the surrounding villages gather to primly sip beer and whisky, and smoke and watch each other. There, strobes throbbing, Madonna crooning in her little-girl voice, you'd never know you were on the edge of a Roumlouki plain, until the music shifts. An electric piano thumps out a fast 5/8 rhythm, and teenage stars of the local folk dance troupe, showing off the fancy improvisations they've been learning, lead a long line of pressed bodies through the taut, tiny movements of *tik*.

The changing face of the plains: On a drive through the towns and farming villages of the plains, one is struck by the amount of new house construction and farm machinery. Indeed, with tractors and earthmovers and ubiquitous mud, the scene often evokes a real estate venture before landscaping. Postwar economic aid certainly helped rebuild the countryside. But the noticeable bourgeoisification of the wealthier farming villages has also depended on the surplus of farmers emigrating (alone or with their families) to Germany and Australia in the 1950s

pletely, many find themselves imprisoned in a domesticity their mothers never knew. They remember the drudgery of farming in the pre-tractor era with little fondness, yet the oft heard remark that such a housewife "just sits" reminds them of their economic dependency on their husbands. It also betokens a loss of status and power, for men are sceptical when "the little housewives" (*nikokyroúles*) start talking *feminisimós*. "It's men who are oppressed," they protest. "We work so you can eat."

High inflation and rising material aspirations mean that most families want the woman to bring in wages, but opportunities in farming villages are limited. A woman

and 1960s, or to the oil rigs of Saudi Arabia in the 1970s. The village prospered from the handsome remittances sent back to their families; at the same time, relatives and neighbours were often able to rent or sharecrop the fields left behind.

It is one of modernisation's contradictions that mechanised farming has, in a pattern familiar in the Third World, frequently marginalised women, whose farming skills and labour are rendered obsolete. While women have by no means left the land com-

Left, tobacco, grown in the northern plains, is prepared for drying. **Above**, tobacco leaves.

might earn a little extra by contracting with large garment companies to do piecework at her own sewing machine, a practice which alleviates the problem of finding childcare but denies her a secure income and most social security benefits. Other women work in family shops or small enterprises.

It is partly in response to the village's limited work opportunities that parents want an urban bridegroom for their daughter, and a professional job for their son. Here, women with no special skills may find jobs in light industry cutting or stitching in garment workshops, or stuffing sliced pears into cans. In a gesture which promotes – not just anticipates – this move, the "dowry" flat is now likely to be bought or built in Athens or Thessaloníki, or in one of the larger plains towns, like Sérres, Kateríni, Trípoli.

Some farming villages look more affluent, and some farmers are no doubt wealthier than before. Yet farming life is still perceived as dirty, exhausting and unpredictable, and the horizons of village life limited by few jobs and a dearth of entertainment and cultural life. The farmers' children tend to marry out, and the migratory current still flows towards the cities. It remains to be seen whether "decentralisation" schemes – bringing small hospitals, day-care centres, adult education and greater administrative au-

dress unimaginable to the sartorially puritanical natives.

If the tourist regards the island as a temporary escape and the sea as soothing and benevolent, the perspective of those who live, and who have lived for generations, on the island, is rather different. In the early days of tourism, islanders seldom knew how to swim, and children who ventured too far into the waters were regularly snatched by shrieking mothers who had no reason to romanticise the sea. To them, the sea was no less treacherous for its beauty. "There are three things to fear in the world," goes an old proverb, "fire, woman, and the sea." Death by the sea is both a memory and an expecta-

tonomy to the countryside – and the increasingly unlivable conditions of Athens, can turn the stream.

In the islands: When the foreigners began to descend on the islands, first in dribbles and then in droves, it was perhaps their worship of the sea which first amazed the island inhabitants. But tourists, who appear in the summertime, are to the sea only fair-weather friends, lured by its tranquil visage, azure and clear and benign. They lie dreamily on the sands, courting the sun for a golden-brown colour eschewed not so many years ago by the island aristocrats as the mark of a common labourer, in a state of public un-

tion to those who live, winter as in summer, at its edge. They know the winter squalls, the convulsions of rain and wind that erupt without warning and toss fishing *caïques* like so many toy boats in a bathtub. The sea gives life with its fish and its sponges, but also takes it back.

Geologically, the 1,425 isles in Greek territorial waters are born of the meeting of sea and mountain, for the isles are merely the crests of now submerged mountain ranges. About one-tenth of these are inhabited, some by only a few monks and goats. It is tempting to stretch the comparison, for the individuality of each island in its architecture, costume and dialect is striking, and would seem to suggest an isolation reminiscent of high mountain villages. Yet this individuality is not a simple matter of remoteness. On the contrary, there has always been frequent and intense contact among clusters of islands, and within each island group the central Cycládes, the eastern Dodécanése, the northerly Spórades and the Iónian islands of the western coast – songs are traded, wives are sometimes sought, house styles remain familiar. Rather, embedded in the houses and faces and words of each island is its own particular history of labour, ecology and foreign domination.

The pre-modern economy of sea-piracy

of the European principalities was to extract wealth passing as merchandise through the islands, some wealth stayed on the island, concentrated in the hands of an indigenous elite. This local elite owned land (as in the Iónian Islands) or ships and shipyards, on islands spread from Hydra (Ídra) to Chíos (Híos), and often cooperated with the Europeans on mutually profitable terms. At the turn of the century, many islands had a clear class hierarchy.

On islands blessed with good soil and adequate water resources, some inhabitants lived then, as today, as farmers, and farmed very much as their compatriots did on the mainland. Grapes, melons, figs, tomatoes,

and plunder, shipbuilding and manning vast merchant fleets, sponge-diving and trade made the islands until this century among the richest and most coveted territories in the Mediterranean world. The Ottomans held a much more tenuous and intermittent grip on the islands than on the mainland. European principalities, from the "Hospitaler" Knights of St John to the Venetians, the Genoese, the French and the British, sought through political control and trading privileges to exploit the strategic position and trade of particular islands. Though the object

Left, octopus being cleaned and, <u>above</u>, drying.

oranges and lemons thrive in the arid summer heat of many islands, and beans and onions can be coaxed to grow as well. On luxuriant Corfú (Kérkira), tenant farmers laboured on the estates of local aristocrats in a system not so different from Turkish *chiflikia*, while in the pre-independence Cycládes, the rocky hills were shared, as on Tínos, between the islanders and a powerful monastery.

In many ways, the distinctiveness of each island is a legacy which speaking in the present tense obscures. The island economies of the present, for all except those blessed with fertile land and plenty of water, depend largely on the remittances of island migrants (and their pensions when they return home to retire) and on the development of tourism. The elegant mansions which rise along the hill encircling the Sími harbour bear mute witness to the incredible wealth of the sea traders and shipbuilders, and renowned sponge divers, but they are empty now, mausoleums, mute testimonies to a way of life which collapsed when upstaged by a steamship economy. The wealthy pulled out their money and moved – to Athens, to Tarpon Springs, Florida, to Argentina. On the skeleton of this affluence a new prosperity is being built. For it is the stark and lovely grandeur of these abandoned

sighted (and un-bespectacled) young driver of the motor-scooter decided on a very fast late-night ride. With his friend riding postilion he roared up a dark road in a braggadocio of blind speed (so to speak) and crashed headlong into a tractor coming the other direction. It was a tragedy – but all too typical, for the rate of motorcycle deaths, of both passengers and unwary pedestrians, is horrifyingly high on Kálymnos. Driving a motorcycle very fast is just a new manifestation of a very old code of male bravado.

The Kalymnians like to think of themselves as wild and fearless, rather like their own harsh mountains, and they scorn the soft life of the farmers of verdant Kos, who they

houses and harbours which tourist agencies translate as "picturesque" and which draws the concrete-weary foreigners.

A Kalymnian close-up: If you happened to be on Kalymnos in November 1984, you would have seen the twisted wreck of a motor-scooter and a tractor, entwined in a grotesque metallic embrace, standing like a civic sculpture of some patriotic local hero on the central quay. The authorities put it there as an "example," the crumpled outcome of yet another act of suicidal swagger. The death of two men and the crippling of a third resulted, or so a shocked and grieving town whispered to each other, when the severely short-

sneeringly dub *kótes* (hens). But the tradition of swagger is almost certainly derived from the sponge-divers, who pushed themselves relentlessly in quest of wages and prestige, and profits for their captains, and who daily raced death (in the form of the "bends") in the sea.

The sponge industry is much diminished now, but there are other ways that Kalymnians show their *andrismós*, the Greek version of "machismo." Becoming summer *kamákia* (see pages 285–86) is popular among the less imaginative, but this is not unique to Kálymnos and, anyway, tourism is not well developed here. Others show prowess with more dangerous feats. Throwing dynamite off the mountain tops announces, and honours, the Kalymnian who perishes tragically at sea; it is also thought the only seemly tribute to the old sponge-diver who disembarks the Athens steamer in a coffin. It is also thrown on a dare. Very much in the tradition of noise-makers everywhere else in Greece, the crack of dynamite marks the beginning of Easter.

Fewer men dive for sponges now, though many sign on with the merchant fleets for a few years in the island male's rite of passage, drinking and whoring and spending lavishly in the raucous pattern of sailor life, until they decide it is time to come home and get

daily management of the island to the women, as their fathers and grandfathers had done before.

The myth of the island woman: In the mythology of the land, the mountain man finds his apogee in the island woman. Mainland Greeks contrast their own heroic traditions of the "masculine" mountains with the "femininity" of the islanders. Island dances are soft and undulating, like the sea, and very quick, they insist, while theirs are upright, rigid and proud, like warriors dancing on mountain peaks. (They forget the low, quick, sweeping *zonarádhiko* of the Thrácian hills.)

The music, too, is "sweet." In this, they have given a sexual nuance to what is prob-

married. From the 1950s onward, hundreds of men also left for periods of five to 25 years abroad, building highway bridges from Ohio to Florida or sweating in the factories, of Darwin, Australia, a city so full of Kalymnians the Australian-Greek taxi-drivers simply call it "Kálymnos." Sometimes these men married a Kalymnian bride and returned abroad with her to raise a family (re-emigrating to Kálymnos again a generation later). Just as often, though, men emigrated alone, with cousins and compatriots, leaving the

Left, transporting fish between the islands. **Above**, a *kafeneíon* in late afternoon; fisherman.

ably more accurately the difference between a refined urban sound and a raucous, rustic style. Never mind that the ubiquitous synthesiser has infiltrated the *nisiótika* of popular cassettes – it cannot destroy the lightness of that most popular and familiar genre of island music, a music developed in a network of wealthy Aegéan port cities, including the sophisticated Greek-dominated Asia Minor cities of Smyrna and Constantinople. This style uses an ensemble of stringed instruments: a dolorous, hauntingly human-voiced violin; a *santoúri* – hammer dulcimer of the Orient – whose resonating strings create a waterfall of sound; and the long necked and deep throated voice of the Turkish *ud* (in Greek, the *úti*), or its smaller substitute, the strummed *laúto*. (The reedy island bagpipe, the *tsambúna*, goes unmentioned.) Island songs, with an almost courtly and Venetian chivalry, celebrate love, courtship, beauty: from the Cretan verse-romance *Erotókritos* whose verses still tunefully resound throughout the Aegéan, to the improvised teasing couplets, the *pismatiká*, of the Cycládes and Dodécanése.

The "femininity" which mainlanders attribute to the islands is no doubt intertwined with their suspicion that women actually run things there. And indeed, the seasonal exo-

months and years at sea? Tales of bored housewives and exhausted island-bound lovers proliferate even on the islands, though their veracity remains quite unverifiable.

Yet on some islands, the family of an unmarried girl guards her reputation against slander ("Better your eye come out than your name," the proverb warns) with a vehemence rarely found these days on the mainland. On Kálymnos, for instance, co-education in secondary schools was long resisted; it is only a few years since island teenagers began to attend class together, and some parents are skeptical that the camaraderie of these mixed student *parées* can really be innocent.

dus of men as they followed the ships, the fish, the sponges or the factory job in Mannheim or Melbourne, has given many an island a strikingly female character. If tourism has enabled many men to return, the "feminine" quality is still perceptible in the way women dominate neighbourhood spaces. "A man is a visitor in his own house," Greeks say, and islanders with even more reason, as men are shooed out of the house every morning so women can get on with their chores. Mainlanders slyly insinuate that island women not only dominate their men, but cuckold them. After all, how do they manage while their husbands are away

Consequently, an explicit moral and religious conservatism accommodates a tradition of feisty women with most peculiar results: the same community which, pleading local "custom," petitions the bishop to negotiate a Kalymnian exemption from Greek law, giving them permission to marry daughters off at 14 before they lose their hallowed chastity – amiably tolerates the 25-year extra-marital liaison of a lusty yet commendably fastidious "housewife".

This last word translates badly. *Nikokyrá* (house-mistress), though an entirely ordinary title, holds no slur, and all the more so in the Aegéan, for here, houses belong to women. If mainland brides used to move in with their mothers-in-law on many Aegéan islands, the mother still gives her house to her oldest daughter when she marries, moving herself (and her husband) to smaller quarters: a tiny flat in the basement, a shed on the edge of the property, a rented room nearby. Second and third daughters, who once could expect little in the way of dowry, now almost always get a house as well.

Today, now married, that island daughter probably shares a room or two of this house with strangers. Like innumerable island houses, hers features a scrawled sign: "ROOMS. CHAMBRES. RAUME" and, summer after summer, countless blonde and sleek for-

everyone say – and she says it, too but sometimes she wonders.

In the city: Viewed from the heights of Pendéli, which flanks the city to the east, Athens resembles – as the novelist John Fowles put it – a mass of dice scattered across the Attica plain. Block after block of more or less identical six-storey cement "multiple dwellings" (as they are known in Greek) do not make it the most beautiful urban centre in Europe. Moreover, the rapidity with which the city was thrown up effectively postponed questions of urban planning, zoning, and the siting of local parks to some later date. With close to 4 million people living in its greater area, Athens is

eigners skip down her stairs on the way to the beach and struggle back up after a bout in the disco. They may pass in the hallway, but in many ways their worlds remain separate. She sells postcards in the family tourist shop, while her husband works in the construction crew of a new hotel. She watches *Dallas* as she crochets another doilie for her daughter's trousseau. She worries about her son becoming a *kamáki* and about her daughter passing her university examinations. "Tourism is good. It brings money," she hears

Left, musicians serenade newly-weds. **Above**, a tourist portrait painter confers immortality.

today a concrete matter of fact.

Planners and politicians are attempting to make it more attractive by protecting those few houses still standing which possess any architectural merit and by converting certain side-streets into pedestrian walkways or turning the odd vacant lot into a playground for children. It may be a question of too little too late, but a good many political points are nonetheless scored for trying to make Athens more livable.

Of course, none of this ever stopped people from both visiting and enjoying the Greek capital. Beneath its horrific architectural visage Athens conceals a palpably human heart. Nowhere better than here does the ancient formulation "Man is the measure of all things" ring true. More than just a heart, Athens has soul and some districts, such as Athinás Street around the meat market or Pláka on a hot night, are downright funky.

What makes Athens attractive are its temperamental inhabitants. Clicking their worrybeads, making funny gestures with their hands, by turns provocatively rude or unexpectedly friendly, arguing and laughing… it is enlivening to walk among these people. Athenians do not hesitate to show their feelings and it often seems that emotional states constitute a more powerful communcative device than words. After a

the influx of Greek refugees from Asia Minor. These newcomers were exceedingly poor, in many cases arriving from Turkey with just the clothes on their backs. At first they were settled in makeshift barracks around the city in areas such as Néa Ionía or Néa Smyrni, names which recall their land of origin. Thus the trend of urban expansion was founded and other characteristics such as inner city poverty, the dark underworld of petty criminals (*mánges*) and *rembétika* music (see pages 299–301) came to form part of the capital's image.

Athens has mushroomed in the past 60 years, a period which saw the city's population soar from 453,000 to more than 3 mil-

few days, visitors who expected to remain casual observers find themselves expressing long-forgotten feelings, exercising new facial muscles and vocal chords; unexpectedly at ease and unselfconscious. Aristotle described these as the effects of watching good drama and labelled them catharsis. In modern Athens catharsis is always on offer, only there is no strict demarcation between audience and actors and the drama never ends.

It should be kept in mind that Athens, as sprawling urban metropolis, is a very recent, and unforeseen development. The city was suddenly transformed, increased by one quarter practically overnight, in 1923 with

lion. That's a 568 percent increase over a stretch of time when the population of the country as a whole rose only by 93 percent. Clearly, there has also been a significant movement from the countryside into the city. All roads lead to Athens.

The sheer density of people makes for monumental traffic jams twice a day and four times when there is late shopping. Automobiles are a prime cause of smog (the so-called *néfos*) which chokes the city during windless periods. This smog also mixes with atmospheric humidity to form an abrasive acid which has been dissolving stone monuments that have stood for millennia in the city. Recently a restricted area was drawn around the city centre in order to alleviate the problems of traffic and smog. On alternate days private cars with even and odd license plate numbers are allowed to circulate within this exclusion zone. This is great for taxi drivers but there are not enough cabs to cope with the rush-hour demands. Be prepared to accept a jitney-like arrangement where other people share stretches of the ride with you.

Urban attraction: While the disadvantages of the metropolis are all too apparent to the casual observer, the benefits which Athenians enjoy are perhaps less obvious. There are more doctors, medical specialists, and hospital beds here than in any other region of

thing from chocolate factories and breweries to the massive dockyards and refineries sited along the coast at places such as Pérama, Scaramánga and Elefsína (Eléfsis). The drive from Athens to Córinth is virtually a tour of Greece's industrial heartland.

Those who hold a high school diploma are eligible for a number of prestigious civil service positions which mean anything from working for the electric company to serving as a government adviser. Such positions are desirable because salaries are inflation-indexed and hiked every year, best of all they are secure for life and include a pension scheme. This permanence and security are highly prized in a society which is emerging

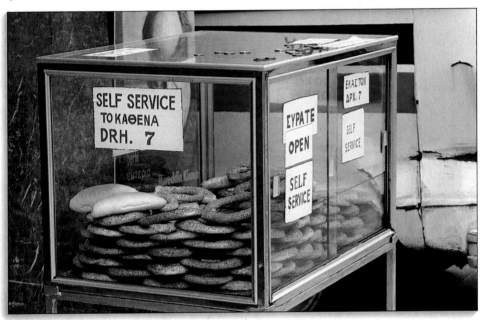

Greece. Educational opportunities are also superior. There are more schools, teachers and university places per capita in Athens. And when the studying is finished, there are jobs. Furthermore, Athenians are often more highly paid than workers in other parts of the country.

Greece as a whole may be underdeveloped industrially, but 50 percent of the nation's industries (employing 10 or more people) are located in or around the capital; every-

Two kinds of self-service: Italian ice cream and Greek doughnut, *loukoumádes* (left) and *kouloúria*, a favourite breakfast (above).

from a primarily agrarian mode of existence (until 1960 more than 50 percent of the population were living on the land).

Whereas in former times it was hoped that a son would work his father's fields and flocks, such a proposition is now scoffed at by young men in villages. Supreme admiration is no longer accorded the rugged, autarchic shepherd able to provide his family with goats' milk, cheese, meat and other basic needs. The image of the educated civil servant or professional has usurped earlier ideals, office workers do not dirty their hands or sully their clothes, and some civil servants will allow the fingernail on their little finger to grow extra long as evidence of their non-manual employment.

Education is thus consummately valued as it facilitates upward social mobility. In this striving for knowledge and in the fascination for foreign goods and ideas – for which the Greeks have a word, *xenomanía* (see pages 312–13 in the Cultural ABCs section) – one may discern many symptoms of the "developing country" syndrome. People are engaged in the effort to secure white collar employment which they associate with an image of modernity and sophistication. Yet Greece has neither the industrial base nor the GNP to support such aspirations at present. In relation to the GNP there are twice as many

ment would be if they returned to Greece, they remain abroad. Who can blame them when, by some estimates, there are more lawyers in Athens than in all of France.

In the view of villagers, the move from the country to Athens is one which is likely to secure employment, relative financial prosperity, and prestige, though in which order it is not exactly clear. In any case it is not easy to move back to the village except for holidays or retirement because this would mean re-adapting to village life, which pales after a stretch of time in the city. Athens is the centre of Greek political, commercial and cultural life. More than 17 major newspapers are printed every day in the capital, account-

students pursuing higher education in Greece as in the United States. Granted that most businesses originate in family enterprises, no real demand has arisen for managers at the executive level. Thus many of those who complete courses of higher education end up in positions which under-utilise their talents.

Some go to work as teachers in the private tutorial schools (*frontistíria*) which one sees all around Athens. These institutions help students to cram for the State University entrance exams. Many talented students go abroad to study and, aware of how limited their opportunities for research or employ-

ing for 90 percent of national circulation. National government-sponsored, and most other Greek television also emanates from Athens, a fact apparent in the advertisement of products designed for the city dweller or in the promotions for Athenian stores not to mention the weather reports, which concentrate on conditions in the capital. Living in this city, one feels oneself to be connected to the navel of the Hellenic world. It is difficult to cut the cord.

East meets west: Athens is the primary point of entry into Greece. In 1981 close to 2 million tourists, over half of all those arriving by air in Greece, landed at Athens'

Hellenikon Airport. In this and in other respects Athens is the main interface between Greece and the rest of the world. Here, villagers from outlying rural areas will probably encounter European and international culture for the first time. This is also the place where most Europeans will form a first impression of Greek culture.

It is said that approached from the east Athens is the first European city, and approached from the west, it is the first oriental city. This interplay of east and west may be put to use in making sense of the cityscape as well as the types of people living and interacting within it. On the western pole, ideally speaking, is Syntagma Square bounded by

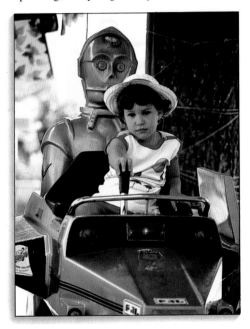

the offices of international airlines, deluxe hotels and the House of Parliament. Syntagma bears a smart Western look; Gucci, St Laurent and Chanel vie for the allegiance of the heart in this zone where English is the *lingua franca*. Visitors from rural Greece are totally awed when they stray into this area. Yet they feel slightly uncomfortable for there is nothing here to which they may readily relate. One humble man from a Cycládic island expressed alarm at not being able to tell who was Greek from who was not.

Left, cosmopolitan Athens. Above, international marketing has reached even the smaller towns.

Less than a mile away is the opposite pole, Omónoia Square. Here one may savour a Greek coffee in some of the largest coffee houses (*kafeneía*) to be found anywhere in the country. (Try the "Alexander the Great" or the "Neon".) Women are served but one cannot help noticing that they form a distinct minority in these male domains. Omónoia is filled with hawkers and small merchants who peddle anything from wristwatches to rice pudding. At night, men appear wheeling large copper samovars with a warm drink called *tselépi*; a creamy, slightly gingery concoction said to be the perfect antidote for an oncoming cold. Here, it is the tourist's turn to feel foreign.

Omónoia and Syntagma are representative of two extremes of Athenian, one could even say Greek, identity. These two styles, the traditional and the modern, are to some degree apparent in every individual in what amounts to a cultural bi-polarity. As a hypothetical illustration, if a *Romaiós* (that is, a Greek of traditional leanings) needs to go from Pláka to Omónoia, he would possibly choose a course so as to pass Athens' cathedral, the Mitrópolis, then proceed through a district of small shops selling cloth, jewellery, household and religious objects; that is, if it is decided against dropping down to Athinás Street, which is itself practically a full-scale bazaar. The more progressive Greek, the Hellene, would probably take a course so as to pass through Syntagma and then proceed down Stadíou Street past numerous cinemas showing subtitled foreign films, department stores and neat shopping arcades. At one point there is a museum of folk art with a statue of Kolokotrónis, the hero of the Greek War of Independence, standing before it. For the Hellene, Greek traditionalism is a strange sign of backwardness and an embarrassing indication of Eastern influences. It belongs in museums.

In the different routes which they might choose, the imaginary Hellene and *Romaiós* confirm two very separate experiences of the capital – and life in general. This mixture of east and west may possibly account for the popularity of Greece as a holiday spot, and the attractiveness of Athens in particular. One explores and lives out romantic fantasies linked with the east, but in a constrained fashion. There is always the familiar, Western aspect of the city to fall back on.

"ATHENA, MY GRANDMOTHER"

One of Greece's best contemporary writers, Cóstas Taktsis, has written a collection of short stories, Athéna, My Grandmother, *the title referring to both his grandmother and his city. This extract shows how Athens evokes feelings of pride and melancholy.*

I am an Athenian and indeed one of the few fifth-generation Athenians. For the past 40 or so years I've watched Athéna change – for the worse. It's one thing to learn something from books – *"Perhaps Sócrates and Phaédris once sat here, where we are standing now"* – and quite another thing to know it first-hand, so you can say: *"Do you see that busy avenue swarming with cars and exhaust? When I was a child it was a trash-filled ravine with a thin stream which watered the few surviving plane trees."* What I want to say is that I see Athéna over time, in a way which would be impossible for provincial folk or foreigners, and with this same temporal perspective I see myself... As the years pass I begin to feel not simply Athenian but also as if I am a small piece of Athéna, like some microscopic archaeological monument in motion. Sometimes in the evenings when I go out on my terrace to water my flowers – geraniums, jasmine, basil and hibiscus – and I see the provincial folk and tourists hanging from St George's bell tower to get a good look at Athéna, I have the strange, overprotective sense that I am, even if they don't know it, a postcard like the ones they buy to send back home.

I have lived in many cities. A few of them – Sydney, New York – I love dearly, and I would gladly see them again for a bit, even if only once every five years. But more than anywhere else I would like to live out my life here in Athéna, and when the time comes I'd like to die here. And unless something unexpected happens my wish will come true: I'll die someday when the population reaches five million (five-and-a-half million, in high tourist season). By then, I sometimes think, nothing will be left of my Athéna, the Athéna I loved. But something inside of me tells me that I may in fact be wrong. Because – unless something earth-shattering happens – for a long time, forever I hope, there will still be the Lykavitós (Lycabéttus) and Philoppápou hills. By then of course they will have become 'protected' by some tacky public or state organization, and they will have been fenced off with barbed wire. But children and lovers will always find an opening, a hole just big enough to squeeze through. No matter how polluted the air gets the Athenian honey autumn won't change much, nor the gentle Athenian winter, with its kingfisher days, nor the intoxicating spring, nor the narcotic summer, with its rare light breezes. Even if the Sarónic Gulf gets dirtier there will always be a few clear swimming spots. People in, the meantime may have gone to the moon to find jobs but the magic of the moon when it pokes up from behind Imetoú (Hyméttus) peak will always be the same.

Two or three times recently late at night I let my car drive me to Saint John of Rendi. In between the factories that spit up infected vapours and the workers' apartment blocks there are still a few cabbage patches... Driving back I passed the Kerameikós cemetery where I played as a child. Once I couldn't resist the temptation: I left the car in front of the new kitsch Christian church and walked up to the railing. I glued my eyes to the spot where the memorial tomb of Fgesus was, and suddenly, I swear, I saw my grandmother, God rest her soul, quite alive watching me with a look of gentle reproach, as if to say, "So there you are, at least you didn't turn out worse" and then she disappeared. Thanks to her, no matter what my identification papers claim, I am Athenian. Thanks to her I love Athéna. Some say the way she's ended up she's the ugliest capital in the whole world. I don't know, nor does it concern me. Beautiful or ugly, for me she's unique. She's the city in which I was born, in which I have lived and in which my grandmother died. Naturally I have to admit that from some vantage points – just like Athéna the city – she was a monster, and she put me through hell a great portion of my childhood and adolescence but what can I say? She's the only woman... I ever loved.

All Greek males serve two years in the army.

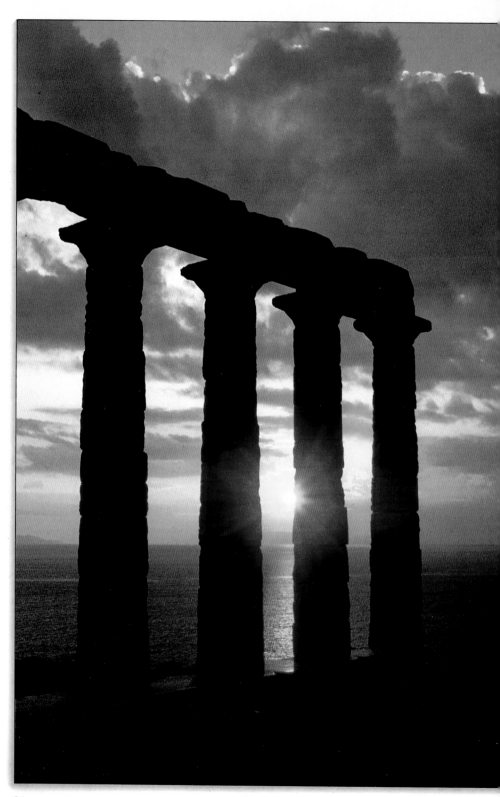

"Marvellous things happen to one in Greece," wrote Henry Miller in *The Colossus of Maroussi*, "marvellous *good* things which can happen to one nowhere else on earth. Somehow, almost as if He were nodding, Greece still remains under the protection of the Creator. Men may go about their puny, ineffectual bedevilment, even in Greece, but God's magic is still at work and, no matter what the race of men may do or try to do, Greece is still a sacred precinct – and my belief is it will remain so until the end of time."

In this section, our writers will take you on 10 individual journeys, each writer to the part of Greece he or she knows best. Starting in the northeastern corner near Turkey and Bulgaria and travelling in a zigzag fashion down to Crete, you'll find the history, geography and local culture of each area covered in detail.

The 10 sections have been loosely designed as two-week itineraries, but of course the longer you stay, the better. Perhaps, like Lord Byron, you will one day be able to declare: "It is the only place I ever was contented in."

Preceding pages: girls during an Easter Epitáphios procession; fishing boats off Kálymnos; the town of Kastráki in Thessaly; olive trees on Crete. **Left**, sunrise at Cape Soúnion.

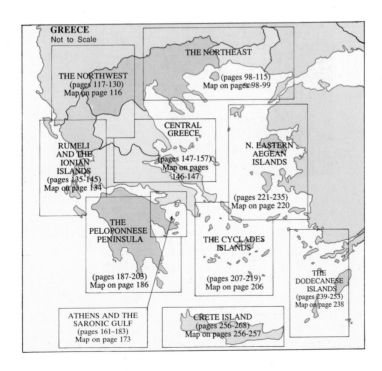

GREECE
Not to Scale

THE NORTHEAST

THE NORTHWEST
(pages 117-130)
Map on page 116

(pages 98-115)
Map on pages 98-99

CENTRAL
GREECE

RUMELI
AND THE
IONIAN
ISLANDS
(pages 135-145)
Map on page 134

(pages 147-157)
Map on pages
146-147

N. EASTERN
AEGEAN
ISLANDS

(pages 221-235)
Map on page 220

THE
PELOPONNESE
PENINSULA

THE CYCLADES
ISLANDS

(pages 187-203)
Map on page 186

(pages 207-219)
Map on page 206

THE
DODECANESE
ISLANDS
(pages 239-253)
Map on page 238

ATHENS AND THE
SARONIC GULF
(pages 161–183)
Map on page 173

CRETE ISLAND
(pages 256-268)
Map on pages 256-257

THE NORTHEAST

Thessaloníki stands about halfway between the Iónian Sea to the west and the Évros River to the east. It is the second largest city of Greece and is often referred to as co-capital with Athens. A line projected north of Thessaloníki reaches the tripartite border between Yugoslavia, Bulgaria and Greece. This line also divides the Northwest of Greece, comprising Épirus and West-

ern Macedónia (Makethonía), from the Northeast including Eastern Macedónia and Thrace (Thráki).

The history of the Northeast is dominated by the movement of tribes, races and nationalities across its territory. The local Macedónian and Thracian populations were subject to constant invasion and flux. On his way to fight Athens and Spárta (Spárti), the Persian Xerxes marched countless troops across the north Aegéan land route, while his fleet followed along the coast. It was from here that Alexander the

Preceding pages: Edward Lear's watercolour of Thessaloník

Great set off to conquer the east, and here that the Romans established the Via Egnatia stretching from the Adriatic coast to the Hellespont (Dardanelles). Later, the disintegrating Byzantine Empire would face continuous incursions from the north due to Slavic expansion. And the Ottoman Turks, advancing from the east, would make a circle across the Balkans, conquering the Macedónian and Thracian lands before closing in on Constantinople.

The sea provided an important access to the northeast, despite the fact that the coast is tucked away at the northeastern-most corner of the Aegéan. Odysseus, leaving Troy for his return journey to Íthaca (Itháki), drifted to the land of the Kikones, the ancient site of Maronia. Southern Greek cities, especially Athens and Chalkis, began their colonisation of the Chalcidice (Halkíthikí) peninsula via the sea as early as the 7th century BC. Later, when Thessaloníki became the second largest city of the Byzantine Empire, Venetians, crusaders and other seafarers skirted the coast to and from Constantinople.

KEY

Road Network

Road Under Construction

Distances In Kilometers 12, 62

National Road Number 15

European Road Number E-92

Shipping Routes

Car Ferry

Airport

Airfield

Yacht Supply Station

Altitude In Meters •2310

Camping

Mountain Hut

Prehistoric Site

Archaeological Site

Byzantine Site

Medieval Site

Monastery

Spa Resort

Cave

Beach Facilities

Ski Center

Golf Course

Scale

1:1,000,000

The northeast does not offer the traveller the magnificent large-scale archaeological sites and stunning temples of central and southern Greece. However, its proximity to other Balkan states and its rather late acquisition by Greece give it greater ethnic variety and more unspoiled natural beauty. Both these features are rapidly changing due to modernisation and integration into a more uniform national culture. The region's sites fall into two categories: either they are too bare to astound, or they are palimpsests where layers of civilization can be read one after another. One of the best examples of the latter category is Thessaloníki itself.

Thessaloníki: To the visitor approaching it by sea, the modern city presents the solid facade of apartment blocks characteristic of many Mediterranean seaside cities. At the beginning of this century, the same view was marked by elegantly rising minarets, which were destroyed either by the Great Fire of 1917 (which turned nearly three quarters of the city to ashes), or by Greek nationalism retaliating for previous Turkish desecration of churches. Behind today's high-rise facade, encircled by the Roman and Byzantine walls, and scattered in the midst of main traffic arteries and pedestrian alleys, lies the city's historical wealth. Roman ruins, Byzantine churches, Turkish buildings and Jewish tombstones are hidden away behind the greenery of *plateíes* or the colourful houses of the old Áno Póli (upper town).

Thessaloníki was founded in 315 BC by the Macedónian king Kassander, who named it after his wife. It was not an important city during the rise of the Macedónian Empire in the 4th century BC. Today its **Archaeological Museum** houses Macedónian, Hellenistic and Roman finds from the whole region, including the notable Sindos and Vergína collections. The latter comprises the magnificent treasures of what are alleged to be Philip II's royal tombs.

Macedónian sites: Philippi, north of Kavála and founded by Philip II himself, has little that is Macedónian to

Below, a quiet moment on the Thessaloníki waterfront.

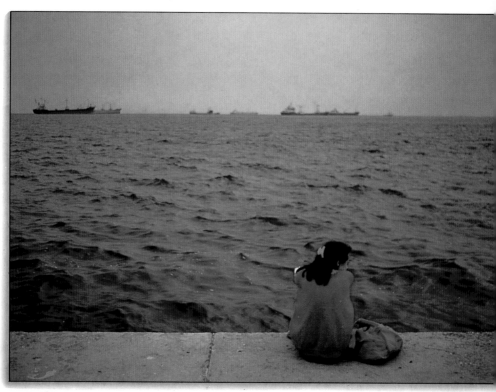

show, for it developed in later Roman times. **Vergína**, on the way to Véroia, was the capital before Pélla and remained the royal cemetery.

The tombs of Philip of Macedónia, discovered in 1977, are closed for further excavation. But there are other tombs and a half-standing palace situated in a pleasant landscape. **Díon**, at the foot of Mount Olympus (Ólimbos) farther south, was founded by Macedónian kings as a place of worship to the Olympian Zeus (Zefs) and, most likely, as a Macedónian show-case to the rest of Greece.

Pélla, on the road to Édessa, is the most outstanding site. The rather small scale of its revealed grounds, and its location right by the side of the road, give it a humbleness which doesn't correspond to its past glory. Standing in the courtyard of the **House of the Lion Hunt**, surrounded by graceful Iónian columns and the exquisite floor mosaics that have survived (some on site, some in the local museum), one cannot help but sense that here stood the imperial

court which became master of the Greek world in the 4th century BC. It is here that Philip of Macedónia planned the conquest of Greece. And here his son, Alexander the Great, trained at arms and was taught by the philosopher Aristotle in preparation for a brilliant though short-lived career as conqueror of the east.

City tour: Thessaloníki gained renown as a Byzantine city. It has yet no Byzantine museum, but an interesting exhibition outlining the city's history is housed in the **White Tower** by the waterfront. This is the city's landmark. Built in the 15th century, it served as a prison under Ottoman rule. In 1826, it was the site of a massacre of mutinous Janissaries, the Sultan's guard, which earned it the name of "Bloody Tower." The memories of this event were brushed away with a coat of whitewash and a consequent change of name. Today this name is misleading, for the tower is no longer white. The steps going up in a spiral around the inner wall are flanked by small deep-set windows which frame partial views of the city and gulf. One can then assemble the different pieces into a single panorama from the battlements.

The Roman ruins are distributed along the two main avenues leading to the waterfront: the **Forum** and **Odeon Galerius Palace Complex** along Dimitríou Goúnari Street. Caesar Galerius built this complex at the beginning of the 4th century, when he chose Thessaloníki as his seat of residence. He was famous for his ruthless persecution of Christians, including the martyrdom of St Demétrius, patron saint of the city. The palace ruins are scattered in the midst of busy **Navarínou Square**, lined with *tavérnes*, snack bars and ice-cream parlours. The triumphal **Arch of Galerius** was built to commemorate the emperor's victory over the Persians: relief panels at its base depict scenes from the campaign.

Churches: Undoubtedly the most important building in the complex is the **Rotunda**, or **Church of Saint George** (**Ághios Yiórgios**), one of the few sur-viving examples of circular Roman architecture. Galerius intended it for his mausoleum, a function it never fulfilled as the emperor fell in battle and his enemy did not return the body to Thessaloníki. With the spread of Christianity, it was soon turned into a church and decorated with glorious wall mosaics which only partially survive around the upper part of the interior. The Rotunda is flanked by a half-standing minaret from the days when it served as a mosque. It dominates the views down to the sea from above and up to the **Chain Tower**, from the seafront marking the northeastern corner of the Byzantine fortifications.

Another early Christian building is the tiny **Church of Óssios Davíd**, tucked away in the old part of town up the hill. It was allegedly built by Galerius' daughter, Theodóra. The unique 5th-century mosaic in the apse is one of the earliest samples of its kind. Its outstanding beauty derives from the *naif* depiction of Ezekiel's vision, the rare representation of a youthful Christ, the

Understatement in argument is not a Greek characteristic

fine colours and elaborate symbolism.

From Ossios Davíd one can continue a visit to the city's important Byzantine monuments by following one of two paths: one goes back down the hill to the major 5th to 8th-century basilicas while the other makes a long semi-circle across the old city past 14th-century churches.

The early Christian basilica was a plain rectangular building. In a sense, its plan derives from the classical Greek temple, replacing the exterior colonnade with walls. Both the 5th-century **Ahiropíitos Church** and the heavily restored **Church of St Demétrius (Ághios Thimítrios)** are such examples. Both have been badly damaged by fire and the surviving mosaics must be sought out: in the first under the arches, in the second above the pillars on the east and west sides of the church. The crypt in St Demétrius is supposed to mark the site of the Roman bath where the saint was martyred. The **Church of Aghía Sophía** (Holy Wisdom) shows a first attempt to convert the basilica into

a domed structure. The inside of the dome, which represents the heavenly vault, is covered with a surprisingly well-preserved large-scale mosaic depicting the Ascension, illustrated by the corresponding scene of the 12 apostles, two angels and the Virgin Mary, separated by trees and gazing up at the "Pantócrator," the Almighty Christ.

The great controversies: During the Byzantine period, Thessaloníki lived through two major theological debates. The Iconoclast Controversy raged in the 8th and 9th centuries when excessive worship of icons led to an equally extreme reaction against them. The Óssios Davíd mosaic was covered with cowhides to save it from destruction, while the original mosaic of the Virgin in Aghía Sophía's apse was destroyed and restored after this storm had passed. The focal point of this controversy was Constantinople, while the 14th-century Isihast Debate centred in Thessaloníki itself. Isihasm (from *isihía*, meaning peace) was propounded by the monks of Mount Áthos, and claimed that "by

n exchange goods in hessaloníki's market.

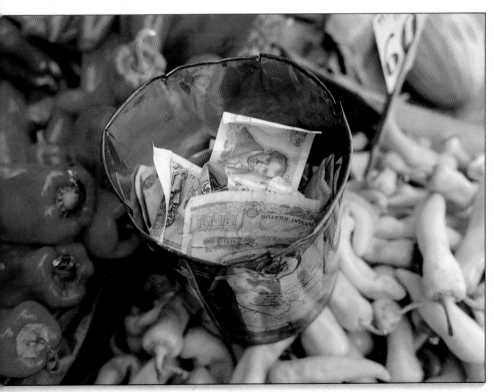

holding the breath, by making the spirit re-enter into the soul, and by gazing fixedly upon the navel they could attain to the vision of the uncreated light which shone on Tabor." This creed was ridiculed by the Calabrian monk Barlaam, leader of the Zealot opposition. A struggle ensued which was at least as social and political as it was theological. Isihasm's major theorist, Gregory Palamás was Archbishop of Thessaloníki; his reliquary is kept in the city's cathedral.

If you take the second walk from Óssios Davíd, you cross the charming **Áno Póli**. A 20-minute walk from the downtown centre takes you to this part of town which still lives like a village. Here and in the Acropolis, the highest part of town enclosed by fortifications, you can find good *tavérnes*. In the 14th century the hill was covered with small monasteries of which only some of the chapels survive. The **Church of St Nicholas Orphanos** has exquisite frescoes. The **churches of St Elias and St Catherine** represent interesting devel-

opments in the cross-in-dome architectural form, which culminates in the **Church of the Holy Apostles**. The latter's fine mosaics with scenes from the life of Christ are so high up that they can only be appreciated with a pair of binoculars.

Other Influences: Thessaloníki was conquered by the Turks in 1430, just 23 years before the fall of Constantinople. Churches were conveniently turned into mosques by plastering over the interior decoration and building minarets up their sides. Fifteenth-century Ottoman monuments develop the style of elaborate dome constructions of late Byzantine churches. There are two mosques of particular interest: the graceful **Alaja Imaret**, now turned into an exhibition hall, and the **Hamza-bey Jami**, now the Alcazar movie theatre. Drapers and goldsmiths sell their wares as they did long ago in the **Bezesten**, a six-domed covered market. The **Yahoudi**, once a Turkish *hamám* (public bath), now shelters an open-air flower market and a small fish *tavérna* which is

Left, a priest stocks up. Right, an early Christian mosaic at Ossios Davíd

recommended. Around it spreads today's central market area, displaying a colourful array of mounds of fresh fruit and vegetables, fish and meat, heaps of olives, sweets and spices, wooden utensils and straw baskets. A more contemporary Turkish monument is the house where Mustafa Kemal was born, today the Turkish consulate. Later known as Ataturk, he was the leader of the Young Turk Movement that overthrew the Sultan and founded the Turkish Republic in 1928.

Contemporary things: Modern Thessaloníki spreads far beyond the old city walls. The University gives it a bustling student life which gathers at the bars near the seafront and White Tower at night. The International Fair held every October makes it an important trade centre for the Balkans. Along the eastern quay, modern apartment blocks stand beside grandiose old mansions. One of them, now the **Folk Art Museum** offers an exhibition on ethnic differences in Northern Greece.

Further along, the suburb of **Kalar-**

nana provides good seafood restaurants right on the sea. **Panorama**, an affluent suburb to the northeast, affords views which justify its name and features delicious triangular cream pastries called *trígona*. On a clear day, look out far to the south as you sip coffee by the waterfront or pause on the sinuous uphill pathways of the Áno Póli; you may see the massive form of Mount Olympus (Ólimbos) blocking the entrance to the bay, a link between modern Thessaloníki and ancient Greece.

Going east: Many roads lead east out of Thessaloníki. One of them first leads north to the town of Kilkis and the shore of the Greek half of Lake Doiran, then up the mountains to the Rupel Pass (the only access route to Bulgaria), and further east to Sérres. This route is also followed by the railway.

Sérres is best reached by the road branching off northeast of Thessaloníki. Both Sérres and Drama, further east, were important in Byzantine and Ottoman days, and continue to be prosperous provincial towns. Both of-

MOUNT ATHOS

*What can I do for you if you wear the
shameful garment
of the flesh and have not laid bare your mind
and made
naked your soul, if you remain covered in
darkness and
do not have the strength to see the light?*
— Seymeon the Mystic

From the northern seaboard of Greece three
long arms of land known as Chalcidice
(Halkíthikí) reach into the Aegéan. At the
extreme end of the third and most easterly
arm, the mountain which has given the peninsula its name, **Mount Áthos**, rises in
solitary magnificence. The fame of Áthos
rests on its large monastic community; these
saints and humble monks have earned it the
epithet "holy," now an intrinsic part of the
name: Ághion Óros, the Holy Mountain.

The history of the monastic settlement
begins with the advent of hermits in about
the mid-9th century, roughly 100 years before the foundation of the first monastery. St
Peter the Athonite, perhaps the most famous
of the early monks, is supposed to have lived
in a cave here for 50 years. The first monastery, the Great Lávra, was founded by St
Athanásios in AD 963. He was a friend and
councillor of the first historical benefactor
of the Holy Mountain, Nikephóros Fókas.
Thereafter, the foundations multiplied under the royal patronage of the Byzantine
emperors who supported the building of the
various settlements with imperial resources,
in the form of money, land and treasures.

Thus all the monasteries share a rich heritage. The names of Byzantine emperors are
still commemorated in their churches and
imperial charters are zealously guarded in
the library of each monastery.

The monasteries are divided into two
categories: Coenobite and Idiorrhythmic. In
the Coenobite monasteries all monks keep
to strict regulations under the direction of an
abbot or *Igoúmenos*. Property is divided and
meals are eaten in common in the *trápeza* or
refectory. In the Idiorrhythmic monasteries
(which include the three largest: Lávra,
Vatopédi and Iviron) there is no property in
common, and each monk provides his own
food and clothing from his own resources.
All monasteries are Greek except for the
Russian Pantaleímon, the Serbian Chilan-

**Xenofont‹
monaster**

dari and the Bulgarian Zográfou, and they all, with the exception of Vatopédi keep the old Julian calendar, 13 days behind the rest of Europe, and Byzantine hours which begin at sunset and so vary every day.

The monasteries, however, form only one part of this "holy" community. A great number of monks prefer to live in smaller monastic establishments, the *skétes* and *kelliá* dotted around the peninsula. The *kellí* or cell is a single building containing a little chapel inhabited by a smaller number of monks. The *skete* is a small monastic village composed of a few cottages clustered round a central church. Both *sketes* and *kelliá* are dependent on one of the 20 monasteries. There are also monks who choose to live like hermits, following the traditions of St Peter the Athonite, in an *Isihastérion*, a rough unadorned hut or a cave, perched precipitously on a cliff's ledge. The hermits live in great poverty and are rarely seen.

If Áthos continues to exercise a singular compulsion over the hearts and minds of others, this is not because of the scenery, spectacular though it is, nor on account of its being one of the richest museums of Byzantine art and culture. Ultimately it is because it lays claims to represent the highest form of spiritual life known in the Orthodox and indeed in the entire Christian tradition. Through the pursuit of a discipline demanding scrupulous attention to both outer action and inner prayer, the monk aspires to purify his body and soul from various alien attachments by which he is bound, and thus traverse the road that leads, by way of ascetic practice and the higher forms of contemplation to his "deification."

All visitors to the Holy Mountain will recognise that they themselves have also traversed a road that leads to a very different realm, a realm which by ordinary human standards may even be conceived as divine. Thus the description of Áthos by one of its poets as the "domain and garden of the Holy Virgin" echoes the feelings of most men who have had the luck to be born male, and so gain privileged entry to this holy place.

Visitors applying for "visas" to visit the Holy Mountain will be asked why they have come. Many have been turned away because they supplied the "wrong" answer: to see the treasures, to hike in the unspoilt woodland. The only acceptable reply, of course, is: "I have come to grow as a Christian, and to praise God." By the time you leave, it may well be the only *true* answer.

nt Athos
unrise.

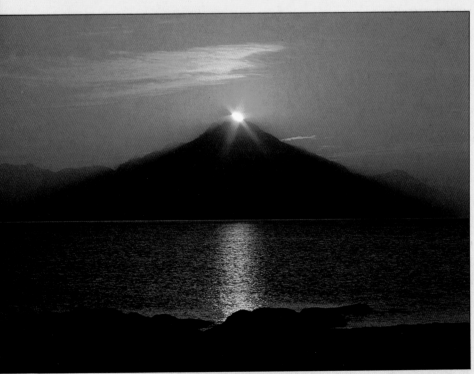

fer pleasant resting spots in shady central plazas and give access to hiking and skiing in the mountains behind them. Sérres was burnt down by the retreating Bulgarians in 1913 and was completely rebuilt, but two important Byzantine churches remain: the 11th-century **Church of the Holy Apostles** and the 14th-century **Church of St Nícholas (Nikólaos)**. A domed Ottoman building in the central square is a museum.

The land and villages lying between this area and the sea are mainly agricultural. Some come alive at specific times of the year. The Sarakatsánides, a nomadic tribe of herdsmen, assemble in summer for their *panayíri* (saint's day) near Sérres and Dráma. **Langadas** is the site of an old Thracian ritual of treading barefoot on red-hot coals, held on 21 May by the descendants of refugees from a Thracian village.

Chalcidice (Halkíthikí): The main road east of Thessaloníki runs along the base of the Chalcidice Peninsula, skirting lakes Koronia and Volvi. The huge hand-like peninsula stretching three fingers out into the Aegéan was sparsely populated until a recent tourist and development boom.

Little is left to show its important role in classical times when the colonies of various southern Greek cities served as the battlefield for the Peloponnésian War between Athens and Spárta (Spárti). **Potidea**, on the first finger, triggered off Spárta's declaration of war in 432 BC, while the Battle of Amfipolis put an end to the conflict in this area ten years later. Armies clashed across the land, and fleets fought off the shores. Finds from the area are kept in a museum at **Poliyiros**, the region's capital.

The peninsula also bears marks of other times. At the **cave of Petrálona**, fossils and a Neanderthal skull have revealed the existence of a prehistoric settlement. At **Stayira**, a modern marble statue overlooking the Ierissos Gulf marks Aristotle's birthplace. **Xerxes' Canal**, now filled up, was built around 482 BC to help the Persians avoid the fate suffered in their previous campaign, when its fleet was wrecked sail-

The aqueduct at Kavála.

ing round Mount Áthos. This and Xerxes' bridge over the Hellespont were considered by the Greeks as products of Persian megalomania: "marching over the sea and sailing ships through the land." The medieval **Potidea Canal** still separates the first finger from the mainland and serves as mooring ground for fishing boats.

Billowing hills and the beautiful forested slopes of Mount Holomon cover the peninsula's palm. You may drive around the first two fingers, **Kassándra** and **Sithonia**, always finding an idyllic spot: charming inland villages alternate with seaside fishing hamlets, luxury hotels with camping sites, protected coves with sandy beaches, pine-clad slopes with bleak promontories. Sitting on the beach at **Sarti**, on the middle finger, you can make out the form of Mount Áthos rising like a pyramid from the haze across the gulf. Here, women travellers should sign off, for the Holy Mountain is a male preserve.

Back north: The main road leading east skirts the popular beaches at the head of the Strymonic Gulf on its way to **Amfipólis**. The city was founded by Athenian colonists in the 5th century BC on a Thracian site called "The Nine Ways" where, according to Heródotus, the passing Persians had seized nine boys and girls and buried them alive as a propitiatory sacrifice. Its new name, meaning "the surrounded city," was derived from its position in a loop of the River Strymon, strategically commanding the inland flatlands, the mouth of the river, and the coveted gold mines of Mount Pangeon. Here was fought the battle that decided the first phase of the Peloponnésian War. Today the table-top plateau is strewn with limbs of broken statues, Hellenistic mosaics and the foundations of early Christian basilicas.

Crossing the Strymon over a bridge guarded by the **Lion of Amfipólis**, a colossal statue re-assembled from the 4th-and 3rd-century BC fragments, the road forks out to Kavála. The old road runs the length of the beautiful green valley between Mounts Pangeon and

eturning om night shing.

Simvolon, passing through slate-roofed villages with panoramic views. The new highway, faster but less scenic, follows the coastline.

Rising in the shape of an amphitheatre from the harbour up to the pine hills, **Kavála's** magnificent location and manageable size make it one of the most pleasant towns in Greece. A colony of Thásos by the name of Neápolis in antiquity, it became an important port with access to Philippi during Roman and Christian times, while today it is the major export centre for tobacco from the surrounding plains. The local museum houses finds from Neápolis and Amfipólis.

The harbour has two parts: the modern part, and the old fishing harbour with small fish restaurants and a market backed by the arches of a 16th-century aqueduct. The old town surrounded by Byzantine walls rises on a promontory to the east. Walking up the narrow winding streets, you will notice a set of golden half-moons, the Sultan's symbol, shining above an outer wall. This was the Imaret, a Turkish almshouse, also known as *tembelhane*, the loungers' home, as the lazy had soon outnumbered the needy. You can push open the heavy wooden gate and ramble through its now desolate courtyards.

At the top of the hill, **Mehemet Ali's house** is a fine example of traditional Turkish architecture. Born in Kavála in 1769 of Albanian descent, Mehemet Ali became Pasha of Egypt and founder of the Egyptian royal dynasty which lasted until this century. In the square, his statue looks out to the south, the direction of the country he set out to rule.

Philippi, although named by Philip II of Macedónia, contains little that is Macedónian. From the Acropolis, where three medieval towers rise on the ruins of Macedónian walls, you get an extensive view of the battlefield which made this site famous. It was here that in 42 BC one of the decisive Roman battles was fought between the republican forces led by Brutus and Cassius, who had taken part in the assassination of Julius Caesar in 44 BC, and the latter's avengers, Antony and Octavius.

Justice was meted out as both Cassius and Brutus committed suicide upon seeing their forces defeated. It was left to the Battle of Actium some 11 years later to decide the final struggle between the two victors of Philippi. The Roman ruins, mainly to the south of the highway include the foundations of the **Forum** and the **Palaestra**, as well as the **Public Latrine** at the southwest corner of the grounds.

The beginning of Christianity: Philippi is reputed to be the first place in Europe where St Paul preached the gospel, nearly a century after the famous Roman battle. He arrived in AD 49, but was soon thrown into prison as the local religion was still a form of Thracian paganism. Six years later, however, he revisited the town to which he would later address his Epistle to the Philippians. By the 6th century, Christianity was thriving at Philippi, as the foundations of several early Christian churches of the basilica type testify.

Ferries for the island of **Thásos** leave regularly from Kavála or, if you are

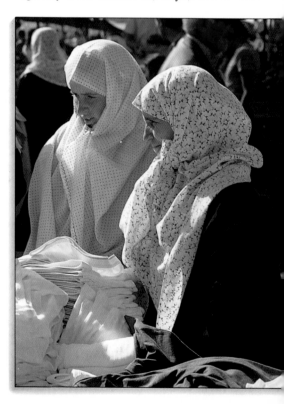

Pomack women in the Xánthi market.

travelling by car, from Keramoti further east. Thásos is endowed with great natural beauty. On the east, pine trees slope down to golden beaches, pine-scent mingling with the salty sea breeze. The western shore is flatter, serene and spectacular at sunset when the sun's rays catch the silver-green of olive groves. Between the two main seaside towns, **Limen**, the capital, and **Limenaría** on the other side of the island, small groups of houses along the shore alternate with large villages perched on the slopes. The slate roofs, running waters and shady plane trees of **Panaghía** and **Potamia** could easily trick you into thinking you were deep in the mountains, were it not for glimpses of sand and sea far below. **Theológos**, reached from the southwest, is the site where the medieval capital moved for protection from pirates. In antiquity, Thásos was a Párian colony and, later, a colony of the mainland shore opposite. In Limen, traces of the ancient naval and commercial harbours can still be seen. You can also make a long walking tour of the ancient walls enclosing the modern town. The theatre has been informally restored with wooden benches placed amongst the pine trees. If you take the walk in late afternoon, be sure to carry a flashlight; it may be dark by the time you reach the crescent-shaped rock-hewn **Sanctuary of Pan** at the top of the hill and if you are not prepared you might experience the "panic" known to have been induced by this mysterious half-man half-goat god! A detailed guide of the grounds can be obtained at the museum.

Back on the mainland east of Kavála, the **Nestos River** flows through the **Yellow Plain** (known in Turkish as "Sari Saban"), a vast expanse of corn and tobacco fields. The Nestos marks the boundary between Eastern Macedónia and Thrace. Its estuary is surrounded by poplar plantations used as a hideout by birds. It can be reached only by dirt roads leading to the fine beaches facing Thásos. Some beautiful scenery along the Nestos Gorge can best be seen by train between Drama and Xánthi.

urist
tigue on the
rry to
ásos.

Muslim presence: Ancient Thrace (Thráki) used to stretch deep into present-day Bulgaria and the European side of Turkey. Greek colonisation of the coast often led to conflict with the native Thracian tribes. The Roman Via Egnatia spanned the area, leaving scattered traces of Roman and, later, Byzantine fortifications. Thrace was overrun and settled by Slavs and Ottomans. It was eventually divided between Bulgaria, Turkey and Greece, as a result of 19th- and early 20th-century nationalist struggles. Although there was a population exchange between Turkey and Greece in 1923, the Turkish inhabitants of the Greek part of Thrace were allowed to remain in return for protection granted to Greeks living in Istanbul. The Turkish minority is distributed between Xánthi, Komotiní and the tobacco-growing plains south of the two cities. Gypsies who espoused the Muslim faith and the Turkish language are also settled here. Another Muslim minority, the Pomaks, live in the mountains of **Western** and **Eastern Rodopi.**

They appear to be of Slavic descent as they tend to be fairer than Turks, and traditionally cultivate tobacco on the lush Rodopi terraces and valleys. This border area is a military zone and can only be visited with permission from the Ministry of Defence. Applications for permits should be made at the Xánthi police station, but the process can take a week.

The best place to see a motley crowd of Greek citizens belonging to different races is in the hubbub of **Xánthi's** Saturday **open-air market.** The Muslim women look very graceful in long black satin overcoats and white *yashmaks* (scarves), which are gradually being replaced by gray or brown shorter coats and printed scarves. The Gypsy women stand out in their colourful wide trousers and their scarves tied behind the ears exposing their chins. Many of the men still wear burgundy-coloured velvet or felt fezzes, or white prayer caps. Greek priests, their cassocks blowing in the wind and tall black hats sticking out of the crowd, also do their week's shop-

For sale: pirated audi tapes.

ping. This market mainly caters to local needs, so you may find little to purchase, but it is worth spending a Saturday morning here to see a facet of Greece which you will not find in the rest of the country. In the evening, you can witness another aspect of Xánthi life; a street off the main square is closed off for the Saturday night *nifopázaro* (brides' fair). Traditionally this was the time for young men and women to exchange glances. Today it is more an opportunity for the whole town to meet and promenade.

Xánthi became a prosperous commercial and administrative centre in the 19th century. Renowned masons were brought from Épirus to build merchant homes, tobacco warehouses and *hans* (inns). The *hans*, large square buildings around a central courtyard, were resting-spots and trading-centres near the marketplace. South of the square, an intoxicating aroma of tobacco fills the air; this is the area of the tobacco warehouses, some still in use and featuring extraordinary facades. The white-washed houses and slender minarets of the Turkish quarter rise up north.

In **Komotiní**, Muslims constitute more than 50 percent of the population. Two central mosques fill up with the faithful at prayer times. In the surrounding cobbled streets, small shops spread a colourful array of everyday items. Old men wearing fezzes sit solemnly outside coffee-houses, playing with their worry-beads. The museum houses archaeological finds from all over Thrace, two of the most important sites being Abdera south of Xánthi, and Maronia south of Komotiní.

Both sites have little to show apart from the foundations of layers and layers of civilization, but both are of historical significance. **Abdera**, especially affluent in the 5th century BC, was the birthplace of two major philosophers in antiquity: Demócritus, who expounded an atomic theory of the constitution of the world, and the sophist Protagoras who incapsulated his relativism in the phrase, "Man is the measure of all things." Further east,

A photo store window in Xánthi.

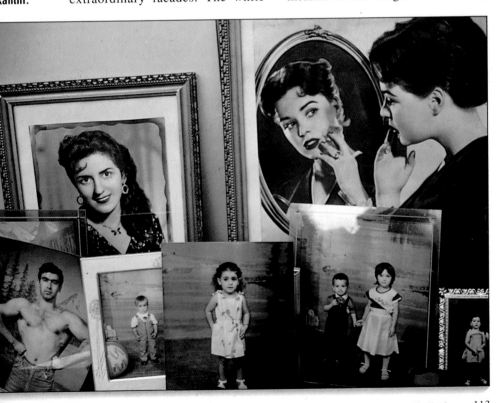

Maronia marks the site where Odysseus' ship is supposed to have strayed after leaving Troy for the return journey to Íthaca (Itháki). Although the natives were unfriendly, it was their sweet-smelling red wine which later saved Odysseus and his companions from the terrifying cyclops Polyphémus. Trapped in his cave, they managed to get Polyphémus drunk on the delicious wine and then while he slept they poked his single eye out with a huge red-hot pole and escaped by hiding under his sheeps' bellies. A cave to the north of Maronia retains the name of Polyphémus' Cave.

The Évros valley and Samothrace (Samothráki): The road from Komotiní zigzags through barren limestone hills before coming down to the vast Évros plain and leading on to Alexandroúpolis. Formerly a charming seaside town, **Alexandroúpolis** has developed into an unruly urban conglomeration. Dirt roads lead to the western part of the Évros delta, an important wetland for migratory birds from northeast Europe, including flamingos. Ecological tourism will soon provide better access and facilities for observation. No access is permitted to the river itself, for it belongs to the border military zone. Ferries leave the harbour for the island of Samothrace (Samothráki), while the road continues east towards Turkey and north along the Évros valley.

Unlike the other island of the Thracian Sea, the green and golden Thásos, **Samothrace** raises its forbidding granite heights above stony beaches and murky waters. The landscape was not always so inhospitable. Hómer has the mighty Poseídon watching from here the action in the plains of Troy: he "sat and marvelled on the war and strife, high on the topmost crest of wooded Samothrace, for thence all Ída was plain to see, and plain to see was the city of Troy and the ships of the Achaíans."

With time, the forest has receded, leaving the desolate lunar landscape of the aptly-named **Mount Fengári** (Mount Moon). Traces of the old luxuriant vegetation survive in the north-

east, where a variety of butterfly mingles with the spray of small waterfalls formed by creeks gurgling down the mountainsides. The ancient native cult of the Great Gods was retained after Greek colonisation of the island in the 7th century and flourished up to the 3rd century. This site and the **museum of Paleópolis** display evidence of the cult, its grounds and its mysteries.

The road from Alexandroúpolis leads northeast past the Roman staging-post of Trajanópolis to Ferai, where the 12th-century **Church of the Virgin** discloses fine but faded frescoes. Corn and sunflower fields, which are spectacular in midsummer, stretch as far as the eye can see.

Soufli was once famous for its silk production. The land sloping down to the Évros used to be planted with mulberry trees whose leaves nourished the silkworms. Today the trees have been replaced by corn fields and the single silk factory still in use imports cocoons from the East. A variety of silks are for sale at a shop near the central crossroads. **Didimótiho** has a Byzantine fortress with a commanding view of the Évros valley, and an abandoned pyramidal-roofed mosque. A folklore museum offers an interesting overview of the region's traditional culture and handicrafts.

Cross countries: There are two ways to cross from here into Turkey. One is by train from the small railway station of **Pithio**, a sleepy village below its once vigilant fortress. The other is from the border outpost of **Kastanies**. The passage cannot be made on foot, so you must either have a car, take the one-day bus trip leaving twice a week from **Orestiada**, or wait at the border for a lift. Just across the border, the four minarets of the 16th-century Selimiye Mosque, the architect Sinan's last masterpiece, rise above swaying poplar trees on the opposite bank of the Évros River. From the Turkish town of Edirne, built on the site of Roman Hadrianople, you can look back to the once Byzantine city of Thessaloníki, and forward to the combined Byzantine and Ottoman grandeur of Istanbul.

Looking across the Turkish border at the Selimiye Mosque.

EPIRUS AND NW MACEDONIA

Épirus and the northwest corner of Macedónia (Makethonía) are worlds apart from the azure, sun-bleached Greece of Zórba (Zorbás). Here instead, you will find jagged limestone peaks and deep sunless gorges, mountains mantled by forests and rimmed with snow, villages cut from the same stone mountains and timber.

This tough, austere land sets the scene for a different way of life. You can feel the weight and sobriety of this existence when you walk down the stone streets of a village lined with stone houses or witness the slow, plodding steps of an Épirot dancing to the wailing clarinet. You can sense the social closure and restraint in the architecture of the Zagorahória houses set off far from the street by large gates, or when, at a village festival, you are not asked to join in the dance, but rather expected to stand apart, forever the foreigner.

More of the same: Even the rain which falls here more abundantly than anywhere else in Greece reminds that you are not in Naúplia (Náfplion) or on Náxos. Still, the contrasts between this Mountain Greece and that of the Mediterranean are today beginning to blur in the increasing homogenisation of the modern Greek nation.

In their massive postwar migration to Athens, the Épirots have brought a bit of the mountains to the city, and, with each holiday vacation spent in their native villages, bring a bit of the city back to the mountains. These days the Sarakatsáni shepherd can finish milking his herd at noon in a highland pasture and, flying from Ioánnina, still make a doctor's appointment in Athens at 5 p.m.

How it started: While Épirus becomes more and more integrated into and unified with the Greek nation, it is crucial to appreciate how distinct its past history has been from the rest of Greece. It achieved Greek statehood less than 80 years ago, in 1913, some 80 years after most of the mainland had achieved sovereignty. At that time, moreover, it was

hardly evident that this region was, in fact, Greece: the population of this wide strip of land was a melange of ethnicities, languages, religions and customs: Greeks, Turks, Albanians and Macedónians, as well as the nomadic peoples – the Sarakatsánides, Vláchoi and Koútsovláchoi.

Following World War II and the Civil War, this region suffered a rapid loss of population to Greek and foreign cities. By the 1970s, many Épirot villages were in a state of rapid physical and social decline. Houses were left to decay, and the few ones still inhabited sheltered an ever-diminishing population of old, economically inactive men and women.

But in the past decade, things have changed. The government has worked to integrate the region into the national economy, emigration trends have been reversed and attitudes towards village life modified, the "traditional" now viewed less as a stumbling block to economic prosperity and more as a cultural heritage to be preserved.

The associated benefits and tensions of this new era for Épirus are most visible in Zagóri. Stiff government regulations of building permits and low interest loans and subsidies have led to the restoration of many buildings both public and private so much so that whole villages have been preserved as traditional settlements in their pre-19th century architectural character. Simultaneously, new roads are being built, often right over old mule paths, giving access to the tiniest villages and most distant pasture lands.

Conflicting interests: Behind all these manifestations of "modernisation," the astute observer will see a microcosm of the Greek reality today – a stage for conflicting interests and world views. Conservationists who want to preserve the land as wilderness versus entrepreneurs who would like to develop skiing facilities on the slopes and aerial tramways in the gorges; farmers who rely on the constant flow of rivers versus the state-owned electric utility which has embarked on a series of low-head hydroelectric projects; mining versus land reclamation; and the ultimate question: what sort of tourism to develop?

The new concept that is emerging here is that of "low impact" tourism, or "ecotourism." It is being promoted by conservation organisations and most agencies of the central government but resisted, predictably, by many local interest groups. Perhaps the "cultural centres" composed of village youths who study in the major cities will help resolve this urgent question.

The territory covered here is vast by Greek standards, spanning some 233 miles (375 km) from Igoumenítsa to Édessa, by the most direct route. A minimum of 10 days is suggested for this tour, but the more time you have the better. Note, too, that the coastal region of Párga, Efira, the Nekromantíon of the Ahéron, Kassopi, Préveza, Aktion and Árta (briefly treated in the Roúmeli section) forms an historically important part of Épirus and that the Igoúmenitsa-Árta-Ioánnina loop is an appropriate addition to the route indicated here.

Igoumenítsa: The modern port of Igoumenítsa which welcomes a great share of the travellers entering Greece from the west is the major port of Épirus and indeed of northern Greece. You may not even notice you are in Épirus unless, walking by the man with his table of cassettes set up in the central square, you hear the plangent, bleating *klaríno* – the Épirot clarinet. Realise it or not, you have set foot in the land of the *klaríno*, whose sounds you will hear across the entire region in summer at the local village festivals, in winter in the town *tavérna*, and almost always on any bus you board.

The road from Igoumenítsa to Ioánnina winds its way up through the valley of the **Kalamas River**, the ancient Thiamis, with every mile climbing further into the highlands of the **Píndos mountain range**. To the north lie the villages of the **Morgana**, one of which, **Liá**, was rendered infamous in recent years with the book (and movie) *Eléni*, which polemically recounts the tribulations suffered in this area during the Civil War. The Píndos is the largest

A priest in Kónitsa, Epirus.

118

Greek mountain formation and one of the largest in all of the Balkans, extending from Mount Morava in Albania to the Ágrafa range in central Greece.

Ioánnina: On entering the upland plain near the Konitsa road junction, the stark face of Mount Mitsikeli appears high above Lake Pambiotis and Ioánnina which lines its shores. Over the past 1,000 years, **Ioánnina** has perennially been one of Greece's great cities, a centre of Hellenic culture and education, an international crossroad of traders and in its last glorious epoch, the citadel of Ali Pasha, the "Lion of Ioánnina," the famed maverick-tyrant who broke away from the Sultan to set up an autonomous Épirot kingdom. Today Ioánnina remains one of Greece's most lively provincial centres and a home to one of Greece's six universities. Apart from its own interest and the beauty of its setting, Ioánnina makes for a convenient base from which to explore the surrounding area: the Zagorahória, Métsovo, Dodóna (Thothóni).

Unlike most other large Greek cities, the history of Ioánnina does not extend back to ancient times. It has distinctly medieval origins, supposedly taking its name from a local monastery of St John the Baptist. In 1204 it burgeoned in size and importance as a result of the Latin conquest of Constantinople and subsequent establishment of the Despotate of Epirus. Refugees from "The City" swelled its population and in the late 13th century it achieved the status of an archbishopric. It fell, with the rest of Greece, to the Turks in the 15th century, and in the late 18th century Ali Pasha made this city of 35,000 inhabitants (large for that time) his headquarters.

Ioánnina today testifies ambivalently to Ali's legacy – for while he left behind the city's most distinctive monuments (its mosques and the redoubtable walls of the citadel), he also burned much of it to the ground during the siege by the Sultan's troops in 1820. This, along with the postwar penchant for building large apartment blocks, has left Ioánnina with a decidedly modern face.

ánnina is mous for its astry, ougátsa.

The people's square: The wide expanse of Ioánnina's central square, lined by the regional army headquarters and various other public buildings, is the most obvious place to orient yourself for a tour of the city. This is where the people of Ioánnina meet: the students at noon at the bright sidewalk cafés, the old men in the traditional cafés lining Avérof Street playing *távli* and cards, families and old friends walking arm-in-arm for an evening *vólta*. Here too you can eat some of the *bougátsa* for which Ioánnina is famed – fine cheese or custard-filled pastry.

After a bit of nourishment, the **Archaeological Museum** at the north end of the square makes a good visit. It has a fine array of Épirot archaeological artefacts spanning from Paleolithic to modern times. Odós Avérof descends finally to the **Kástro**, the fortress of numerous Épirot despots and, lastly, of Ali Pasha himself. In this tangle of buildings and alleyways set on the promontory jutting out into the lake are the most salient reminders of Ioánnina's past – the massive walls and its gateways, the **Aslan Pasha** and **Fetiye** mosques. The first mosque now houses the Municipal Museum with a diverse collection of Épirot costumes, jewellery and other relics.

The area around this mosque is the supposed scene of one of the famous stories linked to Ali Pasha in the popular imagination. Kyra Frosíni was the beautiful mistress of Ali's eldest son. In the most common variant of the story, the Pasha took a liking to her as well. But she resisted his advances and paid the price: a watery death. Ali had Kyra Frosíni and 17 of her female companions tied up in weighted sacks and dropped in the lake. Further down the waterfront we reach the sealed-up Fetiye ("Victory") Mosque and the tomb of Ali Pasha in front of it. In these buildings the "Lion" ruled over his pint-sized empire – taking his pleasure in his Seraglio, entertaining such guests as Lord Byron in grand style, and ordering the death of many an enemy.

Monasteries, paths winding among

Even in Greece, it rains sometimes.

fragrant flowers and trees, and a *tavérna* serving local freshwater specialities all fit onto the islet of **Lake Pambiotis** a brief boat ride from the city. **The Monastery of Ághios Nikólaos** near the fishing village houses vivid frescoes, one depicting unusually gruesome martyrdoms, another peopled by such ancient luminaries as Plato, Aristotle and Thucydides. At the **Monastery of Pantaleímon** is one last piece of Ali Pasha memorabilia – the house into which he fled in 1822 when hunted by the Sultan's troops. Here his luck ran out, however. Stuck on the first floor, Ali was doomed when the soldiers fired through the ceiling from below. The bullet holes are still there today.

Zeus's sanctuary: South of Ioánnina lies **Dodóna (Thothóni)**, Épirus' main archaeological attraction. The road winds up **Mount Tomaron** (with views of Ioánnina, the lake and Mount Mitsikeli in the background) to a small valley where the sanctuary is located. Hómer calls it "wintry Dodóna," emphasising again Épirus' alpine other-ness; its distance from Odysseus' "wine-dark sea." And it is a desolate site indeed. In antiquity the Dodóna oracle was regarded as the oldest in Greece. Dodonian Zeus who was worshipped here was thought to reside in the trunk of the holy oak tree.

Heródotus tells us that the tree (the second oldest in Greece after the willow in the sanctuary of Héra at Sámos) became holy when a dove flying from Thebes (Théva) in Egypt landed on it, began speaking in a human voice and ordered that an oracle of Zeus be set up there. Thereafter priests interpreted the rustlings of the holy oak tree in the wind. As at Délphi (Thelfoús), their pronouncements were enigmatically worded. The importance of the sanctuary diminished by the 5th century BC as that of Délphi increased.

The beautifully restored amphitheatre which dates from the 3rd century and the days of Pyrrhus, the great Épirot king who defeated the Romans in battle at the high price of most of his soldiers' lives, has a capacity of 18,000 specta-

me for ssip at a s stop in étsovo.

tors and hosts a festival of classical drama during the summer.

Worthwhile diversions: The road north out of Ioánnina leads to the mountainous heart of Épirus – the Zagorahória. If you are unable to take this extraordinary trip and are instead heading east into **Théssaly**, you can partially console yourself with a visit to **Métsovo**, 36 miles (58 km) from Ioánnina. On this route you first pass **Pérama**, one of Greece's most spectacular caves. Then, after a long circuitous ascent just before the **Katára Pass** ("the Damned"), the only motor-crossing of the central Píndos, Métsovo appears to the southeast. It is a singular Greek village, justly famed for its stunning location, its popular architecture and handicrafts, its cheeses and its inhabitants who still dress in their traditional clothes.

A fine display of the baronial side of Métsovo's culture is at the **Tosítsa Mansion**, an *arhóntikó*, or lord's manor, with much in common with the mansions of Siátista and Kastoría. Inside are fine examples of Metsovite woodcarving, weaving and carpets. Perhaps one other aspect of Métsovo will strike you – its fine state of preservation. This is thanks to the financing of the town's son, Evángelos Avérof, patriarch of one of the richest and most powerful families in Greece, the same family which left its name on such august monuments as the Olympic Stadium in Athens.

The Zagorahória: The Zagoriá District is a culturally and geographically distinct region of Épirus comprising 46 villages, the **Zagorahória**. Its physical boundaries are the imposing mountains and deep gorges that define the Ioánnina-Konítsa-Métsovo triangle. The region enjoyed relative autonomy during the Ottoman occupation, since wealth from trading allowed local leaders to pay off the Turkish overlords. It became a centre of learning and the seat of affluent professional classes who emigrated to major commercial centres in the East and in Europe subsequently returning to their homeland with even **A bridge in Zagorahóri.**

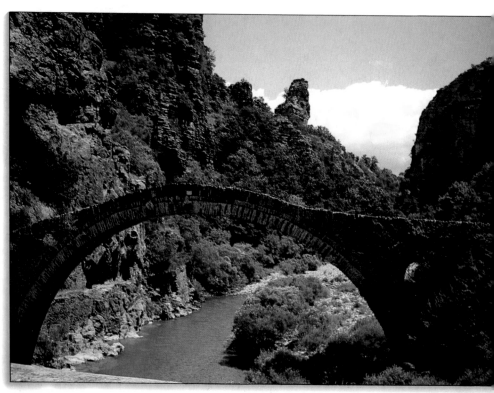

greater wealth. The West and East Zagóri villages are themselves somewhat distinct from one another in history and present appearance.

The East is an area populated in large part by Vláchoi, while the West bears the signs of more Slavic and Albanian influence. A more recent difference resulted from East Zagóri's fierce resistance to the Germans during World War II. In retribution the Germans ravaged the area, so that today the West Zagori bears an architectural testimony to its past, while the eastern villages were almost entirely rebuilt following the devastations wreaked by the war.

The Zagoriá landscape is dramatic and varied, embracing towering summits surrounded by sheer vertical rock faces, benign alpine meadows, deep forests, fertile plains and sinuous canyons. It is one of the few pockets of wilderness left in Greece and harbours the last remaining populations of wolves, bears, wild boars, lynx, the rare chamois and various types of eagles and hawks. Yet, even in the most remote corner the traveller will find signs of civilization: a Byzantine church; a graceful, slender arched bridge from the Ottoman period; a family of Sarakatsáni or Vlach shepherds grazing their flocks in the high plains.

A Zagorahória itinerary: Here are two suggested circuits in the central and west Zagoriá region which can be done separately or linked together.

For the central route you leave the Ioánnina-Konítsa road just past Karies and follow signs for the Víkos Gorge. The town of **Vítsa** hosts some fine traditional houses and one of the oldest churches in the region, **St Nícholas (Nikólaos)**. To gain access, ask at the local police station.

Just up the road, **Monodéndri** has a fine central square with the huge plane tree and the **basilica of St Athanásios**, not to mention delectable cheese pie at the café there. The short walk to the **monastery of Aghía Paraskeví** and beyond, along the ledge above the **Víkos Gorge** is literally breathtaking.

Next take the route to the villages of

Kipi, **Negades**, and on foot to half-deserted **Vradeto**. An extraordinary three-arched Turkish bridge spans the torrent on the right just before entering Kipi, where, in the upper part of the city, there are well-preserved buildings, a church and school, in a *plateía* overlooking the town. Further up the road, Negades is known for its three-churches in-one basilica dedicated to St Demétrius, George and the Holy Trinity, containing good frescoes. For the excursion to Vradeto, take the road to Tsepelovo. A few hundred yards past the fork to Kepesovo a footpath marked by a sign veers to the left to Vradeto. This one-hour hike includes the crossing of a small gorge, a unique climb on a sinuous Turkish cobblestone path (which is one of the most notable pre-modern engineering feats in the region), and a taste of the eerie stillness of this remote village (population seven during the winter). With another 30 minutes of walking you arrive at **Beloi** from where you can see the entire Víkos Gorge. Finally, for somewhat uncharted adventure into the mountains continue up the road to Tsepelovo and to the remote villages beyond.

Western Zagorahória: For the western Zagorahória continue further north on the Ioánnina-Konítsa road. **Kalpaki** marks one of the most glorified battle sites in modern Greek history. Here in the early winter of 1940 the Greeks met the invading Italian army and rolled them back into the snowy Albanian mountains for a winter of hell.

Soon a sign indicates the road (on the right) to **Aristi** and **Pápingo**. This area, tucked among the high peaks of **Mount Gamila**, comprises some of the best-preserved traditional settlements in Épirus. In recent years the two villages of Pápingo (**Megálo** and **Mikró**) have gradually become known as idyllic mountain retreats. And with good reasons: the *Pírgi* (sheer limestone "Towers") rise 2,000 ft (610 metres) at the villages' back door; some 20 traditional houses, beautifully restored by the National Tourism Organisation, are readily available for rent; good cheese *píta*

A family eating together.

and fresh trout are served at the various local *tavérnes*; and lastly, just off the road between the two villages there is an unusual swimming hole for a bit of alpine aquatics. From here too you can set out on various hikes in the mountains around Mount Gamila.

Leave the valley of the ever ice-cold spring-fed Voidomatis River and enter that of the temperate Aoös by way of the Ioánnina-Konítsa road. Just before entering Konitsa, an old Turkish bridge, the region's longest, spans the river alongside the new one. A three-hour walk on the southern bank leads through the thick forest of the National Park to **Moní Stomiou**, magnificently perched on a cliff inside the gorge.

Konitsa is a regional centre with a distinct military presence. It is a good place to take on provisions and have a meal either before or after your mountain perambulations.

Northwest Macedónia: The road from Konitsa to Neápolis (and Kastoría beyond) is the single connecting route between Épirus and northwest Macedónia (Makethonía). Out of Konitsa it climbs into the western foothills of **Mount Smolikas** (alt. 8,650 ft/2,640 metres), the tallest in the Píndos range, and then descends into the valley of the **Sarandaporos River**. On this road just below Eptahorio is a 32-ft (10-metre) strip of bold blue letters emblazoned on the concrete embankment: FREEDOM FOR NORTHERN ÉPIRUS – a solemn reminder that, according to the reckoning of many Épirots, half of that region is out of reach in Albania .

On the other side of Mount Víon, having exited Épirus and entered Macedónia, you arrive in **Pentalofos**, which stands like a gateway between the two regions. Its fine gray stone houses, still very much in the Épirot style, drape across the hills which give the town its name – "Fivehills." During World War II some of these buildings formed the headquarters of the British Mission to the Greek Resistance. From Pentalofos the road continues eastward through remarkable limestone formations, waves of rock lying like so many

Epirot llage.

HIKING IN THE PINDOS RANGE

Large tracks of unspoiled nature, a varied landscape with villages scattered at convenient intervals and a vast network of trails make this region of Greece a hiker's paradise – and one which is still not overcrowded. A great number of interesting walking trails can be found in the North Píndos, ranging from strenuous multi-day "*haute route*" traverses involving technical climbing, to a series of interconnected day hikes through wilderness and pasture lands between successive villages, to leisurely nature walks.

Travellers relying entirely on the automobile for the exploration of this region will be amply rewarded by taking short walks around the villages, monasteries, and churches mentioned in the itineraries suggested below. Hikers in good physical condition can opt for a series of day hikes, designing their trip according to time constraints, car availability, bus schedules, and special interests.

Although the train system is extensive, it is not always maintained and clearly marked, and may confuse the first-time traveller in the Greek backcountry. Thus, a good map and compass, a trail guide, a keen sense of direction, an ability to get and double-check trail information from villagers and shepherds, and a good sense of humour are necessary for the enjoyment of foot travellers in North Píndos.

Great caution is good advice for novices and seasoned hikers alike, as weather is known to change very rapidly with little warning. In recent years maps and excellent trail guides have become available (see Dubin, Salmon, Sfikas in bibliography). Here we will not attempt to duplicate in detail descriptions which can be found in these source books.

The hiking loop outlined here passes through a number of different eco-systems, and connects some of the most beautiful villages of the region. It begins and ends in the Pápingo villages where there are ample accommodation facilities (EOT houses, inns), and reliable *tavérnes* and supply stores. It has the disadvantage of being the most popular route by far, though nowhere near as well-travelled as the footpaths of England and Central Europe. August is the peak month.

The mou▮ ridge ab▮ Pápingo.

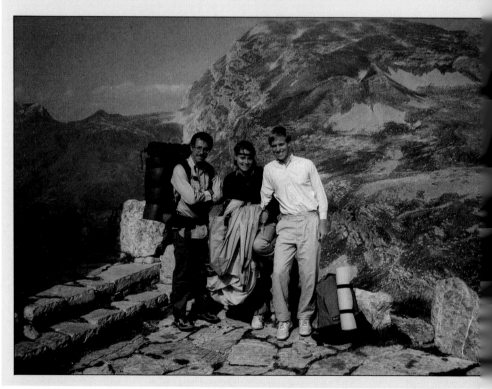

126

a. **Mikró Pápingo–Astrákas Hut:**
(Mountain Refuge visible from Pápingo: get
keys from Pápingo, or plan on bringing tent}
on Mount Gamila col: 3–4 hours (water
available at regular intervals), 3,000 feet
(900 meters) ascent.

b. **Side trip to Drakólimni** (alpine lake at
6900 feet [2,100 meters] altitude). An ideal
site for views, meal, etc: 1–1½ hours each
way. Overnight at the Refuge or camp on dry
bed of Xeróloutsa pond (a 15-minute descent to the east of the refuge on the way to
Drakólinmi: spring water).

c. **Astrákas Hut/Xeróloutsa–Tsepelovo:** a day-long hike through alpine meadows, high plains, gorge (Mégas Lákkos)
crossings, and, eventually, scree slopes,
under the shadow of the sheer rock faces of
Astrákas. Water is scarce, so plan supplies
accordingly: 5–7 hours depending on pace.
Overnight at Tsepelovo (two inns – but it is
necessary to make reservations in advance
during August).

d. **Tsepelov–Vradeto–Kipi:** The first leg
of the trip on foot (about 2 hours), then
another hour down the Kalderimi ("Skála")
of Vradeto onto the main asphalt road. Walk
(2–3 hours), hitchhike, or take the bus to
Kipi. Overnight in Kipi.

e. **Kipi–Vítsa–Monodéndri–Víkos
Gorge–Víko (Vitsiko) Village:** From
Monodéndri follow signs to the Gorge: a
well renovated *Kalderími* (cobblestone
path) takes you to the usually dry bed of
Víkos (30–45 minutes). A strenuous path
(red blazes) covers the length of the canyon,
criss-crossing the river bed. Midway at the
intersection of Víkos Gorge and the side
canyon of Mégas Lákkos (2–3 hours), a
series of freshwater ponds are formed by
nearby spring water (potable). Stop for
lunch and a swim, but do not leave any
garbage. This is bear country, as evidenced
by their huge droppings on and around the
trail and scratch marks on trees. Continue
through thick forest and pass a small
meadow before reaching the source of the
Voidomatis River. Camp anywhere you
want, but stay clear of the trail and hang food
from tree branches out of bears' reach. The
total hiking time is 5–7 hours, depending on
one's pace.

A variation is to take a left fork on the new
cobblestone path to the village of Víkos (1
hour) and hitchhike or take a bus to Aristi
and then to Pápingo, or cross Voidomatis
and follow the path there to Mikró Pápingo
(2–2½ hours).

layers of melted lead atop one another.

Siátista, a small town noted for its fine, 18th-century mansions, is a brief detour from the road to Kastoría. These mansions, called *arhóntiká* because they were the residences of the archons, or town's "leading men", offer a glimpse into the feudal society that flourished there during the middle centuries of Turkish rule. It was a centre of furring, tanning, wine-making and a stopping point for caravans on the trade route connecting the Balkans to Vienna, but fell from prosperity when, after Greek Independence, the commercial networks changed.

With some imagination, plus a bit of resourcefulness to gain entry into these houses, (ask at the café in the main street), you can learn a good deal about the lifestyle and world view of the people who inhabited these dwellings. The most interesting are the Manoussi, Poulikos and Nerantzopoulos houses. They are constructed in an architectural style which is widespread throughout northern Greece: a ground floor of solid stone wall whose few openings are often covered by iron gratings (as brigands abounded and security was uncertain), storage cellars and workshops; a second floor also of stone – the main winter residence; and a third floor of painted plaster board which juts out over the rest of the building, supported by wooden brackets – a kind of summer parlour and reception room. The walls and ceilings of these are often finely painted. After Siátista you will be well-prepared to see the *arhóntiká* of Kastoría, another town which grew wealthy from the fur trade.

Returning north, the road follows the upper valley of the **Aliákmon**, the longest river in Greece, whose 185 miles (300 km) flow in a great arc from high in the Píndos to the Thermaïc Gulf. Soon the road reaches **Kastoría Lake**, which the town, built on a peninsula, seems nearly to divide in half. Before entering town, on the left you pass a formidable military cemetery designed in latter-day fascist style. It commemorates the Greek soldiers of the govern-

A furworker i Kastoria.

ment forces killed during the Civil War in this area, the so-called Grammós-Vítsi where the last brutal stage of the Civil War was fought. The whole scene is one of the most visible reminders of that era between 1946 and 1974 when citizens branded as "communists" were harassed, tortured and exiled. Only now are the communist fighters being commemorated too. Kastoriá, somehow, refuses to let you forget this legacy, for, entering the city proper, the central **General James Van Fleet Square** reminds you that American equipment and advisers helped to decide the Civil War in favour of the Nationalists.

A Byzantine centre: Kastoriá is one of northern Greece's most alluring cities. Its history as a Byzantine provincial centre and as a hub of the fur industry is well-reflected by its 54 surviving churches, many of which were commissioned by rich furriers. Kastoriá's churches embody the fine Byzantine art of a provincial centre, far from the grand imperial mosaics of Constantinople and Thessaloníki. The work here often shows more folk and Slavic influence than that of the first and second cities of Byzantine. If you have a morning you can see at least a few of these winding through the city and ending up in **Kariadi**, the Old City, amidst Kastoriá's fine *arhóntiká*.

Ághïi Arnárgiri sits at the northeast edge of town, not far from the lake. It is the oldest church in Kastoriá, built in 1018 by Emperor Basil II to celebrate his victory over the Bulgars. Note the fine exterior brick walls decorated with various geometric forms, the arched windows above the apse divided by a colonnette, and the frescoes on the west facade of Saints Peter and Paul flanked by Kosmás and Dámian on either side. The dark interior contains frescoes including St Basil and a scene of the Pentecost. This church is also well known as Greece's earliest example of groin-vaulting.

To the south, **Panaghía Koumbeli-díki**, with its unusually tall drum-shaped dome contrasts strikingly.with Ághïi Arnárgiri. It too is from the 11th

eft, the Índos ↑ountains. ight, two ρirot women ↕ traditional ostumes.

century, and has frescoes on the facade, not just in niches but covering the whole wall. Further south it is the interior frescoes of **Ághios Nikólaos Kasnitzi** that stand out in this simple single-aisled basilica. Further south again, the **Taxiárchi** of the metropolis has both external and internal frescoes. It also contains the tomb of the Macedónian liberation fighter, Pávlos Melá, who was killed by the Turks in 1904 just north of Kastoriá.

In the Old City above the city's south bank you find the many *arhóntiká* from the 17th and 18th centuries, with their characteristic painted upper floors which project over the windowless lower ones. Most of these are quite dilapidated, save that of Nazim and Emmanuel, the latter now turned into a folk museum.

Kastoriá's fur industry: Strolling through these streets you'll also notice the most important aspect of Kastoriá's present social and economic life: the hundreds of small workshops crowded with tailors, fur-cutters, rolls of sewn-together furs and patterns for coats-in-the-making, which form the network of Kastoriá's famous fur trade. The history of this trade extends back at least 500 years to when beavers made Kastoriá Lake their home (Kastoría roughly means the beaver-place in Greek.)

As these were hunted out of existence, however, Kastoría became the repository for the scraps of fur discarded by the fur industries of Europe and North America. Here in these workshops the scraps are cleaned and sewn together into one piece and then fashioned into a fur coat which is then re-exported to the same countries from which the scraps originated and is sold at relatively low prices. The Greeks may discuss the economics of the business if you stop to chat with them in one of their shops.

Before leaving Kastoriá take the time for a promenade along its shores. On the south side you can walk to the **Monastery of the Mavrotissa.**

To the Préspa Lakes and east: The road north out of Kastoriá continues along one of the upper branches of the Aliak-mon River. We are now heading towards an unusual corner of Greece, where Greece and all things Greek taper off into the cold blue waters of the **Préspa Lakes** and merge into Yugoslavia and Albania.

These lakes are the nesting ground of two endangered species of pelicans (the Dalmatian pelican and wild pelican) as well as numerous other birds, and are today protected as a national bird sanctuary. Despite statutory protection, however, various construction projects have done much damage to this unique habitat in recent years.

The road to the east leads through Flórina and Édessa and finally to Pélla and Thessaloníki. We pass through **Flórina**, badly battered during the Civil War, and join the **Via Egnatia**, which connected the Roman Empire from Durazzo to Constantinople. To the north is **Mount Vóras**, the scene of numerous Balkan battles, and to the south, **Lake Vegoritis.** From Alexander the Great's campaigns to modern times, this has been a point where people converging from north, south, east and west have vied for turf.

At the turn of the century this was the land of the "Macedónian Struggle," the guerrilla warfare conducted by Greeks against the Turks and Bulgarians. Indeed the area saw little peace in the first half of the 20th century – the Macedónian Struggle 1900–08, the Balkan Wars 1912–13, World War I and II, and the Civil War – a narrative of violence and contestation equalled by few corners of the globe.

Édessa is unlike any other town in Greece, thanks to the streams that wind through it and over its famous waterfall. Walking down its backstreets, or sitting in the square, the sound of rushing water is never far from your ears. A path takes you right down the cliffside and into the waterfall's mist. At the north end of town there is a Roman (or Byzantine) bridge which served the Via Egnatia. Édessa, perched on its high bluff, marks the edge of the Macedónian highlands, and from here you can gaze out to the well-cultured plains that spread towards Thessaloníki and the sea.

Ali Pasha, the famous despot of Ioánnina, in his lake.

ROUMELI AND THE IONIAN ISLANDS

The region of Greece commonly known as Roúmeli is too often visited just for the sake of the classical site at Délphi (Thelfoús). Roúmeli is not, it is true, as rich in classical monuments as the Peloponnése. But a taste for Roúmeli, a part of the country which lets you travel largely in peace, is not hard to acquire and is difficult to lose.

"Roúmeli" is properly "Western Roúmeli," its name originating in the Ottoman term for the Greek nation within the Empire, *Rum Millet*. The word *Rum* is the one the Greeks themselves used: *Romaiói* or citizens of the eastern part of the Roman Empire. The notion of being, in today's Greek, a *Romaiós* is complex and persistent. *Romaiosíni* (the noun) is everything in Greek life and the Greek identity that is *not* classical, *not* Hellenic; everything, in short, that a one-sided view of the Greeks is liable to reject as "un-Greek."

Hellenism and *Romaiosíni* certainly do meet, merge and sometimes clash all over Roúmeli. At Délphi you will see shiny new shepherds' crooks being snapped up by pale Athenian schoolchildren. Or, in the smallest out-of-the-way place, you may ask to see *t' arhéa* ("the ancient remains") and then, following a shepherd up a winding path to the tinkle of sheeps' bells, suddenly find yourself at a little ancient fort or acropolis.

It is probably Roúmeli's natural setting that leaves the deepest impression. The hiker has the chance to see everyday marvellous sights such as a herd of goats tumbling down a slope much greener close up than it seemed from the road below. By contrast, the visitor who goes in search of traditional architecture is likely to be disappointed. The main reason is that much of Roúmeli suffered a scorched-earth policy both in the War of Independence and later in 1940–49.

And the inhabitants of the region have long had a formidable reputation as guerrilla fighters. In the 5th century

BC the Athenians found that with the "barbarian" Aetólians they had bitten off more than they could chew; in the middle of the 19th century the Athenian authorities were still having severe problems with banditry in Roúmeli. Some of the *kléphtoi* who had indeed helped to dislodge the Turks in 1921 were reluctant to give up the lawless, free and profitable life of rustling, kidnapping and roast mutton. More recently, it was from Mount Veloúhi (Tímfristos) in Roúmeli that the communist guerrilla Áris Velouhiótis took his *nom de guerre*.

Banditry, the visitor will be relieved to know, has disappeared, and good roads with buses that go everywhere have put Roúmeli's main towns and villages within easy reach of the capital; but the rural communities continue to live a pretty dour pastoral life. And the Rouméliots' reputation in Greece is not for worldly sophistication. (One reason is their heavy accent: their speech is very short on vowels, which makes it laconic and often hard to understand.)

Towards Parnássus (Parnasós): The **monastery of Osios Lukás** (not Luke the Evangelist but an obscure Blessed Luke) is often visited in a hurry as a small Byzantine concession in the standard classical tour. But this 11th-century monastery with its two churches, an example of late Byzantine grandeur in scenic isolation, is well worth a longer visit. It is the nearest one will get to the experience of Mount Áthos, and Osios Lukás deserves a day to itself before passing on to Délphi.

Crossing the edge of the mass of **Mount Parnássus** does something to prepare one for the experience of Délphi. Parnássus (Parnasós) dominates the centre of Greece from whichever direction one approaches it, whether it be from Lamía north, Livadiá east, Náfpaktos west or by ferry from the Peloponnése south.

It is the mountain's breadth and shape rather than its sheer height – Giónas is taller – that render it so impressive. In fact, the ascent can be performed on a clear day from late spring on – by the fit

Near Arta, a stream is diverted to create a whirlpool for washing rug

136

as well as the fanatical. Ask for details at **Aráhova**, a fresh and invigorating village hung with expensive rural crafts.

Aráhova's skiing facilities are its main attraction; some years back ski-racks became obligatory wear for the Athenian station-wagon. In the upper square by one of the village's many tumbling streams there is an excellent *tavérna*. There is also a St George's Day festival (23 April) in which the air is heavy with the scent of lambs which the ancients offered to the gods above and which the moderns offer to their own senses, being roasted in the open air. Watch out for the old men's race; the old boys, some reputedly over 80, run to the top of a steep slope and then unwind with a cigarette.

Délphi (Thelfoús): From here, it is only a few curving miles down to **Délphi**. This is the place which, of all others in Greece, visitors have found most memorable that is, since its excavation at the end of the last century. Mycénae (Mikínes) and Olympia fascinate; Délphi awes. Abrupt crags rise above as

vultures soar above them on winds that can suddenly turn to storms. The site involves steep climbs with, as their reward, the continual glimpsing of new angles and further treasures.

Délphi's fascination is threefold: its stirring setting, the scale, beauty and diversity of its monuments; and, as a sub-text, its turbulent and often disreputable history. The site may be divided into three parts, each of which deserves a morning at least. (To appreciate Délphi to the full, stay the night in one of the many hotels and get up at first light the next morning.)

At the upper site, dedicated to the Apóllo of the oracle, follow the Sacred Way, past the treasuries given to the oracle by Greek states. The Treasury of the Athenians is of particular interest, covered as it is with inscriptions of Athens' glories and the city's thanks to Apóllo. It is easy to forget that the whole building has been put back together like a jigsaw puzzle in modern times.

From here the path winds up past the oracle itself (a little imagination is re-

he Thólos at
lelphi; and a
estival in
loúmeli.

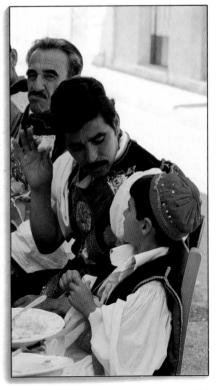

quired at this point) and the theatre to the stadium, the best preserved in Greece. The lower site, the preserve of Athéna, contains the single most beautiful monument at Délphi, a columned rotunda. (From here one can walk down the valley into what is said to be the largest olive grove in the world, a sea of ancient trees threatened by a planned highway.) There's a bus back from Itéa. Finally the museum on the site contains numerous marvels, including the famous Charioteer. The large quantity of Roman statuary – including a bust of the Emperor Hadrian's lover Antinous – is a reminder that Délphi had an enduring attraction.

Today Délphi is the home of a Cultural Centre which sees its task, improbably, as the bringing together of the world "in a spirit of amphictyony." (Yes, you'll need that dictionary – and so do they.)

Galaxídi and Náfpaktos: A few miles below Délphi is the port of **Itéa**, from where we look across the bay to **Galaxídi**, a strange little enclave, in a rugged pastoral setting, of the Greek maritime past before the days of steam. Once the third port of Greece, Galaxídi looks as if it is a bit of Syros perhaps, transferred to Roúmeli. The island atmosphere used to be heightened by the fact that, before the main road was built, Galaxídi was most easily reached by ferry from Itéa. It has a virtually unspoilt core of grand bourgeois houses (*arhóntiká*), some of which rest on sturdy lengths of ancient wall.

Galaxídi is now a well-preserved ghost-town; the ship-owners have long since left for Piraéus and rarely visit their old houses. But with charming details in the town – such as painted ceilings in some of the houses, if you can get a look inside – and impressive views outside it, Galaxídi has much to offer. Parnássus (Parnasós) is magnificently prominent above the villages that scale its slopes; from the hills above Galaxídi, Córinth can be seen on a clear day; and at night the lights of Éyio in the Peloponnése twinkle across the water.

Galaxídi was once spoken of as the **Galaxídi.**

future St. Tropez of Greece. It has escaped such a fate, but the rusting ships that lie offshore – victims of the Gulf War – and the scars from bauxite workings on the coast opposite – Greece's biggest source of foreign exchange – are a reminder that this region remains vulnerable to the pressures of a wider world.

The coast road continues with innumerable windings to **Náfpaktos**. It was here that the Athenians defeated the Spartans in a naval battle in 429 BC and dedicated a ship to Poseídon, god of the sea, at **Ríon** opposite. And in 1571 a famous battle took place (in fact fought just outside the Corinthian Gulf off the west coast of Greece) through which Náfpaktos became famous as Lepanto. An Ottoman chronicler records, "The Imperial fleet encountered the fleet of the wretched infidels and the will of God turned another way." It is well worth the climb up from the toy-like Venetian harbour, past little gardens, to the almost impregnable castle above.

From Náfpaktos, one can return to Délphi by the old upland route, as beautiful as the coast road and more hazardous. On the way, the stone village of **Lidoríki** is near the birthplace of General Makriyánnis, a fighter in the War of Independence whose *Memoirs* are the best insight into the mind of old Roúmeli. Here is a chance to breathe the air and stretch your legs before going on past the shining waters of the **Mórnos reservoir**, which supplies Athens with the water that the locals are denied. Stark rocks are intermittently set off by green valleys with cattle; mountain fauna such as eagles and rock thrushes are noticeable.

Finally the road reaches **Omfissa**, an old town in a crater-like setting. The old tanneries (*ta tabákika*) give you a good idea of an old neighbourhood without the old smells. **Sálona**, the castle above is a reminder of Omfissa's heroic past, the reintroduction of classical place-names is a prime example of Hellenism versus *Romaiosíni*.

Mesolóngion and Agrínio: Continuing from Náfpaktos towards the west coast,

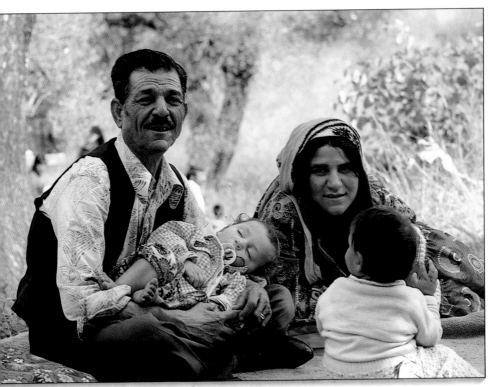

the landscape becomes flatter. Mesolóngion is the best known town here, one as rich in associations as Náfpaktos but with a less attractive present face. The lagoon with its feluccas is an unusual sight in Greece, but after a night in the company of Mesolóngion's mosquitoes it is easy to see how it was that Byron came to die here and leave his name – as *Víronas* – to a good many Greeks since.

Mesolóngion's role in the War of Independence continued with a grim siege and the slaughter of its inhabitants, events commemorated in an unfinished poem by the national poet Solomós. Unfortunately, the poem, however fragmentary, is more evocative than the visible reality.

From Mesolóngion there is a road up through the wild **Klisúra gorge**; further on, you will see tobacco leaves hanging outside almost every house. This is **Agrínio**, a prosperous commercial centre. From here one can take a rough road into the upland district of **Karpenísi** and then skirt **Mount Tímfristos** and continue along the oppressive **Sperhiós valley** to **Lamía** (117 miles/188 km). Alternatively, we can deviate – and that's the word, for it's easy enough to get lost on the way – to the **monastery of Prusós**. The faint-hearted may prefer the shores of **Lake Trihonís**.

The west coast: At first sight Árta is unspectacular, but it is of great interest to the historically minded. The town saw its heyday in the 13th century as the seat of the Despot of Épirus, whose realm stretched all the way up the west coast of Greece to what is now Dürres in present-day southern Albania (Northern Épirus to Greek diehards).

Árta is proverbial in Greece for its bridge, a fine Turkish construction clearly visible to the south of the town. A well-known folk song relates that the bridge's builder, despite his "forty masons and sixty apprentices" could not get it to stay up until he had immured a living thing in the foundations whose spirit would guard it. By ill luck or so the tale has it – this turned out to be his own wife. For impressive and not much vis- **The bridge o Arta.**

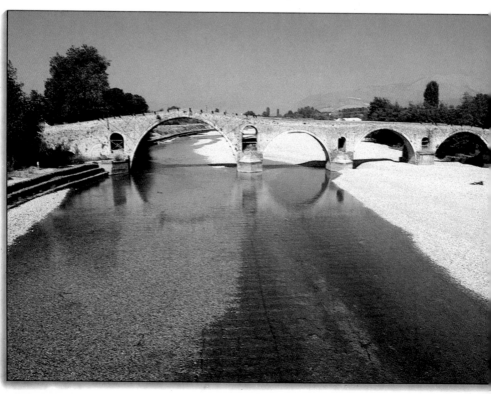

ited ancient monuments try the fortifications at **Strátos** to the south. The older residents of the rather forlorn village there speak not Greek but a sort of Latin, the Vlach dialect more common further north. Just north of Strátos one can turn left for **Astakós**, which has ferry connections with some of the Iónian Islands .

The main road continues to **Préveza**, a town which, like Árta, is known, if at all, through poetry but in a rather unfortunate way. In 1928 a young civil servant who had received a posting there, Kóstas Kariotákis by name, tried to drown himself, failing which, he shot himself in the head. Before accomplishing this he had avenged himself on Préveza by writing a poem really entitled "Province" but which is universally known as "Préveza," in which the town is seen as the archetype of the boring, a place where hearing the band on Sunday is a major event. Even today teachers and civil servants quake at the thought of being sent to Préveza by central government; but the town's

worthies revere the memory of their unwilling citizen.

A few miles away are the remains of **Nikópolis**, the city founded by the Roman emperor Augustus to celebrate his victory over Antony and Cleopatra off Actium in 31 BC. Impressive walls and a theatre survive as a reminder of the hated Roman domination. Foreign domination did bring tourism, however, and in the first two centuries, Nikópolis was a real tourist trap. Visitors arriving there from Rome would either show off their Greek and perhaps pay a call on the philosopher Epictetus or buy Greek trinkets and drink too much Greek wine.

Some certainly visited the **Nekromantíon** (the oracle of the dead) beyond Párga. Here, under the watchful eye of Hades, Lord of the Underworld, visitors would believe or half-believe that they were communicating with the souls of the dead, much as many Athenians today consult the small ads at the back of the newspaper for mediums. Archaeology has revealed what appears to be special effects equipment. A bit

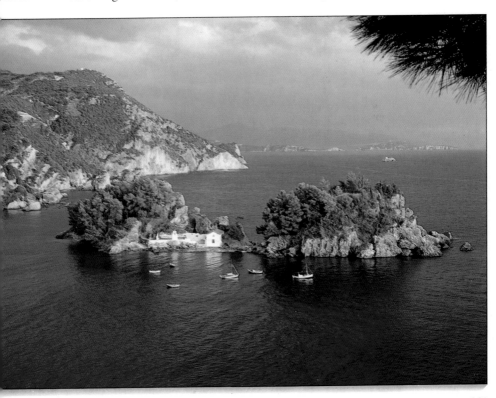

further up the coast we reach **Igoumenítsa**, which is the port for Corfú
(Kérkira) or from there Italy. Roúmeli
has been left behind.

The Iónian Islands: When people speak
of "the Greek islands", it tends to be the
Aegéan that they have in mind. Very
different in flavour, and largely free of
the hubbub of the Aegéan routes, are the
Iónian Islands. (In Greek they are called
Eftánisa after the number [seven] of the
principal islands; one of them, **Kíthira**,
no longer administered with the rest and
geographically an extension of the
Peloponnése, will not be dealt with
here.) The visitor from any mainland
country tends to relish the very insular-
ity of the Aegéan islands. The Iónian
Islands by contrast are in two main
respects far from insular.

In the first place, all of them are near
the west coast of Greece, from Épirus
north to Élis south of the Corinthian
Gulf. From the island of Zánte (Zákynthos), birthplace of the national poet
Solomós, one can see the turtle-shaped
castle of **Hlemútsi** opposite; the poet

himself describes the earth shaking
from the cannon-fire at the siege of
Mesolóngion some way to the northeast. Moreover, a formal and informal
network of communications has always
tied the main islands and numerous is-
lets to small ports on the mainland, and
such intercourse is the natural state of
affairs. Cattle were taken across the
straits in the world of Odysseus; today it
is mainly smaller items – wine or those
mysterious parcels that seem to fill
every Greek mode of transportation.

The Ottoman rulers of mainland
Greece did not want to break this chain,
and an important consequence in the
present is that the population of the
Iónian Islands has remained relatively
stable by comparison with that of the
Dódecanése, where the loss of the mainland coast to Turkey has deprived islanders of their livelihood and led to
large-scale emigration. In the Iónian
Islands a large rural population still exists and the twang of Chicago or Melbourne Greek is rarely to be heard.

The other way in which the Iónian

**An art dealer
on Corfu.**

Islands are far from insular is that they are, in the high culture at least, an amalgam of East and West. Under Venetian rule – which on Corfú (Kérkira), always the most important of the islands, lasted from 1386 until 1797 – the rich were bilingual in Greek and Italian, often educated in Venice or Padua and in some cases honoured with the noble titles of the *Libro d'Oro* in the manner of a European aristocracy.

Many were Roman Catholics, and the religious paintings of the 17th and 18th centuries clearly bear the mark of Western developments, as does the architecture of the churches to which they belong. It was native traditions as much as any interference, kindly or otherwise, by external powers, that made the Iónian Islands the first home, in the lands that now make up Greece, of a university and of a form of representative government.

But the islands' geographical position has been a source of more than a distinctive culture. It has also meant turbulent times for a region of great commercial and strategic importance, ever since Córinth's colonization of Kérkira (now Corfú) in order to secure the Italian trade route. Between 1797 and 1864 the islands were ruled, under various constitutions, by Venice, France, the Ottoman Empire, France again, the United Kingdom and finally Greece.

Corfú (Kérkira) was famous in ancient times for a bloody civil war; more recently it came into vogue through the writings of the Durrell brothers. Much has changed since World War II, and the island is now Greece's single biggest tourist asset. At the same time, however, it remains an island of great agricultural wealth, especially in olives – a blessing of Venetian rule. Its population is still overwhelmingly rural, and in fact Greece's least literate. So it is still easy to escape the "pubs" of the main tourist centres and find a quiet spot, especially to the northwest.

Despite its crowds and considerable war damage Corfú Town remains a unique conglomeration of public and

eorgie
árzas of
Georgie
oves the
eople"
estaurant on
orfú.

domestic buildings in which one can detect all the influences that have affected the island: the emblem of the lion of Venice; a French-style colonnade; houses with a Neapolitan flavour; and a clear legacy of British rule, cricket on the esplanade (fox-hunting never caught on). Opposite loom the forbidding mountains of Albania.

Lefkáda is the least visited of the Iónian Islands; island lovers spurn it as being too similar to the mainland, from which it is separated only by a chain-ferry. Mainland affinities are indeed much more evident on Lefkáda, long subject to a tug-of-war between the Venetian and Ottoman empires.

More often visited because of its name but still very peaceful for most of the year is **Íthaca (Itháki)**. The reason of course is its fame as the home of Odysseus (though envious Lefkáda has disputed the claim). Hómer correctly describes the island as rugged; it is also beautifully green. **Vathí** the capital, a deep port with white houses climbing steep slopes on either side, is the best

place to stay (the north of the island is within easy reach). Go to the little museum, test your connoisseurship on the supposed El Greco in the Cathedral, walk out of town a little way and you will understand why Byron once wished he owned it.

Cephaloniá, the largest and most rugged of the *Eftánisa*, is perhaps the island on which one most feels the loss of old ways and the passing of power and culture elsewhere. Lefkáda and Íthaca were always humble, but **Argostóli** was a charming town before the disastrous earthquake of 1953, and plays from **Lixúri's** 18th-century days have recently been revived on the Athenian stage.

Zánte (Zákynthos) appears from the boat (from Killíni in the Peloponnése) like a little model town. The churches and other buildings restored or rebuilt after the great earthquake of 1953 look just a little too bright and new. But while the atmosphere of the old streets has been largely lost, the public buildings and churches remain charmingly decorous. Less overrun by tourists than Corfú, Zánte gives one some idea of what it was that the Iónian Islands brought to the Greece of today.

One of the greatest contributions, especially valued by the Greeks, is poetry. After the fall of Crete in 1669 many of the aristocrats who had produced the literature of the Renaissance in Crete left for the Iónian Islands and Zánte in particular. And the tradition was combined by the two great Romantic poets born on Zánte, Count Dionísios Solomós and Andréas Kálvos; a third poet, Ugo Foscolo, wrote in Italian, but the Greek government still claims him as Greek on his anniversary.

Off the main square by the harbour there are, in fact, two fascinating museums, one devoted largely to Solomós and the other to the paintings of the distinctive Iónian School.

These highbrow activities apart, it is only fair to mention that swimming on Zánte is as good as anywhere in Greece, and that a subsequent evening meal will sometimes be accompanied by serenades after the Italian fashion.

Left, boatman from the Mesolóngion. **Right**, a woman from Corfú.

144

CENTRAL GREECE

What today we consider Central Greece was, until the end of the Balkan Wars in 1913, Northern Greece. At that point the northern boundary of Greece ran from Vólos through Lárissa, around the wide Thessalían plain, through the southern part of the great Píndos range to Árta on the west coast. Yet again territory in Greece proves to be temporary. But whatever the name of this middle part of the country, the area comprises the best that Greece has to offer: mountains, trees, fertile land, sandy beaches, islands, running rivers, and excellent harbours. Vólos, situated about halfway between Thessaloníki and Athens, makes a convenient hub for our travels in Central Greece which can fan out in every direction.

One's first impression of **Vólos** is that some giant took an accordion made of Athens, Piraéus, Thessaloníki, and all their outlying suburbs, and compressed it. The city has a little bit of everything found in a huge metropolis.

Once there, the visitor senses immediately the unique charm of the small busy town. There is a lovely promenade along the quay. The harbour reminds one of island harbours more than big city ports. Running down to the sea are numerous narrow streets in whose arcades are hidden some great little *ouzeríes*.

Like most important port cities of Greece, Vólos has an incredibly long history, dating back to neolithic times (about 4600–2600 BC). The wonderful tale of the adventuresome Jason who set out from Iolkos, portions of which have been excavated on the outskirts of Vólos, in the famous ship *Argo* to find the Golden Fleece long before the Trojan War, seems to come alive as you gaze out at the gulf named after the ancient port of **Pagasae**. Mythology is everywhere in Vólos.

The Spórades: For those who choose the sea, Vólos is the boarding point for the tiny luscious group of islands known as the **Northern Spórades**.

What a marvellous word! It means scattered, or sown, as the root of the word means seed. It is an accurate designation for these islands, strewn off the coast of Pélion.

Closest to Vólos is **Skiáthos**, whose only rival in small island tourism is Mykonos. This is partly due to its intensely lush greenery, but mostly to its sandy beaches. The most popular of these, Koukounariés, has a sandy stretch more than half a mile long, shaded by pines and shrubs.

Skópelos, the next in the row of the Spórades to the east, has not been as yet devoured by tourism in spite of it being perhaps more picturesque. Its beaches are lovely. The one lying in the curve of the bay of the main town, **Skópelos**, is usually very crowded. Others, smaller and more intimate than those of Skiáthos, are accessible by car or bus. The most lovely are **Stáfylos Cove, Limonári,** near the main town and **Miliá** and **Loutráki** nearer to **Glóssa.** Rent a "put-put" and chug to your own isolated beach, of which there are many.

You should not miss the opportunity to visit this beautifully green island. It has two ferry boat stops, Glóssa, "the tongue," opposite Skiáthos, and past that the main harbour, which as you approach looks like a white-tiered wedding cake, decorated with brilliantly-coloured flowers. The harbour is intensely busy, what with the four-times-daily ferry service and the many private yachts.

For those interested in chapels and fascinating convents (some of these produce handwoven goods), or remote monasteries, Skópelos, for all its tiny size, has about 360 such – white dots on a variegated green landscape of almond, plum, fig, and olive trees and thousands of grape arbours. Skópelos even boasts some antiquities, including the remains of a Cretan colony, and, as everywhere in Greece, a ruined *kástro*.

Beyond Skópelos lies the oblong island of **Alónisos**, with its steep, rocky coastline on the northwest, and undulating hills. On the dock you will witness a phenomenon, not unique to Alónisos by **Skiáthos**.

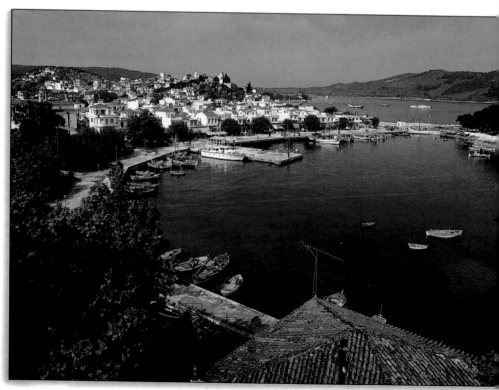

any means, but surprisingly fervent here: that of soliciting rents for private rooms. Some locals hold out discreet cards; others wave large signs. The practice is illegal, so the hopefuls keep one eye on the shore to watch out for the tourist police, and the other on the debarking passengers.

If, by renting a moped, or hiring a "put-put", you can get beyond the harbour town, you will find Alónisos one of the last bastions of unspoiled tourism in Greece. Here are deserted beaches; green pine groves without discarded film boxes and plastic bottles. The only paved road leads from the harbour to the old pre-1950 earthquake town of Alónisos. To get anywhere else you must go by dirt road or skiff. Renting a small boat is worth it because you can make a round-the-island and across-to-Peristéra trip at your own pace.

Peristéra is the small island that hugs the shore of Alónisos on the eastern side. For other areas on the island, such as the beach at **Marpoúnda** on the south, or **Kokinókastro** on the eastern

peninsula, there are regular launches leaving from the main harbour during the summer.

Beyond Alónisos and its small companion, Peristéra, are scattered three or four more islands: **Pélagos** (also called Kyrá Panaghía), **Yiaoúra**, which has a cave worth investigating and **Pipéri**. These can only be reached by *caïque*, or one's own yacht. It was off these rocky promontories that a Byzantine wreck was discovered in the summer of 1968 and subsequently explored by a team of archaeologists, including the famous Throckmorton, under the auspices of the Greek Archaeological Service, supervised by Nikólaos Yialoúris. The brilliantly-coloured Byzantine plates, with their motifs of sailing vessels, fish and border designs, are now in the museum at Vólos.

The fourth major island of the Northern Spórades, **Skyros**, has the most history and legend of the group. It was the island where the two-timing Théseus was put to death by the king of the island, Lycomedes. It was here that

eft, a musician om Central reece. ight, a riest from kópelos.

Thétis hid her son Achílles, disguised as a woman, with Lycomedes' daughters so he would not be drafted for the Trojan War. The main town itself, also called **Skyros**, is built partly on a bluff overlooking the beach to the east, and then dips into lower ground where most of the shops are.

A bust of Rupert Brooke, the British poet who died off Skyros while on his way to fight in the Dardanelles in 1915, dominates the tiny square of the uphill part of the town. From there the view to the sea is out of this world. Just beyond the square is a miniscule chapel, tended with infinite care by a little old woman. This is the chapel so treasured by the Nobel prize-winning poet, Seféris. He loved the island, and often rented "The Mill," a refurbished old mill house close to the beach, sleeping four and having a lovely garden running down to the sea.

Clearly the wealth of legend surrounding the island is an indication of its commercial importance. It was a centre of maritime commerce for thousands of years, and home to many of the Mediterranean pirates who defied law and order from the days of Pompey in 70 BC to the middle of the 19th century. All is calm there now, except during the hectic summer tourist season, when the few houses that have rooms are crammed. Go in October.

Eúboea (Évia): From Skyros' harbour of **Linariá** a ferry boat leaves regularly for the east coast port on **Eúboea** of **Kími**. Up from the noisy broil of the dock, the real village is charming. Stay there a night, if you can. Of course, Évia, as you must pronounce it or no one will know what you are talking about, is more usually reached via the road from Athens to the large sprawling city of **Chálkis (Halkítha)**, the capital of Eúboea. However, arriving on the island via the back way gives you a chance to get a taste of the landscape.

After Crete, Eúboea (about 115 miles/180 km long) is the second largest island in Greece. A thorough exploration of the island is most rewarding. It is a microcosm of Greece. Museums, restaurants, beaches, factories, refineries, **Two landmarks i▶ Metéora: St Nicholas…**

discos, glamorous hotels, pollution, ancient, Byzantine, Frankish, Venetian, 1821 relics – all are there. Chálkis (perhaps named for the Greek word for bronze *halkós*) alone possesses all of these. The bustling city is located on the **Eúripus channel** whose irregular currents change direction as many as 14 times a day. Its maritime significance was as important in the 7th century BC as it was in the period of Venetian dominance (AD 1200–1400), when the island was known as Negropont.

All along the coast going north, and even further to the south, are the latest hotel development projects. Although the beaches are not very desirable for swimming, as they are mostly pebbly, and not very clean, the hotels are always full during the summer. This is true of the whole Miami-like coastline facing the continent, as well as the southern ferry port of **Karístos**, jutting up on its limestone hill.

The beautiful parts of Eúboea are the central and northern portions. The road winds leisurely up and up, settles down in some valleys, and then goes up again. All are green and wooded. A 12-mile (19-km) junket to the west from the main north–south road at **Strophyliá** leads you to the resort of **Límni**, very much the enclave of the British, who maintain summer homes or even stay the year round. It is also a great haven for yachtsmen.

If you get that far you should proceed along the narrow coastal road to the very attractive convent at **Galatáki** with its spotless refectory and peaceful rooms overlooking the sea between the island and the mainland.

In addition to the traces of Frankish and Venetian remains, sad relics of past glory, there are many ancient ruins. Most of these are in the northern part of the island near **Istiéa** and **Oreí**, and are rather disappointing to the non-expert. It is more rewarding to visit the **sanctuary of Ártemis** near **Vathí** on the road to Chálkis from Athens. There, close by the immense cement works of Chálkis, you can visit famous **Aúlis**, where Agamémnon's youngest daughter, Iphigénia, was sacrificed on the altar of Ártemis, the virgin huntress goddess, so that the winds would be favourable for the Greek fleet to set sail for Troy.

A final place to visit in Eúboea is **Edipsós**, with its centuries-old renowned health springs. From there you can take off for the mainland. Sacred to the ancients for their healing powers, the springs were frequented by such famous Roman characters as Sulla, the conqueror of the east. Although the beach is hardly ideal, many large tourist hotels have been built around the small bay. Some of these nearest the springs boast mineral water piped directly into the rooms.

Thermópylae (Thermopíles): The monument dedicated to the men who died at Thermópylae in July of 480 BC, defending the Greeks against the hordes of Persians, is located on the National Road to Lamía, just beyond Kámena Voúrla (a mineral spring centre like Edipsós), mobbed in the summer in spite of mushy beaches and murky wa-

ter. *Thermopíles* literally means "warm gates, or pass" because of the area's innumerable hot sulphur springs which bubble up today as they did in 480 BC.

The last part of Book VII of Heródotus has immortalised the romance of betrayal. How Leonídas and his 300 Spartan men were annihilated because of the treachery of a well-bribed local, Ephiáltes (the word means nightmare in modern Greek) is a well-known tale. Although Leonídas had known of the path over the heights of Mount Frikion, the Persians slaughtered the 1,000 men guarding it, and swooped down upon the Spartan rear. And that was the end of the 300, Persians in front and Persians behind. Their immortal epitaph rings sacred: "O stranger, announce to the Spartans that we lie here, obedient to their words."

Metéora: Suddenly, as you round a bend in the dull road that leads from Tríkala to Kalambáka, erectile, elemental rock formations piercing the sky confront you – the **Metéora**. Nothing you have ever seen in pictures can pre-

Along the coast of Pélion.

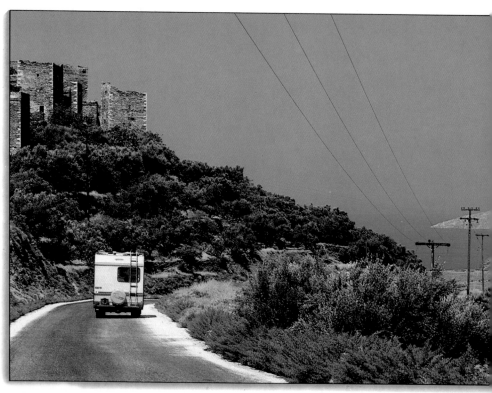

pare you for this. On these projections are some of the most extraordinary monasteries in the world. The name is derived from the verb, *meteorízo*, which means to suspend in the air.

Few places in Greece are so intensely visual. The formations, which once supported 24 monasteries, defy description. Most geologists hold to the theory that the strange outcroppings of rock were created by millions of years of erosion by the **Piníos River** as it split the Píndos range of the west on the Thessalían plain from that of Mount Olympus and Mount Ossa on the east.

Whoever was the first, Andrónikos or Athanásios, depending upon which of the various histories you may read, which aged monk gives you the *real* story, you can only marvel at how long it took to get stone by stone, brick by brick, board by board up to those heights with a basket and a rope ladder.

The largest of the monasteries, the Grand Metéoron, also known as Metamórphosis (Transfiguration) took three centuries to complete, having been founded around 1356. Ághios Stéfanos (now run by nuns) was completed at the end of the 1300s. Of the 24 monastic communities which flourished till the last part of the 17th century, their heyday being in the 14th and 15th centuries, seventeen are in ruins, and only five are open to visitors. Of these, only three are inhabited.

Clockwise, the visible monasteries are: **Ághios Nikólaos** (uninhabited except by someone to collect a fee) built around 1388, with a small chapel containing frescoes by the monk Theophánes of the Cretan School (*circa* 1527); **Grand Metéoron**, looked after by a few monks of the St Basil order with a valuable collection of manuscripts dating to the 9th century and icons displayed in the old refectory; **Varlaám**, with 16th-century frescoes by Franco Catellano, restored in 1870; **Ághia Triátha** (Holy Trinity) which is approached by approximately 139 difficult steps chiselled out of the rock, and whose major claim to recent fame is being an on-sight location for the James

Wildflowers near Makrinítsa.

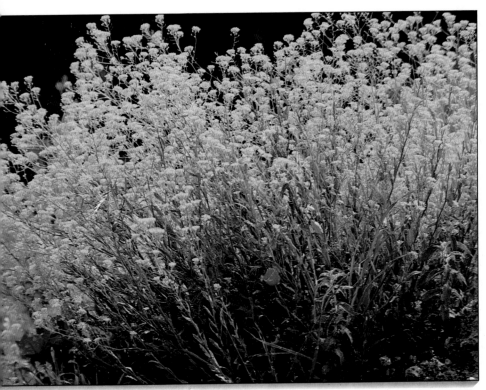

Bond movie *For Your Eyes Only*; **Ághios Stéfanos**, where although the nuns can often be less than friendly, the renovated chapel is easy of access and whose small museum displays ecclesiastical robes, icons, manuscripts and similar treasures.

If you really want to understand the monasteries' beauty and awe, you should try to connect up with some local person from Kalambáka or Tríkala, who will know the entrances and exits and secret low doors out to the grassy meadow-like plots of green nestled in the secret hollows of the rocky pinnacles. While most tourists are shepherded back into their buses, you can explore, and after finding a secluded hedge, gaze out over the plain far below.

Olympus (Ólimbos): Today, as you drive through the beautiful **Vale of Témpe** along the gorge of the Piníos River, you can hardly believe that until 1913, it was not even part of Greece. The Vale, however, oblivious of time and armies remains the same welcome lushness of cool and green as it has been for thousands of years. Even the encroachments of tourism have not changed the river, which forms the 6-mile (10-km) pass severing Mount Olympus from Mount Ossa. Along the way there are several touristy stops. One is the little church of **Aghía Paraskeví** across a narrow foot-bridge over the river. There you can light your candle and fill your canteen. Another is the **spring of Aphrodíte** at the end of the pass. In spite of these tourist traps, no one should travel the "Vale", hymned by so many poets, without stopping somewhere – either to look down at the river and take a picture, or perhaps wander down a path to its edge.

Leaving the cool vale you head north straight for the "home of the gods," Mount Olympus. There are several passages in Hómer where he alludes to Zeus' habit of bringing down the clouds to cover the summit of Mount Olympus so that no one on earth could see what was going on. Well, that is just one way of stating an obvious fact. Very rarely can you get a good picture of the moun-

A Byzantine monastery.

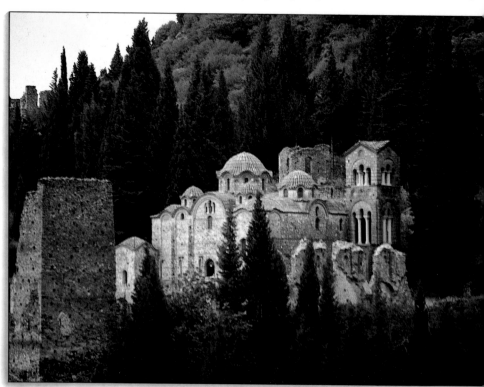

tain from the narrow plain that lies between the mountain and the sea, the **Thermaïc Gulf** (from the word *thermós*, meaning warm because of all the warm springs). Even more rarely can you get a good distant shot, so continuously is the summit girdled with clouds.

There are two major ways to ascend the mount of the gods, the slow and the fast. Basic details can be obtained from the offices of the Alpine Club in Athens, Vólos or Thessaloníki (SEO). If you want to taste the nectar of the gods, the best plan is to go up the slow way, and down the fast. This requires some advance preparation. A direct contact through the Alpine Club or a travel agency is necessary so that the refuge camps and a guide to take you up the last rocky ascent will be available. The lower regions are easy to traverse, as the path from the Stávros refuge camp is easy to follow. This first refuge camp on Olympus is accessible by bus from the village of **Litóchoron**, a 30-minute ride. You can also walk it.

Beyond Stavrós, a dirt road skirts the foothills, and then the real trail takes off along a gentle two hours of climbing through lovely wooded terrain. After some two hours of walking you will come to the "crossing" of the Enípeos stream which, further down, flows into the Piníos gorge. At the crossing the rocks and fresh waterfalls with all the surrounding green are so enticing that you may feel like staying there all day.

Beyond is the steep ascent, through pine, beech, oak and scrub, to the marvellous second refuge camp. This one has three large cabins which together can house as many as 70 people. You will need about five hours to reach this second refuge camp. If you are lucky, while you are panting up the steep trail, a donkey may pass, laden with bottles of orange drink. Its destination is the refuge camp, but the proprietor will sell you his wares on the way.

Most people end up staying at the second refuge camp, after nearly a seven hour climb, and never make it to **Mítikas**, the top. This is because you

ΡΗΓΑΣ ΦΕΡΡΑΙΟΣ

really should have some experience as a rock-climber, unless you have the assistance of the guide. There is only one seam where steps have been cut in the rock face. Theoretically there is a guide who mans the refuge camp six months of the year. He is responsible for keeping tabs on climbers, and stocking the refuge with food and mountain tea (*tsaï tou vounóu*).

Having reached the top of Mítikas, however, you will find the descent via the fast route not-too difficult, once you get down off the rocks. The trail is well marked, a direct plunge into the Thermaïc Gulf. Via this trail, experts starting from the coastal village of **Platamónos** have made the ascent and returned in one day. The item to remember, whichever trail you take, is the water flask.

Pélion: Having navigated the austere heights of Mount Olympus, let us now return to the "hub" of Central Greece, Vólos and **Mount Pélion**.

The mythological explanation for the mountains which circle the great Thessalían plain is wonderfully imaginative. Huge creatures called Titans or Giants (depending upon what version of the story you read – Hómer, Hesiod, Ovid, Virgil) vied with each other to dominate the underlings, Zeus and Poseídon. What modern scientists call earthquakes, ice flows, seismic shifts of plates, or whatever, were simply credited to the Titans. It was they who tried to pile Pélion on Ossa, and both mountains on top of Olympus to reach the heavenly realm of the gods.

The legend is often laughed at as being a tall tale until you have been there. Then the close juxtaposition of the three mountain massifs and the precipitous cleavage of the vale may make you wonder.

But let's leave such great endeavors to the gods and content ourselves with a trip around Mount Pélion, land of the centaurs. These famous beings had the legs and bodies of horses (indicating the importance of the horse in the development of civilization) and the arms and heads of men. These creatures were the teachers of many of the major heroes, Achilles being the most famous. The intriguing historical fact is that the entire Pélion region was *the* centre of learning in Greece throughout the 17th and 18th centuries. A whole slew of monasteries with research facilities grew up in the centaurs' habitat. Many of the important secretaries and governors of provinces in the Austro-Hungarian Empire, the Sultan's inner circle, the Russian court, not to mention many intelligentsia of Europe, were educated on Mount Pélion.

There are few remains of this grandeur, but **Zagorá**, the former centre, still boasts an excellent library and **Makrinítsa**, about 12 miles (19 km) from Vólos, has preserved the 18th-century "Pélion-style" houses. Probably the original reason for becoming such a centre of erudition was its lush water supply, and its inaccessibility to the Turks, which meant no revenues for the overlords.

The beaches, where Mount Pélion crashes into the sea, are beyond the power of words or pictures to describe. The sand is soft and creamy – real sand. The sea is more turquoise and filtered purple than any photograph. Sea-fashioned caves and hidden coves will lure you down the many steps at **Tsangaráda** or the twisty road that ends up at **Ághios Yiánnis**.

You will need a number of days to see all the villages nestled on Pélion's slopes: **Machriráchi, Miliés, Milopótamos, Makrinítsa,** one of Pélion's most beautiful villages with cobblestone streets and spectacular views to the north, or **Drakiá**, **Ághios Lavréndis**, dedicated to folk art, or **Argalásti** in the heel of Pélion's boot.

However, it is worth the time. Indeed, time should be the password for the whole country. You cannot "do" Greece in two weeks. The ancients have left their relics, of which the museums are full. The Romans, Byzantines, Arabs, Slavs, Franks, Venetians, Turks have done the same. That encompasses about 6,000 years of high civilization. Nowhere in Greece has this heavy mass of history, triumph and tragedy made itself more evident than in so-called **Colour coordination** "Central Greece."

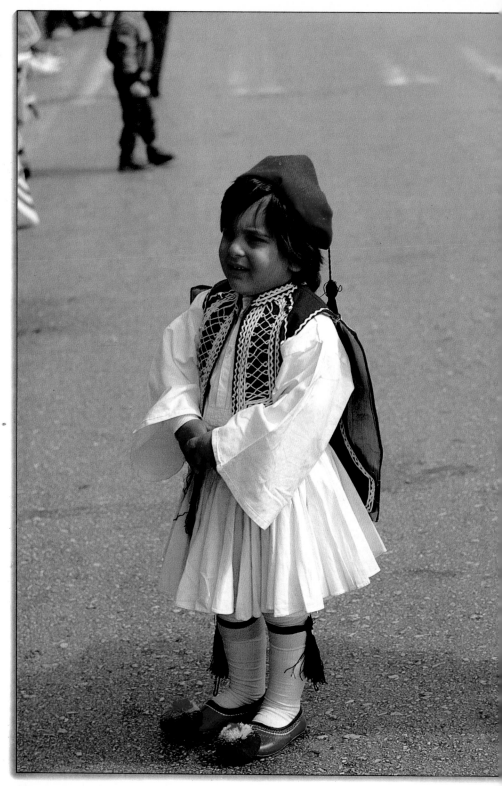

ATHENS

If there is one quality which Athens should be credited with unreservedly, it is elasticity. It might be compared to an indestructible old sweater which has shrunk and stretched and shrunk again through the centuries, changing its shape as circumstances required.

Athens is barely mentioned in Hómer. It emerged as a growing power in the 6th century BC. Then came the Pericléan high noon, when Athens became a great centre of art and literature, commerce and industry. With Macedónian expansion came the first shrinkage, though Athens remained a prestigious intellectual centre with particular emphasis on philosophy and oratory.

In the Hellenistic age, Athens was overshadowed by the great monarchies founded by Alexánder's successors, but not obliterated, the rulers of Egypt, Syria, Pérgamum courted the old city with gifts of buildings and works of art. Yet one can't help feeling it was perhaps already beginning to rest on its laurels, to turn into a museum-city, a "cultural commodity" rather than an active, living organism. Besieged and sacked by Sulla in 86 BC, restored and pampered under two philathenian Roman emperors, Augustus and Hadrian, sacked again by the Herulians in AD 267 and Alaric the Goth in AD 395, Athens entered the Byzantine era shorn of all its glory – a small provincial town, a backwater. The edict of the Byzantine emperor Justinian forbidding the study of philosophy there (529) dealt the death-blow to the ancient city.

Venetian incursion: Under Latin rule (1204–1456), invaded, occupied and fought over by the French, Catalans, Florentines and Venetians, Athens shrank even further. It was only after the Turkish conquest in the 15th century that it began to expand again, but still falling far short of its ancient limits. There were more setbacks, including a devastating Venetian incursion in 1687. Athens finally rose from its ruins after the War of Independence, an "exhausted city," as Christopher Wordsworth noted in 1832, and was suddenly raised, unprepared, to the status of capital of the new Greek state.

Growing up fast: Athens is thus a city that has grown haphazardly, and too fast. It never had a chance to mellow into venerable old age. Old and new have not blended too well, you can still sense the small pre-war city pushing through the huge messy sprawl of today's modern capital, like the proverbial thin man struggling to get out of every fat man.

An unmellow city, then; a city in transition, it is said apologetically. But then one might say it has always been in transition; not the natural kind, but violent and irregular, leaving visible marks, glaring contrasts, untidy seams.

You occasionally come across what must have been a country villa, ensconced between tall office buildings, its owner still fighting against the tide, its windows hermetically closed against dust, pollution, the roar of the traffic. For traffic in Athens has to be seen (and heard) to be believed. For one thing, Athens must have the highest number of motorcycles of any city in Europe: cars are expensive and get stuck in the traffic, motorbikes wriggle through where everybody else fears to tread.

But branching off from these frenzied central arteries are the minor veins of the city, relatively free from congestion: narrow streets where the architecture may be shrilly modern, yet life retains in part some of the old patterns. Most apartment blocks have balconies and verandahs, and there you can see the Athenians in summer emerging from their afternoon siesta in underpants and nighties, reading the paper, watching the neighbours, watering their plants, eating their evening meal.

The hot weather makes life in the open air a necessity; this in turn means gregariousness, a kind of social exhibitionism – it is no accident that there is no word for "privacy" in Greek – though nowadays the pale blue flicker of television draws more and more people indoors. Yet even television sometimes turns into an excuse for gregariousness; there are improvised World Cup parties, election-night parties; collective viewing while eating, drinking, talking, and playing cards.

Recently taxis have also turned into a sort of communal institution. Taxis are cheap in Athens and therefore in great demand. If you're lucky enough to get a taxi, you soon find you have to share it with others. But what began as a necessity has evolved into one more occasion for social exchange, whether heated argument or comfortable chatting. Are the Athenians then such sociable and funloving creatures? Not really; they are simply easily bored and immensely restless. Byron called the Greeks "an intriguing cunning unquiet generation."

Another foreign traveller, the Frenchman Edmond About, observed in 1852 that the Greeks are vain, curious, furiously ambitious, set on a relentless quest for success and prosperity, as a result of the insecurity generated by decades of poverty; more than poverty, the sheer precariousness of life in Athens in those protracted dark ages. This is perhaps what gives the city its intent, bustling air, often mistaken especially by disciplined northerners – for uninhibited Mediterranean exuberance. It's true that the incessant activity has nothing of the antlike industriousness of the Protestant work ethic. Improvise, make do, contrive and combine, keep going, keep ahead, is more what it's all about. The feverishness is also due, no doubt, to the need for rapid adaptation to the modern world, to the crazy pace created by those abrupt, transitional pangs mentioned above.

It would be interesting to write a sociological study simply noting the kinds of shops that predominated in Athens with each successive transition: the 1960s saw an extraordinary eruption of "Scandinavian" furniture shops, in the 1970s it was fashion boutiques and art galleries; everybody became bathroom-conscious in the 1980s, and shopwindows displayed huge shell-shaped bathtubs, gold taps, an infinite variety

You never know what you might find...

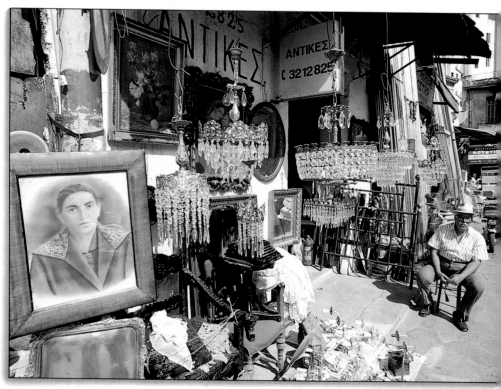

of bathroom-tiles; then came the craze for Video Clubs – understandably, since Greek TV is not all that exciting, and there were, until recently, only two channels, which seemed to copy each other with amazing fidelity. The 1990s are bringing international designers like Armani to Athens, along with cowboy gear (saddles included) for the *nouveaux* urban cowboys.

There is a constant struggle to catch up with the West while clinging to the old traditional ways. *Tavérnes*, competing with pizza and fast-food shops, try to keep up a semblance of *couleur locale* (which is fast turning into *couleur internationale*: you find better *taramosaláta* in London supermarkets than in Athens). Arranged marriages are still going strong, but the matchmaker is now competing with a computer service. Doughnuts and *koulóuria*, popcorn and *passatémpo*; a priest, majestic in flowing black robes, licking an ice-cream cone or riding a motorbike – unthinkable 10 or 15 years ago. Coexistence – but the edges are still jagged.

City streets: One of the places where the meeting of old and new is most manifest is the commercial area between **Monastiráki** and **Omónoia Square**, at the heart of the city. It is a kind of huge chaotic bazaar, bringing to mind the market described in a comedy by Euboulos in the 2nd century BC, "Everything will be for sale together in the same place at Athens, figs, summoners, bunches of grapes, turnips, pears, apples, witnesses, roses, medlars, haggis, honeycombs, chickpeas, lawsuits, beestings-puddings, myrtle-berries, allotment machines, irises, lambs, waterclocks, laws, indictments."

Beestings-puddings and allotment machines sound mysterious enough, but the weird assortment of objects to be found in the market today is almost equally intriguing. Kitsch-collectors will find much to interest them; Greek kitsch is perhaps the most orgiastically hideous in the world. The modern age has brought mass production tourist trade on a grand scale. Even the shops

God and Mammon side by side.

around the **Mitrópolis**, specialising in ecclesiastical articles, have turned touristy; the manufacturers have perhaps caught on to the fact that tourists often find bronze candle-stands just the thing for a garden-party; a priest's heavily-embroidered robes can be turned into a stunning evening dress, while pectoral crosses outshine the flashiest *faux bijoux.*

But if you move away from the robust vulgarity of **Pandróssou Street** to the narrow sidestreets off the **Flea Market**, you step into an almost pre-industrial era. This is the district of traditional crafts (crafts minus "arts"), wholesale shops selling refreshingly non-decorative, down-to-earth stuff like screws, all sizes and shapes, locks and keys, chains of varying thickness, boxes and crates, brushes and brooms, mysterious implements like futuristic sculptures, mousetrap shops, herb-shops (the mountains of Greece are reputed to be a botanist's paradise), shops selling incense, resin in big amber-coloured chunks, contrasting bright blue chunks of sulphate of copper used for plants (and fishing octopus) – a whole serendipitous accumulation of things no longer to be found in our brave new ready-made world.

Head for the hills: There's a peaceful busyness in these narrow streets. Only a few steps beyond, you are back in the great melting-pot, the high-rise buildings, the fumes, the heat. You panic, but not for long. The saving grace of Athens is that there are easy ways out; better still, visible ways out. Just when you're feeling buried alive in the asphalt jungle, you see at the end of a street a fragment of mountain, a slice of open country, trees, breathing outlets.

Athens is full of bumps, some big enough to deserve the name of hills, others mere excrescences. Eight of them have been counted, (one up on Rome!) but there may be more. There's **Mount Lycabéttus (Likavitós)**, of course (you can't miss it); the equally conspicuous rock of the **Acrópolis**, flanked by the **Pnyx** on one side, and the hill of **Philopáppus (Filopápou)** on the other where it is the custom to fly kites

on the first day of Lent; the hill of **Árdittos**, next to the marble horseshoe **Stadium**, built by Hérod Átticus in AD 143 and totally reconstructed in 1896 (the first modern Olympic Games were held there); the hill of the **Nymphs**, capped by the gray dome of the **Observatory**; the barren, windblown **Tourkovoúnia range**; and the hill of **Stréfi**, the poor man's Lycabéttus, far less touristy, where the efforts of landscape-gardeners appear more strenuous than on the other hills.

There are small hidden cafés and a measure of coolness on some of these hills. Still, these small pockets of green don't really deserve the name of oases – you have to go further afield for that, up one of the three mountains that encircle Athens. **Mount Hyméttus (Imitoú)**, beloved of honey-bees, glowing violet at sunset, provides a real oasis. Driving up the winding road past the monastery of **Kaisarianí** (15 minutes' drive) you reach a vantage-point of beauty and tranquillity from which to contemplate the whole of Áttica. (Also see page 171.) The city is panoramically visible, yet totally, eerily inaudible. On **Mount Párnes (Párnitha)**, only two hours away, you can walk in a dark wilderness of fir trees, play roulette at the casino, ski in winter. **Mount Pendéli** is crowded, lively, popular, with all the ensuing disadvantages: air thick with *souvláki-smoke* and the screams of overactive children.

But if you're not much of a climber, if you're simply "*las des musées, cimetières des arts,*" as Lamartine said, you can still escape to the **National Gardens**, within a stone's throw of the Byzantine, Benáki and War museums. You walk down **Hérod Átticus Street**, watch – if you must – the changing of the Évzone Guard (whom Hemingway refers to as "those big tall babies in ballet skirts"), then turn right, into the park. Suddenly there is thick shade, tangled bowers, romantic arbours, and relative quiet.

Do not expect anything lush, the generous green expanses, the grassy carpets, the lakes and cascades of other European parks. Here are only modest fish-ponds, thin but constant trickles of water running along secret leafy troughs; a few forlorn deer, and a large population of cats, fed, and neutered, by Athens' few committed animal-lovers. Cicadas whirr away, peacocks cry, mournful for all their spotted blue-green glory. Here you can observe the Athenians at rest; here students come to study, lovers meet, old men meditate, mothers brood, weary hitchhikers sleep on a bench, under a roof of wisteria, even the busy briefcase-men use it sometimes as a bridge, an interlude in between two hurried appointments.

There is a solitary, unexpected stretch of green lawn on **Vass. Sofías Avenue**; beautifully designed, it serves as the setting for the giant bronze statue of the eminent statesman Venizélos (1864–1936), who seems on the point of plunging into the traffic, and then thinks better of it. If you climb over the green slope to the back of the site, you come upon the **Park of Freedom**. It is not a park, by no stretch of the imagination; as for the word freedom, it has here a

propitiatory (expiatory?) function, for during the military dictatorship (1967–74) this was the HQ of the dreaded military police, where dissidents were detained and tortured.

There is a pleasant café, a lecture-hall, a tiny open-air theatre. The torture-chambers have been turned into a museum; posing again that difficult moral problem: what does one do with places like this? Cover them up, preserve them, embellish them? Remember or forget? Remembrance may breed hatred, oblivion begets apathy. Here the effort seems to have been to preserve and transform at the same time; to commemorate the horror while creating around it an atmosphere in which the ghosts may be laid to rest. An optimistic, perhaps utopian message: life goes on, the present takes over without disowning the past. The Greeks are good at carrying the burden of the past, they've been doing it for ages; but like all burdens, it sometimes interferes with their sense of balance.

Not particularly green, but certainly

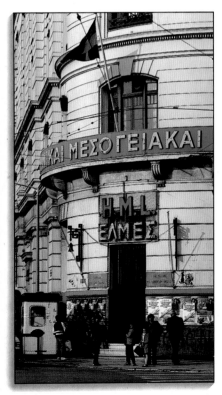

an oasis, **Pláka**, the old quarter clustering at the foot of the Acrópolis, has now been refurbished, restored to its former condition, or rather to a fairly good reproduction of it. The garish night-clubs and discos have been closed down, motor-vehicles prohibited, for the most part, houses repainted, streets tidied up. It has become a delightful, sheltered place to meander in; you almost think yourself in a village, miles from the urban monster below. You come upon small architectural beauties: Byzantine churches, the Tower of the Winds, the Old University, fragmented arches and walls.

Night moves: The night is sure to provide some respite from the heat, as most nocturnal activities take place in the open air: restaurants, cafés, theatres, cinemas. (Even the clattering garbage collectors work at night). Do not mistake the open-air cinemas for drive-ins; they have rows of seats like ordinary cinemas, and the only customers on wheels are the midnight babies brought there in their pushchairs by their harassed mothers and silenced with ice-cream. As for theatres, apart from the **Hérod Átticus Theatre** which is the official venue of the Athens Festival, there is a large theatre on Mount Lycabéttus, used mostly for concerts of modern music, and several abandoned quarries (Áttica, land of stone…) converted into theatres that put on some very good productions and provide a starkly dramatic setting.

The night is long in Athens; Athenians fiercely resist sleep, or make up for lost night-sleep with a long afternoon siesta (caution: *never* telephone an Athenian between 2 p.m. and 6 p.m.). Cafés and bars stay open until the small hours; bars and "pubs" here are unlike those of other European capital; they are larger, they have tables, provide music (usually loud) and serve food (usually expensive) as well as drinks.

Three o'clock in the morning, and the traffic still won't give up; groups of people linger on street-corners, goodnights take forever. The main streets are never entirely deserted; per-

Colossal lion at the foot of Hymettus.

haps this is one of the reasons why Athens is a safe city to walk in at night, except for the occasional bag-snatcher, but real violence is rare. The "unquiet generation" finally goes to bed; verandahs and balconies go dark, cats prowl, climbing jasmine smells stronger – and all the conflicting elements in the patchwork city seem momentarily resolved in the brief summer night.

Seeing the sites: Seen from the right angle driving up the Ierá Odós (the Sacred Way) or looking up at its rocky bulk from high in Pláka – the Acrópolis still has a presence that makes the grimy concrete of modern Athens fade into insignificance. Climb up in early morning in summer or early afternoon in winter, when the crowds are thinnest and a strip of blue sea edged with gray hills marks the horizon. On a wet or windy day, walking across its uneven limestone surface feels like being on a ship's deck in a gale.

Until the year 2000 or so, the Acrópolis will look like a stonemason's workshop, much as it must have done in

the 440s BC when the Párthenon was under construction as the crowning glory of Péricles' giant public works programme. Some of his contemporaries thought it much too extravagant: Péricles was accused of dressing his city up like a harlot. In fact, the Párthenon celebrates Athéna as a virgin goddess and the city's protector. Her statue, 39 ft (12 meters) tall and made of ivory and gold plate to Pheídias' design, used to gleam in its dim interior. (It was carried off to Constantinople in late antiquity and disappeared.)

Conservators have installed a folding crane inside the Párthenon to lift down several hundred blocks of marble masonry and replace the rusting iron clamps inserted in the 1920s with non-corrosive titanium. Rust made the clamps expand, cracking the stone. Acid rain turned carved marble surfaces into soft plaster.

The restorers also succeeded in identifying and collecting about 1,600 chunks of Párthenon marble scattered over the hilltop, many blown off in a

1687 explosion of an Ottoman munitions dump inside the temple. When they are replaced, about 15 percent more building will be on view. New blocks cut from near the ancient quarries on Mount Pendéli (9 miles north of Athens), which supplied the 5th-century BC constructors, will fill the gaps.

The **Eréchtheion**, an elegant architecturally complex repository of ancient cults going back to the Bronze Age, is already restored. The original Cáryatids who supported a porch over the tomb of King Kekrops, a mythical founder of the ancient Athenian royal family, have been replaced with copies to prevent further damage from the *néfos*, the ochre blanket of atmospheric pollution that hangs over Athens.

Completed in 395 BC, a generation later than the Párthenon, the Eréchtheion also housed an early wooden statue of Athéna, along with the legendary olive tree that she conjured out of the rock to defeat Poseídon the sea god in their contest for sovereignty over Áttica. In Ottoman times, the building was used by the city's Turkish military commander as a billet for his harem.

The **Propylaía**, the battered official entrance to the Acrópolis built by Mnesikles in the 430s BC, was cleverly designed with imposing outside columns to awe people coming up the hill. Parts of its coffered stone ceiling, once painted and gilded, are still visible as you walk through.

Roped off on what was once the citadel's southern bastion is the small, square temple of **Athéna Níke**, finished in 421 BC. It supposedly stands on the spot where Théseus' father, King Aégeus, threw himself to his death on seeing a black-sailed ship approaching harbour. Théseus had promised to hoist a white sail for the return voyage if he succeeded in killing the Minotaur on Crete but carelessly forgot.

The sculptures that Lord Elgin left behind are in the **Acrópolis Museum**. Four Cáryatids stare out from a nitrogen filled case, scarred but still impressively female. The coquettish "koraï" reveal a pre-classical ideal: looking

Tourists "romancing the stone".

closely, you can make out traces of make-up, earrings, and the patterns of their crinkled, close-fitting dresses (the spikes discouraged birds from sitting on their heads).

North of the Acrópolis, the **Agorá**, the ancient city's political centre, looks like a cluttered ruin field. If archaeologists had their way, the whole of Pláka would have been levelled. But the reconstructed **Stoá** of Áttalos, a 2nd-century BC shopping mall, is a cool place to linger among scents of ancient herbs replanted by the meticulous American excavators. And a look at the stolid **Thisseíon temple** opposite will make you appreciate that the Párthenon is truly a masterpiece.

Across from the Agorá, on the far side of the Piraéus metro line, one corner of the Painted Stoá has been exposed in Adrianoú Street. This famous ancient building gave its name to Stoicism, the stiff-upper-lip brand of philosophy that Zeno the Cypriot taught there in the 3rd century BC.

On the south side of the Acrópolis lies the **Theatre of Dionysios**. The marble seating tiers that survive date from around 320 BC and later, but scholars are generally agreed that plays by Aéschylus, Sóphocles, Eurípides and Aristóphanes were first staged here at 5th-century BC religious festivals. A state subsidy for theatre-goers meant that every Athenian citizen could take time off to attend. Doves nest in niches in the Acrópolis rock, which would have blocked the chill north winds at day-long performances during the Anthesteria celebrations early in the year.

Past Monastiráki, the **Kerameikós Cemetery** in the potters' district of the city was a burial place for prominent ancient Athenians. An extraordinary variety of sculptured monuments – tall stone urns, a prancing bull, winged sphinxes and melancholy scenes of farewell – overlooked the paved Sacred Way leading to the Dipylon Gate from Eleúsis, where the mysteries were held.

Most of the original grave *stélai* are in the National Museum, but the replicas are still eloquent. It's the perfect place

facelift for e Cáryatids.

to recover from a hard day's sightseeing; tortoises lumber through the undergrowth and frogs croak beside a slow-moving stream.

The Museum's collection of grave goods forms a magnificent guide to Greek vase-painting: from a squat geometric urn with a rusting iron sword twisted around its neck to the elegant white *lekythoi* of classical Athens and self-consciously sophisticated Hellenistic pottery.

Hádrian's Arch: A few Roman monuments recall a time when Athens was a city to be revered, but stripped of its movable artworks. The 2nd-century Emperor Hadrian, a fervent admirer of classical Greece, erected an ornate arch marking the spot where the classical city ended and the provincial Roman university town began. He also finished off the **Temple of Olympian Zeus**, a vast building abandoned when its original constructors ran out of funds around 520 BC, and dedicated it to himself.

Later in the century, Hérod Átticus, a wealthy Roman administrator, built the steeply-raked theatre used now for Athens Festival performances, as a memorial to his wife.

And a 1st-century BC Syrian was responsible for the picturesque **Tower of the Winds**: a well-preserved marble octagon overlooking the scanty remains of the Roman Forum. It is decorated with eight relief figures, each depicting a different breeze, and once contained a water-clock.

Byzantine Athens is scantily represented: a dozen or so churches, many dating from the 11th century, can be tracked down in Pláka and others huddle below street level in the shadow of the city's tall, modern buildings. They are still in constant use: Passers-by slip in to light a yellow beeswax candle, cross themselves and kiss an icon in near-darkness before returning to the noise and jostling outside.

One of the handsomest is **Ághii Theodóri**, just off Klafthmónos Square. It was built in the 11th century on the site of an earlier church in char-

Relics in the National Archaeologic Museum: Mask of Agamemnon.

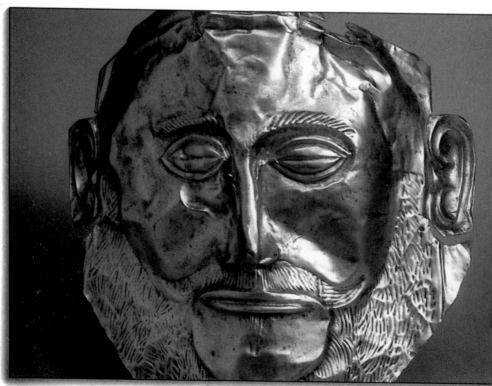

170

acteristic cruciform shape with a tiled dome. The masonry is picked out with slabs of brick and decorated with a terracotta frieze of animals and plants.

Ághios Nikodémos on Filellínon Street dates from the same time but was bought by the Tsar of Russia in 1845 and redecorated inside. It now serves the city's small Russian Orthodox community; the singing is renowned.

On Athens' eastern and western limits lie two famous monasteries: Kaisarianí and Daphní.

Kaisarianí on Mount Hyméttus, surrounded by high stone walls, is named after a spring which fed an aqueduct constructed on Hádrian's orders. Its waters, once sacred to Aphrodite, the goddess of love, are still credited with healing powers (and encouraging childbearing). The monastery church goes back to AD 1000 but the frescoed figures who gaze out of a blue-black ground date from the 17th century. Clustered around are stone-built cloisters, a kitchen and refectory and a former bath-house. The monks' wealth came from olive groves, beehives, vineyards and medicines made from mountain herbs.

Daphní, a curious architectural combination of Gothic and Byzantine decorated inside with magnificent 11th-century mosaics, occupies the site of an ancient sanctuary of Apóllo. A fierce-looking Christ Pantócrator, set in gold and surrounded by Old Testament prophets, stares down from the vault of the dome. The present building dates from 1080 and the Gothic porch was added in the 13th century when Daphní belonged to Cistercian monks from Burgundy and was used as the burial place of the Frankish Dukes of Athens.

Museum notes: Going back to 3000 BC, the **Goulandrís Museum** displays a unique collection of slim, stylised Cycládic idols in white marble, beautifully mounted and lit. They were scorned by 19th-century art critics as hopelessly primitive, but their smooth, simple lines attracted both Picasso and Modigliani. Mostly female and pregnant, the figures come from robbed

.and a onze rider.

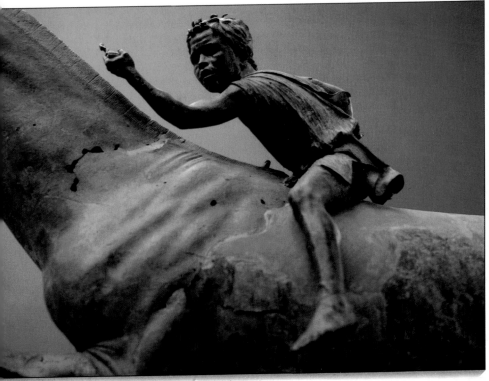

graves in the Cycládes islands; scholars are still uncertain of their purpose.

Crammed with badly-labelled treasures from every period of antiquity, the **National Archaeological Museum** should be visited early in the morning before the guided tours turn the echoing marble halls into a deafening Babel. Not to be missed are the Mycenaéan collection, the Thíra frescoes and the major bronze sculptures.

The **Mycenaéan Gallery**, containing Schliemann's finds from the shaft graves at Mycénae, is stuffed with treasures from the 2nd millennium BC that repay close examination: miniaturism was prized on coloured sealstones, daggers and signet rings. Gold gleams everywhere, barbaric and sometimes tawdry but a clear indicator of prehistoric Greek wealth.

Upstairs, the Thíra Fresco Room reveals a lighter side of Bronze Age life: small rooms decorated with Aegéan island scenes of dark-eyed boys boxing, blue monkeys swarming up a mountainside and statuesque, black-haired women with heavy make-up.

Few large-scale ancient bronzes have survived, but the statue of Zeus coolly poised to hurl a thunderbolt, which was netted by a fisherman off Cape Artemision in Central Greece, is one splendid exception. It dates from around 470 BC when classical naturalism in sculpture was just about to take off. By comparison, the bronze child jockey on his Hellenistic racehorse, cast two centuries later when heightened realism was the fashion, has a strained, almost frightened expression.

The bronzes in the **Piraéus Archaeological Museum** are more workmanlike but still fascinating. Both the graceful, rivetting archaic Apóllo, one of the earliest fullsized bronze statues, and the soulful, helmeted, Hellenistic Athéna were found in a sewer excavation in 1959, and perhaps belonged to a cargo of Rome-bound loot awaiting shipment.

The **Byzantine Museum**, a mock-Florentine mansion built by an eccentric 19th-century duchess, contains a brilliant array of icons and church relics from the 13th to the 18th centuries. Across the street, the **Benáki Museum** houses a wonderfully eclectic collection of treasures – including jewellery, costumes and two icons attributed to El Greco in the days when he was a young Cretan painter called Domenico Theotocópoulos.

The **Canellópoulos Museum**, a 19th-century mansion, is a similar treasure trove of objects from every period of Greek art acquired by an erudite, obsessive collector. And the **City of Athens Museum**, an accumulation of 19th-century furnishings, pictures and fittings in a house where teenage King Otto lived while waiting for his palace to be completed, evokes the atmosphere of upperclass life in newly independent Greece.

Outside Athens, a 43-mile drive to **Cape Soúnion** on the windy tip of the Áttica peninsula takes you to Poseídon's temple. Completed in 440 BC its slender, salt-white columns are still a landmark for ships headed toward Piraéus. Lord Byron carved his name on a column on the north side. The marble came from nearby Agríleza, where the Athenians also mined silver and lead. Following an impressive classical fortification wall down the hillside, you come to the remains of ancient shipsheds in the bay below: the Athenians once organised warship races off Soúnion and it later became a pirates' lair. Sunset here is often as dramatic as the tour organisers claim.

More out-of-the-way is the **Sanctuary of Ártemis** at **Braúron** – now called Vravróna – on the east coast of Áttica, 22 miles (35 km) from Athens through the wine-growing Mesolóngion district. A 5th-century BC colonnade visited by owls at twilight is flanked by a 16th-century Byzantine chapel, built on the site of an altar to Ártemis. In classical times, well-born girls aged from five to 10 and known as "little bears" performed a ritual dance at a festival honouring Ártemis as goddess of childbirth. Their statues are displayed in the site museum: plump with appealingly solemn expressions and dressed like miniature adults.

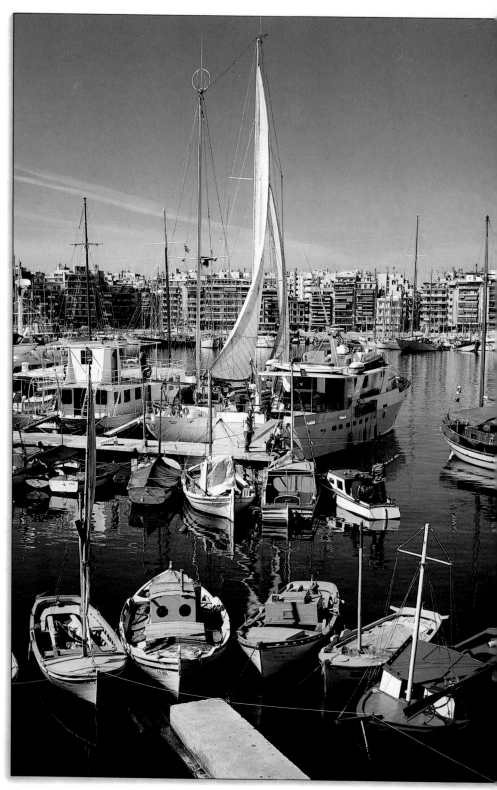

ISLANDS OF THE SARONIC GULF

Athens and the islands of the Sarónic Gulf are often lumped together in guide books. There is sense to this since many Athenians frequent these islands on weekends, while during the summer these islands are veritable extensions of the more fashionable Athenian neighbourhoods. Yet this view of the Argosarónic islands doesn't take into account their separate identities. They are islands, not suburbs. Each has its own character and deserves more than a page of our attention.

Aégina: This is a privileged island, rich in natural beauty and prized for its healthy climate and clear air. About an hour and a half by ferry from Piraéus – or half an hour by the "flying dolphin" hydrofoil – Aégina has had little trouble attracting visitors. Although the island bears some of the scars inflicted by an expanding tourist industry it is large enough to allow refuge from the crowds. Long a favourite Athenian retreat, it remains more popular among weekend smog evaders than among foreign tourists from elsewhere.

Shaped on the map like an upside-down triangle, Aégina's southern point is marked by the magnificent cone of **Mount Óros**, the highest peak in the Argosarónic islands, visible on a smog-free day from Athens' Acrópolis. The centre and eastern side of the island is mountainous; a gently-sloping fertile plain runs down to the western extremity where Aégina Town overlays in part the ancient capital of the island.

When the world was small and a city or an island could aspire to be a Great Power, Aégina, strategically situated between the Peloponnése and Attica, looking out upon the Aegéan and all the Mediterranean beyond, became a wealthy trading state with shipyards, fleets and a sophisticated banking system. In the 7th century BC Aégina produced the first Greek coins – the silver "tortoises" – and with these gained great financial leverage throughout the ancient world.

With the onset of the Persian Wars in 491 BC the Aeginétes first sided with the Persian army, to the chagrin of the besieged Athenians, but in 480 BC at Salamis, the greatest of all Greek sea battles, they returned to the Greek side and won the praise of the Delphic Oracle as the fleetest navy on the seas.

But Aégina (the "eyesore of Piraéus", as Péricles called it) posed a threat to Athens' expanding maritime empire. In 457 BC and again during the Peloponnésian War the Athenians defeated the Aeginétes at sea, on the second occasion expelling the entire population and replacing it with Athenian colonialists.

After the defeat of Athens in the Peloponnésian War, the Spártan Lysander, in recognition of the help Aeginétes had given Spárta during the war, returned them to their home. After this Aégina played a less conspicuous role until the 1820s when it became the temporary capital of liberated Greece from 1826 to 1828.

The Aégina Town one confronts today is typical of small Greek cities a century ago. A number of classical mansions stand at the edge of town. Several buildings constructed after the liberation of Greece in 1828, from the time of the island's first governor, Ioánnis Kapodístrias (1776–1831), are also preserved. The **Archaeological Museum** in the centre of the town displays a number of interesting artefacts from the island's history. The modern harbour oval in shape and crowded with picturesque *caïques*, was the city's commercial wharf in antiquity; small additions were built in the Roman period and under Venetian rule.

The **Military Harbour** lies near the village of **Karantína**; remnants of ancient moorings can still be seen there. To the left of the port as you enter is the hill of **Kolóna** with the remains of the **Temple of Apóllo** (formerly attributed to Aphrodite). All that is left from this famous temple is a single *kolóna* (column). The temple (Doric, six columns by 12, built in 520–500 BC) was superseded by a late Roman fortress, fragments of which survive on the sea-

he busy
acht basin at
Piraeus.

AÉGINA: A PLACE OF RETURN

The well-loved poet Katerína Angheláki-Rooke gives her impressions of Aégina....

Aégina is a place of return. It is a place that opens, receives, consoles and heals. Other islands are points of departure; you leave them behind and set off on expeditions, exploits, conquests. Dry, arid islands like Hydra, Íos, Mykonos and Santoríni inspire action. Aégina, on the other hand, is a feminine island; as the boat turns the corner, the horse-shoe shaped harbour – the church of the little Virgin on the one side and the old yellow house on the other – provides the perfect enclosure for an aching heart. When I was small I thought the yellow house had become yellow from the passing of time, like an old photograph.

The harbour is alive. It is as alive in the winter as it is in the summer. Tourists barely alter this island. They make a brief appearance and then disappear mysteriously, like the summer sirocco, the hot, humid wind that sweeps in from the south, the Sahara. In September the air smells of resin from the pistachio nuts that are harvested there and the freshly washed barrels ready for new wine. The light is soft and caressing, having lost the harshness of August. Across the water the mountain of Methana turns a dusted blue. I sit at Skotádis' *oúzo* shop watching the *caïques* unload fruit and vegetables, while Babouas, the Down's Syndrome sufferer who owes his name to the only sound he can produce, paces up and down and smiles at the familiar faces. He is grateful for this place which forgives human and divine mistakes and accepts us all.

Inland, the landscape is reminiscent of Attica. Perhaps the island retains something from its motherland, across the water, in the same way we often keep the facial characteristics of our parents. The curves of the hills and the tops of the olive trees follow and at

The poet her dog Henry.

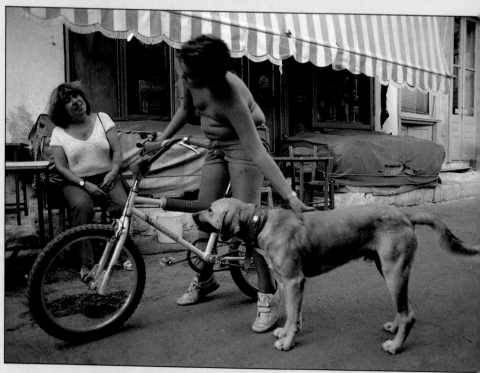

times interrupt the sky. The clouds add a touch of frivolous imagination in the midst of so much blue seriousness. These are the elements Aégina shares with Attica. But Aégina is distinctly an island; your nostrils quiver in the salty air which reaches you wherever you go. There's a sense of being cut-off, set apart; there's an atmosphere of independence, of autonomy, of solitude. A dual personality then is the key to this island's charm. Aégina is both the sweetness and the severeness of life, all in one slight stretch of land.

"Oh! to be in Aégina again!" wrote my godfather, the novelist Kazantzákis when he was abroad, away from the island and his house by the sea. From his window on Aégina the adventures of Odysseus opened in front of his eyes like water-flowers of incredible intricacy and beauty.

Sometimes Kazantzákis would leave his rock promontory and go to town to buy sweets from Prokopis, the Greek from Asia Minor, a master when it came to Oriental pastry or to chat with the village idiot – a different one then, at the end of the 1930s. "Tell me, Thomas, have you ever gone to school?"

"Couple of times, boss, I wasn't very good at it, but then I got sick, I became an idiot and now I don't have to worry about a thing!" Kazantzákis marvelled at the wisdom of Thomas.

The deaf and mute man cleaning fish in the market, the baker with his eternal grin and his apron covered with flour, the fishing boats nonchalantly bobbing in the little harbour, the dogs relentlessly sniffing the butcher's doorstep, the whole island stops as the sun sets across the sea. Ah! the sunsets of Aégina, the gold and red glories that envelop us for a short instant, filling us with nostalgia and anticipation.

I leave Skotádis' and the harbour and take the road up the hill back to my house. The trees and walls fence off my private history. What is here contains me and I contain it. Its presence is my continuity, the impersonal continuity of someone who has lived and loved a place: Aégina.

tádis' shop.

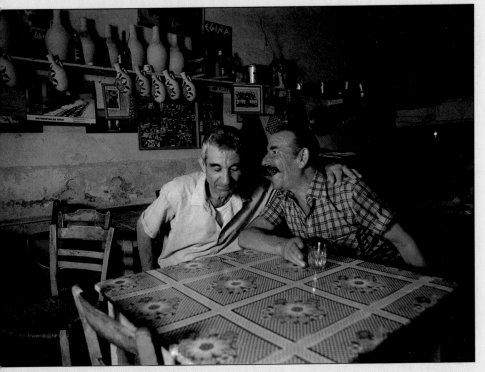

ward side. Although from the sea the position of the temple looks unimpressive, the view from the hill in late summer is breathtaking. Apart from the usual day trips to small resort towns (**Souvala, Pérdika, Aghía Marína**) or to the two neighbouring islands of **Angístri** and **Moní** you should, even if Greek ruins or Byzantine churches are not your cup of tea, visit the **Temple of Aphaía** and the **Monastery of Ághios Nektários**.

The Temple of Aphaía stands at the top of a hill above the cape of Aghía Marina in a pine grove commanding a splendid view of the Aegéan. Built in celebration of the victory at Salamís, it has been called "the most perfectly developed of the late Archaic temples in European Héllas." It is the only surviving Hellenic temple with a second row of small superimposed columns in the interior of the sanctuary.

Aghios Nektários (Anastásios Kefalás: 1846–1920), Metropolitan of Pentapolis, was the first saint to be canonised (1961) by the Orthodox Church in modern times. The monastery named after him stands on a hill across from another which is covered with ruins of more than 20 churches and monasteries, survivors from the 13th century and later, some with remarkable stone iconostases (especially the **Monastery of Panaghía Hrisoleóntissa**). These churches were once part of the old hóra of the island (*Paleóhora*) where the islanders sought refuge from sudden attacks by pirates (the town was twice destroyed by the famous pirate Barbarossa and once by the Venetians). When the Turks were thrown off the island in the 1820s the Paleohorítes came down to the port leaving their churches behind.

A final word of advice: avoid the town of Aghía Marína (a dreadful package holiday centre), though its beach is worth a visit. The beaches on the little islands of Angístri and Moní, admittedly not the most beautiful in the Aegéan, are still a good bet. Aégina Town with its loud fishmarket, its picturesque port where *caïques* unload **Pistachios.**

their fruits and vegetables, its lively *ouzeriés* and *tavérnes* and its traditional pistachio sellers make up for a possibly uneventful swimming trip.

Hydra (Ídra): The island of **Hydra**, once Idrea, "the well watered," is now ironically a long barren and waterless rock. The heart of the island is its harbour-town. All around the picturesque bay white houses climb the slope accented by massive gray *arhóntiká*, the houses of the gentry. Along the quay are the colourful shops of the marketplace, with the marble tower of the Holy Virgin Cloister in the centre. The harbour, girded by a little thread of a breakwater, forms a soft and perfect crescent, its two ends flanked by 19th-century cannons.

Hydra has aspired to be a fashionable artists' colony and retreat for intellectuals, and has also attracted a less orthodox fringe of idlers. The combination of Hydra's raw natural beauty and the wonderful harbour town continues to be irresistible. Hydra is the Mediterranean island *par excellence*.

The foundation of Hydra's greatness

was laid in the 18th century, when the reviving commerce of the Peloponnése coupled with the grain trade with South Russia provided the Hydriots with an outlet for their abilities. Hydra, once no more than a small port in the Venetian empire, gradually became the dominant maritime power in the Aegéan. During the War of Independence the Hydriots threw themselves heart and soul into the fight with merchant families, notably that of Koundouriótis, converting at their own expense their trading vessels into war ships.

The well-preserved and imposing houses of all these families are now little museums and open to visitors. In the huge **Mansion of Admiral Tombazis**, the Athens School of Fine Arts has established a branch which hosts artists of international acclaim. A Merchant Navy Training School occupies the **House of Tsamados** and across the way are the Hydriot Archives.

The higher reaches of the town and the hills beyond remain surprisingly untouched, charming and full of Greek

Égina waterfront.

colour. Narrow alleys and steep staircases lead from one quarter to the next. The uniformity of white walls is broken again and again by a century-old doorway, a bright blue window frame, striking scarlet steps, or a dark green garden fence.

With plenty of *tavérnes*, cafés, bars and nightlife, Hydra should also appeal to the tourist who may have no interest in the island's glorious past and its various historical monuments. For many Hydra is just a point of departure, a base from which to organise a series of expeditions to the mainland and other islands. For others Hydra, this immaculate little town bathed in white and blue colours, is the Greece one is so eager to rediscover time and time again.

Póros: The island of **Póros** is separated from the Peloponnése by a small passage of water – the word *póros* in Greek means "strait." The island can be reached not only by ship and "flying dolphin" but also by driving along the Peloponnésian coast via the **Isthmus of Córinth** and **Epídauros** to the little town of **Galatás** which lies opposite the main harbour. As one sails in through the northern entrance, the harbour opens up. It is almost landlocked and one of the finest anchorages in the Aegéan. Your first glimpse of the island will be of the white houses and bright orange rooftops of Póros Town.

Built on a hill with its highest point at the centre, the town resembles an inverted amphitheatre and the effect is disarming. On the mainland opposite, the village of Galatas with its white steps and dark alleys and its *Lemonodasos* where lemon groves grow amidst water-mills, makes a wonderful sight. It is easy to understand Henry Miller's enthusiasm (in his book *The Colossus of Marousi*) as he sailed between Póros and Galatás. "I don't know which affected me more deeply – the story of the lemon groves just opposite us or the sight of Póros itself when suddenly I realised that we were sailing through the streets. If there is one dream which I like above all others it is that of sailing on land. Coming into Póros **Gypsy girl.**

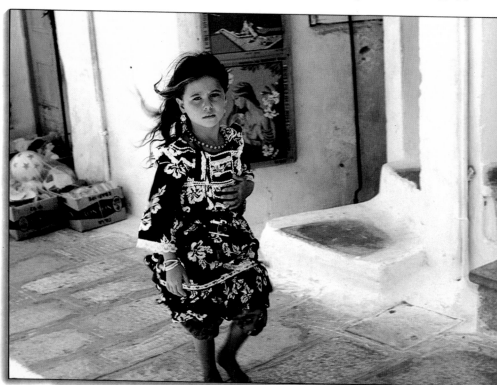

gives the illusion of the deep dream. Suddenly the land converges on all sides and the boat is squeezed into a narrow strait... To sail slowly through the streets of Póros is to recapture the joy of passing through the neck of the womb. It is a joy too deep almost to be remembered."

It is not an illusion that one is sailing between houses; friendly faces actually hang out of the windows just above your head while the scents of *retsína*, *oúzo*, lemon and grilled fish fill your nostrils.

Although a number of hotels have been built on Póros and prominent Athenians have owned vacation houses here for decades, the island has never been fashionable like Hydra or Spétses, but during summer it gets as crowded as Aégina.

On the southwestern coast are the remains of the old military harbour that the Russians laid out with the Sultan's blessing. In 1830 the first naval arsenal was established here which survived until 1877 when it was closed in favour of Salamis. The building now houses the **Boys' Naval Training School**. The famous Greek warship *Avérof*, which played a major role during the Balkan Wars of 1912, is docked in front of the School. The anniversary of the battle (6 December) is marked by a celebration (*panayíri*) and parades.

The main sight on Póros is the **Monastery of Panaghía Zoodóhou Pigí** (Virgin of the Life-Giving Spring) beautifully situated in an overgrown glade. Only a few monks still live there today. Noteworthy is a wooden, gold painted iconostásis dating from the 18th century and adorned with late Byzantine illustrations from the New Testament. It was presumably brought to Póros from Asia Minor.

In front of the monastery a new road encircling the heights to the east climbs through the pinewoods to the plateau of **Palatia**, where the ruins of the **Sanctuary of Poseídon** are situated in a saddle between the highest hills of the island. The temple was excavated at the turn of the century and little remains but its setting is rewarding.

Yachts docked at Hydra's fashionable port.

The ancient town of **Kalávria** was situated nearby, and the sanctuary was the headquarters of the Kalávrian League, a religious association of several towns that included Athens as well. The sanctuary served as an asylum for shipwrecked sailors, pirates and political refugees. It was here that the famous Athenian orator Demosthénes, in flight from Antipater's emissaries, took refuge, trusting that not even the Macedónians would dare to profane so ancient and famous a shrine. When they did, he poisoned himself.

The visitor to Póros must not leave without making a side trip to **Troezen** on the Peloponnése. To reach it you can take a boat from the harbour of Póros to the town of Galatas and then a bus to the ancient town. En route between Aégina and Póros, the boat stops at the town of **Méthana**. There is no need to stop in this tourist village. Póros is by far a more exciting choice.

Spétses (Spétsai): At the southern end of the Sarónic Gulf, **Spétses**, the ancient *Pitiusa*, or "pinetree" island, offers the most picturesque beaches and the most sophisticated nightlife of the nearby islands. As a British commentator has rightly observed, "Spétses lacks only titular recognition as a possession of the United Kingdom." On any given weekend one is likely to find as many British tourists on Spétses as Athenians on Aégina.

Although Spétses Town is full of new hotels, noisy bars and cheap fast-food places, the eastern side of the island, the *Palió Limáni* (**Old Harbour**) still radiates a gentle grace, a particular magic that is apparent to even the short-term visitor.

The 18th-century *arhóntiká* one sees in this part of the town are now the property of wealthy Athenian families who despite the summer invasion of tourists return to the island with the hope of finding their special *tavérna*, their favourite boatman and their "old acquaintances" in the fish market.

Like Hydra, Spétses was one of the main centres of activity during the Greek War of Independence, having

The *Flying Dolphin* hydrofoil from Piraeus calls regularly at Poros.

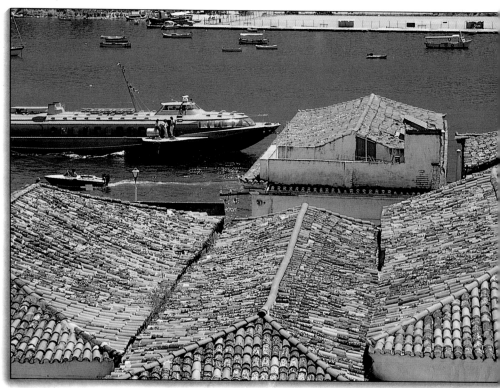

contributed a fleet of 100 ships to the Greek cause. The island is distinguished for being the first in the archipelago to revolt against the Ottoman rule in 1821 and the fortified point, still bristling with cannons now forms the town's *Platia*, the **Dapia**.

Bouboulína, Greece's national heroine, was a Spétsiot woman who took command of her husband's ship after he was murdered by the Turks. According to a story, the Turkish fleet arrived one day off the coast of Spétses when all of the men happened to be away, so Bouboulína and all the other women of the island, rather than hiding on the hills, collected all the fezzes they could find (all Turkish subjects had to wear these hats) and placed them on the asphodel plants that grew in masses along the shore.

From a distance the fezzes swaying in the wind looked like warlike hordes and the enemy fled at the sight. This "victory" and the more engaging one of 8 September 1822, when Spétsiot brigs and fireships repelled a superior Otto-man force is celebrated annually by a *panayíri* in the name of *Panaghía Armáta* (her little chapel stands on a hill close to the Old Harbour). A mock battle is staged, a Turkish flagship made out of cardboard is burned in the middle of the harbour and there follows a display of fireworks.

Although after the War of Independence Spétses' fleet declined with the emergence of Piraéus as the main seaport, the traditions of shipbuilding continue unabated. The small naval **museum** in the imposing 18th-century *arhóntikó* of Hadziyiánnis Meksis, Spétses' first governor, contains coins, costumes, ship models, weapons and other memorabilia from the island's past including the bones of the famous Bouboulína. The house in which she lived is behind the **Dapia**.

Outside the town near **Xenía beach** is the **Anargírios and Korgialénios College**. John Fowles taught here and memorialised both the institution and the island in his novel *The Magus*.

The town's beaches of **Aghios Mámas** and **Ághios Nikólaos** are polluted and quite unattractive in contrast to the beautiful beaches of **Zogeria**, **Vrélo**, **Aghía Paraskeví** and **Áyii Anáryiri** which are appropriately situated on the pinewooded part of the island. In addition one can go to the various beaches opposite Spétses on the Peloponnésian coast. The prettiest of these is probably **Hinitsa** and for those who enjoy water-skiing, **Pórto Héli** with its protected bay provides the perfect setting.

Spétses can also be used as a useful communication link. From here one can get to Naúplia, Árgos, Epídauros, Mycénae or to the southern town of Monemvasia where the Greek poet Rítsos was born. During the summer months when the Ancient Drama Festival is held in Epídauros a trip to one of the performances is a definite must.

An evening walk in the Old Harbour or in the woods of Ligoneri, a ride in a horsedrawn carriage to Aghía Marina, a taste of fish cooked *à la Spetsiota* are but a few of the pleasures that await the visitor on Spétses.

he ophistication f the Saronic ulf islands s mirrored n Spétsai.

THE PELOPONNÉSE

The **Peloponnése** (Pelopónisos) takes its name from the fabled hero *Pelops*, and the word for island, *nísos*. But it is scarcely thought of as an island. Should you blink, however, in passing over from Attica (Attikí) you might miss the slight isthmus that joins the Peloponnése to the mainland.

The Peloponnése is divided into seven *nómoi* or provinces: Corinthia in the northeast; Argolis, the eastern peninsula, that juts towards the Aegéan; Elis, pushing west towards the Iónian Sea; Achaéa, to the north; Arcadia, in the central mountains with a brief shoreline along the Argolis Gulf; Laconía, the two southern prongs; and Messenía, the last promontory to the southwest.

The Peloponnése stands a world apart. Not only is its landscape unsurpassed in archaeological importance and variety, its history mirrors every major shift throughout the Greek peninsula, from the Mycenaéan period to modern times. Even Athens has not been prone to so much upheaval. No other part of the Greek world has suffered so many changes, so many invasions, so much political strife.

Ancient ruins: The ruins of ancient **Córinth (Kórinthos)** convey a melancholy reality. The city was destroyed several times by earthquakes and what can be seen here, particularly in the walkways with marketplace stalls, is of Hellenistic-Roman vintage and comparatively late. The city was completely razed to the ground by the Romans in 146 BC, and well into the next century, by order of Julius Caesar, Córinth was "founded" once again by the Roman Empire. It moved quickly into prosperity and influence. When St Paul delivered his "Epistle to the Corinthians," the Apostle had God say to the city, "I will destroy the wisdom of the wise, make void the intelligence of the intellectuals..." Apparently Paul thought that this self-confident and affluent centre of paganism needed instruction.

The ancient site is to the southeast of the modern town and built on rising plateaus with its acropolis at the top of the mount, the Acrocórinth (Akrocórinthos). What stands of the Greek city today is the great temple of Apóllo, or rather seven of its columns.

The rest is the Roman city with many homey touches along the walkways. But what makes the whole trip here worthwhile is the climb up to Acrocórinth. Here we find the most complete 17th-century Venetian fortresses. And the view from up here is spectacular: to the east, the expanse of the Sarónic Gulf; ahead, near the shore, lies Isthmia where the second most important games of the Hellenic world occurred every other spring. Next in the line of vision from this height lies the old part on the Sarónic side where St Paul had his head shaved; and nearby, the healing springs, called the Baths of Helen.

Nowadays a road runs along the shore which will get you to Epídauros in half the time you need by the inland route. The modern road is well engineered with spectacular views: you travel high up above the sea, looking down at the white-sand beaches; on a clear day you can see the islands of Salamís and Aégina. Looking in the other direction, to the west of the Acrocórinth, the Corinthian Gulf, with the mountains of the Peloponnése, is on your left.

The road along the shore to the west is a modern highway that leads to Pátras the port city. The shore towns along the whole coast to Pátras are very lovely as are the beaches; the landscape is tame and refined with a spattering of soft pine trees, particularly around Kyato and Aigion. It is only with a glance southward that you are brought up against a harsh contrast, the sheer cliffs of the Cyllene mountain range – wild nature close to the tame shore – a motif of the Peloponnésian terrain.

Leaving Córinth: The road south to Árgos is a bad road and treacherous for the newcomer. It crisscrosses several times the same rickety railroad line for no apparent reason.

The Argive valley is most spectacular when approached from the other end, the descent along the coiling road of the Arcádian mountains. In early morning, as you take the last turn for Mount Parthenion, you find yourself before a breathtaking panorama. The salt air from the sea accents the smell of wild flowers that grow on the mountain; the deep shadows of the gorge to your left hang down into darkness; and the peak opposite the gorge is covered in early sun. The descent to the valley takes a short while. When you reach the straight road amid the citrus groves which are in bloom, you will be greeted by the sweet perfumes of lemon and orange blossoms.

There is an amusing tale in Theophrastus about the people of **Tiryns**, a place in mid-valley between Árgos and Naúplia, where Hérakles was born. It seems the people here were incapable of any serious accomplishment because they laughed too much. So they sent an embassy to the oracle at Délphi to find out how they might cure themselves of this weakness. Délphi's answer: they must sacrifice a bull to Poseídon; throw the offering into the sea without laughing once; and the god would cure their affliction. So they prepared for the sacrifice, taking care to keep the children far away, for their laughter could not be easily controlled. After the sacred ceremony, as they were taking the offering to the sea, a little boy who had escaped from the others and followed the procession, asked some ingenuously funny question and brought the entire population to their knees with fits of wild laughter.

Árgos valley: Before you know it, you find yourself in modern **Árgos**. It is a bustling capital, the busy market centre for the entire Argolis province. The people here live well by comparison with the rest of Peloponnése. Their valley produces fruit and olives and their only complaint is they cannot find enough labourers at harvest-time: it isn't rare these days to see German or English students working in these groves. But modern Árgos, apart from its exquisite climate, isn't much fun.

The true elegance of this valley is **The Corinth Canal.**

reserved for **Naúplia (Náfplion)**, perhaps the most classy small city in the whole of Greece. It has a tradition and culture all its own. After the Greek Revolution, between 1829 and 1834, Naúplia served as the first capital of Greece. Some of its neoclassical houses, its carefully planned streets along the sea, and the large official looking buildings date from this period. This small city seems to have retained its dignity: anybody who is anybody in Peloponnése seems to live in Naúplia.

The road to Neméa breaks off from the main pass at Dervenákia. At the southern end of the Neméan fields a decisive battle was fought in the 1820s, cutting off the Ottoman empire armies who came to squelch the revolution of the Moréa. *Moréa* was the alternate name at this time for the Peloponnése; named so, they say, because of the abundance of mulberry trees (*moriés*) in the land. Others suggest that its name came from the fact that its shape resembles the mulberry leaf. Nowadays that name is rarely used. At the great battle the "old man of the *Moréa*," General Kolokotrónis himself, with his fierce revolutionaries, massacred the Pasha's superior armies in what surely was in fact a Herculean feat.

The Neméan games: The Neméan plain beyond this road was the roaming ground of the famous lion that Hérakles defeated. Here, too, is the place where the Neméan games were held, which rivaled those of Isthmia and Olympia. Part of the stadium can still be seen.

The whole of the Argive plain: Naúplia, Tiryns, Mycénae (Mikínes), Neméa and the full distance of the fertile valley, can be seen from the castle on the top of Lárissa hill that rises at the edge of Árgos. The townscape below, undistinguished cement and brick buildings, dissolves into the primary shades of fields and groves in every direction.

On the other side of the gulf lies Naúplia, while a little more than half way there the solitary Cyclopean walls of Tiryns rise up. To your left, and a bit northeast, stand the majestic ruins of

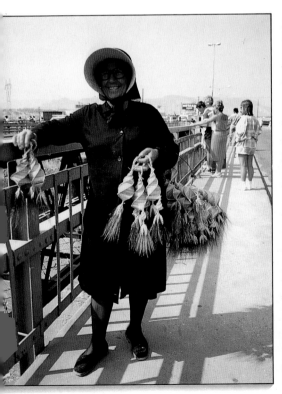

An old lady sells souvenirs to travellers crossing the canal.

Mycénae, and a little further, straight north, beyond Dervenákia pass lies Neméa. To the northwest and behind, you can always see Arcádian Cyllene and Artemision and their snow peaks, even in summer. You can even make out the white-stoned river-bed of Inachos, mostly streamless since ancient times and on a clear day, far down along the cape, a very deep blue sea.

The Tiryns ruins: The ruins of Tiryns, though not a fine spectacle, have their own majesty. The ruins here are older than those at Mycénae, and, as legend would have it, this is where Pérseus came to settle with Andrómeda (though some say he was born here), bringing from Lydia the Cyclops who built the great walls. The blocks of the wall are 100 cubic feet each, making Pausánias marvel: "Why should we bother to visit the pyramids when we have something like them right here?" The tower and the several gates with a triangular gap, suggest a sophisticated knowledge of building long before architecture became a developed art.

Mycénae's buildings and walls are somewhat less impressive than those of Tiryns. The Cyclopean structures do not look as powerful or sturdy, but these are more tragic stones. Here Klytemnéstra received her husband Agamémnon entering the Lion Gate, on his return from Troy. She decked the gate with purple carpets and insisted he step on them along with his slave-paramour Cassándra. Then, when he relaxed in a bath, she hacked him to death with an axe. Agamémnon's is one of the beehive tombs below the citadel. Here, in a shaft tomb, Schliemann excavated the famous golden death-masks and the other exquisite gold ornaments that excite the visitor upon entering the Mycenaéan room of the National Museum at Athens.

Away from Mycénae we pass again through Tiryns and Naúplia to reach the sanctuary of Epídauros to the east. Naúplia is more impressive when compared with Mycénae. Palamídi, its citadel, has 1,000 steps to the top. Legend has it that the city was founded by

Taking provisions to the monastery.

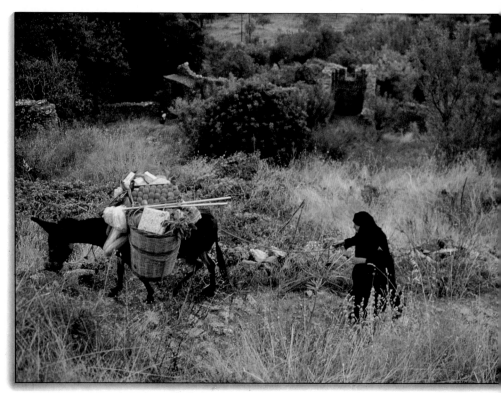

Nauplius' son, Palamidis. On the promontory, there is a fortress which has a varied history. The dungeon was used during the late 1940s civil war as a prison for the whole Peloponnése.

The lower portion was built during the first years of the 18th century by the Venetians. The Senate of St Mark at Venice decided to sacrifice the walls and temples of Aégina, and transferred the stone slabs here to build this fortress. The Greeks won their most decisive battle against the Ottoman armies on this hill in the 1820s. And while Naúplia served as the first capital of a newly independent Greece, in 1829 trouble was not far away. Here, outside the church of St Spyridon, not far from Palamídi, the first president, Capo-dístria, was assassinated. You can still see the bullet that struck a pillar.

Only a short distance from the first step of Palamídi lies the port, and in the centre of it the islet Bourtzí. This islet has a marvellous castle which covers nearly the whole of it. During the 19th century, after the revolution, it was the residence of the executioner. Now it is a pleasant inn and worth a short boat ride.

The theatre at Epídauros: Epídauros lies just beyond the short Arachneon mountain range to the east along the Argolid peninsula. Epídauros comprises three towns: Ligourio, which is about a mile (2 km) from the ancient sanctuary serves to receive the traveller; Old Epídauros, which is the port town as it was of old, and New Epídauros, above on the hillside, hidden behind the bend. Old Epídauros is now a resort town of exceptional charm; you are more likely to see a spattering of yachts coming and going than the arrival of pilgrims to the healing grounds. The beaches to the left of the town are memorable in early summer.

New Epídauros, on the other hand, is virtually a mountain village; and in the old days most of its inhabitants were shepherds. Now they cultivate the small valley below which leads to a tiny gulf. The beach at the end of the fertile grove has grey-black sand and is clean, warm and secluded. Ligourio is an over-

Women wait patiently with their rabbits.

crowded village. Too small to accommodate the hordes who come during the theatre festivals, it has become a place where every home-owner rents rooms in summer. So during the tourist season this village changes character altogether. During normal times the inhabitants cultivate a rich olive grove that extends all the way to the sanctuary.

The sanctuary, less than a mile off the main road, is surrounded by pine trees. The ruins themselves present no special fascination, but the grounds have that sacred aura about them, a kind of mystical quality. This place exudes good health: the air, the trees, the aesthetics of it transmit a healing quality. When you reach the theatre, the crowning glory of Epídauros even to this day, you feel sure this is a place of healing and celebration.

The annual festival, begun in the early 1950s, has hosted some of the great performers of our time, from María Cállas to Katína Paxinoú. In any given summer you can see up to six or more tragedies mostly by the National Theatre of Greece, though in more re-

cent years other groups have been permitted to perform as well. The performances are geared for the tourist, but it wasn't long ago when the shepherds and people from the surrounding villages came here on star-studded nights, and shed a tear or two over the plight of Agamémnon's daughter or Medéa's children. This still happens on dress-rehearsal nights when the local townsfolk are admitted free of charge.

The theatre at Epídauros faces west and is the finest extant example of its kind. Its design and acoustical engineering have never been matched. In our own day, it stands as the sacred monument – a kind of patron saint – of every theatre artist the world over. It is every artist's dream to play at Epídauros. Britain's National Theatre has played at Epídauros, and each year many companies ask to perform here.

The main road before the turn for the sanctuary continues in a southeast direction to end up at Galatas on the cape. The view of the *Lemonodassos* (forest of lemon trees) along the cape with the

Bourtzí, 19th-century island residence of the civic executioner.

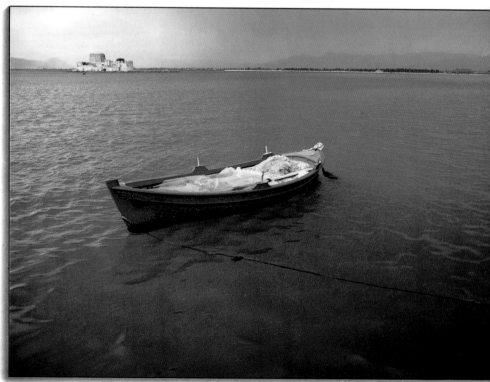

island of Póros in the distance, is an exquisite and refreshing experience. And some of the finest beaches are around Hermióni and Pórto Héli.

Trípolis: Back now to the road towards Arcádia and the central Peloponnése. We climb the face of Parthenion and leave behind the grand view of Argolis, ending up at **Trípolis** (the name denoting the three ancient cities, Tegea, Mantinia and Palladian). **Tegea** was the site of a remarkable temple of Athéna whose pediment Pausánias claimed contained some of the greatest art of his time. Tegea is well-known for its annual fair. Here is the largest animal trading ground in all of Greece. Gypsies come from all over to buy and sell horses, mules and donkeys. **Mantinia** is now simply an elongated valley between two mountain ranges. Its ancient ruins contain a sanctuary. Of the three, **Palladian** is the only one with no ancient history. It was named by a fickle Roman emperor, who stopped there in the Antonine period. Trípolis was the capital of the Moréa for the duration of the Ottoman occupation. It still retains some of its gruff, trading character.

The people of Trípolis are intensely political; you can observe them in the cafés, at the various squares, engaged in heated discussion. Aristotle's "man the political animal" (*zoön politikón*) is everywhere evident. Trípolis is too provincial to attract the traveller. But it has other charms: the best yoghurt anywhere can be found at *Kanatas*, on the side-street behind the Ághios Vassílis Church in the centre of town. The town is sprawling. with the army at one end and the Air Force at the other. It serves as the "big city" of the central Peloponnése, where many young labourers from surrounding villages end up for work. In contrast to the daytime rowdiness of the marketplace, the city's central square has a grace at night, when young couples take their stroll.

All roads that lead away from Trípolis take us into picturesque and important parts of the Peloponnése. Our first direction will be towards the Olym-

hepherd
nd his flock
n the Máni.

pia mountains. A short side-trip northwest of Trípolis warrants attention. Here the traveller encounters a series of upland valleys which are narrowly linked from Tegea and Mantinia to Orchómenos, less than 15 miles (25 km) away. The irrigation of these valleys, lying as they do between mountain ranges, has always been a mystery. Pausánias, in AD 160, speaks of considerable controversy (and strife) when the Mantinians insisted on diverting the water from the Orchómenos valley to irrigate their own crops. By Pausánias' account this water came from subterranean springs, which is borne out by today's scientific accounts as well. It seems the entire Mainalon range converges its subterranean streams in this valley, forming in the winter season a virtual lake, just to the northwest of ancient Orchómenos.

Small villages: The road toward this valley away from Trípolis is an excellent one for travel. The mountain to the left is **Mainalon**. At its highest peak, Ághios Ilías, is a fine ski resort, limited in distances but very charming with a spectacular view of the valleys below. Along the main highway, at the foot of the mountain and just above ancient Orchómenos, is **Levidi**, a village of great beauty. It is built on the hillocks that lead to the lowlands, and provides the centre for the villages which surround the valley. The people of Levidi, which is known for its excellent mountain climate, are the farmers of the Orchómenos valley, where the ancient water controversy has been raging.

This, too, is the birthplace of Aléxandros Papanastasíou, who served as prime minister of the Republic in 1924, after the expulsion of the king. Orchómenos, on top of the hill that rises at mid-valley (and nearer to the Chelmos range on the opposite side), was, like Tegea and Mantinia, an ancient city; it had an acrópolis overlooking the valley as its centre. Three temples: to Apóllo, to Aphrodíte and to Ártemis Mesopolítis, as well as a fairly well-preserved theatre, stood here at one time. A certain loneliness and grace

Naúplia seen from the Palamidi fortress.

characterise this spot nowadays. Its water has not yet been taken away thanks to the clever arguments and civil disobedience of the populace.

Further along on this main highway are two noteworthy places. One is the village of **Vitina** which is a well-known mountain resort, frequented mainly by Athenian Greeks. It has a rather damp climate, since it is surrounded by a pine forest. Summer and winter, this little village is always bustling with visitors. Further on, you will find the spectacular town of **Lagadia**, built along a gorge.

What makes this town remarkable is not only the fact that it hangs on the edge of a mountain, but that it is so sturdy. The houses are built by the stone masons of Lagadia, known throughout the whole of Greece for their skill. They have built most of the fine church walls across the country.

For the remainder of the road to Olympía, the land is tamer. This is the country where the Great Mother, Deméter herself, searched high and low for her daughter Perséphone. She changed herself into a mare, the better to travel through the mountains. At Phigalia, a bit south of here, on Mount Eleos, she was raped by Poseídon who had taken the shape of a stallion for the sacrilege. For a long time after that she hid in a cave on the mountain until Pános, the warm-hearted shepherd boygod, found her and begged her to revive fertility for the earth that had lain fallow in her absence. Nowadays the legend has been expanded to include the Christian mother with a small chapel at Deméter's sanctuary. Still, the old legend persists in local memory.

When the sacred flame burned: The Olympic games were the most renowned of all the festivals in Greece. They took place once every four years, at the time of the full moon in August or September. The sacred flame burned long before the eloquent sanctuaries to Héra and Zeus and the Praxitéles statues were created. These can be seen at Olympía's excellent museum today. All enmity and war ceased during the games. A heavy fine was exacted on whoever disobeyed the Olympic committee. Hard-headed Spárta paid up more than once; so did many other cities. But, for the most part, everyone made a solemn effort to cease all hostilities. So sacred and serious were these games that the Hellenic world starting in 776 BC based its chronology on the four-year Olympiads, measuring its history accordingly.

Today the site is peaceful and green, surrounded by pines, poplars and plane trees and bounded on two sides by the Alphios and Kladeos rivers. All the temples can be traced; so can the stadium and the gymnasium. The best preserved is the temple to Héra, inside whose sanctuary the masterful Hérmes statue (now in the museum) was found.

The great athletes who came here to compete were not the only competitors, and the games were not the only feature. It seems that writers, historians and poets frequented the festivals, coming here to read their work. The historian Heródotus read part of his work at Olympia. And the ever-present poet-for-hire, Pindar himself, read his commissioned Odes.

Pátras city: If you leave the Alphios valley, the road north will bring you to the lush and fertile province of Achaéa and the city of Pátras. If you turn south along the coast, you will enter the province of Messenía and will come to some of the loveliest beaches along the Iónian coast. **Pátras** is Greece's third largest city, after Athens-Piraéus and Thessaloníki. Its patron saint is St Andrew, and many people keep his namesake in the family. Greece's former prime minister, Andréas Papandréou, came from here. Pátras is a sprawling city, both a bustling port and a university town. Being the centre of traffic for the Iónian sea, Pátras is the first place travellers from Italy see. There is also a ferryboat service for the Iónian islands, Zánte, Cephaloniá and Ithaca. Although the various occupations by the Venetians have given the city some finesse, one's first impression is still of an unappealing port city.

Backtracking from the Alphios val-

Climbing among Naúplia's ruins.

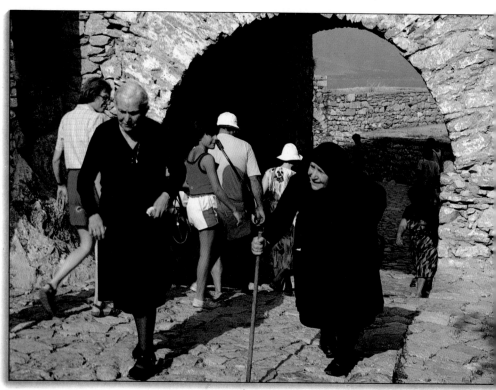

ley, once again through Arcadia, we reach Bassai, where one of the most complete temples to Apóllo (now covered by a protective tent), is located. Next is Megalopolis, and finally down the Aegéan coast of Arcadia through Leonidion to Monemvasia.

The oak trees of Megalopolis look as if they are dying from the pollution of the hydroelectric plant. Megalopolis was always an artificial city. It was built in haste around 300 BC as the new capital. People were brought here from all over central Peloponnése in an ancient experiment in migrant labour and political relations. Today, the electric plant has also drawn workers from other regions. But if the ancient experiment did not work, the modern one is doing no better. Political historians insist, however, that the original experiment was one of the noblest of all in representative democracy, and that had it succeeded, it would have far surpassed the Athenian model.

The shore drive from Astros to Leonidion has a special charm, with a tower-ing mountain range on the right, and brilliant blue sea on the left. After Leonidion, however, the road must veer inland up the mountain, for only eagles can travel near the water as the mountain itself falls suddenly into the sea. The monastery of Elonis perches atop these cliffs. Terracotta red buildings hang from the highest rock. Then, within a short distance past the monastery the world changes again, as we are greeted by soft green almond trees and oaks at the border of Laconía.

Gibraltar of Greece: Monemvasia is the most extraordinary, and perhaps most beautiful place in all of the Peloponnése. Certainly it is the most unique spot in Laconía. It boasts the other history of the Moréa, the Medieval one, and it throws light on all the minor fortresses we have been encountering along the way. Monemvasia is often called the "Gibraltar of Greece." An impregnable fortress, it had the reputation of being self-governed from the 6th century though later it did come under the Byzantine empire. Monemvasia is a

e renowned eatre of idauros.

great rock in the sea, connected to the mainland by a man-made causeway, hence its name *móni embásis* (only one way in). Its fame across western Europe was for the excellent wine that went by the name of Malmsey or Malvoisie, the Western variations of its name. The dark, fruity wine was at first a product of Laconía, but later it came from Crete and other islands. Monemvasia served as the broker and merchant port for its transfer west.

As you walk along the causeway from the mainland town you see nothing ahead of you but a bulky squarish hill of solid stone. The fortress town is well hidden from view. But from inside the gate, though the street is initially dark and narrow, you will suddenly catch sight of the blue Aegéan. On this main street is the home of one of Greece's greatest poets, Yánnis Rítsos. When you reach the small courtyard of *Elkomenos Christos* (Christ in chains), stop and take in the vista. Above you is the old town and further up the great castle. The architecture is of Byzantine

origin, but with the many invasions, the rebuilding and remodelling, it is difficult to date any of the structures.

This strategic place, which commanded the Aegéan from the west, lies on the east side of the Malea promontory and only about 18 miles (30 km) north of its cape. Until 1246 when it fell into the hands of Guillaume de Villehardouin, only the Byzantine eagle flew here. But even under Villehardouin its inhabitants insisted on self-rule and self-taxation with feudal service to the conqueror. After that time it passed again to Constantinople, then later to the Turks, again to the Venetians (and even to the Pope for a brief period), and once more to the Greeks during their War of Independence.

Whether under the Byzantine eagle, the Venetian lion or the Turkish crescent, Monemvasia remained a strangely independent and virtually impregnable community. Its two soft ports far below its retaining wall made it a great trading centre, like a giant battleship setting up business in the middle of the sea.

The last of Spárta's open-air photographe in the museum garden.

Mistrá (Mistrás): While Monemvasia was mainly secular, **Mistrá**, the other great centre of the Byzantine Greeks, was purely a holy place. Only 3 miles (5 km) outside of Spárta toward the sea, it is an imposing promontory, almost like a toy hill in the vicinity of the great Taïgetos range. Mistrá is the most romantic chapter of eastern Christendom, with its churches still standing, many of its icons recovered, and only the perishable frescoes and adornments lost to the conquerors and the centuries.

Among the most notable architectural structures stand the Pantanássa monasteries, Ághios Dimítrios (the Metropolis) Evangelístria and the monastic area of Vrontokion with its cultural centre and the burial place of Byzantine prelates. Aghiï Theodóri, built on this spot in the late 1200s, is one of the last of its kind, with a central octagon as a *thólos*.

Mistrá enjoyed a cultural and intellectual life for much of its existence before 1460, when it went into decline and disuse with the Turkish occupation.

In 1400 Mistrá produced the last of the Greek philosophers, Gemistos Plethon, a Platonist, who lectured extensively on the works of Plato. Some of his students taught subsequently at Oxford. But his views were not in accord with those of the Church, so he was often criticised in Greece.

Spárta (Spárti): **Spárta**, the ancient ruins and the modern town, are best approached from the north, on the Trípolis road. From the top of the pass, flanked as we are by the Parnon range, the view is splendid. Once again the landscape has shifted radically. The Eurotas valley, lush and fertile, extends as far as the eye can see. Alongside the valley, as if leading it by the hand all the way to the sea, Taïgetos rises with such grace that you are only intermittently aware of the optical illusions it is about to play on you. When the light falls at a certain angle the mountain stands right next to you; at other times, crowned by mist, it lurks at a distance.

Spárta's ruins are not well preserved. You can make out a sanctuary and a

ft, steps to e Persian untain in ycenae. ght, prickly ars in the áni.

theatre on the gentle rise, but no acropolis, no grand hillsides with citadels, and no walls to enclose it. The Spartans were warriors of such mettle they needed no walls to hide behind. Besides, the Spartans never put much stock in the aesthetic look of things. These monuments were never spectacular; only functional.

The Spartans embarked on the disastrous Peloponnésian War with some reluctance, goaded by their allies; but once in the war, their nature was not to relent. As late as the 2nd century Pausánias told of how the people of the mountains of the Máni would call themselves Lacedaemónians and look upon themselves as the direct descendants of the ancient Spártans.

In fact, these same Lacedaemónians were still not converted to Christianity as late as the 12th century. They remained self-governed in willful isolation, and no conqueror, friend or foe, would traverse the terrain, fearing the wild Spartans. Their terrible disillusionment and decision to abandon the

social world must have come after the Romans destroyed their city at the end of the Hellenistic era. Neither Augustus later nor the Turks in our own era dared to invade them. They all acknowledged the Máni's independence.

Gythion: Travelling south from Spárta toward Gythion, it's difficult to imagine its dark history. The fertile valley with its olive and citrus trees is peaceful. The road towards Gythion is excellent. We leave Mistrá behind to one side and travel with the mountain always to our right. Along the way signs point to villages deep in the mountains. One such village is **Arna**. This is the place which boasts that all its children make it to the university. This is quite a claim considering how competitive entrance examinations are. The village is the schoolteacher's dream. You can see a certain austerity in the eyes of the children, an intensity and gentleness – boys and girls alike – and your thoughts return to the ancient youth and their austere training for success in the world.

Gythion is a port town, and the as-

In
Monemvasia
a cemetery.

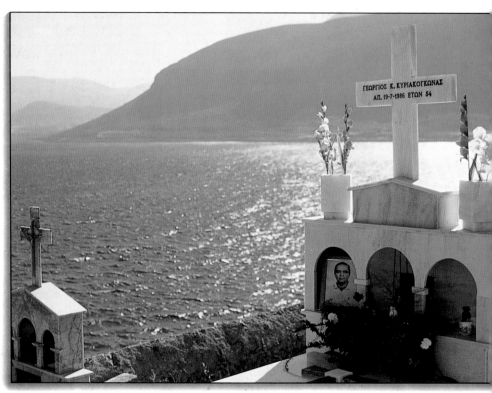

tounding fact about it is that it hasn't undergone what the tourist-minded businessmen call "development." It is still, on any weekday, an unspoilt bazaar. It doesn't put on airs or fancy clothes for the evening promenade, as opulent Spárta does nowadays. The sea, they say makes people different, more refined – it blunts the edges. If that is true, the people of Gythion have much of the sea in them. In ancient times this served as Spárta's port. It was from here that Helen sailed for Troy with Paris. The place where they embarked is marked on the long causeway connecting the islet of Marathonísi with the mainland.

The road that heads for the mountain, towards Cape Matapan (or Cape Tenaron, as it is often called) leads first to Areópolis, across Taïgetos and almost to the other side on the Messenían Gulf. It is best to travel down the cape on the west side and return by climbing the face of the mountain on the east. **Areópolis** is already in the deep Máni, and here you begin to discern a wild nature in the people. Deep isolation, as a way of life, has brought all manner of contradiction to the surface. The church of Areópolis has a telling militant nature. It is the church of the martial saints, *ton Taksiarchon*, and is adorned by primitive reliefs of these warring figures. The war-god Ares would certainly approve of his modern Areópolis.

Here the people of the Máni cultivate olive trees; but the trees are so puny, growing on such tiny patches of red earth, that you wonder how they manage to survive, both the trees and their tenders. The view down the coast is spectacular. After the stalagmite and stalactite Caverns of Diros the road to Cape Matapan becomes more and more forlorn. In the distance you can see the architecturally distinctive cubistic towers breaking the bareness of the landscape (see Vendettas on pages 304–05 of the Cultural ABCs).

The windy vistas and the aura of the sea far below end as we ease down to the fishing village of **Gerolymin**. The few boats of the fishermen lie aslant along the jetty. You can read the surprise in the faces of the villagers whenever they see that anyone has arrived by land.

The remainder of the drive to Matapan is treacherous along unpaved road, but well worth the spectacular view at the cape. You can see the island of Kíthira (Cythera) to your left off the coast of Cape Malea, south of Monemvasia; and you can see, too, Cape Akritas to your right south of Koróni. And here a shiver runs down your spine as you turn your head 180 degrees and take in these three prongs of southern Peloponnése and remember the time-worn stories of the old seawolves who have sailed along these capes. Since ancient times this has been the most dreaded sea for all Greek sailors. Here, at Matapan, the free Lacedaemónians had their headquarters; and, where the temple to Poseídon used to be, the small Church of The Asómaton has taken its place.

From Spárta, embarking on the last leg of the journey, you leave Laconía behind and enter the province of Messenía. The drive is the most spectacular of all, for you scale the highest peak of Taïgetos and begin your descent from the western side high above Kalamáta. Still, one final detail of their "gymnopaideia" should detain you.

The *Keadas*, just before the village of Trypi, is the dark and bottomless pit, marked now by a wire mesh in front of an opening between two rocks, where military-minded Spartans threw their "unformed" children, those unfit for battle. The hole is unmarked; from its depth rises a cold air, a true chill several degrees cooler than the warm atmosphere. The mountain beckons, yet it's hard to get that eerie hole out of your mind.

Messenía province: Leaving Laconía the road travels up the great Lagada gorge over Taïgetos, and already we are in Messenía. The people in this province are famous for always trying to sell you something. They are the butt of many jokes across the Peloponnése. The inn on the descent here is too opulent-looking to belong to any but Messeníans, as are the trinkets that are

sold along the road. These are fine handicrafts and make good mementos of a visit.

Kalamáta down the valley produces olives, the best export olives from all of Greece. You also see the cigarette factory in the distance. It is a city with inexcusable amount of pollution and dull buildings, saved only by a fair stretch along its shoreline and port, which displays some old-fashioned charm: a tumble of docks, jetties and riggings looking in the direction of the sea, the port thumbing its nose at the tawny central plain and sprawling city of Messenía.

In the 1980s Kalamáta suffered a tragic earthquake that showed the sham of its building contractors who profited from not making the buildings earthquake-proof with extensive foundations and steel girders as the law requires. The best way to cope with Kalamáta is to leave it and head directly for the Iónian coast. After a brief detour to the Methóni and Koróni promontories, where splendid Venetian castles will remind you once more of medieval Greece you can head for Pylos the city of old Nestor from Hómer's *Odyssey*.

You should stay at **Pylos** as many days as you can for this is a quiet, restful place by the sea. The fish is inexpensive and plentiful. The walk along the beach, beyond the high school, under the pine trees, comes as a healing and celebratory experience, after one had braved all these many centuries of the Peloponnése. And you can contemplate, if you wish, the terrible battle that took place at the islet across the way, Sphacteria, between the Spartans and the Athenians, described in masterful detail by Thucydides.

You might prefer to contemplate the later battle at Navaríno Bay, the one you're looking at, for in the 1820s the Bay at Sphacteria was called Navaríno. Here, the three fleets, French, Russian, and English decided to help the Greek Revolution by engaging the navy of Ibrahim Pasha, and destroying all his ships. The people of Pylos have erected bronze busts of three admirals in their town square to commemorate the event.

Tradition lives on at Olympía's stadium.

EGEO PELAGOS

KIKLADES

THE CYCLADES

The Cycládes are the quintessential Greek islands. They are what people think of when they think of Greece. Images of white and blue: whitewashed houses and domed churches surrounded in all directions by a shocking blue – the sea, the sky, even most doors and window frames are painted an electric blue.

Mykonos, Santoríni, Folégandros… they are as magical as their names sound. But should you go in search of an unspoiled haven, beware; the Cycládes have been the site of mass tourism of late. It's best to avoid peak summer months, and visit instead in June or September.

The Cycládes islands – 39 in all, 24 inhabited – offer diversity, something for everyone. Mykonos and Santoríni have more "action" than most large cities. In fact, single folk visiting any Cycládic island can expect not to remain single for long; here are better meeting places than any pub or club at home. Greek men look forward to the tourist season for *kamáki*, which translates roughly into "picking up" women. They've got it down to a science, staking out the discos in twos and threes, and using the basic English they know and think women want to hear.

Couples wanting a romantic holiday will find it in the narrow winding lanes of each island's *hóra* (main town), in the turquoise-green sea you dip into to escape the blaze of the Aegéan sun, and at *tavérnés* where dining is alfresco and wine abounds. If money is no object, fine yachts can be chartered for personally designed "island hopping" tours, or villas rented for lengthy and decidedly non-touristy stays.

There is another version of island hopping: Strap on a backpack and use the inexpensive network of Greek ferries to rough it at island camp-grounds. It's a way of travelling much favoured by Europeans and young Americans, though islanders disdain it as it brings them little monetary profit. To their credit, backpackers discovered Greece's lesser-known islands. Greeks themselves followed the backpackers' example and started touring their own islands; Athenian youths can now be seen sleeping bag in hand, wearing jeans and writing postcards from tiny villages they would never have thought to explore 20 years ago.

No matter what mass tourism has done or will do to the Cycládes, they simply must be seen. Visually, they compare with nothing else in this world. Cycládic architecture is so unique and impressive, it has influenced the work of many famous modern architects, including Le Corbusier.

No nymphs: Some say the "Cycládes" are named after nymphs who were transformed into rocks when they refused to offer sacrifices to Poseídon. The truth is, the inner ring of the archipelago forms a circle, or *kyklos*, around the holy island Délos.

The Cycládes were inhabited as early as 6000 BC. The heyday of Cycládic civilization came during the Bronze Age (2800–1100 BC) and paralleled the rise of Cretan and Helládic civilizations. The Cycládes islanders traded with Crete, mainland Greece, Cyprus, even Asia Minor and Africa. They enjoyed a high standard of living, judging from jewellery and household wares found by archaeologists. Toward 2000 BC, Cycládic maritime activity declined because of competition from Crete, and by 1500–1000 BC, the Cycládes fell under the domination of Mycenaéan civilization.

Later, in 487 BC, the islands came under the rule of Athens, but when Athens' power waned, a succession of foreign conquerors ensued: the Romans (second century), the Venetians (13th century), and finally the Turks (16th century). It wasn't until after the Greek War of Independence (1825) that the islands became Greek again.

Geographically, the Cycládes are flung like boulders in the Aegéan Sea, south of the mainland between the Peloponnése and the Dodécanése islands. As you approach they look like huge, sterile rocks, grayish-brown in colour, jutting ungracefully from the sea; their

eceding ges: ykonos.

only inviting quality is a cove here and there, with turquoise water lapping onto a tiny bit of shore. Still, their aridness takes on a charm of its own; then there is the bustling harbour, and all the whitewashed houses you've read about.

When travelling to the Cycládes, the only unpleasant task is deciding which island to stop at. Asking friends or even Greeks won't help much. Each island has a distinct appearance and personality. But chances are you won't want to miss Mykonos and Santoríni, the most trumpeted of all Greek isles.

The tourism trade on **Mykonos** began 30 years ago, unlike other Cycládes islands which only recently have drawn tourists' attention. In the 1950s, Mykonos must have been surreal, otherworldly. Even today, under the trappings of souvenir shops, glitzy watering holes, Mykonos' natural beauty is astounding – and evident at first sight of its semicircular harbour, sugarcube houses, and whitewashed windmills.

Every year from May to October, Mykonos comes alive. Owners of bars,

boutiques and hotels flock back to the island from their winter homes in Athens, Europe or New York to open for "the season." The hordes descend; frenetic holidaying has begun. Though local inhabitants may frown at the intrusiveness of tourism, they prefer the new standard of living to their pre-tourism poverty. Land that was in their families for generations suddenly became an unimagined source of income. Fortunately, through zoning laws which dictate that buildings on Mykonos may be only two storeys high, their island has maintained its human scale.

Mykonos has two scenes: beach and bar. At the beach you take off your clothes; at bars you put them on – your expensive, most fashionable clothes. It's a chic island where people come to see and be seen: Scandinavian models, Austrian doctors, Hollywood actors, Greek shipping types and the international yachting set. You may have heard Mykonos is a gay haven. True, true. Mykonos' first bar, Pierro's, opened in 1955 and is still operating.

208

A typical day on Mykonos goes like this. You wake up late and go out for a large breakfast at around 11 or 12 (not a Greek custom at all but probably imported from America to ease hangovers). You swim and sun-worship at your choice of beach: Paradise, Super Paradise, Eliá (all nude), or Ághios Stéfanos, Platí Ialós, Psaroú and Ornós (at least topless). In the evening, showered and carefully dressed, you stroll down streets lined with designer boutiques and galleries. You can shop or drop into an outdoor café for people-watching, a favourite pastime.

Dinner is late, around 10 or 11 p.m., at the waterfronts of Little Venice or the harbour, where you dine on grilled octopus and crab, fried kalamária, french fries, salad – all washed down with *retsína* or cold frosty beer.

Mykonos has elegant restaurants as well, serving continental cuisine; it's best to take advantage of them here as this type of establishment is a rarity on the islands. At midnight, the nightlife that never stops begins. Take your pick:

Remezzo (celebrity-studded disco), Astra (new wave), the City Bar (with its drag show), Argo (a mix), Kastro (classical), the Mykonos Club (Greek dancing) *et al.*

With all this club-hopping, it's good to know there isn't much of archaeological importance on Mykonos. But nearby **Délos**, an uninhabited isle, should be seen. It's the holy island of the ancients where, as mythology holds, the twin gods Apóllo and Ártemis were born. The entire island is an archaeological site where you see floor mosaics, three marble temples to Apóllo, sites of sacrifices, and the most impressive Street of the Lions – all bathed in a light and mystery that can't have changed much in 5,000 years.

Greece's answer to Lourdes, the island of **Tínos**, is just an hour from Mykonos. Tínos is the site of a spectacular religious pilgrimage every 15 August. Thousands of faithful miracle-seekers flock to Tínos' shrine dedicated to the Virgin Mary, **Panaghía Evangelístria**, and pray to a sacred icon said

Mykonos'
Paradise
Beach.

A HARD NIGHT
ON MYKONOS

"Follow me to Paradise," says the inscription on a van waiting by the waterfront. The bold lettering leads up to the figure of a female Pied Piper, a brown, lithe girl dancing under a huge yellow sun. Below, in small letters: *Paradise Camping, Mykonos.*

Even after discovering this is simply an advertisement, the invitation retains its potency. During these brilliant summer months, the small brown-and-white island seems to reiterate the promise: Follow me to Paradise. And the crowds raptly obey the summons.

The search begins the moment you set foot on the swarming landing stage, where the knapsack tribe with their huge Quasimodo humps mix with returning islanders (the jet-set tribe prefer to fly), gleaming motorbikes collide with primitive wheelbarrows, beach-buggies with heavily laden lorries. First, the search for accommodation. A frantic question rings in the air: "Room? Room?" In August, the cruellest month of tourism, a note of despair creeps in; the question changes to "Roof? Roof?" Even a roof will do (the white, cube-shaped houses all have flat roofs), a verandah, a balcony, anything. If you walk around late at night, you will see them: dark shapes, like Egyptian mummies, lying side by side in some sheltered corner, or on the beach. With the first rays of the sun, stray dogs will nudge them awake, or the steady slap of a fisherman beating an octopus on a nearby rock.

The provident or fortunate ones who have secured a roof over, rather than under their heads, sleep on till mid-morning. Most shops, geared to the needs of the late sleepers, don't open before 10.30. Serving breakfast is a thriving business; some places are famous for their gargantuan breakfasts, which are really brunches. Then there is the exodus to the beaches. Public transport is surprisingly good. Some people prefer to walk: brown leathery health-fiends in sensible shoes and straw hats. At Pláti Ialós the man who runs the boat-shuttle lures undecided bathers with the familiar summons: "Paradise!" he shouts. "This way to Paradise!" And if you think Paradise isn't good enough, there's Super-Paradise (Super for short) farther along the coast.

The choice of a beach requires subtle consideration. I've heard it said that there are 200 beaches on Mykonos. Let us play safe and say there are at least a dozen easily accessible ones, with fine yellow sand, blue-green waters like great sea-chambers of flawless glass, tawny rocks all around, as smooth as giant pebbles. Nudism varies; choice ranges from fully-clothed "family-beaches" (rare) to those exhibiting pure, Edenic nakedness. But the nuances are finer than that. Innumerable small cliques subsist on mysterious distinctions: There are those who only bathe at Super and those who will consider no other beach than Eliá; both look down on those who go to Rolex Beach, so designated by the initiates to indicate it is frequented by the nouveaux riches. The same goes for bars and discos at night: On Mykonos you *are* where you *go*.

In the late afternoon, after the return of the bathers, Mykonos hoists its pennants, flies the banners of summer: huge mauve beach towels; flimsy, elementary swimsuits; *pareos, sarongs, loongies*; are hung up to dry in the wind, while their owners sink into a late, late siesta.

Around 11 p.m., the pleasure-seekers emerge, spangled, draped, tasselled, painted, scented, ready for the festivities of the night. They squeeze through the narrow, meandering streets – conflicting currents, this way, that way – wherever the call of pleasure sounds stronger. Here and there small knots of people form, instantly attracting more people; the knot becomes a group, a crowd, what's going on, who is it, what are they doing, let us in.

Sometimes there is a real centre of attraction: a film star; a man impersonating a robot; a drag queen; a woman sporting a live snake like a long, undulating scarf. Actors and spectators, insiders and outsiders. Some people look exhilarated, almost surprised at themselves, at the ease with which they have slipped out of their city-bodies. Others are simply drunk, comfortably or miserably so. There are the over-eager, or the timid and the lonely, and those who look sullen, restless, having searched but not found. Pleasure is a hard and capricious taskmaster, and is it not a commonplace that the only paradise is paradise lost?

Here is a large blonde woman with burnt thighs tapering into extremely tight white cowboy-boots blowing thoughtfully into a pink balloon. Here is a hybrid figure in striped bermudas, top-hat, high-heeled lamé sandals, stranded with a loadful of wasted efforts, allurements unused and useless. And all through the night, you hear the steady beat of music, picked in relays by one disco after another.

The old lovers of Mykonos, who "discovered" it in the 1950s, keep lamenting the desecration. The place has become another St Tropez, they sneer – or worse, Capri, or worse still, Blackpool; yet they still come back every summer, carrying

middle of summer is often defaced by advertisements and graffiti, stained with the brown blood of melted chocolate ice-cream.

There are still donkeys carrying large baskets of melons, figs, tomatoes, bunches of flowers interspersed with fresh basil and verbena; but you suspect it's a deliberate touch of *couleur locale*; most other peddlers switched to three-wheelers long ago. You are never sure what is genuine and what is there for show. A local boy rides bareback on a white horse along the beach, a romantic image if ever there was one. He gets off the horse, picks two white sea-lilies in the sand, sticks them behind the horse's ears. Two ladies in flowing djellabahs come up and talk to him; he offers them the lilies. Was it all stage-managed?

No matter how crowded, there is a peculiar

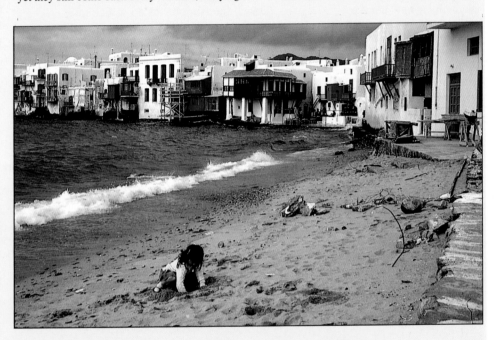

around their bile and their scorn, putting on proprietary airs, betrayed but persistent lovers. Perhaps it is the invincible beauty of the place, the purity of the light, the linear perfection. Perhaps they are dimly aware that this island can never be totally "spoilt."

Long before the "beautiful" people wake up, the Mykoniots go about their business as if the invasion hadn't taken place. They gossip, discuss the coming municipal elections, cluster round the fishing-boats that have just come in with the night-catch. The sleepy idyllic island of the 1950s? Not quite. Many of the boats' names have changed: fewer *Aghíes Marínes* and *Thomadákia*; more fancy names like *Troubadour*, *Romantica*, *Super*. The ubiquitous whitewash that makes Mykonos look like a snow-city in the

sense of *lebensraum* on Mykonos – dare one call it a capacity for freedom? It is a quality that can easily topple into destructive excess at one end, indifference at the other; yet somehow, most of the time, a delicate balance is maintained.

Consider this scene. A little, withered old woman, bundled in black clothes from top to toe, trudges every morning along one of the more dedicated nudist beaches selling fresh figs. She picks her way carefully through the tangle of naked bodies; looking neither right nor left, she hands out figs, pockets money. When she reaches the far end of the beach, she sits down on a rock and puts away her basket. Very cautiously, she lifts the hem of her black skirt and dips one foot, then the other, in the shallow waters – untouched, in her small pool of privacy.

to have healing powers. Tínos is more than this famous church; notable are its pretty interior villages and over 1,000 whitewashed dovecots – masterpieces of folk architecture.

If Mykonos is cozy and like a storybook town, **Santoríni** is shocking, its topography an impossible triumph of nature and man. The island, also known as Thíra, has the misfortune of being located where two of the earth's plates meet. Brutal volcanic activity has destroyed the island again and again, yet people continue to live on the precipice, cultivating whatever is left of the land and building new homes.

It is eerie, chilling, exhilarating, to look from your white terrace at a volcano's crater floating in the sea. This dark, amoeba-like mass of land is surrounded by an ominous haze; though dormant, the volcano emits gas and steam at 80° C even today. Again from the terrace you look down at the sheer drop of cliffs, actually walls of the caldera. Chunks of land have been blown away, exposing coloured layers of pumice and lavas – grey, brick, black, each stripe the trace of a different volcanic eruption. Once more from your terrace, you look right and left at the band of white cylindrical cottages surrounding yours, carved into the cliffside and fitting together like a jigsaw puzzle: your terrace is someone else's roof.

This land is a ghost of what it once was, a crescent remnant of what used to be a perfectly round island, "Strongyle." The volcanic eruption *circa* 1500 BC which shattered Strongyle is said to have taken Crete's Minoan civilization with it. Santoríni's geological history is much too complex to do justice to it. Suffice it to say that what you see and learn supports the most spine-chilling theories: could Santoríni be Pláto's lost Atlantis?

Today, approaching the island by boat, you see what seems to be a snow-capped mountain. Sailing closer, you realise the snow is actually white-washed houses perched atop cliffs. Six hundred spiral stairs lead up from the harbour to **Firá**, the island capital, but **"Plug-in" Christianity.**

212

you can hire a mule for what proves to be a rollicking adventure, or ride the modern funicular donated by one of Greece's shipping families. Firá is a disappointment though, drowned in a commercialism of "B" class *tavérnés* and pushy jewellery store salesmen who live for American cruise passengers, the proverbial "big spenders." Santoríni's population swells from 9,000 to 70,000 in summer, and most of its visitors congregate in the capital. You should stop in at **Franco's Bar** or the **Kira Fira Jazz Bar** one night, a landmark on the island, and eat seafood at **Zorba's**, but it's best to stay elsewhere on the island.

From Firá, a 10-minute walk along the cliff path brings you to **Firostefáni**, the ideal spot to unpack your bags. Firostefáni offers the best view of the volcano on the island, and the most dramatic streaks of red and violet during sunset. It's almost exclusively residential, with fabulous villas tucked inconspicuously away, plus it affords easy access to the hub of Firá.

Oía, the village on Santoríni's northern tip, is billed as the most picturesque on the island. It is the old commercial centre where elegant mansions (damaged by a serious earthquake) testify to the wealth of the seafolk who lived here. Life is marginally quieter here than in Firá, with fewer bars and *tavérnés* ,and earlier closing hours.

Renting a jeep is a good way to see the island. In the morning, set out for Akrotíri, one of the greatest archaeological finds in recent decades. Here, under a roof built to protect the excavation, is the 3,500-year-old city found buried under pumice and volcanic ash from the explosion which destroyed it around 1500 BC. A civilization of great wealth thrived here, as revealed by paved streets (which you actually walk on), two-and three-storey homes complete with toilets, wood furniture, elaborate pottery and wall paintings. No bones were found, which means the inhabitants knew of the coming eruption.

The wall frescoes, similar to those of Minóan Crete, were found in surprisingly good condition and are on display in Athens' National Archaeological Museum. They depict monkeys, antelopes, and papyrus that never lived or grew on Santoríni, thus suggesting commercial ties with Egypt and Africa. Today, the dig is carried on by Athens University students during the summer, under the direction of Professor Christos Doumas; it may take 100 years to complete the Akrotíri excavation.

By midday on Santoríni, it's always time to swim. **Períssa Beach** is a favourite; lamentably, also with package tourists. The bay is packed with travellers who've arrived by bus from Firá, the stretch of black sand is 5 miles (8 km) long and there are plenty of isolated spots. **Kamári Beach** is also popular if crowded; often you won't find a place to lay your towel. It is separated from Períssa by a mountain which houses the site of ancient Thíra, a steep climb but well worth the hike. **Monólithos Beach** is far from the madding crowd and features three of the island's best *tavérnés*.

To be perfectly fair, tourism has had positive side-effects. Previously, the whitewashed cylindrical houses so characteristic of the island were deserted, crumbled caves. When the island was "discovered," natives moved back and rebuilt Santoríni. The architects who came were committed to maintaining the traditional style in restorations and new constructions and they succeeded.

Today, Greeks and even foreigners will pay 2 to 7 million drachmas (US$13,000 to $46,000) for a cottage, and almost twice the buying price for restoration. It's hard to imagine paying hard-earned cash for so primitive and dilapidated a dwelling, but easier to fathom once you step into a would-be bedroom and witness the view.

If you can't find accommodations on Mykonos, **Páros** is a good second choice; it has begun of late to rival Mykonos in its vibrant nightlife and cosmopolitan atmosphere although underneath, Páros is an uncomplicated, not especially distinctive fisherman's island with excellent beaches and **Santoríni.**

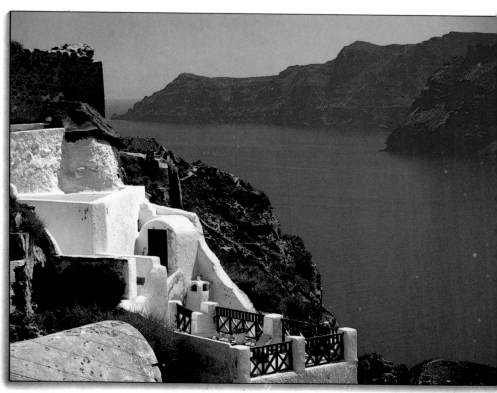

whitewashed villages.

Parikiá, the harbour town, and tiny **Antíparos**, a nearby island known for its stalactite caves, are backpackers' meccas. For more "class" and fewer crowds, a Greek magazine recommends **Naoússa**, the snow-white fishing village on the northern coast. The truth is, it's too late: Naoússa is overrun by "Rooms for Rent" signs and droves of trendy youths dressed up for drinks at **Labyrinth Bar** on the waterfront.

Forty years ago, the Greek poet George Seféris called Páros the loveliest of all the Cycládes. From Naoússa, rent a jeep and head west to **Kolibithres**, a swimming beach with giant rock formations reminiscent of Greece's Metéora.

A five-minute drive east from Naoússa, in the direction of Santa María reveals splendid beaches which – for unknown reasons – are empty. The water is shallow here and deliciously transparent. But the best beach on Páros is on the east coast just past Molos where a small hand-written sign indicates "Kalogiros." This small bay is framed by cliffs that jut in and out, creating semi-private spaces for nude bathers. A swim here affords a fine view of Náxos. Continuing south, you arrive at the coastal towns of Pisso Livadi, Logaras and Drios, all commercial but with pleasant, sandy beaches.

Lefkes, an inland mountain village and the old capital of Páros, is off the beaten track and too often missed by travellers. If there is time, visit **Marpissa village** and the ancient quarry at **Marathi**, where the coveted Parian marble was mined.

Páros' central location in the Cycládes makes it a hub for boat connections to almost any place in the Aegéan. The standard sea route brings you to **Náxos** next, the Cycládes' largest and most fertile isle, where in mythology Théseus abandoned Ariádne after she'd helped him kill the Minotaur. Náxos is still a fairly well-kept secret and offers a fine complement to Páros with its orchards and vineyards, medieval fortresses, and giant archaic stone *kouroi*.

Shopping trip in Náxos.

From Náxos, boats leave two or three times weekly for Koufoníssia, a group of microscopic Robinson Crusoe islands (only six of 23 are inhabited) with names like Donoussa and Skinoussa, virgin beaches, and only a few rooms to let. Íos, next on the ferry route from Náxos, has an idyllic Cycládic harbour and spotless white town. But Íos – allegedly where Hómer died has been claimed by "party-ers" and counter-culture types, as you can see by the nudists sunning on cliffs as your ferry passes by.

Folégandros, the next stop, is worth getting excited about. Don't be fooled by what could be the blandest harbour in the Cycládes, save for neighbouring Síkinos'. Folégandros gives you a sense that you are unearthing it; you are partaking in island life rarely glimpsed by tourists.

Visually, it's astonishing: rough, mean terrain, arrogant and forgotten. Its bald gray hills look like lunar landscape, while here and there efforts by the inhabitants to build terraces have succeeded, giving rise to olives and vineyards, though preciously few.

Folégandros, named for a son of King Mínos, has a population of 800. Since there is only one road and very few cars the islanders get around on foot and donkey. Public transportation consists of two minibuses, one running from Karavoslasi harbour up the steep mountain to **Hóra**, and one from Hóra to Folégandros' only other village, tiny **Ano Meria**.

There are inexpensive rooms to let and at least one second-class hotel in Hóra, a whitewashed village typical of the Cycládes but perhaps less self-consciously so. **Kástro**, the old quarter, is built on a huge cliff and has an entrance and exit which used to be sealed off each evening to give protection against pirate invasions.

You wake up early on Folégandros to a breathtaking view of whitewashed **Panaghía Church** towering over Hóra on a hillside. As you go in search of morning coffee, you soon discover island life revolves around three squares, **Folégandros.**

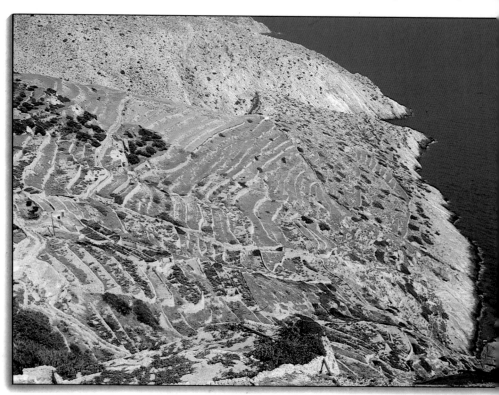

216

situated back-to-back and framed by white churches. Breakfast, lunch and dinner are served here, and tourists can be seen at all hours of the day reading and underscoring book passages, writing postcards, holding hands, staring into space. You easily adapt to the lazy island pace, and as you walk through Hóra to get ready for the beach, you take in the smells of onions and olive oil cooking. Villagers still stare curiously when they see *xénoi* (foreigners), and watch as they collect a day's water supply from the fountain.

Folégandros' **Angali Beach** is also memorable. Yes, for its crystal-clear bay, two good *tavérnés*, and a funny sign saying "Please, no nude bathing here, you have Firá and St Nicholas Beaches for that." But mostly for how one gets to and from Angali. The minibus lets you off on the paved road, high above sea level, and you climb down a steep mountain path for some 20 minutes, using whatever leg muscles you own for brakes. The return? Either you are wise enough to take the six o'clock *caïque* to Karavostasi, or you hike back up the mountain. There are donkeys to aid your trip, but there's something to be said for beating this forbidding terrain.

A Folégandros evening begins with coffee and the sunset, both readily available at the **Rainbow Pizzeria**, where you are served on a terrace overhanging the cliffs. Next, you'll want to compare dinner menus at **Kritikos'** and **Niko's**, Hóra's two main *tavérnés*. Don't expect to eat fresh fish on the island; your choice usually includes Greek salad with *souroto* cheese instead of féta, stuffed tomatoes, meatballs, *souvláki*, *tzatzíki*, french fries, and delicious local bread. After a leisurely dinner, it's time to move on to one or another square for coffee, or better yet to Hóra's only pub, **Laoumi**. Finally, just before bed, stop back into Rainbow Pizzeria for homemade *baklavá* that is out of this world.

You may get stuck on Folégandros, not wanting to leave. It's a harmonious existence where tourism for once hasn't upset the traditional balance (save for a

igs drying in he sun.

few large hotel constructions now underway). A waiter says visitor traffic has been on the rise since 1980. When asked the secret of keeping tourism controlled, he tells how the islanders chased out 50 undesirables, literally ran them off Folégandros.

Another island which maintains its natural flavour is **Syros (Síros)**, capital of the Cycládes. This is a thriving metropolis, not a fisherman's town, with an economy based on Greece's first boat yards and textile factories, not summer tourism. Don't misunderstand; Syros is pleasant for vacationing. Actress Catherine Deneuve spent her first-ever trip to Greece here in 1986. But Syros has an opulent, independent past and is proud to live in it. The island capital, **Ermoúpolis**, was Greece's greatest trading centre, its most important port until the rise of Piraéus at the turn of the century.

Ermoúpolis (named for Hérmes, god of trade and commerce) is built on two "peaks," one crowned with a Catholic church and the other by an Orthodox. It is full of Italian-designed neoclassical mansions, many open to the public today. Skylights, sweeping spiral staircases, painted ceilings and chandeliers are testimony to the fortunes made here, many in black market racketeering.

Ta Vapória (The Ships) is the city's most aristocratic corner, a line of neoclassical homes along a cliff over the sea, where waves crack against rocks in the style of Gothic thrillers. One of these mansions has been luxuriously transformed into the **Hotel Vourlis**, which in 1985 won an award as one of the seven best renovated buildings in Europe.

High above Ermoúpolis, on the Catholic peak, you can walk through 13th-century **Áno Syros**, the typical Cycládic old town built up high for protection against pirates. **Lili's Tavérna** offers a terrace view of the city and harbour below; on a clear night, you can even make out the lights of Mykonos.

Syros has lovely seaside towns, including Vari, Achladi, Megas Ialos and Galyssas, the latter featuring a popular campground. But the most impressive resorts are Delagrazia (or Posidonia), with its enormous Italian villas and castles, Agathopes and Finikiá. All are within a five-minute drive of each other and offer a good alternative to staying in Ermoúpolis.

While most Cycládic islands can be reached by ferry from Piraéus, there are several which require leaving from Rafína and Lavrion – Ándros and Kea, for example. Being slightly out of the way has kept their beauties unsung, to the point of being omitted from guidebooks on the area, though certainly not for long.

Ándros, the northernmost of the Cycládes and home of many Greek shipowners, has two ports, **Gávrion** and **Batsí**, plus all-white villages with red-tile roofs. The island has much green, good beaches, and a noteworthy museum of modern art which opened in 1986. South of the Paleópoli-Andros road is the most spectacular of the island's 13 monasteries, **Panahrandou**, which is more than 1,000 years old.

Kea, also known as Tziá, heads the westernmost chain of Cycládes. It's just south of the mainland and has been popular for years with weekending Athenians who have summer homes there. What the island lacks in sandy beaches it more than makes up for in rocky coves and red-tile roof homes like Ándros'. Neighbouring **Sérifos** and **Sífnos** are particularly attractive islands and often pictured on Greek postcards. Today there are no traces of the gold mines for which Sífnos was celebrated in antiquity, but over the past few years it has become a favourite with tourists seeking the "out of the way." There are ferry connections direct from Páros and other well-known islands.

Also part of this westernmost chain, **Kinolos'** chalk-white cliffs add to the already dazzling brilliance of its towns. Finally, you arrive at **Mílos**, where the famous *Venus de Milo*, now in the Louvre, was found. The island's 5,000-year-old civilization was on a par with Crete's; thus there are plenty of cultural attractions to enjoy in addition to good swimming and eating.

Amorgós' celebrated Kozoviótissa, the convent o the Presentation of the Virgin founded by Aléxis Comnénus.

SAMOS

N.Karlovassi
Potamio
Drakei
Marathokambos
Kalithea
Ag.Kiriaki
Paleohori
Ormos
Kambos
Pagondas
Limnonaki
Idroussa
Platanos
Pirgos
Koumeika
Potokaki
Ireo
Vourliotes
Mitilinii
Hora
Psili A
Ag.Konstandinos
Ampelos
Kambos
Kokari
Kalami
Vathi
Paleo
Po
Pithagorio
Ag.Dimitrios
Ag.Ilias
Avlakia

Samos
Kama

Hrissomilia
Fourni
FOURNI

AGIOS MINAS
SAMIOPOULA

MAKRONISSI

STRONG

AGATHONISSI   Megalo

LESVOS

Mithimna (Molivos)
Petra
Skoutaros
Gavathaso
Sigri
Eressos
Skala Eressou
Andissa
Hidira
Messotopos
Apothikes
Skalohori
Filia
Vatoussa
Parakila
Agra
Lisvori
Skala
Kalonis
Vassiliki
Ipio
Pelopi
Stipsi
Napi
Ag.Paraskevi
Keramoti
Aris
Anemotia Kaloni
Skala
Agiassos
Paleokipos
Papados
Megalohori
Plagia
Plomari
Ag.Issidoros
Vrissa
Vatera
Paleohori
Akrassio
Sikaminia
Klio
Kapi Mandamados
Mistegna
Komi
Keramia
Moria
Pigi
Pamfila
Panagiouda
Loutra
Neapoli
Varia
Perama
Skopelos
Skala
Kratig
Enalou
Argenos
Lepetimnos
Skala Sikaminias
Agios Stefanos
Aspropotamos
Nees Kidonies
Skala Mistegnon
Koutropoli Thermis
Paralia Thermis
MITILINI
Politnitos

HIOS

PSARA
M.Kimissis Theotokou
Psara
ANDIPSARA

Agiasmata
Nenitouria
Agio Gala
Melanios
Keramos
Parparia
Agia Markela
Limia
Volissos
Sidirounda
Anavatos
Elinda
Nea Moni
Lithio
Ag.Georgios Sikoussis
Agia Irini
Passa Limani
Mesta
Olimpi
Pirgi
Ag.Georgios
Emborios
Komi
Kalamoti
Neinita
Armolia
Elata
Kalimassia
Ag.Minas
Thimiana
Kardamila
Kartas
M.Frangovouniou
HIOS
Halkio
Karies
Vrondados
M.Mersinidiou
Langada
Sikiada
Pitious
Fita
Potamia
Kambia
Amades
Vikio
Marmaro
Kastro
Inousses
INOUSSES
Vessa
FANA

ANDROS
Ag.Nikolaos
Stenies
Andros
Sineti
M. Panahrandou
Ormos
Korthi
P.Meria

TINOS
Ormos Panormou
Panormos
Isternia
os Isternion
Kardiani
Kionia
Tinos
Agapi
Kaloni
Komi
Falatados
Steni
M.Kehrovouniou
Ag.Ioanis

IKARIA
Armenistis
Ag.Dimitrios
Hristos
Vrakades
Langada
Manganitis
Gialiskari
Avlaki
Kambos
Evdilos
Keramo
Karavostamo
Frandato
Kossikia
Plagia
Hrissostomos
Kioni
Perdiki
Mavrikato
Therma
Agios Kirikos
Therma Lefkadas
THIMENA
Fanari

220

NORTHEASTERN AEGEAN ISLANDS

Lésvos (Mytilíni), Chíos (Híos) and Sámos form an extraordinary, if slightly arbitrary, trio. They are grand by Aegean standards and, marking the extreme eastern edge of Greek territory, are far from mainland Greece. They lie, moreover, at considerable distances from each other; geographically they are not a chain of islands but extensions of the Asia Minor mainland, to which they have been bound for millennia. Clearly they have distinct personalities, proud and resistant to being grouped together. They do, however, share a common East Aegéan history, which merits a moment's reflection.

On Lésvos, Chíos and Sámos, Turkey is a constant presence. It manifests itself in everyday life in many ways: as a threat to the Greek soldier who mans the pillboxes and camps that spot the coasts and hills, and who peers out across those narrowest straits that separate him from the Turk; as the lure of another world, "Asia," for the tourist who wants to venture beyond; as a lost homeland to the elderly Greek refugee who, seeing it from her window, remembers what she left some 70 years before. For it was here, along this coast around Smyrna that the Greeks were driven into the sea in 1922 by Mustafa Kemal's troops. With this the dream of taking back their city, the "Megáli Idéa," vanished in flames and smoke and a millennial cohabitation was cut in two.

In the formidable depths of these islands' histories an interplay of shared and divergent fates can be traced. The early (3rd and 4th millennium BC) inhabitants of these islands appear to have been closely linked to the East – both "Chíos" and "Sámos" are said to derive from Phoenician words. But it is in the west, in the dusk of the Bronze Age, that these islands' early destiny was forged. Around 1100 BC, shock waves of the Dórian invasion of the Greek mainland rippled across the Aegéan to the coast of Asia Minor – whole peoples, Iónians mostly, transferring their homes to safer shores. Here too the first seed of difference between the three islands was sown – Iónian Greeks, apparently from Attica, settled on Chíos and Sámos; on Lésvos it was the Aetolians from Théssaly who differed in culture, language and customs from the Iónians.

Separate ways: These differences soon became clear in the civilizations that evolved on these islands between 900 and 500 BC – Lésvos developed as an independent island-state, achieving great economic and cultural prosperity in the 6th century under Pittacus, one of the Seven Sages. This was an era of innovation in music and poetry, the age of Alcaeus and Sapphó. Meanwhile Chíos and Sámos were prospering as well, but as a part of a great economic and cultural network – the Ionian Confederacy, a league of 12 Iónian cities. Out of this matrix came Pythagoras of Sámos, Thales of Miletus and, it is said, Hómer of Chíos.

This efflorescent moment in the East Aegéan was soon shaken, however, by the new political force in the east Aegéan – the Persians. Just as the islands' history had been shaped by the shock waves of the Dórian Invasian moving east, they were the first to be hit by westward moving Persian tsunami which shortly struck, and, in so doing, galvanised the mainland Greek world. From around 550 to 480 BC, the three islands were overrun by the Persians. Their loyalties were somewhat divided in the Greco-Persian conflict – Sámos, for example, fought *against* the Greeks at Salamis, with the Greeks at Mycale, only to revolt against and be crushed by Péricles' forces decades later.

The middle of the 5th century belonged, of course, to Athens and consequently during this time the three islands "belonged" to the Athenian sphere of power. But by the turn of the century they began to sway this way and that with the arrival and departure of Spartans, Macedónians and Ptolemies, finally finding some stability and favour under the Romans.

Little is known about life on the islands in the centuries following Roman decline. With the growing force of

Christianity the Byzantines gained control of them, though not without devastating set-backs at the hands of Saracen pirates in the 8th and 9th centuries. The year 1204 roughly marks the rise of Latin power – first the Venetians and then for two centuries the Genoese (1350–1550) who established important centres of trade and commerce on Lésvos and Chíos. The Turks then arrived to rule for three and a half centuries; Greek independence was declared in 1821, and the Turks were defeated at Sámos, yet the islands did not join the Greek state until 1913.

In the Middle Ages and the Modern Period it is the differences as much as the similarities which strike us. Sámos, for example, was nearly deserted for much of this time, while Lésvos and Chíos were dynamos of the Genoan trade machine. Their participation in the Greek Independence struggle varied too. Chíos was the favoured island of the Sultan and its wealthy traders, shippers and landowners enjoyed semi-independence. They were not eager to rock the boat that kept them afloat. The Samians, with less to lose, were fiercely opposed to the Sultan and dealt him many defeats; "to go to Sámos" was a Turkish periphrasis for certain death.

Today, too, the islands are an admixture of the common and unique. Since independence Lésvos has been a somewhat "cosmopolitan" island with developed olive and spirit industries and a tradition of artists and poets. Its tourism is varied from lesbians to meditators to beachcombers. Chíos, on the other hand was drastically depopulated in the 19th century by its two catastrophes, only to become the home of Greece's wealthiest shipowners. It is a rich island and does relatively little to solicit tourists who, at least until recently, have not visited there in great numbers. Tourism has probably changed Sámos the most. It has given a great boost to the formerly exiguous economy of wine producing, olive growing and lumbering.

Sámos: This island of dense forests and vineyard-clad hills, wild mountains and Byron-praised wines can, in its rich

A beach near Kokári, Sámos.

222

diversity, accommodate nearly every type of traveller. The island tour proceeds in a circle around the island beginning from Pythagóreio (though you may arrive at Sámos Town or even Karlovassi). One word of caution though: Pythagóreio is just the beginning and is the noisiest part of the island.

Pythagóreio is on the site of the ancient city of Sámos whose three surviving monuments are the town's main attractions – the Temple of Héra, the Tunnel of Euplinius and the harbour mole. They are all worth a visit, but perhaps the last of the trio is the most pleasant. Strolling down that immense arm originally constructed by Lesvian slaves you can watch the majesty of Cape Mykale, Turkey, fading into the golden evening.

By day Pythagóreia's neighbourhoods are alive with children playing hopscotch, vegetable vendors selling their wares from their pick-up trucks and an occasional baby gurgling under the shade of a cypress tree. These are the endlessly repeated rituals that go on just

a block in from the loud clamour of the waterfront. This is the "frying-pan" (*Tigáni*) as the town used to be called for the harbour's shape, a name in keeping with the sound of motorcycles, the smell of suntan-lotion and the sizzling disco-beat that prevails here. Disco-cocktail bars lit with candles rim the frying-pan, booming out an aural smorgasbord.

A change of names: The name "frying-pan" was perhaps too prophetic of what the town actually turned into. And so in 1955 the town fathers changed it to Pythagóreio, harking back to its most famous "son", Pythagoras. This breeds a second irony for it seems that Pythagoras exiled himself from Sámos (for southern Italy) in disgust over King Polycrates' policies. But, under Polycrates, Sámos achieved its moment of glory between 550 and 500 BC, earning Heródotus' highest praise: "I have spoken at greater length of the Samians because of all the Greeks they have achieved the three greatest projects."

The ruins of the **Temple of Héra** lie

outside of town past the airport. One unusual column and the temple foundations are all that remain to suggest the immensity of what was once one of the largest Greek temples ever built. The **Tunnel of Euplinius** is perhaps even more notable (certainly better preserved) as it presents an under-emphasised aspect of the Greek civilization – their technological expertise. The tunnel was built as an aqueduct to carry water through the mountain to the city and in later Byzantine times served as a refuge from pirate raids. Today you can walk through a good part of it.

The minute **Archaeological Museum** has a number of beautiful *anthemia* (flower tops) from grave steles and some fine Roman busts. On the other side of town the **Logothétis Castle** and the **Church of the Transfiguration** with its graveyard is an interesting complex of buildings strewn with architectural fragments. On this site overlooking the sea the Samians, commanded by General Logothétis, defeated the Persians in 1824.

Vathí, the capital: Sámos Town or Vathí lies facing a large bay on the north coast. It is the island's capital and, in contrast to Pythagóreio, its civic life is not dominated by tourism. In both size and population (8,000) it is a large town and has a bustling social and economic activity of its own. Its most striking area is **Ano Vathy**, the "old city" a few miles up the hill from the town centre, the red-tile roofs of its old Turkish houses visible from afar. An hour's walk will take you through the winding streets (built for donkey and cart, but now used by cars), of a traditional Greek community which carries on a rather separate life from the rest of Sámos Town. The style of these wooden houses with the overhanging second floor is architecturally linked with that of the Turkish houses of Macedónia but worlds apart from the whitewashed stone Cycládic houses.

In the town centre there are some fine shop-lined streets, and a colourful garden across from the post office and Archaeological Museum. The road to the western part of the island takes you

Painting boats in Pythagóreio harbour.

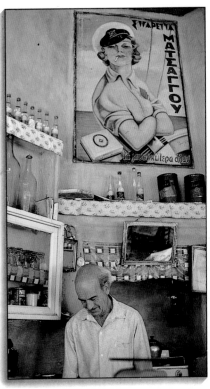

along the harbour, winding through lush stands of pines and along the north coast to **Kokkari**. With its long, pebbly beach it is one of the island's favourite resort spots. A small fishing village built on a spit of land forms the original centre of this town which now sprawls down the entire beach, and there at the edge of all the bars and *tavérnes*, the bare-chested fishermen string out their nets for mending. Kokkari lies in the craggy shadow of Mount Karvoúnis.

The road continues west from Kokkari and traverses the mountain's vineyard-clad foothills. **Tsamadou** and **Avlakia** beaches come at intervals. Just after Avlakia a road on the left leads towards **Moní Vrondiani** founded in 1566, the oldest on the island. It is a pleasant 2-mile (3-km) walk from Vourliotes to get there. The road continues to Karlovassi and for one fine stretch passes right along the sea's edge.

Karlovassi is a strange town. It may fascinate you, or disenchant you – but it probably won't bore you. First of all it is difficult to get your bearings here, for it is divided into at least four parts – **Old Karlovassi** at the far western edge perched on the mountain next to the Aghía Triátha church; the **waterfront**, a kind of no man's land; **Middle Karlovassi**, full of old mansions from the turn of the century when the town was set up as a tanning centre (which collapsed after the war when that industry was centralised in Athens); and, perhaps the most interesting, **New Karlovassi**, which, like most towns in Greece prefaced with "neo," was settled in 1922 as a community for refugees from Asia Minor.

Like the old city of Sámos, it is filled with fine old houses, lovely winding lanes and, best the voices of *yiayias* yapping in their little gardens, of children arguing over who won the game, and, even an occasional man's voice, a carpenter squaring a wall. Most of the men, though, are off in town, working in the stores, sitting in the *kafeneía*. Just beyond Karlovassi on the coast lies an immense and usually deserted pebble beach called **Potami**. The sea here is clean and outrageously blue. This too is the end of the line; to get to the rugged west end of the island you will have to walk (a fine walk at that), to take a boat or come around from the south side.

Karlovassi roughly marks the halfway point in this circle around Sámos. From here all roads lead into the island's mountainous interior, dotted with small villages, few of which have any special "sites" to be seen, all of which have the simple attraction of being what they are: quiet, old settlements where the men drink coffee in plane-shaded squares; where the well in the square bubbles cool spring water for the mothers washing their families' clothes, the greengrocer and the laden donkey; where wooden Turkish houses line the streets with the typical Sámian churches of golden sandstone and a blue-and-white-striped cupola standing in the centre of town. These are villages for quiet exploring, for sipping a coffee in the *kafeneíon* and for mustering all the Greek you've learned so far.

There are three possible routes through this territory: one takes you most directly back to Pythagóreio, bypassing the island's west side, through Koudeika, Plátanos and eventually Pyrgos before reaching Pythagóreio. (**Pyrgos** is a fine old town worth visiting, and, **Spatherei**, just down the road, has one of the finest views on the entire island.) The second takes you on the best road to the Ághii Theódori junction where you can head for Marathokampos or back to Pythagóreio. And the third leads you up and around the slopes of **Mount Kerkis** which rises to the west 4725 majestic ft (1,440 metres). This is a rough road at spots.

Mount Kerkis covers the west of Sámos and dominates the horizon of the eastern Aegéan. From the summit you can take in Pátmos and other Dodécanése islands, Chíos and Turkey. Climbing it is a worthwhile challenge, requiring most of a day for both the ascent and descent. Start from Kosmadei, from Drakei or even from Votasakia Beach, the trickiest route. In the days of pirate raids, Samians left

Left, groves of mastic trees on the slopes of Chíos. Right, scraping resin off the mastic trees.

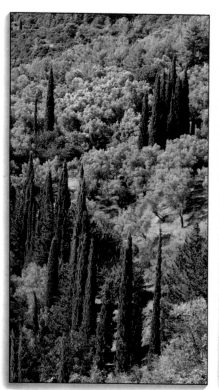

their villages and took refuge on Mount Kerkis. More recently Greek guerrilla fighters in World War II and during the Civil War made it their hideout. Some 400 guerrillas are said to have held out here during the Resistance.

The Resistance links Mount Kerkis to the destiny of the village of Kastanea, where 27 villagers were shot by an Italian firing squad in 1943. Every year on 30 August the villagers in the area walk to the site to commemorate the event.

A rough road leads from Kastanea south crossing the bizarre, burn-out landscape of a more recent local tragedy. In mid-summer 1986 a man-made fire ravaged much of this area, destroying not only precious forests but century-old olive groves as well. And for some residents of Marathokampos this has meant economic ruin. The same sunny dry weather that attracts tourists also makes Greece extremely prone to forest fires in summer. By being cautious with cigarettes and matches, travellers can play their part in preventing such disasters.

From Marathokampos you descend to Ormos Marathokampos which has a long beach extending to the west. The beautiful, untouristed west coast will reward you for the troubles of travelling its unpaved road with the forested hillsides of Mount Kerkis, deserted coves only to be reached by foot, and the few quiet villages that lie between here and Karlovassi.

Chíos (Híos): "The history of Chíos is too voluminous to be brought into the compass of a letter" the French traveller Tournefort wrote in 1701. Since then three history-filled centuries have gone by rendering a survey of this island's past all the more formidable. Chíos, in contrast to Sámos, thrived during much of the Middle Ages and the modern era. The foundation of Néa Moní, Chíos' renowned Byzantine monastery, in 1049 marks the beginning of a millenium in which Chíos would play an important commercial and cultural role in the East Aegéan. During the centuries of Genoan and Turkish rule (1333–1556 and 1556–1912) Chíos be-

the central actory in lóra, the raw lastic is rashed and rained.

came wealthy trading in silk, wines and, most important, mastic, the milky resin of the lentisk tree. Today Chíos prospers in the shipping trade, home to some of Greece's wealthiest shipping dynasties.

Between Chíos' former glory as Genoan and Turkish trade centre and its present modern shipping wealth stands Chíos' catastrophic 19th century. In the span of 60 years most of its people were either killed or driven away, its social and economic order decimated, and its cities destroyed. Chíos had enjoyed great privileges and favour from the Sultan. In 1821 as movements for independence were stirring on the mainland and on neighbouring Psará and Sámos, the Chíots were disinclined to disturb the order that brought them such prosperity.

On the night of 22–23 March of 1822 General Logothétis and 1,500 men arrived from Sámos to instigate an uprising on Chíos. Word reached Istanbul immediately and the Sultan allegedly ordered: "Every Chíot must die."

Within a week the Turkish troops landed and began a massacre which would last some two months. Some 30,000 Chíots were killed and another 45,000 enslaved. Life on Chíos as it had been known was over. Sixty years later, in 1881, the worst earthquake in modern Greek history destroyed what was left, killing 4,000 people.

Starting from scratch: It should be no surprise then that Chíos greets you upon arrival with a waterfront of concrete and steel buildings, not the quaint old houses of a fishing village. It almost seems from the look of Hóra that, building on nothing, the Chíots have been so much the more enterprising. Chíos today is a bustling shipping centre of some 25,000 inhabitants and so preoccupied with that trade which provides over three-quarters of the island's annual revenues that it pays little attention to tourism. To many this is a relief. Nonetheless, Hóra is not all shiny modern businesses. In at least three places it preserves a strong link with its past: in the "old city" inside the Kástro; in the

Left, machines flatten and press the mastic leave into "chicklet" shapes. Right, a Jewish cemetery.

Archaeological Museum and Koraïs Library; and in Kampos, the southern suburb of old aristocratic gardens and mansions.

The **Kástro** with its towers and massive walls was the fortress built and modified by the Byzantines, Genoans and Turks. It formed the protected civic centre for the town – here were the state offices and churches and aristocrats' homes. Under the Turks it was the Turkish quarter, the Greeks living in the settlement outside the wall. Today you can still walk through its alleys and by the old Turkish houses, visit the rather sumptuous church of **Ághios Yiórgos**, the "dark dungeon" where the Chíot nobles were imprisoned in 1822 and the **tomb of Kara Aly** in the Turkish cemetery – the Turkish admiral who supervised the massacres and was blown up by one of Admiral Kanáris' fireboats the same year.

The more archaeological and archival side of Chíos' past is preserved in the **Archaeological Museum** (housed in the mosque on the far side of Plateía Vounakia, presently closed) and in the **Koraïs Library**, which with 95,000 volumes is the fourth largest library in Greece. In the same building you will find the **Argenti Ethnographic and Folklore Museum**. Also, before leaving the centre of town walk through the "bazaar" of old shops on **Aploteria Street**.

On the way out of Hóra heading south you pass through **Kampos**, a "suburban" area of old mansions and country gardens and former residence of the Chíot aristocracy. Only a few remain from its former glory of 200 when European travellers described this place as a kind of paradise. Today you can see the high stone walls that enclosed these luxuriant abodes; the arched gateways, some etched with fine Turkish calligraphy and; peeking inside here and there, buildings in varying states of disrepair. One house has been restored, that of the historian Phillip Argenti. Inquire at the tourist office at the port about seeing it.

Beach, villages and the coast: The road leads out of Kampos towards the fascinating southern end of Chíos. First comes the turn-off for **Empório**, a fine, black pebble beach set on the side of some cliffs of unusually textured brown rock. This was the site of different settlements starting in the early Bronze Age and ending in the early Middle Ages. Returning to the interior we enter the mastic region around the villages of Pyrgi and Mesta.

Chíos is the unique source of mastic whose name is derived from *mastazo*, meaning "to chew" in Greek (like *masticate* in English). Once used as chewing gum it was extremely popular in Istanbul and allegedly freshened the breaths of the Sultan's concubines. The Romans had their toothpicks made from mastic because it kept their teeth white and prevented tooth decay. Even the "father of medicine," Hippócrates, praised its therapeutic value for coughs and colds.

The first stages of the mastic production process are basically the same today as in ancient times. The villagers set off in the morning for the mastic groves, some on donkey, some in a pick-up. They carefully scrape the resin "tears" from the bark of the lentisk tree and then bring them home to be separated from the leaves and twigs. In the last stage the material is sent to a central processing plant where the "tears" are washed, baked and formed into "chiclets." Some 150 tons of mastic are produced annually, most of it exported to France, Bulgaria and Saudi Arabia for up to 35 dollars a kilo.

Pyrgi, the first of the two fine mastic villages visited here, still showily displays the wealth it accumulated over the years in the mastic trade. The facades of many of its houses are designed with black and white geometric shapes. In its fine square you'll also find the **Church of Aghio Apostoli** colorfully frescoed and with an imposing "pantokrator" in the dome. A walk through the alleyways of Pyrgi will take you under the stone arches built to protect buildings from earthquakes, by cellars where a donkey eats hay next to the woman making coffee on a gas stove and, on certain midsummer days, around corners where the breeze blows thick with oregano, the men sifting truck-loads of it to send to New York.

Mesta, to the west is a graver, more sombre village which lacks the colours of Pyrgi. Here one is left with the brute sensation of stone – of deep arched alleyways, walls, streets and homes. The NTOG has set up some guesthouses there and tourism has begun to stir things up somewhat. For those with adventuresome spirits (and motorbikes or a sturdy car) the beautiful and quite deserted western coast awaits. Between **Limnos Meston** and **Siderounta** are some very fine coves and pebble beaches set among scenic promontories. The freshly cut gravel road (quite rough in places) eventually takes you to **Volissos** in the north. Otherwise you will pass through Hóra again in order to explore the island's middle region, Nea Moni, and, if you want to push further, the "ghost towns" of Avgonima and Anavatos.

Nea Moni is one of the finest surviving examples of mid-Byzantine architecture, founded in 1049 during the Patriarchate of Constantine Monomachus IX. It suffered along with the rest of Chios the double disasters of 1822 and 1881, its monks being killed and relics and manuscripts pillaged, in the former and cupola cracked, in the latter. Its mosaics, cracked as they are, are outstanding. The refectory and ruins of monks' cells evoke the days when a religious life thrived there. Ask the caretaker to see the charnel house where the skulls of deceased monks are kept. Those bones, stacked as they are, mark how differently they conceived of an individual life not that of one man but of legions of men passing their existence on earth under the knowing gaze of the "Pantokrator" depicted in the dome. It is said that many of these bones date from the massacre of 1822.

The deserted villages of **Avgonima** and **Anavatos** are further along the gravel road. Perhaps Anavatos gives the best idea of Chíos' 19th-century fall from prosperity. The village set up on the hill for defensive purposes was inhabited through the 19th century. To-

Stringing tomatoes on Chíos.

day it crumbles away, its houses and churches losing their human forms, slowly merging into the dry brown hillside. Meanwhile, an old man runs a makeshift *kafeneíon* at the bottom of the hill, and a woman tries to eke out a living selling figs, honey and spices to the few tourists who pass by.

The north of the island is a sparsely populated area of ruined towers and fortresses, semi-deserted villages and a few good beaches. Certain parts were severely scarred in the forest fires of 1981. Perhaps in compensation for its relative poverty, the richest shipping families come from the north of Chíos, the town of **Vrontados** in particular. Just north of Vrontados is the so-called **Stone of Homer**, where local tradition says that Homer sang his rhapsodies and taught his pupils. There are also some fine little Byzantine churches in the north, such as **Panayia Ayioga-lousenas** in Ayios Galas.

The island of **Psara** can be taken in as a side-trip, either by scheduled boat from Hóra or by leasing a fishing boat from Volissos. It is a quiet island with a small fishing village. It became famous as one of the most active islands in the Greek Revolution and the home of Admiral Kanaris. For continuously harrying Turkish troops it paid dearly; in 1824, 14,000 Janissaries landed in the north. Three thousand islanders escaped. The other 17,000 died.

Lésvos: Lésvos has always been "an island with a touch of class", as the Ionian poet Anacreon enviously put it in the 6th century. A lot has changed; and yet today Lésvos stands for roughly the same things it stood for in antiquity: poetry, culture, education and a democratic spirit. In those days one thought of the poetess Sappho, the Philosophical Academy where Aristotle and Epicurus taught, and the democratising rule of Pittacus, one of the Seven Sages. Today the Nobel prize poet Odysseus Elytis; the folk painter Theophilos; the educated, cosmopolitan Lesvian upper class and a tradition of progressive leftist government come to mind.

There may be few real continuities

ackgammon ame in yrgi, Chíos.

between the Lésvos of then and today, but something about its vast size, its fertile olive-green expanses and its position on the margins of the Greek world seems to have favored a Lesvian identity not wholly bound to the present. Lésvos is the opposite of the *nissáki*, the quaint little island; it is, in fact, Greece's third largest, measuring 44 by 24 miles (70 by 39 km) at its extremities, with a population of 90,000.

Throughout its history it has set itself apart, culturally and politically, from mainland Greece. Its earliest inhabitants probably formed a part of the Trojan race. At the time of the Trojan War both Achilles and Odysseus came with Achaean forces to punish and plunder Lésvos for siding with Troy. In the wake of the Dorian Invasion, Lésvos was settled, not by Ionian Greeks (who occupied the whole Asia Minor coast to the south), but by the Aetolians of Thessaly, a different ethnic group.

Through centuries of struggle between the island's five cities Lésvos as a whole developed into a cultural dy-namo, exporting to mainland Greece such poet-musicians as Terpander and Arion whose particular Aetolian styles and innovations helped to shape the new cultural movement from the Homeric epics and Hesiodic narratives to the lyric and later to classical tragedy. With Alcaeus and Sappho the lyric reaches unparalleled heights of refined thought and sentiment. At the same time the ruler Pittacus (who was no friend of the aristocrats Alcaeus and Sappho) was busy initiating democratic reforms.

But the Lesvian heyday soon ended as the Persians gained control of the East Aegean. Lésvos sided with Athens for some years, only to rebel against her in the early years of the Peloponnesian Wars, an incident made famous by Thucydides. Lésvos generally then shared the vicissitudes of Chíos and Sámos, dominated by Macedonians, Romans (who made it a favorite holiday spot), Byzantines, Venetians, Genoese and Turks.

During the early modern era a land-owning aristocracy developed on **Lésvos harbour.**

232

Lésvos along with a large population of labouring peasants. Peasant and working-class movements took hold here and to the present day it has been a centre of progressive left government, earning the title of "the red island" among fellow Greeks.

Accompanying such economic and political activity, the arts and education have flourished since independence, producing numerous writers, thinkers and painters as well as an upper class noted for its high level of education. Since World War II Lésvos' social and economic fabric has shrunk considerably with steady emigration to Athens, Australia and America. And yet the foundation of the University of the Northeast Aegean has been a hopeful sign for the continuation of Lésvos' cultural autonomy and strength.

Sightseeing: Mytilíni is a bustling port town of around 25,000 inhabitants facing the Asia Minor coast. The Mytilíni waterfront is lined with some fine old *kafeneía* behind which runs the main thoroughfare of the market. On the pier-arm which extends out into the harbour, opposite the ferry landing, there are a number of fine *tavérnes*. which the Mytilineans frequent, dining late into the evening. Look for the taverna with the ancient juke box playing *rembétika* classics. Behind the ferry landing, you find the small, delightful **Archaeological Museum** housed in a villa, containing Roman mosaics depicting scenes from Menander's comedies, a rare Aetolian capital and some other nice sculptural knick-knacks.

Just around the wooded hill stands the Genoan castle, a remnant from the 100-odd years of Gattelusi rule (1354–1462). If you have the inclination for folk culture you can visit the **Popular Art Museum** behind the bus stand on the harbour. But even more noteworthy is the **Theophilos Museum** in Varia, 21 miles (4 km) south of town. This has paintings by Theophilos, one of Greece's most noted "primitive" painters. The road to Varia passes through the part of town where Lésvos' aristocracy built their mansions, living there

Rooftops of Yiássos, Lésvos.

until after the last war when most left for Athens and abroad.

The road running north from Mytilíni skirts the coast facing Turkey. To the west of Moria a few arches still stand from the Roman aqueduct that supplied water to Mytilíni. **Madamados** is the site of the **Taxiarchon Church**, famed for its black icon of the archangel Michael. Here, too, a strong ceramics tradition survives. South of Madamados, in the village of **Aghia Paraskevi**, an unusual festival takes place in the period after Easter. In this "festival of the bull" a procession of costumed men and women and cavaliers parade to the village chapel. After the church service a bull is sacrificed, a banquet held and horses raced.

At **Kari** the road divides, the north fork descending to the seaside village of **Sikaminia**, the west fork skirting around the edge of **Mount Lepetimnos** and eventually reaching the sea at **Petra**. Petra has a long pebble beach which spreads out below the **Church of Panaghia Glikofiloussa** (Virgin of the Sweet Kiss) perched on a cliff. Petra is also the home of the Women's Agricultural-Tourist Collective.

Molyvos, a hillside town of old stone and mortar houses with red tile roofs surmounted by a Genoan castle, is Lésvos' favorite tourist retreat. In Molyvos' *tavérnes* you may sit next to a group of transcendental meditators, members of a health food conference or a group of Lesvians on pilgrimage.

In pursuit of beaches: The west of Lésvos lies at an imposing distance from Mytilíni and, if you are pressed for time, you will probably want to limit your travels to the east of Kalloni. If you do have the time you'll find the west more barren and rugged than the east, consisting in large part of lunar volcanic terrain. Many of those who do venture west do so in pursuit of some of Lésvos' finest beaches. **Skala Eressós** probably wins the prize, and is turning into quite a little tourist resort. **Sigri**, to the north, is a quieter, less touristy village with a good beach.

The southeast of Lésvos is striking in its diversity. On the south coast **Plo-mari** combines a moderate orientation towards tourism with its indigenous industry – the production of *oúzo*. The **Varvaryianni distillery** is just east of town and produces a "deluxe" *oúzo* which is arguably the best in the world. Stop in to see the process and try a free sample. There are some decent beaches along the coast here, the best being at **Aghios Isodoros** which is located just east of Plomari.

Perhaps the most remarkable place on Lésvos is the village of **Aghiassos**. Tucked away from the thoroughfares of tourism on the shaded hillsides below Mount Olympos, Aghiassos seems, indeed, to live by rhythms remote from the modern world. Its traditions of weaving and pottery still continue, and the dialect spoken here is quite distinct from standard modern Greek. The Church has a renowned miracle-working icon and on Assumption Day (15 August) it is the site of pilgrimage for men and women from all over the island. Carnival is celebrated with gusto here as well.

Below, café cards in Vath old town, **Sámos.** **Right,** festival-goer in Lésvos.

THEODOR ELIAI...
FRANKFURT A/M

TH. ELIADIS · ELIADIS

PLAKAT-FABRIK
WÜSTEN & KORNSAND, FRANKFURT A/M.

Die Sch

1. Ein Schwamm-Taucher, welcher von einem Haifisch verschlungen wird.
2. Ertrunkener Taucher, weil er Tau und Ballaststein verloren.
3. Schwamm-Sammler.
4. Taucher, das Zeichen zum Aufziehen gebend.
5. Taucher, die Wurzeln eines grossen Schwammes ausziehend.
6. Taucher, der die Besinnung verloren hat und ertrinken muss.
7. Zu Hilfe eilender Taucher.
8. Taucher, welcher sein Tau verloren hat und nach oben zu schwimmen versucht.
9. Zu Hilfe eilender Taucher mit Tau und Stein.
10. Taucher, im Moment des Aufziehens.
11. Taucher, welcher Tau und Stein verloren, mit Hilfe der Ankerkette heraufgezogen wird.
12. Ta...
13. und...
14. Ob...
15. Ta...gri...
16. Ta...

SCHWAMM-GROSSHANDLUNG
EIGENE SCHWAMM-FISCHEREI auf der SPORADE-INSEL KALYMNOS.

THE DODECANESE

The names of places in Greece often tell much about their past history, and the **Dodécanése (Thothekánisos) Islands** are no exception. Dodécanése is a new name by Greek standards. For the 450 years of Turkish rule they were called instead, the Southern Spórades. In this period the Turks granted these islands considerable privileges and tax-breaks by, generally, treating them with benign neglect. Thus, for the most part, these islands administered their own government, schools and medical care. But when the Ottomans hit on harder times they annulled the privileges, and 12 islands (*thótheka nísia* in Greek) banded together in protest in 1908. Though the protest failed, the new name stuck: Dodécanése. This, despite the fact that today these islands number 14, not 12, but who's counting?

Today the Dodécanése form Greece's southeastern-most territory. Indeed, they were Greece's last territorial acquisition, making the Greek map we know today. In 1912 the islands passed from the Turks to the Italians, who promptly re-named them the "Italian Islands of the Aegéan." The Italians were busy colonialists in their brief 20-year stay, building numerous odd edifices from Pátmos to Rhodes and imposing their language and culture in the schools. Today many middle-aged islanders can still utter bits of their scholastic Italian. In 1943 the Italians surrendered the islands to the Germans who in turn surrendered the islands to the British two years later. Finally in 1947 these islands, spread in an arc across the Turkish coast, were united with Greece to be ruled by Greeks.

Today the people of Dodécanése live largely, as they always have, off the sea. Recently the sea has brought them a novel catch and one of vital importance to the local economy: tourists.

Rhodes (Róthos): Rhodes, the best known of the Dodécanése islands, is rich with natural beauty, architectural variety and bears the signs of a colourful history. Hillsides greet the visitor with extravagant displays of rock roses – it is known as "The Island of Roses." Another name, "Butterfly Island," does not take much imagination to appreciate – butterflies are everywhere. And of course there is the sun and the exquisitely clean sea whose currents combined with summer winds, keep the air and water pure. Endless sandy beaches only a few miles from the hotels are so pristine that it is easy to imagine oneself the first to set foot there.

The City of Rhodes is one of the most architecturally varied cities in all of Europe. Within a few steps one can pass from the ancient splendours of Apóllo's Temple, through the little Odeon Theatre, probably used for rhetoric lessons in Hellenistic times, to Byzantine churches some of which were turned into mosques by the Turks. A beautifully decorated Turkish bath is here, too. And still working. The best way to enjoy it? Go and take a bath!

Greek neoclassical examples are contrasted with heavy state buildings, an ugly legacy of fascism, in this case the World War II Italian variety. Amidst this architectural variety travellers talk with animated gestures, catch each other's attention, and flirt in a babel of languages as they wander past ancient monuments, improvised record and souvenir stores and small *tavérnes*.

Far across the Aegéan from the Greek mainland, separated from Asia Minor by only 7 miles (11 km), Rhodes in ancient times was renowned for its wealth and aggressive navy and was Athens' most feared enemy. In the 5th century BC, Athens attacked and pillaged what were then three independent villages, Líndos, Kámiros and Iálysos. The elders consulted the Olympian gods and decided it was time to join forces and become one, the City of Rhodes. Secretly and with great speed, fortifications and a city wall were completed in 408 BC. Well-defended, the city prospered. Because its strong economy was built on trade, Rhodes tried to stay on good terms with its neighbours.

But twists of history brought trouble. Allied to Persia at the time when Alexander the Great laid siege to Tyre, Rhodes had to endure a Macedónian garrison. As soon as Alexander died, the garrison was thrown out and it was back to business. Wars followed, but Rhodes sided with Rome and prospered. Ptolemy I came to its aid when the city was besieged by Demétrios Poliorketes in 305. Demétrios was defeated but was so impressed by the defenders' valour that he left them his artillery when he and his armies were forced to leave. The citizens sold this unneeded military hardware and used the proceeds to build a monument that became one of the Seven Wonders of the World, the Colossus.

The Colossus: The work of a local sculptor named Cháris of Líndos, the Colossus, by most accounts, stood 70 forearms high, about 102 ft (31 metres), and was a representation of Apóllo. Impressive by any standards, rumour made it even more so by describing the figure standing with one foot on either side of the harbour entrance so that ships passed between its legs! But to do

so it would have had to have been 1,650 ft (500 metres) high, an impossible architectural feat. Nonetheless this beacon to passing ships and monument to peaceful prosperity stood for over a century before it fell to the ground during an earthquake in 226 BC.

Rhodes remained at peace and at the height of prosperity until, ironically, she tried to reconcile the warring Romans and Macedónians only to have Rome take revenge in 168 BC by declaring Délos an open port and ceding it to Athens. Rhodes lost 15 percent of its trade. This punishment and the threat of more forced Rhodes to give up much of its independence and become subservient to Rome, which was not an easy course to take because the Romans were forever engaging in civil wars. Rhodes' trading partners took a dim view of her alliance with the trouble-making Romans. In one chapter of Roman intrigue, Rhodes sided with Julius Caesar only to have Cassius, after Caesar's murder, destroy its fleet, plunder the city and fill up Rome with its treasures.

Antelopes indicate the entrance to the Mandráki harbour on Rhodes.

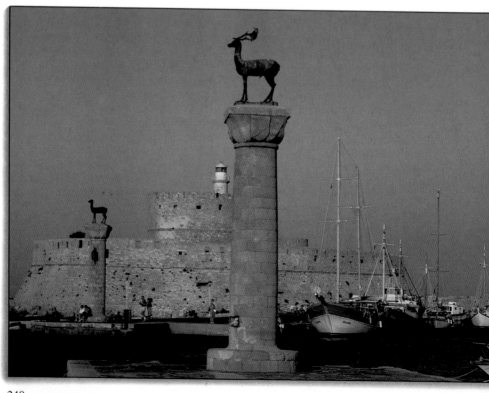

240

Two years later, in 42 BC, Octavius triumphed over Cassius who committed suicide and Rhodes regained much of its autonomy. However, its fleet was gone as was much of its wealth. But Rhodes did regain its cultural influence and for three centuries was the place where many statesmen and literary leaders of the age were educated.

Changing tides swept Rhodes into obscurity after the 2nd century. It moved in and out of anarchy on the fringes of a waning Roman Empire, the Byzantine Empire and the Crusades. In the 14th century, the Knights of St John took control, ruling the island for two centuries until 1522. During this period the walls and fortresses that stand today were built around the medieval city. Even Suleiman the Great and his Turkish armies could not invade the city. A chain stretched across the harbour and the fortress Castle of St Nicholas at the end of the breakwater kept his ships at bay; the walls were impregnable. Finally, hunger, disease and spent ammunition forced defeat. The wall was breached and the Turks marched in as the 180 surviving brethren of the Knights of St John capitulated on honourable terms and were given safe passage. Their churches were turned into mosques.

A Christian order, the Fathers of the Mission, was admitted to care for Christian slaves in 1660; French Franciscan Sisters came and built schools in 1873; the Brothers of Christian Doctrine founded the College of St John in 1889. The 20th century brought other visitors – once again armies. In 1912, the Turks, then the Italians and, during World War II, the Germans. British and Greek commandos liberated Rhodes in 1945 and with the other Dodécanése it became united with Greece in 1947. The **Castle of St Nicholas**, once an armed fortress, is now a lighthouse that welcomes today's visitors.

Island resorts: Rhodes is a big island, and it has more to offer than this marvellous city. Summer resorts are scattered across the northern part of the island;

Líndos, a very old city, dating back to the Bronze age, continues to thrive. It's the only natural harbour on Rhodes, except for the small **Mandráki**, the ancient defence harbour, now full of yachts. Its medieval city is extremely well preserved; an ancient acrópolis also remains with two re-erected classical temples and later Byzantine and Frankish elements.

Near the main square there is one of the most beautiful Byzantine churches on the island, with well-preserved frescoes. The water in the fountain still runs through the ancient water pipes. Líndos' large harbour with long sandy beaches adds the finishing touch. However, it's the light that has made Líndos so famous. The jagged barren mountains which surround Líndos reflect the light so that it almost blinds you. Italian and German painters were the first to rediscover Líndos; some moved there for good. Only later did the tourists catch on. The small city can't hold too many people so most come on day trips by bus or in small boats.

Ancient **Kámiros** is well worth a visit. There's no new Kámiros so that what has been uncovered of the acropolis has been beautifully laid out and gives the visitor an unadulterated picture of ancient life. This is partially true for **Filárimo** as well. At the top of the low hill the ancient acropolis of Iálysos is preserved. Over to the south we find the most beautiful Dóric fountain with its water system amazingly still intact. The **Butterfly Valley** is also a must. Here a small stream meanders through the plane trees and creates little lakes. On the banks the vegetation grows thick as in a jungle. The plane trees are a particularly wonderful kind; the scent of their resin draws red-winged butterflies by the thousand. One abrupt movement or a cry and the butterflies rise up around you.

Kos: Kos is the second largest island in terms of population (20,000), and third largest in terms of size, after Rhodes and Kárpathos. It is a flat island with only one high mountain, **Mount Díktaio**, almost exactly in the middle.

Hellenistic fish, ancient and contemporary

Mandráki is its only protected port. In 1933 a horrible earthquake destroyed the city but the damage was restricted to a very small area. So, although it flattened the city, it hardly touched the nearby towns. Italian archaeologists took advantage of this and excavated the area which they knew overlaid the ancient city. For this reason Kos' archaeological site offers more to the visitor than any other in the Dodécanése islands. It is in the middle of the new city and constitutes a functional part of this urban centre which was rebuilt after the earthquake. The castle is the only part left from the medieval city. And, since it was only used for defence, it doesn't offer much information about the culture at that time.

In **Áspri Pétra** (literally "White Rock") in the western part of the island the finds from excavations go back even further, and it is obvious that there once existed a neolithic settlement there. Quite a few archaeological finds from the Mycenéan period have been found in the city of Kos. Astypálaia, the second most important city of this period is also referred to but it still hasn't been located. Other cities have been lost; for example, it is written that Alkibíades in the 5th century BC defended Meropída, but no one is sure where it was.

Clinging on at the top of Díktaio is **Gía**, the most beautiful town on the island. The houses are built way up on the rocks and look like the monasteries of Metéora. Water rushes down in small streams and large walnut trees grow alongside.

Kos follows exactly the same course of fate as Rhodes. It reached its heights and declined during the same epochs; it suffered the same invasions and adventures. Its most famous ruin is the **Asklepeíon**, built in the 4th century BC, where Hippócrates, the father of medicine, conducted classes and cured the sick. The island from the time of the Romans has been used as a place for rest and rejuvenation; it has a long tourist tradition. But in tourist developments and economic achievements too it follows Rhodes. Hotels spring up like huge

Seeking the shade.

mushrooms on the sandy beaches that surround the island.

Kárpathos: The most dramatic way to arrive at Kárpathos is on the *Panormítis* from Rhodes. This old but sturdy ship serves all of the Dodécanése islands, stopping at various obscure ports while its crew – who are as old and as strange-looking as the ship itself – frantically unload provisions (everything from watermelons to *Pampers*) to cover local needs. After seven hours of travelling on seas which are often rough in this part of the Mediterranean, Kárpathos comes into view with its imposing cloud-capped mountains.

The first port-of-call is Diaphani, a fishing village in the northeast, where passengers are ferried to shore on a small boat, as there is no pier for large ships to dock at. The few passengers who continue have the opportunity to enjoy another hour and a half of the *Panormítis* and its bizarre crew (the one-eyed deckhand, the foul-mouthed captain, and the tattooed navigator to name but a few), as well as to get ac-quainted with Kárpathos itself. All down the 40-mile (25-km) coastline the slopes rise steeply, and the pine-forests which cover much of the island dip right into the sea. The massive forest fire which swept over much of the island in 1983 has left behind a charcoal scar on much of northern Kárpathos but even this somehow seems to lend an added mystery to the unworldly landscape. Occasionally, the slopes give way to large, white, empty beaches – proof that the island was a good choice.

After these magical first impressions, the main port of **Pigádia** is inevitably a disappointment, with little to recommend it beyond the fact that it is well situated.

If you like warm seas, deep clear water with interesting underwater rock formations splashed with colour, and large beaches with white pebbles, then the southeast coast has some of the best (and least crowded) specimens in Greece. Try, for example, **Appella, Ahatá** and **Kyrapanaghiá**. You can visit them by boat, but the land route

Ólimbos, Kárpathos.

will give you the chance to see some of the villages, as well as enjoy the breathtaking view of the beaches from the road above. If you hire a moped, though, be warned – the roads are very bumpy, the cliffs are high, and in places the wind is strong enough to blow you across the road.

The villages are mostly grafted high on the mountain slopes, primarily for historical reasons of security. Piracy was rampant in this region. The wealthiest villages are in the south (**Apéri, Othon** and **Ménetes**), as is evident from the number of traditional and contemporary villas. What is less evident is the source of wealth, for there is hardly any flat farmland, industry is non-existent, and there is no mass tourism. In fact, most wealth is created outside the island, by Karpáthian seamen and emigrants (mostly in the United States), who send remittances to family members left behind, or to their native village in order to build churches and other public buildings, and who also boost the local economy when they return on holiday to see their homeland (and show off their fortune).

This economic structure has profound effects on local culture and attitudes, from their attitudes towards tourists (which range from indifferent to negative – you won't find cultivated smiles or servile behaviour on Kárpathos) to the position of women (who are both more dominant and more traditional than the men due to the fact that they used to stay behind while their menfolk sought their fortune abroad). One of the "cultural imports" has resulted in the establishment of a football tournament every summer, through which the traditional rivalries between villages can be played out on the field rather than by the more violent means of former times. Another area where modernisation and emigration have left their mark is on the architecture and decoration of houses.

You can trace these changes easily as nearly all houses bear the date of construction (as well as the initials of the owner and very often a decorative em-

joke bridges the generations.

blem – such as a mermaid or an eagle) painted or sculpted above the entrance.

The traditional Karpáthian houses consist of one room which is split into two parts. In one corner is the *dórva* which is a wooden platform, bordered by an intricate railing at a higher level than the rest of the room, which generally has a mud floor. This platform houses the trunks where clothes and linen from the woman's dowry are kept, as well as straw mattresses which are rolled out every night for the family to sleep on; in the day they are rolled up to leave more living space, and they are covered with embroidered cloths for decoration.

In the centre of the room stands a wooden pole which reaches to the ceiling, also covered with embroidered cloths and beads. This is the "pillar of the house," and to complete the symbolism a painting or photograph of the couple is pinned to the pole under their wedding wreaths (*stéfana*) – perhaps this custom developed in order to acquaint children with their fathers, who

were mostly absent. The walls are decked with rows of shelves with hundreds of decorative plates and other ornaments. Local handicraft products? Mostly not – they are plates from Hong Kong and France, dolls from Spain and Japan, and a myriad other seamen's trinkets from ports all over the world. The impression is of a splurge of silver, gold and bright colours which miraculously avoids being kitsch.

In modern villas needless to say the house is not limited to one room. However, although the external neighbourhood wood oven has been replaced by an electric stove, and although bathrooms and washing machines have become a necessity, Karpáthians still model their living-room on the traditional style. And here Karpáthian women still display their embroideries and the presents they have received from abroad with the same pride as their foremothers.

In fact the most fascinating aspect of Kárpathos – beyond its natural beauty – is the way that foreign influences have

Skála port and the bay c Pátmos.

246

been adopted and adapted to fit local needs and tastes. For example, in many villages, women still wear traditional clothes, whereas the well-travelled men have worn Western clothes for as long as anyone can remember.

The women's pantaloons, tunics and boots are all traditional local handicrafts, but the costume is completed by a woolen scarf which is imported from Ireland and modified to satisfy local tastes by adding a trimming of sequins and tassels.

At festivals, the tunics are replaced by magnificent dresses, in shades of silver and gold as well as fluorescent pinks and lime-greens on which families spend a small fortune. The ultimate decoration is a collar of gold coins, the number of which indicates a girl's economic position. It is well worth attending one of the major festivals in order to see the young girls decked out in all their finery, on display for prospective suitors, patiently dancing to the monotonous *mantinádes*.

One of the main annual festivals takes place in **Ólimbos**, a village in the north. Perched on a mountain ridge, windswept and literally in the clouds, it is close to how one pictures the abode of the ancient gods at Olympus. The mountainside is cut into with endless terraces, giving the impression of a roughly chiselled sculpture. It is difficult to imagine that these terraces were cultivated as recently as World War II.

Ólimbos is very isolated and its inhabitants seem almost unaware of the 20th century. They marry among themselves and speak a dialect which retains many ancient Greek constructions. The women, dressed traditionally, bake their bread in neighbourhood ovens and even get their flour from a windmill which still functions. You are left with a bitter-sweet taste: on the one hand feeling privileged to have seen the windmill's sails still turning, and on the other sensing that your very presence here, as a tourist, is speeding up the process by which they will inevitably grind to a halt.

It is this same taste that you carry with

A monk from the Monastery of St John.

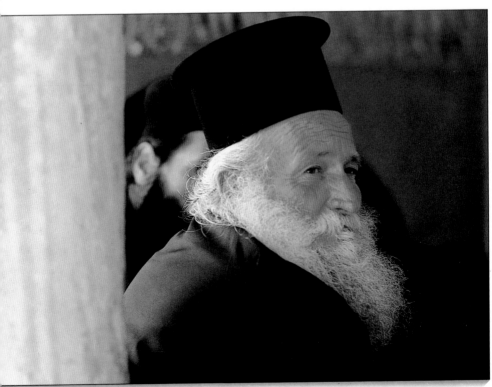

PATMOS

If Délos, the holy island in the Cyclades, was the sacred place of worship for the ancients, its modern equivalent must surely be Pátmos. Pátmos has been a place of pilgrimage ever since the discovery that this small, rocky island is where St John the Divine is said to have dictated the text of "Revelations" to his pupil Prochoros in AD 95.

Greek Orthodox tradition identifies St John with the Apostle John although this has never been proven. Nevertheless, in AD 1088 the monk Christodoulos Latrenos founded a great, fortified monastery in honour of St John, and it has been a place of scholarship and religious enlightenment ever since. At Easter and on the saint's day, 21 May, the faithful flock to its shores to worship and give thanks. Pátmos is included on summer itineraries out of Piraeus, but a convenient approach is via Kos, which has an airport. Pátmos is less than two hours away by hydrofoil (*Flying Dolphin*) in season. But tourists should take note: in any season Pátmos attracts more scholars than sun-worshippers. This is one island that, for

the past two decades, has resisted attempts to establish a nudist beach.

Although the island is no longer ruled by monks, their presence, along with the fortress which looms into view at almost every turning, tempers the rowdier elements found on most holiday islands. Tourists are much in evidence, but those who elect to stay (as opposed to those who arrive by hydrofoil from Kos or Rhodes) appreciate the unique, even spiritual, atmosphere which Patmos exudes. Conversations in the cafés tend to be elevated, night sounds are muted, and many people return season after season to enjoy what one resident calls "the classical life".

Skála is the main harbour, best appreciated late at night when crickets serenade and the sailboats are illuminated against a dark sky. The lights of Hóra on the hill above are indistinguishable from the stars. A few paces from the sea lies a tiny cemetery. Its symmetrical tombstones, when lit by candles, provide a ghostly spectacle.

In the daytime Skála loses charm but gains in efficiency; all island commerce is here, from shops to banks to ferryboat agencies. Buses leave regularly from the main square for Hóra and the monastery. Bearded

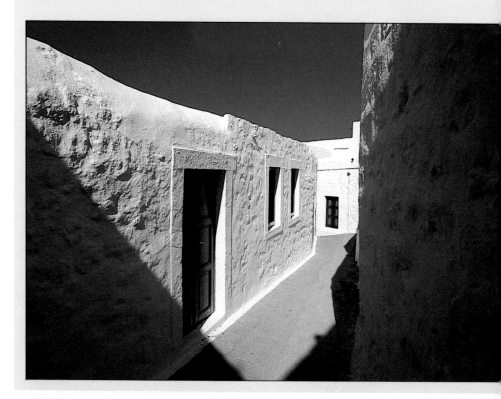

priests in long, hot cassocks vie for seats with sandalled and shorts-clad tourists; the priests, familiar with the tussle, usually win.

Halfway between Skála and Hóra is the **Cave of the Apocalypse**. A silver band marks the spot in the wall where St John is said to have composed "Revelations"; just at the mouth of the grotto is a great cleft in the rock through which the voice of God spoke. This small, immaculate monastery is largely the province of one aged monk, who will gladly conduct you to the grotto. Light a candle here and make a small donation for the upkeep of the church.

The bus stops again at the monastery terrace where there is an unrivalled view of the Aegean. On a cloudless day it is possible to see, not only nearby Sámos, Ikaría, Kálymnos and Léros but also the far away Cycládic isles Amorgós, Páros, Náxos and Mykonos.

The **Monastery of St John the Theologian** is built at Hóra's highest point. A brooding fortress surrounded by defensive walls, just inside is a stall where monks sell illustrated guides. These are well worth buying for a comprehensive interpretation. Within one of its five chapels is the body of the Blessed Christodoulos, the monastery's founder, which lies in a marble sarcophagus. The Treasury houses the most impressive monastic collection in Greece outside Mt Athos; priceless icons and jewellery can be viewed, even handled, but only by special appointment.

Of invaluable importance to scholars is the Library which contains 2,000 printed volumes. It, too, requires special permission to enter but the greatest treasure, 33 leaves of the *Codex Porphyrius*, embellished with gold and silver, can be seen in the public part of the Treasury. Written in the early 6th century on purple vellum, the book contains most of St Mark's gospel.

The silent, shuttered windows in many of **Hóra's** (Pátmos) villas highlight the fact that they are privately owned by Athenians. For this reason rooms are hard to come by, but Hóra's discreet restaurants and, at night, silent, echoing streets are worth savouring. Taxis can be found for the return trip to Skála.

Most of the island can be visited in a day. Buses connect with the beach resort **Groikos** and the fertile village **Kambos**; caïques from Skála call in at beaches at **the bay of Lambi, Livadi ton Kalogiron,** and **Merika.**

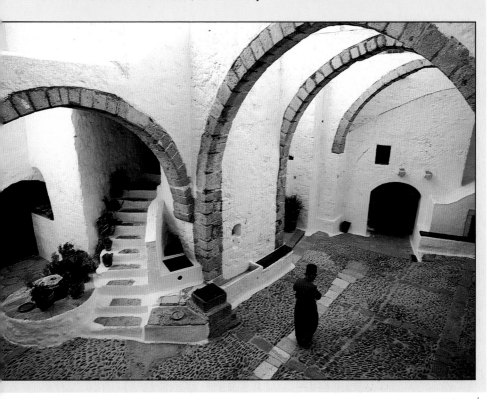

you as you leave Kárpathos, an *ex ante* nostalgia for a less frenzied way of life which you fear will not be there the next time you return.

Sími is the closest island to Rhodes, 24 miles (40 km) from one port to the other. Completely barren, it doesn't even have enough water for drinking, so people gather rainwater in cisterns.

This island was at its height at the end of the 19th century, mainly thanks to the sponge divers and merchants. The **Panohorió** (literally upper city) was an important city, both for its large population, over 20,000, and for its wealth and even more for its extremely well-organized local government.

Interestingly enough, the provinces of this local government didn't go under with the Italian occupation; sponge fishing developed even more, even when the Italians occupied the Libyan coasts so rich in sponges. Somehow the Greeks managed to hold the monopoly on the trade in which they had always excelled.

It's worth a digression to talk about the way the local government organized itself at the time of the island's prosperity. The local elections occurred every year on 25 January. The brief term of office implies that the voters were informed of common problems – otherwise their voting power made no sense. Voters had to be under 80, literate, energetic, impartial, capable of bearing witness, and with no penal sentence hanging over their head. The number of voters was unlimited. They called the local ruler a *Demoghérontas*, and his council was voted in for life by general assembly until 1902, and later by secret ballots. All male youths over the age of 21, who had paid their taxes had the right to vote.

The reason for the election of a first and second *Demoghérontas* is straightforward enough. The first presided over the council and commanded the executive and judicial matters of the community, as well as relations with the High Gate and Turkish generals. The second took care of the community's revenues.

In the middle of this time of prosper-

Quiet times on Kálymnos.

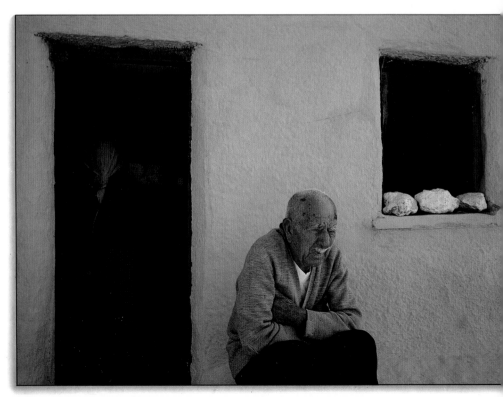

ity World War II broke out. The sponge fishing stopped, sea trade was destroyed; even the ferrying of food to the island became problematic and the islanders deserted their island. The end of the war didn't bring back many of the inhabitants, who were scattered all over Rhodes, Athens and abroad, and the island never grew back to a population larger than 3,000. In the past few years the island has become more lively because of the tourists who come by day boats from Rhodes, to see the distinctive city, and the famous **Monastery of Panormítis**.

Pátmos: In the morning at sunrise the sea in the closed bay looks like a mirror. Beyond the bay stretches the *archipelagos,* where a handful of islands seems to have been flung. And **Pátmos**, the last of the Dodécanése islands in this direction, must have landed farthest north.

Legend has it that St John wrote "Revelation" in the cave which later was walled in and made into a church. You can still see the rock where the holy man and his scribe sat inside the **Monastery of Revelation** halfway up the hill to Hóra.

The island's port, **Skála**, is touristy with many hotels. However, **Hóra**, 40 minutes by foot uphill, is one of the most beautiful traditional towns. Bulky and well built, the town huddles around a medieval castle.

Inside the castle is the famous Monastery of St John the Divine and the large, beautiful church bearing his name with its great wealth of icons, consecrated vessels and votive offerings. The monastery was the object of the Byzantine emperors' devotions and countless private contributors and was certainly the richest in the Dodécanése. Its great wealth helped it to establish a theological school on Pátmos which still attracts students. It is situated just below the Monastery of Revelations.

Kálymnos is even more famous than Sími for its sponge-diving. Although the island on first acquaintance looks austere and dry, it is well worth further investigation. There are many lovely

The colourful houses of Kálymnos.

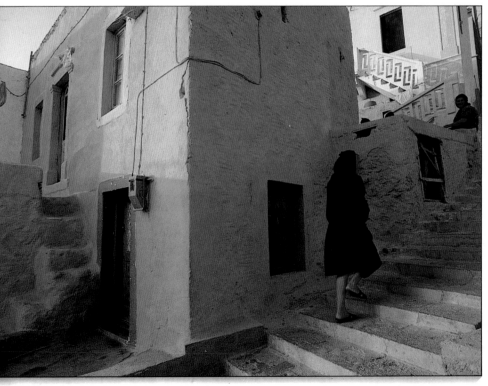

swimming coves and small out-of-the-way villages which offer simple pleasures – a plane tree for shade or a *kafeneíon* for a Nescafé or *Sprite*. But these you can easily discover on your own. The history of sponge diving is more difficult to come by. Signs of this dying trade are everywhere: Kalymnian mantelpieces laden with huge sponges and shell-encrusted amphoras, old men crippled from the bends, women in black, mourning the divers who never came back, but the visitor is often left with more questions than explanations.

Sponge story: Here is some background information. The sponge is a living organism, a colony of sea animals. Its size increases by a third each year. For this reason it is necessary to farm sponges selectively. Unfortunately this rule is rarely obeyed, with the result that the sponges of the Aegéan are rapidly disappearing. The coasts of Libya and Cyrenaïca have also been exploited – although to a lesser degree since these countries impose prohibitive taxes.

The *ímero* (cultivated) sponge is different from most of the common black sponges you see at the bottom of the sea. But only a well-trained eye can tell which is which. The *ímero* is softer and can be cleaned and shaped with clippers while the wilder version is less pliable. There are various grades of *ímero* sponges. The heavier ones are for industry and the finer ones for cosmetic use.

The preparation of sponges for the market has two stages. First the divers beat them hard on the *caïque* deck "to get the milk out of them." Then they string them together and drop them back into the sea for two to three days of cleaning. The soft fleshlike part dissolves and only the golden brown sponge skeleton remains. Then they compress them so that they fit in sacks for export.

Although artificial sponges have taken over the market there are still some people who will pay for the more resilient natural sponge. Be careful, though, that the natural sponge you buy has not been bleached; bleaching may make the sponge look more inviting to the uninformed tourist, but it weakens the fibres.

Over the years fishermen have developed various methods of gathering sponges: spearing the sponges in shallow water, dragging a heavy razor and net behind the *caïque* along the bottom of the sea, so that everything – stones, seaweed as well as the odd sponge gets pulled up together, and finally, diving. In the old days the divers used to sink themselves by tying heavy stones to their waists. Holding their breath, they scraped the sponges off the rocks which they had spotted from the surface; they could usually get two or three before they had to return to the surface for air. There were divers who could dive 40 fathoms deep long before the "machine" was introduced.

The "machine" is what islanders still call the diving apparatus. This consists of a rubber suit with a bronze helmet which connects to a long rubber hose and a handpowered air-pump. The diver is let out on a long wire and given enough rubber hose for the distance he is diving. He can stay down as long as he wants because he has a constant air supply.

The sponge industry aided by the "machine" gained renown while the sponge divers were less lucky: they got the bends. The air hose allowed the divers to go deeper, but the human organism couldn't withstand the new depths; many were paralysed and many died.

Although this "machine" now appears quite outdated, you can imagine what an innovation it was when it was first introduced. It made both the captains and the sponge merchants rich but, ironically, the increased consumption of sponges also brought upon the downfall of the industry. The seabed was stripped bare to meet commercial demands. *Caïques* had to go farther and farther to find sponges. Today, sponge fishing is a dying art but there are many Greeks fishing for sponges in Tampa Springs, Florida and a fleet of *caïques* can still be seen setting out from the Kalymnian harbour for six months of sponge fishing on St Yiórgos' day.

Kálymnian sponges for export.

CRÉTE

The soul of Crete lies in its mountains: the Díkti peaks to the east, Psiloritis in the centre, and the White Mountains to the west, including Pachnes (8,020 ft/ 2,450 meters), the island's highest point. Dramatic, savage, awesome, they have for centuries provided the metaphors for the embattled *palikária*, the warriors of Crete. The mountains recede or come closer, sometimes a translucent shimmering white, other times, a burnt umber. But they are omnipresent, and dominate, exemplifying the history and psychology of the ferociously proud and independent people of this "Great Island." If you want to know the "real" Crete, head for the mountain villages you see from the main coastal road, nestling in the foothills of the mountains and looking almost as if they had sprouted there.

Access to Crete is easy from April until early October, and not difficult outside these periods. Domestic flights within Greece are both plentiful and cheap; in the summer months, there are six flights a day from Athens to Irákleion, and four from Athens to Hanía. But the most romantic way to arrive on Crete is on one of the many overnight ferries from Piraéus.

One can visit Crete at any time of the year as the winter is mild by British and American standards, and the south coast is always warm – it is only 200 miles (320 km) from the coast of north Africa. But the best seasons for many are spring and autumn. From the end of March until the end of June, Crete is breathtaking. It is pleasantly warm without the relentless heat which can characterize July and August. September and October are also temperate months, although a sudden downpour is not unusual in October. But these autumnal harbingers of winter blow themselves out in a day or two, and the sun soon returns.

Background: Crete has always been divided into mountain, plain and coast.

Preceding pages: an olive grove.

In previous centuries invaders remained within the walls of their strategic coastal forts whilst the peasants in the outlying villages acknowledged a change of master. Less than 100 years ago, there were only five miles of paved road on the entire island.

Tourism has changed many of the coastal villages throughout the island and encouraged people to move from more remote parts into the towns. Between a quarter and a third of the island's inhabitants now live in towns. But behind the statistics the old ties with the land linger on. In winter and summer the towns are more populous. Many people spend winter in the towns, and return to their upland villages in the spring. Some are attracted to the towns to work in the tourist industry during summer. During spring and autumn, people return to their villages for planting and harvesting, for most Cretans have some land, and all Cretans are emotionally close to the soil.

Once on Crete, the few major towns on the north coast, each the capital of its respective province, make good bases for exploring the island. Excellent networks of local bus routes fan out from each of these towns.

Irákleion is the largest town in Crete, and is noisy, bustling and dusty in the July heat. Until this century it was known as Cándia, the Venetian corruption of the Arabic *El Khandak*, "The Ditch." It was given this name by the Saracen marauders who seized it in 827. Its history is one of long and violent sieges. Byzantine admirals made repeated efforts to wrest it back from the Arabs before Nikephoros Fokas succeeded in 961, perhaps helped by his habit of catapulting the heads of Muslim prisoners over the city walls to break morale.

The Venetians had less trouble in capturing the town in the 13th century, but their rule was ended by one of the longest sieges in history. For 21 years the Turks besieged the town, kept out by the massive fortifications which had been erected in the previous century, before finally gaining control in 1669.

Today only isolated traces of their past remain. But there are two excellent museums: the **Archaeological Museum**, whose vast collection from Knossós and elsewhere is the best introduction to Minoan Crete, and the **Historical and Folklore Museum**, filled with mementoes of the island's more recent past, as well as a well-displayed collection of textiles.

Just south of Irákleion (there are frequent buses) lies **Knossós**, the extensive late Minoan palace complex excavated and partially reconstructed by Sir Arthur Evans earlier this century. The site is well-known and usually crowded. For those who prefer their ruins untouched and more peaceful, there are several other Minóan settlements in this part of the island: **Festós** and **Górtyn**, to the south, and **Malía**, to the east are all an hour's drive from Irákleion. Also in the vicinity is the **Church of Asómatos**, near **Acharnés**, with Byzantine frescoes, and the Byzantine church complex at Ardon.

Ághios Nikólaos is the most popular resort in Crete. It is a clean well-organized tourist town, though bathing is surprisingly limited. Although it has become an international playground for the tour operators, it remains a good base for the adventurous visitor. The foothills of Mount Díkti are sprinkled with fine painted churches, including perhaps the best on the island – the **Church of the Panaghía Véra**, with its superb Byzantine frescoes, at Kritsa. Nearby lie the deserted ruins of the Dórian city of Lato, just several hours' walk from Ághios Nikólaos.

A little further afield to the west is the windmill-studded Lassíthi plain, one of the most fertile areas of the island and worth visiting as an antidote to the tourist culture of the coastal towns. For a good day's swimming, leave Ághios Nikólaos and head south to the old port of Ierápetra from where you can catch a boat to one of the small coves that dot the south coast.

Réthimnon: From Irákleion there are two routes westwards to Réthimnon. You can follow the main road along the

Below, rocky coast of southern Créte. **Right**, shepherd in Aghía Galíni.

coast and through the foothills of **Mount Ída**. The bus does this regularly in just over two hours. Alternatively. if you have more time you can head south on the Dafní road. This brings you much closer to the overwhelming massif of Ida itself. Following the road which skirts the mountain, you come to the town of **Záros**, and just beyond that, two monasteries, **Vrondísi** and **Valsamonerá**, which contain some of the most beautiful Byzantine frescoes in Crete. The road north to Réthimnon gives some idea of the rare beauty of the Cretan landscape. Below lie the lush orange groves of the Mersara plain and high above on your right tower flanks of the mountain itself which remains capped with snow till well into May. From Plátanos the road winds through unspoilt country to emerge at Filakio at the head of a valley 15 miles (24 km) north of Réthimnon.

Réthimnon itself is an attractive, small port with an Oriental feel. When the Venetians took it over as a stopping-point for ships on the run between Haniá and Irákleion its inhabitants were, largely Greek Orthodox. Under Ottoman rule many people converted to Islam, as they did throughout Crete. These converts continued to speak Greek and failed to follow their new religion with any fervour, drinking wine, for example, and marrying Christians. By the 19th century the population was largely Muslim and even today the old town behind the Venetian harbour, with its narrow lanes, and painted wooden houses with their over-hanging upper stories retains a Turkish air.

In 1923 most of Réthimnon's Muslim inhabitants were uprooted in the compulsory exchange between Greece and Turkey: their melancholy departure is described in the Cretan novelist Prevelákis' work *Chronicle of a City*. But the slender minarets which punctuate the Réthimnon skyline are a reminder of their presence. The Venetian harbour with its attractive waterfront restaurants, is a good place to eat but it is worth exploring the back streets below the fortress where several less pre-

Beach in Irákleion.

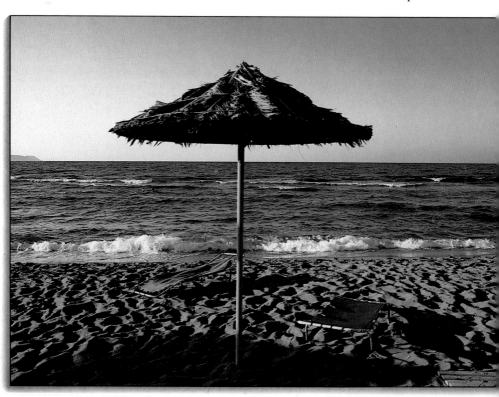

tentious *tavérnes* are hidden away.

Haniá is by far the most attractive of the provincial capitals. A bustling and vigorous town, Hanía has a superb waterfront dominated by the "Old Harbour," comprising a Venetian mole, shipbuilding slip, lighthouse and fortifications. The town has an excellent range of hotels, pensions, *tavérnes*, and restaurants – and not all of them cluster round the Old Harbour, which tends to be more expensive. The **Kavouriá Restaurant**, at the east end of the waterfront under the Hotel Plaza, is a good place to while away an evening, watching the lights reflected in the water, the local Greeks leisurely pursuing their evening *vólta*, or promenade, along with the Technicolour tourists. The large and genial owner, Dimítris Vrettós, is an expert chef in both Greek and European cuisines, and can be patient in several European languages.

Haniá has a superb market with small but seductive *tavérnes* where you can see the stall-owners and market-porters having an early lunch of fish soup or a roasted sheep's head. Haniá is a town which infinitely repays a slow investigation on foot. The Kastéli quarter behind the Kavouriá is a maze of narrow, mysterious alleys, of starkly contrasted light and shade, of tiny artisans' shops and *ouzeriés*. Outside the houses, caged finches and linnets sing in the sun, while high above your head, housewives chat from their geranium-bedecked balconies only a few feet from each other.

Slightly farther out, in the **Halépa** neighbourhood, there are many fine houses dating from the occupation of Crete by the Great Powers at the turn of the century. Here you can still find neoclassical villas which look for all the world as if they have been magically transplanted from Paris. Haniá has – compared with Irákleion – a small but interesting archaeological museum, several art galleries, a surprisingly good public library, a municipal swimming pool and a beach. But an easy bus ride from the centre brings you to the more attractive beaches of **Kalamáta**, a few miles to the west of Haniá, or to **Stavnó**, to the east, on the Akrotíri Peninsula. The town also contains the central bus-station from Nómos Hanión, the province of west Crete.

Mountain excursions: If you want to explore the mountain villages of this scenic province from Haniá, you must first of all acquire a map and a bus timetable. Here you encounter your first problem. The rural buses are quite properly scheduled to suit villagers, not tourists. Hence they tend to leave the outlying areas for Haniá at about 6 or 7 a.m, and return in the late afternoon. This is a nuisance. But remember that on Crete, taxis are plentiful and cheap, and cars can readily be hired. Take a taxi out early one morning to one of the villages – for example, **Thérisso**, about 11 miles (18 km) south of Haniá. If you return the locals' greetings you may be asked to sit down for a glass of *tsighoudiá*, the local *rakí*. (*Rakí*, or *tsípouro*, is the Greeks' answer to "White Lightning." It is distilled from the skins of grapes after pressing.)

A word of advice: Cretans, even in the mountain villages, are inured to the sartorial eccentricities of tourists. But though they are used to women walking about in bikinis, or men in shorts, they do not approve, and at the very least, regard such people with amusement. Mountain villages are not the places for trendy and revealing beachwear. Dressing with modesty will certainly make it easier to pass among the morally conservative people of the mountains.

From Thérisso, a dirt road climbs up and contours along the mountains, heading initially south, then west. It passes through the tiny but impressively situated village of Zourvá, and drops down to the attractive village of Mesklá. Wear light sports shoes and always carry a sun hat, water and a picnic basket. This walk will take you no less than three or four hours at a slow pace but the views are splendid: the ramparts of the White Mountains tower above you to the south, split by dizzy ravines and small gorges as they tumble down precipitously to the foothills. To the north, there is extensive agricultural develop-

Goat cheese and fresh vegetables i the Irákleior market.

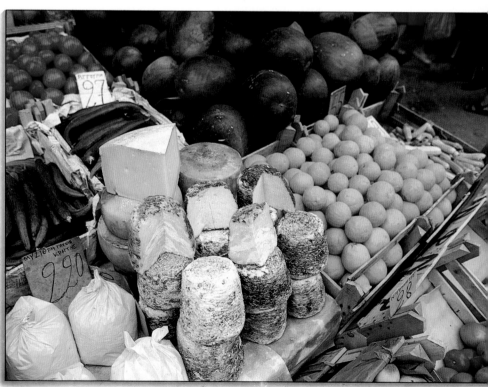

ment among these hills, which are patterned like a patchwork quilt with small fields of wheat, olive-and orange-groves, vineyards and pasture.

On the outskirts of the villages, you are likely to come across a curious bald circular patch, perhaps four to five yards in diameter, and rimmed by stones stuck vertically into the ground. This is an *alóni*, or threshing-ground, still used to this day in many of the villages. If you are about in the right season, you may be lucky enough to see a donkey being driven round and round the *alóni*, towing a heavy wooden sled over the grain. A couple of women sit on the sled with a pan and brush; their function is not immediately clear. Suddenly, however, amidst much laughter they dart forward to catch the donkey's droppings before they get mixed up with the wheat!

Again, you may see a small group of women and children peering up into a tree and shouting encouragement and directions. As you approach, you will see the head of the household perched up the tree in his bare feet, knocking down walnuts with a long pole. The women below husk the green fruit with a knife, their hands are stained a dark brown from the natural dye of the husk which is also favoured by some women as the local substitute for henna. Inevitably, you will be offered an armful of walnuts.

In spring, Crete is garlanded with a seemingly limitless array of wild flowers, and the roadside meadows are ablaze with colour. You should easily be able to identify – by smell, if nothing else – the wild herbs such as mountain thyme, oregano and rosemary, which grow in clumps along the roadside. Birdlife, too, is rich; you will certainly see swooping flights of gold-finches, many kinds of warblers and buntings, and high up, planing on the thermals, you may see griffon vultures, or lammargeyer.

There are two areas which perhaps particularly repay exploration in west Crete. The first is the tangle of villages southeast of Haniá and west of Vámos,

Cretan wildflowers.

west of the main road to Réthimnon: Frés, Tzitzífes, Kiriakosélia, Mahéri. Secondly, there is the grouping south of Kastéli in northwest Crete: Vúlgaro, Kalathénes, Sfakopigádi, Horitianá. This area contains two interesting sites at **Poliriniá** and **Falasárna**. The small sleepy town of **Kastéli**, with its lovely beach, makes an ideal base for exploring this area. The monastery at Kolimbarión, with its impressive frescoes, and Turkish cannonball embedded in its outer, seaward-facing wall, is easily accessible, and there is pleasant walking on both the Rodópou and Grambúsa peninsulas. A boat-trip to **Grambúsa island** for swimming and a picnic makes an exciting and unusual excursion and, weather permitting, can be easily arranged in Kastéli. A longer trip, perhaps necessitating car hire for the day, is to the spectacular coral beach at **Lafonisos** on the southwest tip of Crete. This is a truly beautiful spot, totally undeveloped, although there is a proposal to build a large hotel there. In the meantime, if going there, take a picnic

and adequate water – there is no water supply in the neighbourhood.

No visit to west Crete would be complete without a visit to Ómalos, and the Gorge of Samariá. The **Ómalos** is an upland plateau characteristic of the limestone of the Cretan mountains. It is rimmed by mountains, and is perhaps 2½ miles (4 km) across, with the Gorge of Samariá starting from its southeast corner. This area was the very epicentre of resistance against the Turks, celebrated in a famous Cretan ballad, roared out when mountain men are eating and drinking together:

When will the sun break out,
And when will February come,
That I can take my rifle,
My beautiful Patróna
And go down to the Ómalos…

Today, it is a tranquil place where potatoes are grown, and where the shepherds of villages like Lákki and Aghía Iríni bring their flocks for the summer grazing. Alas, a plethora of white concrete *tavérnes* is beginning to appear at the entrance to the plateau. The two or **Haniá port.**

three modest *tavérnes* already in existence are more than capable of handling the current tourist traffic.

Most people hardly see the Ómalos. They take their tourist or public bus up from Haniá about 6 a.m. to do the Gorge. Thus they miss the spectacular nature of the drive itself, which is undertaken in the dark. A better way is to take the day's last public service bus up to the Ómalos, where you can spend the night and enjoy its still beauty in the evening. The **Ómalos Tavérna** is recommended – simple, clean rooms and good food; tel. 0821-93269. It is delightfully tranquil to sit outside the *tavérna* in the last hour of sunlight, looking south out over the Ómalos, watching the face of the mountains glow in the evening sun, and being slowly mesmerized by the sound of sheeps' and goats' bells.

The "Wooden Steps": In the morning, you can be up early to catch the first bus to Ksyloskalo the "wooden steps" – the abrupt start of the Gorge of Samariá. A word of warning: while there is a well-made path all the way down the gorge, and while there is plenty of water, and while first aid facilities are available at the deserted village of Samariá in the park ranger's house, wear something sensible on your feet! At the very least sneakers are necessary. Strapless slip-on sandals and stiletto-heels are definitely not recommended.

The view from the top of the "wooden steps" is spectacular. Directly opposite you is the massive crenellated face of **Gíngilos** (6,834 ft/2,083 metres), a fine, imposing mountain. Although it is hardly credible from this position, the summit is easily accessible along a well-marked path...to the experienced *and* properly-equipped mountain-walker only. (For information on this and other mountain-walking routes, contact the Greek Alpine Club hut at Kallérghi, above the Ómalos, or the author of this piece via the travel agency given in the Travel Tips section). The gorge is a National Park; the route through it is 11 miles (18 km) long, and the park authorities have done an effi-

Worry-beads for the man; tree-pruning for the woman.

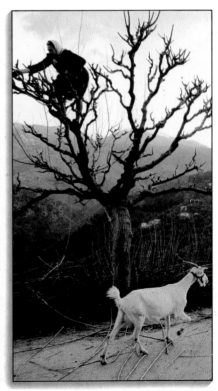

cient job of fencing the path, providing water-and rest-stops, and information boards. It is impossible to get lost. The best advice is to start early, take your time and gape! The Gorge is without a doubt one of Europe's great wonders.

Coastal visits: When you finally leave the gorge on the south coast, you may well be surprised at the intensity of the heat. As you head into the sea for that well-deserved swim, beware: The stony beach is red-hot! The village where you end up, **Aghía Roúmeli**, is an unlovely place designed only to hoover money from as many tourists as possible. But one can sympathize with the villagers' need to make money while the sun shines – Aghía Roúmeli is a desolate and deserted spot in winter. Take the first ferry-boat out, and go to the idyllic coastal village of **Loutró**, along the coast to the east. Loutró, the ancient port of Phoenix, surrounded by interesting and picturesque ruins, used to be a fishing village; now it subsists totally on tourism. However, as it is very small, there is an absolute threshold to the number of tourists it can absorb. But it is still a lovely spot, ideal for lotus-eating, swimming and idle contemplating. The water around Loutró is crystal-clear, this is because there is a layer of fresh-water over the sea-water.

A short hour's walk to the west brings you to an attractive deserted pebble beach. A small *tavérna* not far away supplies cold drinks and basic food. You can leave Loutró by boat, or preferably, walk east along the coast on a clearly marked path until you come to Hóra Sfákion.

Hóra Sfákion serves principally as the boat/coach interchange point for tourists coming down the gorge. But there is an attractive walk from there, along the coast road to **Frankocástelo**, about 7 miles (12 km) away. Here, there is superb swimming in a lagoon under the ruined but still impressive ramparts of a Venetian castle. This road passes through several east Sfákiot villages which although not particularly impressive in themselves, *are* working villages where many traditional agricul- **Rugs drying.**

tural and pastoral activities persist. From Frankocástelo, it is easy to return to Haniá by bus via Hóra Sfákion, while for the more adventurous, a walking trip can be made inland on clearly marked paths, either to the village of **Kalikratés**, or up the **Gorge of Imbrós**, on a smaller scale than that at Samariá, and much less known, but equally spectacular. A little elementary map-reading is necessary for either of these expeditions, plus some help from the locals. Exit from both places is possible by public bus.

While on the south coast, those who like boat-trips have the option of hopping between Hóra Sfákion, Loutró, Aghía Roúmeli, Suyía and Paleohóra. Indeed, this route is strongly recommended for those who are not into walking. These trips afford unbeatable views of the southwest coast of Crete, where the mountains drop dramatically into the sea. It is a stunning, and at times – particularly in the evening – a slightly sinister coastscape; the sense of profound depth in the sea is inescapable.

Every now and then, you will see a small white church nestling close to the sea, or perched upon a high promontory. It is a feature of rural Greek Orthodox churches that they are frequently constructed on sites with good views – and often, water. If you are in one of these coastal villages, and you see a church high above, it is well worth the effort to find the way there – there is bound to be a path. There is a chapel above the long beach at Paleohóra, for example, which gives a complete panorama out over the peninsula. Some of these chapels, for example at Anídri, an hour on foot northeast of Paleohóra, have fine Byzantine frescoes dating from the 14th or 15th centuries. Resist the temptation to take flash photographs; this inevitably exacerbates the process of deterioration.

"The Cretan bus": While talking of travel, mention must be made of "The Cretan Bus" – not the big, efficient coaches which make the regular runs east-west along the main road in the north of the island, or to the popular

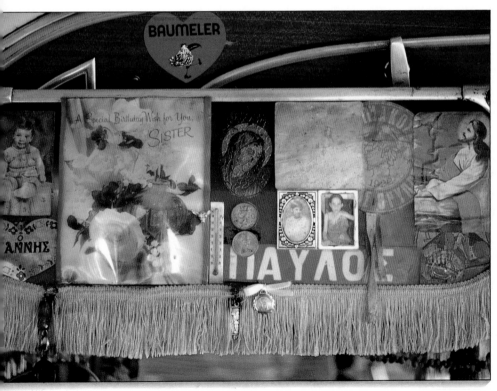

tourist destinations such as Hóra Sfákion, Ksilóskalo, or Paleohóra. Instead these are the much smaller sturdier, and more battered village buses which make the run into Haniá in the early morning and out again in the afternoon. The driver and conductor are usually regulars, often residents of the village in question. The bus takes passengers, of course; but it also takes an amazing range of parcels and boxes, the mail, and carries messages and gossips up and down the district.

Although there is a timetable, there are infinite minor variations in its operation, and the bus is more likely to go when full rather than exactly at the appointed hour. So the way to outwit the driver is to check the departure time on the big destination board in the main bus-station; then ask for the *number* of the bus at the information desk (displayed on a round sticker on the windscreen – never mind what is said on the bus's destination-indicator); then find that bus, and watch it like a hawk! These rural buses, however, are a safe and reliable way to travel, and afford a unique opportunity to meet locals.

Food: A word now about food. The food in restaurants is by-and-large very good. But one must distinguish between "tourist-Greek-food," and food which the Cretans eat in the villages. In the former case, dishes such as *moussaká*, stuffed tomatoes and aubergines, *stifádo*, *taramsaláta* and so on are common and excellent. But these are not daily foods in the villages. Villagers eat what is in season, so their food, while wholesome, often lacks variety. In winter and spring, snails and *hórta* are common; the latter is a wild green, not unlike spinach, and full of iron.

Cretan snails are widely favoured outside Greece as well as by locals, and many are exported to France. They – and dishes like chicken and braised meat – are often served with a *piláfi* of rice cooked in the fat and juices of the meat. It is delicious. All meat, of course, is cooked in olive oil. Roasted sheeps' heads are common, and are eaten down to the bone: flesh, brains, tongue, and eyes. Another popular dish is *kokorétsi*, a very tasty sausage-shaped dish made of roasted lambs' intestines and giblets.

All kinds of lamb are eaten: boiled, roasted, stewed; including the liver, of course. A common proverb in the mountains of Crete says that the best tasting mutton is that which is stolen! It is all cooked in plenty of oil, and always, always served with bread. Similarly, wine is drunk with all meals but never on its own. Bottled wine is distrusted intensely; locals drink their own draught red wine, which is of good quality, having a slight "afterburn" like sherry, and is highly recommended. Bottled Greek wine is ridiculously expensive, with the exception of *retsína*. So, ask for *krasí mávro*, dark wine, or *híma*, wine on draught; it comes by the kilo, or multiples thereof. Fresh fish is comparatively rare and very expensive. Off the south coast of Crete, many fishermen can only make ends meet by using dynamite. The sea is terribly overfished. Fishing with dynamite, although prohibited, continues with predictably tragic consequences.

Left, snowy mountains at the head of Ómalos gorge. **Right**, the Samariá Gorge.

A	
B	
Γ	
Δ	
E	
Z	
H	
Θ	
I	
K	
Λ	
M	
N	
Ξ	
O	
Π	
P	
Σ	
T	
Υ	
Φ	
X	
Ψ	
Ω	

CULTURAL ABCs

Newcomers to Greece are often baffled by the Greek alphabet. Even if they have trouble understanding other European languages they can at least read road signs and figure out which is the Ladies and the Gents. In Greece even international catch words like EXPRESS have a bizarre appearance. Perhaps as much as anything else it is the strange alphabet that makes foreigners throw up their hands and utter the ancient words of despair: "It's all Greek to me!"

The cultural ABCs that follow won't help anyone overcome their fear of Js, Fs, or Cs, but it may provide a key to another set of symbols that are equally strange. Greece is full of untranslatable concepts. What follows is an alphabet's worth of these indigenous phenomena. From E for Evil Eye to K for *Kamáki* to Z for *Zórba*, these entries introduce the newcomer to aspects of contemporary Greek culture which are not immediately obvious. Here readers will find out why no one bothers about birthdays (see Namedays), why kiosks dot every corner (see *Períptera*), why old women dress in black (see Women), and why Greeks are at odds over tourism (see *Xenomanía*).

Of course, this kaleidoscope of incongruous items is only one of many possible collections. The various writers who have contributed to this alphabet are not set on fixing Greece's cultural topography: on the contrary, each – whether linguist, anthropologist or journalist – is interested in tapping the shifting assumptions that go into making myths and shaping cultural identity. Sometimes humorous, sometimes serious, these entries map out another Greece, as important as the Greece already represented by geographical region in the previous section. As a dictionary or as a set of social commentaries, use these pages as you please.

ACRONYMS

Even classicists who can bumble their way through the more conservative newspapers with their many archaisms and purist forms would have a difficult time deciphering the strings of acronyms that appear in most articles today. Always used for the names of political parties (KKE, PASOK, ND, KODISO, EPEN, DIANA), acronyms now stand in for everything from social services (IKA, EES, ANAT, IKY, DEH) to soccer clubs (PAOK, AEK).

A contemporary Greek painter, commenting on the recent proliferation of acronyms, chided that soon the Greek novel would consist solely of abbreviations. It could be he was merely denigrating language as a lesser medium – we all know that, according to photographers, a picture is worth a thousand words – but even so he had a point: acronyms are the fast food of modern Greek discourse. Just as Americans have begun to wonder what McDonald's really means, so Greeks are beginning to wonder what acronyms are all about. Why have public announcements and newspaper articles started to resemble their ancient stone predecessors with their long lines of unpunctuated capitals?

Acronyms, like fast-food hamburgers, have an uncanny ability to camouflage what they contain. One soon forgets what an acronym really stands for. It suddenly has an association all its own, completely separate from its components. Former prime minister Andréas Papandréou took advantage of this slippage and decided to use the same acronym for the Greek police force as the left-wing resistance fighters had used during Greece's civil war. ELAS now stands for both; so an acronym became a subtle way of legitimising a moment of left-wing history.

But subtleties aside, even if it would take a lifetime to decipher the politics of acronyms it doesn't take long to learn those that are most frequently used. And although Greek phrase books rarely mention them, you would be hard pressed to phone overseas if you didn't know that the public phones in every Greek town or city were housed in a building called OTE (pronounced "*oté*"). You might save yourself quite a bit of time if you knew that the Greek tourist organisation is called EOT (pronounced "*eót*"), and embarrassment if you knew that the great hordes shouting PAOK (pronounced "*paök*") in the streets of Thessaloníki on Sunday were not political activists but soccer fans.

BYZANTINE CHURCH MUSIC

Q: In most parts of Greece on Sundays and Namedays (see Namedays) radios are turned on full blast and towns resound with the nasal half- and less than half-tone dips of the Athens' Mitrópolis' cantors. Why does this chanting sound "Eastern" to a Westerner?

A: Traditional modern Greek music has many oriental features, as indeed had the music of the ancient Greeks: not only tones and semitones, but other smaller and larger intervals, oriental chromatic scales, a nasal quality in the voice and characteristic motifs decorated with grace-notes such as are particularly common in the East.

Q: How did Byzantium give birth to two such different church musics as the Roman Catholic and the Greek Orthodox?

A: Were these two kinds of music really so different 1,000 years ago? Plenty of scholars doubt this. For example, this is what Igor Reznikoff believes: "At the end of the 19th century French Benedictines wanted to revive the Gregorian chant and created melodies based upon notes with identical time-value, often indeed beautiful, but which have no connection with the genuine ancient chant as we know it from manuscript sources on the one hand and from the tradition of model music on the other."

Q: What does Orthodoxy have to say about music? Has it always been an integral part of the Greek church service? Has there ever been any instrumental accompaniment?

A: Music has been used in the Christian

Church since Apostolic times, and is regarded by the Orthodox Church as an integral part of the liturgy, to be preserved by each generation as a holy relic and to be performed contritely, humbly and with due decorum. Ancient ecclesiastical tradition, which is still maintained, holds that musical instruments are alien to the spirit of Orthodox worship, because their sounds are associated with worldly festivity. That is why Orthodox church music is purely vocal.

Q: The history of Western music seems closely connected with the evolution of church music. Has there ever been any attempt in the Greek Church to compose new masses as in, for example, the Protestant and Catholic traditions?

A: A number of pieces of Greek church music have been written in a more modern style. Theodorákis, for example, has composed a polyphonic Requiem for choir a *cappella*. These works could be performed in certain churches, but neither the congregations nor the clergy would ever wish to replace the traditional chant.

Q: How has this music survived? Are cantors trained or are they just expected to pick it up from their elders?

A: The church music of the Byzantines, and of the Greeks in general, began to be written down around AD 950, and for that purpose a special system of notation was worked out. Thus, up to AD 950, religious music was handed down by oral transmission. From then onwards, however, it was transmitted with the help of manuscripts, and later, since 1820, in books. But the pupil has to overcome a very considerable obstacle before he can be considered a good *psáltis* or cantor. He must learn to chant in the appropriate style, and in this no written music can help him, only his teacher.

Q: Are there any women cantors? Do women play an active role in church music?

A: If a woman becomes a nun and has a good voice, then she may chant in her nunnery. Otherwise, it is not usual for her to chant. Nevertheless, a number of women in Byzantine times did occupy themselves in writing hymns and setting them to music. An interesting recent study on this subject was written by Diane Touliatos-Banker, under the title of *Medieval Women Composers in Byzantium and the West*.

Q: If visitors want to hear chanting at its best where should they go?

A: There are churches with good cantors and choirs in every Greek city, and also in Constantinople. In Athens, Insight Guides recommend the liturgy at Aghía Iríni (St Irene's), where Lycourgos Angelópoulos and his choir may be heard.

COFFEE

"Would you like a cup of coffee?" It's the classic come-on, from Syntagma to Sámos. Fair enough, women tourists should not be fooled by the sobriety of the homely brew for coffee has long been the drink of erotic encounters.

Among Greeks themselves, offering coffee to a stranger is a gesture of hospitality and an excuse for light conversation. A chance invitation for coffee with an acquaintance and his or her *paréä* (circle of intimates) isn't easily refused. It's the perfect drink for "exploratory" sociability, for jokes and mild flirtation, and many a romance has begun with shy glances over the cups.

Its place in more mundane social intercourse is just as prevalent. Greek men drink it in the ubiquitous *kafeneía*, housewives drink it at home with their neighbours during breaks from their chores. Working people drink it, too, but you won't find a coffee machine at their workplace. They "order out" from the local *kafeneía*, and on downtown streets, ducking in and out of office buildings, you can often see the white-aproned proprietor carrying an ingenious deep-dished tray crowded with coffee cups, the dish suspended, lantern-like, by three, bowed metal supports.

In name, as in quality, it's much closer to the Arabic original, *gahwah*, than the West's watery brew. Ground into a fine powder and boiled with water and varying amounts of sugar, *kafé* is served in tiny cups. You can order it sweet (*glikó*), very sweet and boiled (*varí glikó*), medium (*métrio*) and unsweetened (*skéto*) – and if those few teaspoonfuls don't satisfy your caffeine addiction, double (*thipló*). Connoisseurs know that what distinguishes the exquisite cup from the mediocre is a thick topping of froth (*kaïmáki*). Greeks used to call it "Turkish coffee" (*toúrkiko kafé*), until the 1974 war in Cyprus, when it was angrily crossed off menus across the land. Cyprus is still a sore point, so unless you want to risk angering the waiter, ask for Greek coffee (*ellinikó kafé*).

Even the dregs have their uses. If you leave a trace of liquid so that the dregs can be swished around the cup, you can turn it over and let the wet residue run down the sides into the saucer. It leaves swirling patterns, and many a Greek woman can decipher symbols embedded in them to "predict" the future. Most men wouldn't be caught dead "saying the cup", and since the Church frowns on it, many women hesitate to admit to it. But in their houses, women trade cups and interpretations "for a laugh". Wedding rings and tall, dark, handsome men seem to populate the cup. But one wonders now that Nescafé has become fashionable, what will become of the next generation's fortunes?

DELECTABLES

"And I, hungry once more, gaze at the sweet biscuits." This heartfelt yearning, expressed more than 2,000 years ago by a female character in one of Sóphocles' lost plays, is still experienced in today's Greece, where sweets supply an important national need. The *zacharoplasteíon* (sweet-shop) is indeed a mouthwatering sight, with its mounds of crescent- and cone-shaped biscuits decorated with chocolate, almonds, sesame, apricots or coconut; with its giant baking-tins (*tapsiá*) crammed with diamond wedges of *baklavá* glossy with syrup and bulging with nuts; with its extravagant European-style *pástes* too.

No less tempting are the smells of rose- or orange-flower water, roasted almonds and cinnamon which drift from the kitchens often open to the street, where the curious may peer at the skills of the chef.

The *zacharoplasteíon* is more than a shop. One can often sit for some time, as in a café, eating a *kadaïfi* (finely shredded pastry stuffed with almonds and soaked in honey) or a *profiterol* (not the light French *choux* pastry but sponge softened with syrup and liqueur, covered with chocolate custard and cream), always served with a glass of iced water. In the northern cities – where the abundance of almonds and fruit and the presence of a large population from Asia Minor have fostered a sweet tooth among the inhabitants – sweet-shops are plentiful and often very smart. The city-dweller will eat a *baklavá* – or the even sweeter zeppelin-shaped *touloúmba* – in the early evening, after a siesta and before dinner. Surrounded by glass cases packed with all variety of cakes (which present a constant temptation), one is usually not enough.

At home deliciously fragrant sweet rusks, *koulourákia*, are dipped into tea or coffee at any time. On entering a home you are likely to be offered – refuse at your peril – a piece of preserved fruit in syrup, a *glikó tou koutalioú* (off the spoon), a cross between jam and crystallised fruit. All sorts of fruit and vegetables are preserved in this way; especially delicious are the green walnuts and little damsons of Thásos. The more adventurous will sample a jar of baby aubergines or marrows such as cram the stalls in Thessaloníki's street market. The humblest variety of the "spoon" family is the "submarine", a spoonful of vanilla (a vanilla-flavoured mastic cream) served in a glass of iced water which then makes a delicately perfumed drink.

The range of Greek confectionery is greater than the disgruntled visitor supposes. Foreigners rarely meet with more than the ubiquitous stale *baklavá* or the oily *halvá* packaged in foil. The best *baklavá* is to be found on Thásos, made unusually with walnuts and heavily spiced. Two variants of this oriental pastry found less often in shops are *galaktoboúreko*, milk pie (*fílo* pastry filled with a thick egg custard flavoured with orange flower and cinnamon) and *reváni*, a Madeira-type sponge made with semolina and soused with a cognac and orange syrup.

(Be sure to try them when visiting Aégina.)

Halvá comes in many types. Smyrnan *halvá*, now alas hard to find in shops, is made in huge flat circles and is of a coarse, grainy texture and rich amber colour. Pharsalian *halvá*, to be found in Théssaly, is more gelatinous, closer to Turkish Delight (be sure to call it *loukoúmi*!). Both are excellent when sprinkled with lemon and cinnamon. *Halvá* should be bought in the street market, sliced from huge loaves, spotted with pistachios and almonds or marbled with chocolate. Even more sybaritic is *karidóplastos*, a rich "paté" made from chocolate and walnuts. When surrounded by the proliferation of unknown delicacies, don't be overwhelmed. Ask for a bag of *amigdalotá* – almond macaroons of numerous shapes and flavours – and you can't go wrong.

EVIL EYE

Greeks seldom call it the "evil eye" – just "the eye" (*to máti*). Perhaps the malevolence of "the eye" goes without saying. Belief in the existence of "the eye" is not confined to those from remote or provincial places. The jet set, the middle-class as well as the prole-tariat, and not a few university-educated, swear that it exists. They insist that even doctors acknowledge its reality, just as the Church accepts the existence of demonic possession. Undoubtedly, the experience of "being eyed" is real and widespread, however much one might quarrel with the diagnosis of it.

Concepts of "the evil eye" abound in Mediterranean societies. Whether these different concepts are about the same thing is hotly contested by scholars of this region. But the debate itself underscores just how much "the evil eye" is a social affliction rather than anything particularly metaphysical. Probably, the "evil eye" is about envy. It tends to appear in communities relatively undifferentiated by social class or wealth – "egalitarian" in a sense, but where resources are scarce and competition over them keen. In such places, the increments of "superiority" of one family over another are tiny, yet all-important. Prestige or honour, variously, requires one to "stand out" from one's neighbours – but not too much, for that invites jealousy and bad will. Out of this paradox – the need to be better, the need to be the same – comes "the eye". It is a consequence of envy, but it is envy expressed surreptitiously, even unconsciously.

This qualification is important. A Greek will rarely give "the eye" to someone intentionally. What we'd call "sorcery" – saying

276

special words or doing special actions in order to make something happen to someone – falls into a rather different category, that of "magic" (*máyia*). "The eye", by contrast, is cast by accident. The kind of person who casts "the eye" on you or yours is probably a neighbour or an acquaintance, someone with whom relations are – if not warm – at least cordial. It can happen inadvertently when something is praised, or even silently admired. This is why people take precautions by spitting delicately ("Phtoo! phtoo! phtoo!") on an infant they cuddle or admire, to forestall any ill effects.

The sorts of living beings and inanimate objects most vulnerable to "the eye" are those of unusual beauty, rarity or value. Tiny babies, appealing toddlers, pretty girls and twins are all at risk. Horses and cattle can be afflicted as well. When automobiles "die" for no apparent reason, people blame it on "the eye", and in certain parts of Macedónia you can find one tractor after another with an apotropaic string of blue beads hanging from its front fender. On a parched islet in the Dodécanése, the water supply for one household is stored in whitewashed barrels on its rooftop; on each barrel has been painted, with unabashed simplicity, a large blue eyeball.

Certain people are said to be prone to casting the eye. Often, an individual so labelled (sometimes called a *grousoúzis*) is quarrelsome, odd, or marginal in some way to the community. Blue-eyed persons (a trait Greeks associate with Turks!) are also especially hazardous. Wearing blue – blue beads or the little blue pupil encased in plastic – repels that danger. Many adults place one of these blue plastic eyes next to the cross they wear on a chain around their neck. And until recently all children had some sort of charm – a cross, an eye, an image of the Virgin and Child pinned to their underclothes to protect them.

There is no way to know precisely who has cast "the eye". First, the effects are noticed, and only afterwards is a culprit surmised. All concerned anxiously pool their memories to reconstruct the recent past, straining to identify possible suspects with possible motivations. This response of suspicion reinforces belief in "the eye". It also reinforces its precipitating conditions: those of superficial cordiality and subterranean mistrust

among unrelated families. Oddly enough, then, identifying the culprit is usually quite irrelevant to the cure's effectiveness.

Symptoms of affliction are fairly well-defined: in humans, they include sudden dizziness, headaches, a "weight" on the head or a tightening in the chest, a feeling of paralysis. Significantly, the head and chest are the sites of "breath" and "spirit". Animals show their affliction by bizarre behaviour or suddenly falling sick, while vehicles break down. When it happens, people know who to go to. It's often an old woman who is trusted and respected and who "knows about these things".

The cure has many variations, but this one is typical: the curer takes a glass of water and makes the sign of the cross over it three times. Then she repeats three times silently to herself a special, secret set of holy words, usually a short passage from the *Bible*, and simultaneously drops from her finger three droplets of olive oil into the glass. If the oil remains in globules, the person is not afflicted with "the eye". If it dissolves, this is both the proof and its cure. The curer may yawn and her eyes may tear, while the afflicted person may feel a dramatic "lifting". This blessed water is then dabbed on the forehead, belly, and two points on the chest – that is, at the points of the afflicted's crucifix.

Often enough, it works. Why it works isn't clear, but the moral is: illness isn't about germs alone, it's also about social relations. If that fact has eluded the Western medical establishment, Greeks know it all too well.

Friends or Paréä

American visitors in particular find it hard to put a name to it. "My gang" or "my buddies" sound embarrassingly corny. "My crowd"? Maybe, but most opt for the delicately vague "my friends". Yet these are seldom more than conglomerations of individuals, drifting together and then apart in a conspicuously mobile society. It's only in team sports, campus "Greek" societies and fringy cults that Americans experience that sense of a small tight-knit group that most of the world takes for granted.

Across the Atlantic, Europeans seem more sociable. The English working classes have their "mates" from cradle to grave, but the French, with their *companie*, perhaps come closest to the Greek notion of *paréä*. For *paréä* combines both senses of the French word: of companionship, and of the group of friends itself.

"Do you have *paréä*?" means "Do you have company?" In Greece, without *paréä*, things aren't worth doing. Living alone, going off by yourself for a vacation, taking a lone stroll, these are not signs of independence but of desperation. This is a society whose language has no word for privacy. The closest translation is *monaxiá* (isolation), connoting deprivation, loneliness and loss. Who would choose such a state? Young women on their own are especially suspect: surely they're "looking" for something. Before mass tourism, big-hearted Greeks felt obliged to "adopt" lone tourists wandering their countryside, to "protect" the woman and befriend the fellow. Even today, "Do you have *paréä*?" is less a question than an offer: "I'll come along."

The "naturalness" of *paréä* for Greeks is fostered in their family experience where a myriad of what we'd call "incompatible" activities happen all in one place so that nobody is left alone. Traditional peasant houses had one main room for cooking, eating, working and sleeping, and even in new village houses and Athenian apartments, everything seems to happen in the living room-kitchen. With television droning in the background, the teenage girl pores over her school books while her father passionately argues politics with his brother-in-law, her brother shouts into the phone and her mother clangs pots and scolds the grandchildren.

People often say that the primary unit of Greek society is the family, not the individual, and this is manifested in a different sense of personal boundaries. Greek families are not a place for "respecting the other person's space". They are interactive – indeed, interfering. How else can they show they care? This is where "Greek individualism" is different. Americans and northern Europeans believe they have the right to "do their own thing" and should allow others the same. Greek individualism is rooted in the family and the *paréä* with their intense loyalties and equally intense conflicts. Greeks advise, criticise, make sacrifices for and demand them from those they consider "their own". No laissez-faire here. If American individualism is about the lone cowboy, the Greek version is about the leader of the pack. "Twelve Greeks," they remark in wry self-recognition, "13 captains."

Paréä partakes of both fixity and flux.

"My *paréä*" can mean a fairly fixed group. For young Greeks, it's usually school friends. For those still childless, or far from home at university, the *paréä* becomes an alternate "family". Such a *paréä* can last for years. Its members are always together, and think and talk about each other obsessively. They create a shared history. For their parents, especially if they've lived most of their lives in one town or one neighbourhood, the *paréä* combines long-time friends with relatives and new in-laws with their spouses, people with common interests and common responsibilities.

For the young and unattached, the *paréä* can be all-consuming. Its members meet for coffee before lunch, coffee after, a brandy at 4 p.m., and a meal in a *tavérna* at 10 p.m. Their political convictions probably don't diverge much (only kinship sometimes bridges political quarrels), yet over these little cups of coffee, they debate the fine points of their differences incessantly. They also joke and tell stories, and in their fragmented state of twos and threes, take up their other favourite subject: relationships. Friendships, family relationships, the continuing saga of lovers – all are minutely examined and deep emotional intimacies are thus forged. Friends measure their closeness by the pain they've shared.

Like a family, such a *paréä* sometimes has a kind of incest taboo. Jokey flirtations are part of the *paréä's* spice but, for serious affairs, members of the opposite sex are quite literally so "familiar" that they seem more like siblings. Lovers are brought to the *paréä* more than found within it. Except perhaps at marriage, people don't leave the *paréä* to form a "couple". "Dating" itself is alien to Greek experience.

The *paréä* nurtures vehement loyalties, especially in the face of outsiders' criticisms. But such relentless intimacy can also be suffocating and breed a kind of bitchiness. *Paréä* life can verge on melodrama: imagined slights take on huge proportions. Sooner or later, there's a fight, or a cooling, and the membership changes.

Paréës fluctuate over time but flux is also built into the notion itself. The *paréä* is always expandable – a Greek doesn't fuss about bringing along a new friend uninvited. He expects from the rest the implicit response, "your friend is our friend". They, in turn, don't fuss over this new person's "unique individuality" – the point is to make him part of the group. At the *tavérna*, where the *paréä* typically gathers for long hours of jokes and singing over food and wine, chairs are always being added for friends who happen to come by. They cram chairs in until no more fit. Then everybody squeezes in, two broad bottoms sharing each lumpy, hard-backed chair. Comfort succumbs to sociability, but nobody complains.

For *paréä* life has its own etiquette. "Being together" is its object, not eating or drinking. In the *tavérna*, the *paréä* members submit these creaturely needs to a grander, collective ideal. Endless plates of food come to rest not at each individual's place but haphazardly on the table. Each wields his fork to spear a morsel, then rests it. Meals like this can last for hours. That is the point. The table must be brimming – stinginess Greeks find contemptible, but greediness in *paréä* is almost as bad. So, for all their exhortations to others to "Eat!" they can be surprisingly reticent themselves.

The same goes for drinking. Greeks drink only with food, and never alone. The point is not to get drunk. Drinking is only a means to "opening up", to entering a pleasant and sociable state that Greeks call *kéfi*. For all they drink (and that's usually less than it first seems) there are fewer alcoholics here than anywhere else in Europe.

They regard with distaste tourists who drink to stupefaction – especially tourist women. Greeks may grudgingly respect a woman who can hold her liquor, but they are unforgiving when she can't. It's seen as another proof of the immorality they already take for granted. So the double standard operates here with a vengeance, and in more puritanical locales, females ostentatiously spike their retsína with quantities of soda water or Coca-Cola.

As they've eaten collectively – so do they pay. It used to be that men always paid for women, splitting the bill equally among themselves. Things are more in flux these days. Men will pay for wives and girlfriends, but in university *paréës* everyone is equally impoverished, regardless of sex, so all contribute. Guests, especially if they are foreigners, are a stickier matter. Greeks are proud of their reputation for hospitality. And they would never let a foreigner pay his

– and especially her – way without a fight. But they are sensitive about being taken advantage of. The best policy is always to plunk your money down with the rest – indeed, to show your willingness to pay with as much drama and determination as you can muster – and if you find yourself overruled, to accept graciously.

GRAFFITI

In Procopius' day, Constantinople was brought to a standstill as fans of rival chariot teams, the Reds, Blues and Greens, rampaged through the streets. Nowadays the chariot-racing is gone, but its place in Greek life is filled by politics.

Come election-time, Athens' streets are jammed solid with thousands of banners, flags and posters as supporters flood into Syntagma Square for the big rallies. Walls, bridges, the bare sides of apartment blocks become so many mottled configurations of slogans. Hit squads from the political parties' youth groups head out at night to whitewash opponents' slogans and paint up their own. Outside the towns, it's the same story.

Graffiti are essential to political success in Greece and they impose requirements of their own. Above all, colour. If you think about it, the choice is limited: white is out since it won't show up against whitewash; yellow likewise. Black is confined to the extreme Right. The conservative New Democracy has bagged blue, a light royal which conveniently echoes the national flag. The KKE, the communist party (now split into two) of course uses red.

One of the keys to the success of the socialist party, PASOK, it's said, was its appropriation of the colour green: highly visible, obviously suggesting close ties with the natural world, which helped to offset the party's radical reputation in the eyes of conservative farmers.

The other essential behind effective graffiti is the snappy slogan. Here's where the difference emerges between parties who know what they want and those who can't

make up their minds. One word won the 1981 election for Andréas Papandréou: *allaghí* (change). This simple formula had already worked wonders four years earlier against a feeble array of alternatives such as New Democracy's own "It found Chaos: It created a State" which arguably might have been true but certainly fell flat, failing even to rhyme properly. The centre party's own motto, *allaghí me sigouriá* (change with security), was a laughable imitation of PASOK, a virtual admission of defeat.

PASOK's rise to power took place under the painted rays of a bright green sun, a symbol which did not have the disturbing effects that one might have expected. Defying the laws of nature seemed only to underline the party's potency.

This idea of a political rebirth, the dawning of a new era, was helped by the charisma of Andréas Papandréou himself. Charismatic political leaders recur in Greek affairs, but usually in the guise of elderly father figures, such as the Cretan Venizélos. The sons of such men tend to remain in their father's shadow. But the case of the Papandréou dynasty is different; Andréas' father George achieved charismatic status late in life and was popularly known as "The Old Man". His son, referred to universally as "Andréas", managed to retain his charismatic mantle whilst keeping his youthful image – an unprecedented feat in recent history and one which kept his opponents on the defensive.

But *húbris* is another word coined in Greece, and Andréas' "overweening pride", evidenced by governmental scandals and extramarital shenanigans, finally toppled the wily pseudo-socialist. After a gruelling bout of run-off elections, New Democracy's blue

HOSPITALITY

Almost every travel guide to Greece opens its entry on "hospitality" with the story of Zeus, the disguised stranger-guest. And who are we to break tradition? In its ancient form – and still so, today – the word usually translated as "hospitality" was a bit of an oxymoron. *Philoksenía* is a compound word, combining *phílo*, "to love", and *xénos*, a word meaning – oddly – both "stranger" and "guest".

Now, those were pretty rough times, and people tended to be a little suspicious of strangers turning up on their doorstep. But Zeus, it appears, liked to travel incognito, the better to seduce the lovely mortals he fancied. So Zeus, a trifle opportunistically perhaps, decreed *philoksenía* not just an exalted virtue, but also an obligation.

The *Xénos*, he said, should be treated in a princely fashion, because – who knows? – that stranger might really be a god in disguise, even Zeus himself!

Though the onslaught of mass tourism has jaded it a bit, hospitality remains a virtue. Indeed, it is the very quality Greeks believe most distinguishes them from other peoples, especially the cooler hearts of cooler climes. They're positively competitive about it: every house insists its own hospitality is more genuine than the neighbour's, and "our" village is somehow always more hospitable than the one down the road. In some ways, the "truth" is in the declamation. But certain places achieve a national reputation. Cretans – never a folk for middling gestures – are thought to be as extreme in hospitality as they are in temper. Predictably, the label becomes self-fulfilling. Other locales (Chíos? The Máni?) fare less well in the eyes

of their compatriots – but being an issue of local patriotism, well, it's all rather subjective, isn't it?

Hospitality isn't measured merely by its lavishness. It helps, of course. At weddings or namedays when guests are being fed, Greeks orchestrate an atmosphere of plenty – of copious quantities of meat, wine glasses constantly refilled, of a table choked with platters and bottles – so that all can enjoy themselves, and also, so that none can call them "cheap". Yet poverty is not an insurmountable barrier. Greeks quote little homilies about the poor having little but giving of it freely, and the old woman who brings a glass of fresh water, bread and a few olives to feed unexpected guests (since it's all she has) is thought almost saintly. What counts, ideally, is purity of motive, a selfless generosity which compels one to give whatever one has – however great or humble – without thought of reward.

The reality is more complex. Hospitality creates a relationship, but it is not of equals. The host brings the guest into his own domain; then increases his prestige by giving. The guest, receiving, becomes "obliged" to the host. Once you know this, the common power struggle over food suddenly makes sense. The guest is obliged, ultimately, to receive but is at the same time "ashamed" to seem too eager. Proverbially, the guest was supposed to refuse an offer of food or drink twice, and only – after much coaxing – to relent the third time. It's quite a delicate game, really. It can be disastrous for the unsuspecting traveller. The Greek host thinks your refusals are just politeness, that by saying "no" you really mean "yes". There aren't any magic solutions. You can try to argue "diabetes" or "bad teeth" if you can't bear the sight of another dish of jellied fruit, but be prepared to accept something in the end so as not to insult your hosts. And if you're invited to dinner, it wouldn't hurt to skip a meal or two before.

Most travellers will have more superficial contacts with Greeks, but few will leave without being invited – at least once – into the house for coffee. Fortunately, rituals of hospitality have a fairly standardised form (though this varies regionally). Their formality doesn't compromise their sincerity. And that very predictability can be a boon to the traveller. A few phrases, carefully memorised and strategically deployed, can put you on surer footing.

If you are invited for coffee, you will probably be led to the *salóni*, the formal living room, and left to wait while your hostess retires to the kitchen. She will return in a few minutes with a tray covered in a doily, with a tiny cup of coffee, a saucer of cookies and a glass of water. Take the coffee first: raise it up slightly, and say *Stin iyiá sas*! ("To your health!"). When you've finished, raise the glass slightly, toasting your hostess, and drink the water. When you leave, you can say *Sas ef haristó*! ("I thank you") or even better, *Hárika polí*. The latter is something you say when you've just been introduced ("I'm very pleased [to meet you]") but here, it can also mean "I've enjoyed myself." Hospitality, after all, is about both.

ICONS

To be Greek is, in the case of 97 percent of the population, to be Greek Orthodox. True, many people demonstrate no interest in Orthodoxy. When asked what faith he belonged to, one young man pulled out his state identity card and said, "This card says I'm Orthodox. Personally, I don't really know."

Traditionally, Greek identity has always been strongly bound up with Orthodoxy. This includes the period of the Byzantine Empire when the populace viewed itself as dwelling in a world which had reached its perfect state and was a reflection of the Kingdom of Heaven. Later, after the Ottoman conquest (1453), the Greeks were administered as followers of the Orthodox faith, not as members of a particular national group. The Church was thus the main representative of Greek national identity until independence in 1832.

To those brought up in the largely Protestant if not wholly secular surroundings of northern Europe or North America, the religion of Greece appears threateningly mystical and obsessed with ritual. Any casual visitor to Greece could potentially pass the same verdict as the great Protestant theologian Harnack who wrote: "I do not expect to be contradicted if I answer that this official ecclesiasticism with its priests and its cult, with all its vessels, saints, vestments, pictures and amulets, with its ordinances of fasting and its festivals, has nothing to do with the religion of Christ."

Such a view is uncharitable in the extreme. The use of icons, for example, is one of the most frequently misunderstood aspects of Orthodoxy. These beautiful and highly stylized pictures are not objects of idolatrous worship, but this was precisely the indictment of the so-called iconoclasts in the 7th and 8th centuries. In an effort to purify the religion of this idolatry they proceeded to literally deface thousands of icons throughout Byzantium. Intact pre-9th-century icons are consequently very rare.

The use of icons was ultimately upheld by the Church with the understanding that icons only symbolise the holy person depicted upon them. They are an instrument by means of which this holy person may be venerated. In no instance are they themselves objects of worship. This accounts for the absence of naturalistic realism in their execution. On the contrary, the depiction of each personage is governed by strict conventions and approaches an ideal type.

Through the material icon we are directed beyond to a transcendental glory. As John of Damascus wrote, "I do not worship matter but I worship the Creator of matter, who for my sake became material and deigned to dwell in matter, who through matter effected my salvation. I will not cease from worshipping the matter through which my salvation has been effected."

The icons painted on the walls of churches throughout Greece are an early form of animation. They are a book explaining the Orthodox faith for those unable to read – a writing in images.

Icons are not only revered in church; virtually every house contains an icon stand (*iconostásis*) containing various icons deemed to have a particular importance for the family. They may represent certain saints for whom family members are named. Almost all personal names in Greece are shared in common with a saint and instead of birthdays, saints' days are celebrated (see Namedays). In times of need a person may beseech these saints for help.

Perhaps the single most widely revered icon in Greece is that of the Virgin Mary on the island of Tínos. It is said to have been painted by St Luke and to have special wonderworking power. Every year on 15 August, the celebration of the Assumption of the Virgin, thousands of pilgrims flock to the island to make requests of the Virgin or to leave devotions as repayment for miracles that were performed (see pictures on pages 212–213). In one corner of the monastery which houses the icon a pile of crutches left behind by those healed on the spot can be seen.

In Orthodoxy the miraculous and wondrous seem to be closer at hand than in other Christian traditions. When a miracle happens the people are not particularly surprised. In fact they expect them to happen. Stories abound regarding people who have been "illuminated" by one of the saints and are able to tell the future. Other traditions concern those who imprudently decided to work on the day of St Spyridon, or some other saint, and were smitten for not resting.

Orthodoxy is more than a religion. It is a way of life. Orthodox feasts mark public holidays and so touch everyone. Greeks may not all believe in it, but none can deny that it has exerted an influence over them.

JUNTA

At 2 a.m. on the morning of 21 April 1967, the people of Greece discovered that during the night the army, in a swift, well-planned coup, had overthrown the government and in its place established a military regime. Using a NATO contingency plan developed for use in the event of a communist invasion from Greece's northern neighbours, and codenamed "Prométheus", the conspirators justified their putsch on the grounds that they "were saving Greece from the precipice of communism".

Later in the morning of 21 April a decree was issued proclaiming martial law. Various articles in the constitution guaranteeing human rights were suspended, special military courts were established in Athens and Thessaloníki, political parties were dissolved and the right to strike abolished. Newspapers were submitted to strict censorship and were required to publish exactly what was supplied by the government, and all gatherings, indoors or outdoors, were forbidden.

Many thousands of people with a record of left-wing political views or activity were arrested and sent into exile in bleak camps on remote islands. A large number of parliamentary leaders were taken into custody.

The new government ran true to form. Like other military dictatorships, its measures were alternately savage and ludicrous. Its leaders, the Colonels, were fanatical, if unintelligent, anti-communist salvationists who, no less than Hitler, saw politics in black and white terms: a simple and fierce contest between good and evil. Like the pre-war dictator General Metaxás, they placed much emphasis on the need to discipline and reform the Greek character. They condemned long hair on men and mini-skirts on women and ordered both to go to church.

Even foreign tourists were subjected to some of these regulations, though the government was anxious not to frighten them away altogether. But like other "moralists", they did not escape making themselves ridiculous. For example, through the official propaganda machine they tried to humiliate the Nobel Prize-winning poet George Seféris for handing out a memorable statement of protest against the dictatorship; they deprived the celebrated film star Melina Mercoúri of her citizenship for criticising them; they banned the songs of Míkis Theodorákis, a leading composer, because he had been a left-wing deputy; and they censored the tragedies and comedies of the classical theatre.

After the coup, little was heard of the communist threat which was supposed to justify it, and the seizure of the papers of the left-wing party failed to produce any evidence in support. The coup was a simple seizure of power by a handful of military bigots. The regime resorted to torture and brutality on a big scale as a deliberate instrument of policy to maintain its grip on power. Torture by the police was not unknown in Greece but the extent to which it was practised and approved by the dictators appalled the outside world when the facts became known.

The American government, under Richard Nixon, viewed these developments with no more than embarrassment and after a brief period of indecision gave the regime its accolade in the shape of arms supplies. Greece as a *place d'armes* for NATO seemed more important than Greece as a conforming member of the society of free and democratic nations which NATO was proclaimed to be.

The first blow in the downfall of the junta was initiated by students. In November 1973 a large number of them occupied the Athens Polytechnic and university buildings in Thessaloníki and Pátras. When it became clear that they were attracting widespread sympathy, and when the Athens Polytechnic students began broadcasting appeals on a clandestine radio band for a worker-student alliance to overthrow the dictatorship, Papadópoulous, the regime's strong-man, sent in troops and tanks to crush them. The eviction of the students from the Polytechnic was carried out with extreme brutality, and at least 40 students and other sympathisers were killed, several hundreds wounded and thousands arrested. This ruthless demonstration of force in the centre of Athens turned the stomachs of most Greeks. The days of the dictatorship were numbered.

The regime collapsed eight months later, in July 1974, under the weight of its bungling in Cyprus; this led to a confrontation with Turkey and a military call-up for which the military rulers of the country had prepared with a farcical incompetence reminiscent of the equally empty militarism of an earlier Mediterranean dictator, Mussolini. The conservative leader Karamanlís, who had been living in exile in Paris, returned to Greece in the early hours of 24 July to oversee the dismantling of the dictatorship and the return to democratic rule. The brutal, corrupt and unpopular dictatorship had ended as abruptly as it had begun.

KAMÁKI

Kamáki literally means a fishing trident, but now the word also refers to picking up or "hunting" foreign tourist women, and to the "hunter" himself. While picking up women is nothing new, the Greek kamáki knows that he is playing a well-defined game with its own rules, techniques and vocabulary. Another less romantic mythology has built up around this seasonal activity, fuelled by press coverage, television and, above all, by the exaggerated "fishing stories" of the perpetrators.

The development of kamáki has paralleled the increase in tourism in Greece over the past 30 years. In the 1960s young Greek women were extremely restricted in their movements, and were kept closely tied to the family. There was therefore little prospect for romance, sex, or even an evening out with a young woman for the comparatively independent young man. The arrival of women tourists, who were not only sexually liberated but were sometimes in search of "the four S's" (sun, sand, sea and sex), was an opportunity not to be missed. Kamáki started to be practised wherever foreign women were present, and not only by organized connoisseurs such as the members of the former "Octopus" club in Naúplia, but by any man who cared to try his luck. The "professionals", who roam certain highly touristic areas such as Syntagma Square in Athens, are said to make a living from their occupation, and they are certainly offensive to many tourist women. It could also be that their widely-publicised philosophy influ-

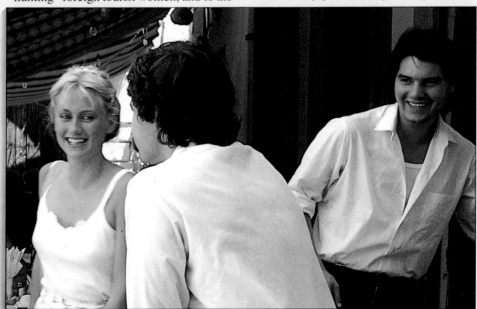

ences the way tourists view the potentially more genuine attentions of other Greek men.

The aim of the pursuit is to have sex and, according to the *kamáki* rules, as soon as possible after meeting a tourist woman, and with as many women as possible. Competitive friends compare "scores" at the end of the summer season, and winter-time *kamáki* conversation dwells on the glory of summertime conquests. It is obviously the chase and not the "kill" that provides the entertainment. Inexperienced men may get no further than asking dozens of foreign women for coffee, and being rejected.

Alternatively, the more sophisticated hunter realises that the initial approach is crucial, and that he has to survey the hunting-ground, lay traps, and be ready to approach, or lay off until the time is ripe.

The intention is to make contact with the tourist woman without her realising that she is being picked up by a *kamáki*. One *kamáki* ploy is to ask the woman the way to the Post Office, and if she does not know, explain the directions to her. The newer the arrival to Greece, the better, because she will not have become wise to the ways of Greek men. Women of different nationalities are said to require different techniques, and among the first questions a tourist woman is asked is "Where are you from?"

There are various theories about which nationalities are easy, awkward, arrogant or beautiful, but all agree that if the respondent is Greek or Italian, there is little hope for success, and one should try elsewhere: Mediterranean women know the old tricks of their men too well to be duped.

If the tourist woman agrees to go for coffee or whatever, she is unlikely to be seen as independent, but rather as naïve. Here lies the contradiction of the game: a *kamáki* will not view himself as the prey of a foreign female *kamáki*. A tourist woman who is evidently out to "catch" men in numbers will probably be labelled a prostitute, as a Greek woman would be. The classic *kamáki* wants at least to appear to be in control; the kudos comes from luring unwilling or unknowing women into bed.

In general among Greeks, *kamáki* has a bad reputation. Most foreign women scoff at these men, and even former protagonists claim that the sport has lost its pioneering glamour, and become crude and vulgar.

However, some see the *kamáki* as continuing the long tradition of hospitality in Greece. He can introduce or add to the delights of being abroad with sparkling sun and sea, exotic music and food, romance, and other elements of the ideal holiday. The foreign woman who understands the rules of *kamáki* can choose whether or not to play the game.

LANGUAGE

Imagine a language which has two sets of unrelated words for basic concepts, such as "nose", "cheek", "shoe", "house", "door", "street", "moon", "red" and "white". Suppose, also, that, together with its own distinct grammar, one set is used in everyday life, while the other is obligatory in official parlance, in education, and newspapers.

That language is Modern Greek, or at least it was until 1974. For the first 150 years after Greece gained its independence from the Ottoman Empire in 1821, there were two versions of Greek, used in different situations, which overlapped in pronunciation and in many areas of vocabulary and grammar, but differed radically in others. This situation is not unique to Greece. The Arabs, for instance, also use different versions of Arabic in different circumstances.

The Greeks have traditionally revered the language of ancient Greek literature and the *New Testament* – almost as much as the Arabs have valued the language of the *Koran*. For centuries they have felt that their writings should depart as little as possible from the language of their illustrious ancestors and the language of their holy book.

Some acquaintance with the history of Greek language is essential for an understanding of Greek culture as a whole over the past 200 years, since the controversies over the language sum up the conflicting attitudes of the modern Greeks to their ancient compatriots. It has never been doubted in Greece that the present-day inhabitants of the country are the direct descendants of the ancient Greeks, who laid the foundations of European civilisation.

This assumption presented the Greeks

who were preparing the way for independence in the 1820s with the problem of what national ideology to adopt in order both to unite the nation from within and to present a national image to the outside world. Within Greece itself – and among adherents to the Greek Orthodox faith in general – a bewildering variety of different languages was spoken and the Greek language itself was split into various dialects, some of them mutually incomprehensible. Nevertheless, Greek was the most widespread language spoken in the area, and Greek (albeit Greek of more than one and a half millennia before) was the language of the Church. So Greek intellectuals of the early 19th century agreed that the best way to cement national unity and to secure assistance from the West in their national liberation struggle was to promote as much as possible their links with Ancient Greece, to which Europeans and Americans at the time had a strong romantic attachment. Their case was supported by the undoubtedly close connection between the ancient and modern Greek languages.

From here on, however, there was profound disagreement. Some Greek intellectuals believed that the modern language was crude and barbaric (this they attributed to centuries of Turkish rule) and that the only way for the Greeks to prosper was a return to the pristine beauties of Ancient Greek, which they saw as a peak of perfection from which any later developments represented a decline. This return would ensure the rebirth of ancient Greek culture, their belief being that anyone who learned to speak like Plato would also begin to think like Plato.

Connected with this was the problem of what the modern Greeks should call themselves. From the early centuries of the Christian era until the beginning of the 19th century almost all Greeks had called themselves "Romans" and their spoken language "Romaic", since they were conscious of belonging to the traditions of the Byzantine Empire, which was historically the continuation of the Roman Empire. They tended to reserve the words "Hellene" and "Hellenic" (i.e. Greek) for the pagan ancient Greeks and their language.

By insisting on calling themselves and their compatriots "Hellenes", some intellectuals were able to envisage the resurrection of the ancient Greek language along with its name; yet at the same time, whereas everyone knows the difference between the Italians and the Romans, the word "Greek" is used indiscriminately and confusingly to refer to the people and language of both ancient and modern Greece.

Others, realising the impracticality of persuading the Greeks to renounce their mother tongue, preferred to look at the example of European nations such as the French, who had reached cultural eminence after abandoning Latin and cultivating their own language. These intellectuals argued that only through the use of the spoken language could the Greeks become sufficiently educated and enlightened to drag their country out of the economic and cultural morass into which centuries of subjection had sunk them. They urged their compatriots to follow the example of the ancient Greeks, who had used their mother tongue to reach the heights of civilisation.

Among those who opposed the imposition of a fully resurrected Ancient Greek was Adamántios Koraïs (1748–1833), a former merchant and physician living in Paris who became the leader of the intellectual movement preparing for Greece's independence. But although he constantly attacked the archaists, he was equally scathing about those who insisted on using the modern language as it was spoken by the common people. Instead he proposed a "cleansed" version of Modern Greek, corrected according to the rules of Ancient Greek grammar.

This language would have the advantage of being not too far removed either from any of the modern Greek dialects (thus avoiding giving an unfair advantage to the speakers of any one dialect) or from Ancient Greek. It would display both the underlying unity among the speakers of Greek in the present day and the profound identity (despite superficial differences) between the ancient and the modern Greeks. Koraïs' compromise language, which was neither fully ancient nor fully modern (and had never been spoken by anyone), was adopted by the fathers of the nation as the basis of the official language, later known as *katharévousa* (literally "the purifying language").

It is difficult for non-Greeks to imagine the almost magic power invested in the ancient written word in Greece. Throughout the 19th century Greek intellectuals, frustrated and disillusioned by the problems facing the Greek state (poverty, disunity, economic and political subjection to the West), seemed convinced that every aspect of modern Greece represented an inferior and tarnished version of some glorious ancient counterpart. The ancient language was looked upon, quite irrationally, as an instrument of absolute perfection; and – precisely because it was no longer spoken, but only written – it appeared to be timeless and eternal, exempt from the change and decay that affect all living bodies (including, of course, spoken language, which is constantly in a state of flux).

It is notoriously difficult to create a standardised language. Look at the differences between the varieties of English spoken within any one English-speaking country, let alone in different English-speaking countries. The Greek intellectual leaders created an added difficulty of trying to forge a standard that would contain material from two separate, albeit related, languages (Ancient and Modern Greek), each of which had never been standardised in itself but was split into widely diverging dialects.

So any user of *katharévousa* had to walk an unsteady tightrope and avoid falling into either incomprehensibility or vulgarity. Those without laborious training in such verbal acrobatics (which meant the vast majority of the Greek population) could choose to ignore the official language altogether and thus exclude themselves from direct access to the law and the state apparatus. Alternatively, they could parrot-learn set formulas which they might not fully comprehend but which would in any case enable them to muddle through.

While the academics were busy deriding the popular language, the poets were writing in it and exhorting people to abandon their prejudices against it. By the end of the 19th century almost all creative writers were using the "demotic" (spoken) language in their works, so that *katharévousa* became solely the language of official parlance and no longer that of cultural life. Nevertheless the struggle continued: people were killed in riots involving adherents of the two opposing linguistic variants in 1901 and again in 1903, and the article of the Greek Constitution specifying *katharévousa* as the official language (inserted in 1911, in response to this violent polarisation) was not abolished until after the Colonels' dictatorship fell in 1974.

During this century the language controversy has often tended to be identified with political divisions; *katharévousa* being promoted by the Right and demotic by the Left. It was partly because *katharévousa* had become tainted by its identification with the Colonels' regime that the more liberal (though still conservative) government of

Karamanlís that immediately followed it was able to begin replacing *katharévousa* by demotic in all areas of public life.

But the Greeks haven't stopped arguing about their language; indeed, it is still a frequent topic of discussion among intellectuals and non-intellectuals alike. Beginning in 1981 Papandréou's socialist government continued the process of dismantling *katharévousa*, and the more laid-back style of its speeches and pronouncements offended many who have found it hard to accustom themselves to a casual use of language for official purposes. The government's abolition of many of the actually functionless diacritics used in writing Greek for 2,000 years (but not in the Classical period), which caused so much misery and embarrassment both to school-children and adults, has been widely criticised.

More justified is the criticism of the official policy on the teaching of Ancient Greek, which used to be a compulsory high-school subject but now cannot be studied at school before the age of 16. These moves are often seen as ploys to cut modern Greece off from its roots, depriving the nation of its firm basis in the past and making it easy prey for Americans, Soviets, or any other foreign power that might wish to exert its cultural dominance.

The Greeks' desire to bridge the gap between their language and culture and those of the ancients has enormously enriched modern Greek life. However, the Greeks need not be ashamed (as generations of school-teachers tried to make them) of the language and culture that developed over the past millennium. Pride in their ancestors often gave the Greeks either an excessive sense of self-satisfaction or, conversely, a feeling of inferiority in relation to their glorious ancestors and their unsatisfactory contemporary condition. Others held the more constructive view that the Greeks should be proud of having kept the Greek language alive through successive periods of foreign domination. Having had their native language wrenched from their mouths in the first grades of school, the Greeks have now been given back their mother tongue.

The Greeks were probably the first people to carry out a successful war of national liberation against an alien imperial power; but the poet Dionysios Solomós warned in 1824, while this war was being waged, that the Greeks would not be free until they had rid themselves not only of their Turkish occupiers but of the pedants who tried to teach them that they were something other than what they were. This second liberation did not come until 1974, a century and a half after the first.

Nevertheless, one positive consequence of the language controversy is a fondness shared by all Greeks – whether peasants,

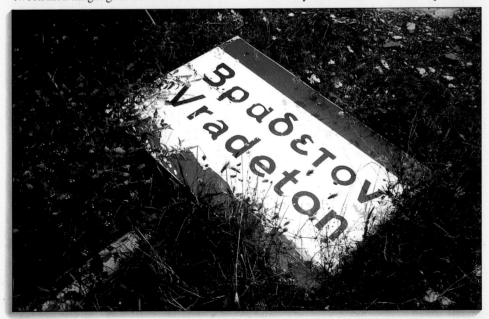

poets, neither, or both – for playing with the different varieties of their language. For the Greeks, language isn't simply a means of expression, but an arena in which they can practise their creativity, display their wits, and generally have fun.

MOVIES

On sultry summer nights in Greece, most of the evening entertainment occurs outdoors, and movies are no exception. Few indoor cinemas are air-conditioned. Some are equipped with a rare innovation: The convertible roof remains closed during the screenings before sundown, then movable panels creakily slide apart to expose the audience to cool breezes and an occasional starry sky.

The rest of the indoor cinemas moved to empty gravel-covered lots, alleys or rooftops where people are usually seated on sagging lawn chairs. According to the union of outdoor cinema owners, a survey of tourists named the open-air cinemas as the number two tourist attraction in Athens after the Acrópolis.

The atmosphere is appropriately relaxed.

Whole families attend and snack bars serve soft drinks, beer, crackers and crisps, but no fresh popcorn. A few operate as cinematic *ouzeriés* where one can sit at little tables and nibble on *mezéthes* (hors d'oeuvres) while sipping an *oúzo*. At drive-in movies, porn films are usually featured and carhops deliver orders of sandwiches, mini-pizzas and chilled bottles of wine to those adult viewers who are reticent about emerging from their vehicles.

Since many theatres are located in the centre of the city, the volume is decreased during the late showing out of consideration for the neighbours. One has a choice of viewing a rather dim picture with adequate sound at the first screening, which starts before dark, or a clearly defined image with a faint soundtrack during the late showings. Fortunately for foreign viewers, Greeks, in contrast to the French or Italians, prefer subtitles to dubbing, so only original language versions are shown.

In any case, open-air cinemas are a relaxing, quaint form of entertainment. No new releases are shown during the summer. But there is a veritable feast of films to choose from, including popular re-releases of the previous season and week-long festivals of older classics by notable directors such as Hitchcock, Bergman or Fellini, plus the inevitable Kung Fu movies and slapstick comedies.

Although cinema attendance has dropped in the past few years, the 150 or so indoor cinemas remaining in the greater Athens area are still doing respectable business. The admission price is low, set at an average of 500 drachmas. Much of the decrease in attendance must be attributed to the increased popularity of video players.

Traditionally, domestic fare topped the popularity list but this has been reversed in recent years when foreign action adventures and romances have sold the most tickets. The heavy European influence in Greek cinema made many of the quality films too "arty" and slow-moving for general audiences who have grown used to a diet of fast-paced imports, or the crudely-made buffoonery of some Greek comedies. Technically speaking, Greek films show high standards in cinematography and sound.

Greeks often wander into a film in the middle and eat and talk throughout it. Yet, lest one think there is no serious audience, a few art houses in central Athens are doing a solid business by booking earnest European imports and a smattering of American independents. Meanwhile, the after-midnight movie trend has re-emerged in Athens in a few central cinemas which show "B" grade thrillers, science fiction and horror flicks. They inspire the spirited and vociferous young audiences to shout humorous commentaries and to create innovative sound effects.

Only a few Greek low-budget farcical comedies and a handful of quality films sold more than 100,000 tickets in recent seasons. The gulf between commercial movies and artistic ones has been great. However, the most popular domestic films of recent years managed to combine "Greekness" with well-developed scripts that have international appeal.

The Civil War, following World War II, had been a forbidden topic in Greek cinema until the election of a socialist government in 1981. Pandelis Voulgaris' *Stone Years*, based on a true story, focused on the romance of a couple who were arrested for their Communist affiliations and were only reunited after 20 years' imprisonment. This film has been on the foreign festival circuit and was included in the second series of the "Seven from Greece" programme which toured the major US cities.

It is painfully obvious, given the country's small population, that Greek films cannot even recoup their initial investment with domestic distribution alone. The Greek Film Centre, now state-run, contributes up to 50 percent of the films' budgets. In order to promote international distribution of Greek films, it has stepped up its festival participation to 35 or 40, including the prestigious Cannes and Berlin Festivals.

The Thessaloníki Film Festival, held each year in October in the National Theatre, screens all of the 20 or so quality films made each year. The notorious third balcony "peanut gallery" is jammed with restless students who are prone to clap and stamp their feet while shouting synchronised slogans if a movie is not appreciated. It can be a gruelling experience for a director. However, those who have not fled down the back stairs might be surprised by an enthusiastic ovation at the end of the film.

NAMEDAYS

"What's in a name?" asked Romeo. He should have asked a Greek! For here, all sorts of stories piggyback onto names, if you know how to read them. Place of origin, for instance: *Theodorákis* is clearly Cretan, for a name ending with *ákis* (meaning "little") bears the slyly ironic tag of this ferocious people. Any *Yánnoglou* is sure to have ties to "The City" (Constantinople), and the common suffix *poulos* (meaning "bird", or "child of") points back to the Peloponnése, as in the case of one clownish ex-dictator, Papadópoulos, "son of the priest".

Since 1983, women are obliged to keep their "maiden" name for life. For legal matters, that is. But before the revision of Family Law, a woman seldom imagined – unless she were rich or Melina Mercoúri – keeping her father's surname. Rendered in the possessive case, female surnames (single and married alike) are grammatically telling: Mrs Papadópoulos really reads "Papadópoulos's Mrs". In mainland Greece, a woman traditionally lost even her first name at marriage, and was known by the feminised form of her husband's: Yiórgos' wife became "Yiórgina". The symbolism persists. At weddings, girlfriends of the bride jokingly write their names on the sole of her shoe, and explain that she whose name is "rubbed out" first will marry first.

Names are not matters of fashion (how many Yuppies do you know named Mildred or Virgil? How many *grandes dames* named Tracey?). You find the odd "Tzimmi" – that Greek-American who made good in Tuscarawa and came home to retire – and "Bábbis", and (as if "Maria" were not perfectly respectable) "Mary". And in eras when neo-classical romanticism rages, mischievous middle-class toddlers are saddled with ponderous names like Kleánthis Andrómachi and Aristotélis. Even Lord Byron, the English poet who, though he never saw a battlefield, died a hero of the Greek Revolution, is regularly reincarnated.

A Greek baby is not fully a person when it

is born, but only when it is baptised and given a name. Baptism, a ritual more solemn than marriage, which initiates the child into the Orthodox community, is celebrated between 40 days and a year after birth. Until then, the child is called simply "Baby", and if (as was more common in past years of high infant mortality) it died before someone – anyone – could baptise it "in the air" by "making the cross" over it three times and uttering a name, it would not be buried in the church graveyard, and its soul was thought to linger in a shadowy nether-world between hell and paradise.

Greeks are amazed at how Westerners name their children guided by little more than fashion and personal whim. They themselves follow strict rules: the first boy is named after the father's father, and the first girl after the father's mother (in mainland Greece) or the mother's mother (in most of the Aegéan islands). Naming the son after the father, as Americans do, is thought extremely unlucky, even vaguely incestuous: a premature usurping of the father's name. But between grandparents and grandchildren, the inheritance is not fraught. The grandmother greets with delight the baptism of a child with her name. While it ritually acknowledges her individual mortality, it nonetheless assures family continuity: "The name will be heard."

Property, too, may be linked to names. On many islands, first-born Kalliópe inherits the house from her mother, Marína, who inherited it from her mother, Kalliópe, and so on in an infinite alternation of Kalliópes and Marínas. Likewise, the boy "with the name" will inherit his grandfather's fields, and he (and his wife) will be obliged to mourn for him when he dies.

Certain events can distort this ideal pattern. A man with many nephews bearing his father's name will yield to his father-in-law's desire for a namesake, or a woman trying to conceive may visit the miraculous icon of a particular saint and entreat its help by promising to give the child its name. These do not alter the Greeks' sense that names connect one to a long line of ancestors, perpetually reproducing itself.

If you are Greek, your name links you not just to your own blood ancestors but to the entire Greek (or more accurately, Orthodox) community. Most Greek names refer to a saint or some holy quality, hence, "Sophía", the sacred wisdom. Birthday parties are for kids; the adult Greek has instead a "nameday", the day when the saint for whom he or she was named was "born into" the life hereafter, usually through a rather unpleasant martyrdom. This day is now "celebrated" by the Orthodox faithful. It's an ingenious system; everybody knows your nameday, sparing you the embarrassment of dropping hints to your friends when you want somebody to celebrate with. But there are a few new twists.

The one who celebrates "treats" the guests. The guest may bring sweets or flowers or a bottle of whisky, but the host provides the feast. On St Demétrios' Day, everyone with a friend or relative named Dimítris or Dímitra must "remember" him or her (and people often know many Dímitrises and Dímitras) by phoning or stopping by, and at the houses of all these Dímitrises and Dímitras, the evening is a jolly chaos of doorbells buzzing, phones ringing and a constant flow of guests slightly green with the evening's fifth peppermint liqueur, proffering formal good wishes, and absently munching roasted chickpeas.

Mortal namedays blend the formal and the festive, but for the saint it's a more lavish affair. Every community has a saint (sometimes several) who specially protects it, and on that patron saint's feastday, the Orthodox community celebrates with a *panayíri*. The word derives from ancient Greek, referring to a public assembly: all (*pan*) those gathered in the marketplace (*agora*). *Paniyíria* of pagan Greece honoured gods and goddesses in a manner which combined worship and pleasure, spiritual obligation and commercial interest.

From the 4th century onwards, however, celebrations of the Christian martyrs absorbed the form and many practices of the pagans, and the *panayíri* with its vast bazaar became a distinctively Byzantine institution. Church fathers then – as now – reviled the more worldly preoccupations of buyers and sellers. A Christian writer of the fourth century warned, "A believer must not go to a *panayíri* except to buy a slave, to take care of life and to buy certain other things fitting for existence."

Today's *panayíri* involves the entire community. The saints are honoured with prayer and processions, followed by feasting and dance into the small hours. Like its Byzantine predecessor, many a *panayíri* resembles a Balkan country fair. Crammed and haphazard on a dusty stretch of ground, often a good mile or two from the village, are parked a wild assortment of carts and caravans. At its edges, wizened old ladies and amputees sit cross-legged on shabby rags, beseeching believers, palms cupped for alms. Next to the van selling Sprite and cloying ice-cream bars is a horsecart spread with roasted chickpeas, peanuts, raisins and sunflower seeds. Wedged in between are tables covered with crocheted doilies and embroidered towels for sale to the girl preparing her trousseau, and next to that a table with religious trinkets. Amidst the crucifixes and "Lives of the Saints" pamphlets you can find tiny blue pupils cased in plastic, dangling alongside a silver cross, amulets against the "evil eye". (See "Evil Eye" on pages 276–77).

Baptismal names are public and fixed, but *paratsoúklia* celebrate the idiosyncrasies of individual lives. Nicknames of a sort, *paratsoúklia* are an insiders' code. Strangers and tax collectors aren't supposed to know them. Rude and ironic, they commemorate quirks of body and character: Manólis' brawny virility is wryly recalled in the feminised "Manola", Yiórgos' philanderings in "Pouli" ("Birdie"), Theofánis' melancholy in "Katsoufis" ("long-faced").

Men get *paratsoúklia* from their comrades, women hardly ever, except by way of men. The man who worked 20 years in America and returned to marry is dubbed "Amerikános", and his wife, "Amerikána", though she's never left Macedónia. Badges of individual peculiarity, they sometimes stick, and get passed on to sons and grandsons, until (with the "real" surname slowly erased from memory) the shaggy, secret *paratsoúkli* slips quietly into the bland respectability of an "official" surname.

ORAL TRADITION

Poetry matters in Greece, and this is due, in part, to the fact that for centuries it was sung, not read. Poetry has always been a kind of performance in Greece, a social event. Even today, contemporary poets can fill soccer stadiums with fans. Until the late 19th century Greek poetry had little in common with the solitary quill-pen traditions of other Western European cultures. This may be because oral poetry was a much more successful way of preserving Greek national identity during the many centuries that Greece was under foreign rule: writing could be censored but no despot could confiscate songs.

Even in this century oral transmission, because of its resistance to censorship, has been necessary. **Yánnis Rítsos** (born 1909), one of Greece's best-known poets, was sent to prison along with many other suspected communists during the civil war. There he continued to write his poems. He would bury them in bottles to keep them from the guards but the only way he could get them to his readers was with the help of freed prisoners who, before leaving, learned his poems by heart and smuggled them out.

The fall of Constantinople (or "The City" as Greeks commonly call it) paradoxically enough marked both the beginning of Turkish domination and of Modern Greek poetry. It is at this point that versions of folk songs still sung today were first recorded or referred to in literary texts. The stock formula "I come from The City", although obviously about the fall, is also found in modern folk songs, and the well-loved 16th-century Cretan romance *Erotókritos* incorporated many verses from folk songs, verses that are still familiar to Greeks. Since oral transmission is an inherently creative process, phrases are not expected to resemble their antecedents word for word; the old phrases serve merely as a structure on which to base new variations. While not all critics believe in a continuous poetic tradition dating back to Hómer, most agree that a certain continuity can be traced from the 15th century.

Until the War of Independence in 1821 and the founding of the Greek State, song and poetry were inseparably linked, whether composed on paper or passed down orally from generation to generation. In fact writing and singing were often equated.

But with the emancipation from the Turks national identity was no longer a clandestine matter. Oral transmission, formerly the *only* transmission possible, now was seen as unreliable. Writing – more fixed and more permanent – became the preferred means for spreading nationalist ideology. The folk song was a stepping stone for poets but not an adequate means of expression in itself. It wasn't reliable enough.

One of the first proponents of a National Greek Literature was the poet **Dionysios Solomós** (1798–1857) from the Iónian Islands. In a letter to a friend he expressed his interest in klephtic folk songs but also stressed that the poet's task was different: "Klephtic poetry is fine and interesting as an ingenuous manifestation by the Klephts of their lives, thoughts and feelings. It does not have the same interest on our lips; the nation requires from us the treasure of our individual intelligence clothed in national forms."

As a matter of fact, Solomós' *Hymn to Freedom* has become the Greek national anthem. Nationalist poets such as Solomós may have criticised the ingenuousness of the oral tradition but their poems always aspired to song. Perhaps a similar tendency in British poetry explains Rudyard Kipling's decision to translate Solomós' hymn:

We know thee of old,
Oh, divinely restored,
By the light of thine eyes
And the light of thy Sword.

From the graves of our slain
Shall thy valour prevail
As we greet thee again –
Hail, Liberty! Hail!

Along with educators who struggled over which Greek to teach, the *demotic* or the purist hybrid of ancient and modern called *katharévousa* (see Language), poets were also frequently debating language. Their indebtedness to the oral tradition and their romantic organicism made them favour demotic Greek over the more synthetic *katharévousa*. Written poetry was not viewed as particularly different from sung poetry; it was just one step further in the natural development of a Greek National Literature.

Kostis Palamás (1859–1943) sets up the homeless gypsy as the modern Greek hero who blasphemes tyranny in all forms, not only the Turk but also the supremacy of Ancient Hellas and those who wanted to reinstate her using *katharévousa*:

I fear no Turk.
Slavery cannot strike me down
Nor can your Hellas dazzle me.
No outworn creed or cult
Can drug me with its incense.
If I discover a papyrus, I burn it
to make heat or light.
Unconcerned I watch it kindle
In whatever mouldering ruin it may be,
Palace, abbey, school or temple...

It would be too simple even in as brief an overview as this to suggest that Greek poetry in the 19th and 20th centuries was all lyricism and nationalism. Over in Alexandria, Greece's greatest modern poet, **Constantine Caváfy** (1863–1933) was doing something totally different. His poetry emphasised writing over song. His poetry seemed to suggest that the human intimacy associated with the oral tradition was no longer possible.

His historical frame was neither the glories of classical Greece nor the emancipation from the Turks but rather the slow decay of the pre-Christian and Christian eras. He invoked the pathos of deterioration, and repeatedly poetry was the only solace.

Written language had the power to construct something material out of what was being lost. Writing for Caváfy was not just a more durable substitute for singing as it was for Solomós and Palamás but a radically different means of expression. The poem took the place of what was missing. It could even fill the geographical space left by the destruction of a city.

Even in his love poems there is the sense that, by writing, a poem becomes a physical replacement for the absent loved ones.

Try to keep them, poet,
those erotic visions of yours,
however few of them there are that can
be stilled.

Put them, half-hidden, in your lines.
Try to hold them, poet,
when they come alive in your mind
at night or in the noonday brightness.

In Caváfy's poetry, memory and experience merge to become one in a distinctly written formulation.

Although the literary establishment to this day promotes poetry that is more indebted to the oral tradition, to the supremacy and intimacy of the voice, an alternative canon might be traced back to Caváfy's more textual verse. This alternative canon would be more concerned with writing as the recognition of a loss, than writing as the preserver of a glorious past.

Outside of Greece, Caváfy is certainly Greece's only well-known exponent of this less lyrical style. But inside Greece there are many poets whose poetry problematises language and prioritises writing over singing (for example, the poetry of Kostas Karyotakis and some of the surrealist poets like Andréas Embiríkos and Níkos Engonópoulos). Yet since the lyrical half of Greek poetry is more readily available in translation we may perhaps concentrate on that and only intermittently refer to the less well-known poetry.

Continuing in the wake of Solomós and Palamás comes another nationalist poet, **Angelos Sikelianós** (1884–1951). But in Sikelianós' poetry "being Greek" has be-

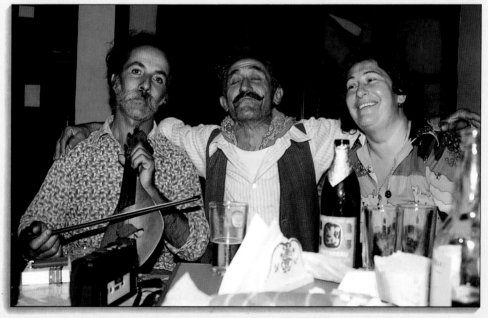

come less of the collective project it was in Palamás' poetry and more a matter of personal identity. The Délphic priestess with her wild, windswept words is the inspiration for the incantatory verse of this modern poet who lived in Délphi. In his poem *First Rain* he writes:

I became a lyre caressed
by the breath's profusion.
Sweetness filled my palate;
and as our eyes met again
all my blood sang out.

Women poets at the turn of the century were also very active defining their particular subjectivity, a doubly difficult task since society and their fellow poets constantly set them up as the object, not the subject, of desire or admiration. **Maria Polidoúri** (1902–30) in her poem *To a Bouquet of Roses* expresses this tension:

If I am the butterfly
you are lacking, open between my lips
the passage, the half-closed heart
that belongs to you.
Or if you wish, I'll rape
your blossoming secret, with a passion
unknown to your generation
the admiration which keeps you young…
My breath, your inspiration,
I do not know which wilted your petals…
which extinguished the light in my eyes…

She cannot speak for the new emerging nation. As the female persona she is the

butterfly, the image of emancipation which the male poets have already appropriated. Instead she takes her positionlessness as the topic and substance of her poem. Like Caváfy and other poets of the alternative canon suggested above, Polidoúri is interested in how the written text differs from a song. The grammatical confusion between the I and the You in this poem is only possible in writing.

Very much a part of the established canon and probably best known of all the modern Greek poets are the two Nobel prize winners **George Seféris** (1900–71) and **Odysseus Elytis** (born 1911). Although their poetry is certainly not devoid of questions about writing, both these poets of the generation of the 1930s draw heavily on the oral tradition. Rather than comprising a Greek avant garde themselves, these poets were just extremely adept at incorporating the techniques of other European modernisms. Seféris introduced Greece to the modernism of T.S. Eliot with its reliance on myth while Elytis imported the other extreme of modernism, French surrealism.

And perhaps it is telling that their poetry gained popularity by the oldest trick in the book, oral transmission, through the ingenious scores of the composer Míkis Theodorákis (see the Theodorákis entry, page 303–04). Often in the most out of-the-way places you will hear people singing Seféris' *"On the secret seashore/white like a dove/ we grew thirsty at noon: /but the water was brackish…"* or Elytis' *"A solitary swallow and a costly spring,/For the sun to turn it takes a lot of work…"*

Some of the poets' phrases may not be as familiar as the old and oral formulas from laments and wedding songs, but in the context of modernisation their words are somehow necessary; they provide a choral response to experiences that are outside the vocabulary of traditional folk songs. As part of his *Mythistórema* (both a history through myth and a myth through history) Seféris constructs a modern mythology where nature is no longer authentic. In his catalogue of the Greek landscape nature is mechanically reproduced like everything else.

For Seféris' argonauts, myth and history have a message; but for Elytis' speaker, myth and history have turned into something more like dream:

*In petticoats of April first and cicadas of
the feast of mid-August
Tell me, that which plays, that which
rages,
that which can entice
Shaking out of threats their evil
black darkness
Spilling in the sun's embrace
intoxicating birds
Tell me, that which opens its wings on the
breast of things
On the breast of our deepest dreams, is
that the mad pomegranate tree?*

As it was with the folk song, the bard in Seféris' and Elytis' poetry speaks for the community. Their poetry is meant to be read in the context of this longer oral tradition.

The various fragments of poems in this introduction, whether read as parts of a continuous tradition or as disruptive alternatives, are all here to entice the reader to read further. Framing Greek poetry in the context of the oral tradition is not meant to trap it there; a strong oral tradition has certainly contributed to poetry's popularity in Greece but exclusive emphasis upon it has also helped to draw attention away from the more textual tradition in Greek poetry.

The generation of the 1970s in particular is indebted to Caváfy's alternative poetics. In conclusion let us return to Yánnis Rítsos whose poetry over the past 50 years has perhaps most dramatically registered this tension between the sung and written text. On the eve of his emergence from the concentration camp on Léros in 1968, Rítsos tried to imagine a new kind of poetry, a regenerative poetry, which would be less concerned with recapturing the past and more concerned with constructing a future. His poem *Return* anticipates the fall of the dictatorship and without being prescriptive, the ensuing poetic activity:

*The statues left first. A little later
the trees, people, animals. The land became
entirely desert. The wind blew.
Newspapers and thorns circled in the streets.
At dusk the lights went on by themselves.
A man came back alone, looked around him,
took out his key, stuck it in the ground
as though entrusting it to an underground hand*

*or as though planting a tree. Then he
climbed
the marble stairs and gazed down at the
city.
Cautiously, one by one, the statues returned.*

[The author is indebted to Rodrick Beaton's *Folk Poetry of Modern Greece*, to Margaret Alexiou's *The Ritual Lament in Greek Tradition* and to the translations of George Thomson, Edmund Keeley and Philip Sherrard.]

PERIPTERA

Although they may appear limited by their diminutive structures, kiosks are really multi-purpose powerhouses. Besides filling the obvious function of newsagent/sweetshop, they may double as mini-amusement parks (with children's rides), sporting goods stores (including sleeping bags on occasion), ironmongers and locksmiths. For customers with problems, the proprietor may dispense psychiatric or medical advice.

Running a kiosk is like directing an orchestra — one eye on the telephone meter, one

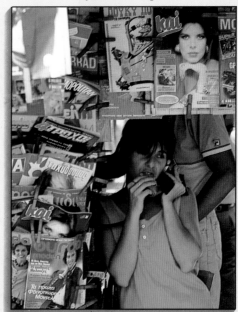

hand giving change and one ear tuned to the voice of a friend who has stopped around the back for a chat. How do kiosk owners cope?

The view from inside a kiosk, or *períptero* as it is called in Greek, is tight, complex and most resembles the cockpit of a DC-9. Down low are a series of tiny drawers in which are sequestered various sewing needles, thread, zippers, antibiotics and usually a supply of condoms; shelved up higher are sweets and the rainbow array of cigarettes, while still higher are assorted shampoos, washing powder and worrybeads. Items of value, pocket calculators, watches and gold cigarette lighters are displayed in little show windows. In the centre sits the proprietor, jammed into two square feet of space yet firmly in control of the till, responding to the images as they appear on the screen – that small opening to the front where customers pronounce their orders.

It is not unusual for a *perípteras* to work shifts of 12 hours in conditions which vary from furnace-like in summer to chill and damp in winter (when most cramp their already tiny space with electric fires or some form of heating). Yet they remain a generally good-humoured lot, eager to oblige the lost foreigner with directions or even the recommendation of a good local *tavérna*.

The kiosks started as gifts from the government to wounded veterans of the Balkan and World War I. Many will remark on the similarity between the architecture of kiosks and that of military guardposts such as those used by the honour guard in front of the Parliament on Syntagma Square. In a symbolic way the *períptera* are also guard houses where old soldiers prolong their duty, emerging from the military into the commercial sector, watching over and serving the community. Happily, they are no longer under attack although thieves do occasionally jimmy their locks in the night.

In Greece people want to run their own business and the more than 3,000 *períptera* in Athens alone obviously make this a possibility. Kiosks are almost all family-run and one cannot help noticing the children or grandchildren of the proprietors stopping by for a sweet on the way home from school, or in summer the whole family sitting around a seafront *períptera* eating watermelon which they may offer to share with customers. Kiosks have a personality and a charm which is part of Greek commerce generally; everything is personal. If a kiosk owner finds that you know a few words of Greek it may take a bit longer to conclude your purchase. They will want to know where you are from.

With only a quarter of the population of England, Greece has nearly the same number of retail shops. Partly this is the reflection of a society which subdivides itself sharply into family and kindred groups, each of which seeks to own a shop, a *magazí*.

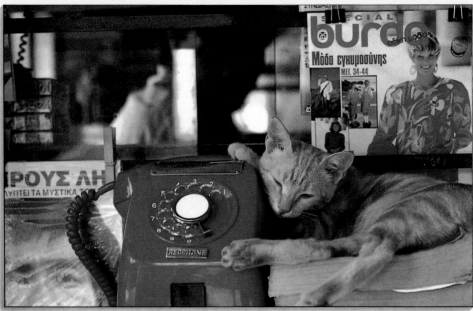

The idea of working for a stranger is odious; in fact, the word for "employee" in Greek literally means "someone beneath another". Consequently, instead of expanding and enlarging, businesses tend to remain relatively small in size while new businesses are opened to accommodate an expanding market. This swollen number of retail shops cause Greece to have the highest mark-up price in the Common Market. Thus the profusion of kiosks throughout Greece is more than just a peculiarity or a coincidence; it is a part of a whole economic mentality – the *períptero* mentality – the basis of which may be summed up in the slogan, "One family, one business".

QUEUEING

Americans call it "standing in line". Born of American "straight" dealing, it falls positively flat next to the elegant British verb, "to queue", from the Latin *cauda*, for "tail". American "lines" exude a democratic egalitarianism; British "queues" fair play mixed with social distance. But both reveal a belief in rationality and order in the ways of the world.

The Greek version is something else altogether. Can you really call it a "queue"? Waiting at a bus stop in Academías in central Athens, you can just make out a semblance of linearity among the bodies, if only because the metal rails installed for this purpose nudge them into orderliness. Once the bus appears, however, the pretence collapses and a chaos of anxiously pressing bodies pushes relentlessly through the doorway. Some Athenians say it's just life in a city bursting its seams – too many passengers squeezing into too few buses. That's indisputable. But you see the same anxious crowding on airport runways where, clutching a boarding pass with a guaranteed seat number, passengers trip all over one another to board the plane.

A different body language is no doubt part of the explanation. Greeks are comfortable with their bodies, and they touch each other constantly – in handshakes and kisses of greeting, in the loving pinch to a baby, in the slap on the arm to a comrade – in ways the "colder" northerners touch only their intimates. So you must interpret no hostility in the face of that old lady whose sharp finger jabs into your back and propels you forward on to the bus. But its blankness can be just as annoying: when you're a foreigner, with a different sense of your personal space, it's easy to feel you're being treated like just a bulky obstacle in the path of somebody else's seat.

This impersonality has a logic, though. It's the inverse of the much-vaunted "personalism" of the Greeks, but not its opposite. Greeks don't imagine they live in a rational universe where all things come to those who wait. There's no place here for the Anglo-Saxon concept of "fairness". For Greeks, the universe is arbitrary and unpredictable – and that goes for God, the Turks and the Greek bureaucracy. Life is a struggle. The goodies are few and the claimants many. You've got to push forward or you're lost.

For centuries, the little guys have survived through personal ties to the landowner, the grocer, the banker, and by making friends with more powerful men who had "means" (*méson*) enough to "help", or who, in turn, had even more powerful "friends". Perhaps these chains of influence linking the peasant farmer to the highest ranks in the centres of power are the nearest thing you get to an indigenous queue!

REMBÉTIKA

Q: What is *rembétika*? The old *rembétika* composer Rovertakis said: "Rembétika songs were written *for* people who sing rembétika by people who sing rembétika. The *rembétis* is a man who had sorrow and threw it out." What political/historical environment originally brought about *rembétika*? How is its early history linked to the 1922 Asia Minor disaster?

A: The *rembétika* is the most original kind of song to have appeared in Greece over the past 100 years. A few examples of the type were already known throughout Greece by as early as 1930, and in the next 15 years these songs became more and more popular, without, however, managing to secure a following among the more well-to-do classes. They received their first recognition from respectable criticism in the 1950s.

Unfortunately we do not know either when or where or amongst whom they originated. Was it in 1850, in 1880, or in 1910? In Smyrna, on Syros, or in Piraéus? Among underworld characters living from hand to mouth by various petty illegalities on the margins of society, or among the deprived and impoverished urban dwellers? The destruction of Smyrna in 1922 certainly increased the production of *rembétika* and speeded up the processes that led to the development of their singular quality.

Q: Do you think that in contrast to the rural folk song which is often a communal expression of a common sorrow or joy, these urban folk songs are an expression of a more alienated individual?

A: The words of the *rembétika* certainly express more specialised and individualised feelings than do the demotic or rural folk songs. They also differ to some extent from the demotic songs in their vocabulary and metrical structure, borrowing new elements from the lyrics of the light songs popular in

the period between the wars, but using the phraseology in a different way, transforming it from the sugary and insipid into something serious and often tragic.

Q: When and why did *rembétika* come back into fashion? What made it possible for a larger audience to appreciate this music?

A: *Rembétika* never completely lost its public. It is simply that in the 1960s this public was not to be found so much in the working-class districts of the towns, where most of the population had succumbed to the craze for "light-popular" songs and "smooth" *rembétika*, but among the students and intellectuals.

These intellectuals initiated the rest of the middle class into the world of *rembétika*, which it had previously despised. Thus *rembétika* finally addressed itself to everyone, because it brought back a nostalgic and picturesque past, poverty-stricken perhaps, but in a way more carefree and certainly more genuine than the alienated present.

Q: Do you think there's any use in comparing *rembétika* with the American Blues?

A: The conditions that gave birth respectively to the *rembétika* and the blues are completely different, and the vast geographical distance separating Greece from

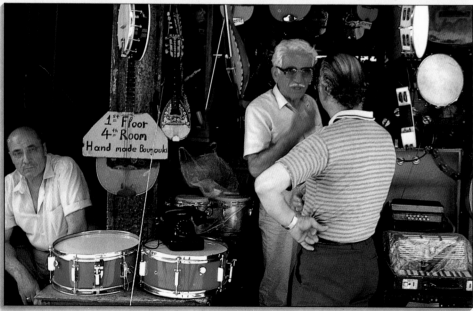

the United States rules out any mutual influence. The occasional similarities one meets in the verses are entirely accidental.

Q: What was the role of the *rembétissa*, the woman who sang with these underworld characters?

A: Woman, as mother, daughter, lover, is the central figure in the verses of the *rembétika*. But the title of *rembétissa* is appropriate only to the woman who follows the shiftless life of the *rembétis*. And she follows him because she has a good voice and wants to *be* someone. She in her turn inspires the men who surround her and, above all, liberates herself, becoming the original of the independent woman in Greek society.

Q: Could you tell us something about the two most important *rembétika* instruments, the bouzoúki and the baglamá?

A: They are very ancient instruments, used by the Assyrians, the Egyptians and the ancient Greeks. The Greeks never ceased to use them, but from time to time simply modified them and changed their names. Thus the ancient *pandoúra* or *pandouris*, the Byzantine *thamboúra* and the post-Byzantine *tamboúras* do not correspond exactly to the modern bouzoúki, but they certainly belong to the same family. It is not known when the word "bouzoúki" came into Greece from the Lebanon, but it is to be found in certain demotic songs.

Q: For the newcomer baffled by all the available cassettes and records of *rembétika,* what do you recommend as a first purchase?

A: Some good records for a first taste of *rembétika* are:
(i) Authentic Songs Recorded in Smyrna and Constantinople before 1922. ACBA 1402 (1982)
(ii) Greek Oriental Smyrnaic-Rebetic Songs and Dances. Folklyric Records 9033 (*circa* 1983)
(iii) Greek Popular Songs in America. Falirea Bros. 22–23 (1984)
(iv) Grèce. Hommage à Tsitsánis. Bouzoúki Ocora. 558.632 (1984)
(v) Grèce. La tradition du Rebétiko. Ocora 558648 (1984)

SHADOW PUPPETS

Shadow puppet theatre, whose protagonist in the Greek version is Karaghiózis, was first recorded in Java, China and India, from where it spread to Turkey and then to Greece. Karaghiózis takes his name from his prominent black pupil or "karagöz" (black eye in Turkish). He is a short balding hunchback with an enormous arm that he uses to club others over the head. He is a poverty-stricken, uneducated Everyman dressed in ragged clothing and usually barefoot.

Yet Karaghiózis is comical rather than pathetic. He is insatiably hungry, constantly preoccupied with finding food for himself and his family. He survives by his cunning and as need arises, impersonates prominent characters and professionals. These ruses provide only temporary solutions to his problems and eventually he is caught and often beaten and thrown in jail. Although he frequently moans "*Ach manoúla mou, ti épatha?*" ("Oh Mom, what's befallen me?"), he always reappears undaunted in the next episode.

The Karaghiózis stage has a screen of any fine white material stretched across a frame. The figures, which are designed by the player, are made of painted leather and synthetic material. They are flat, clean-cut silhouettes held against the screen by the operator and manipulated by horizontal rods with a hinge to facilitate change of direction. A light source from behind, originally oil lamps but now usually electric bulbs, shines through the transparent material of the figures to make them look like stained glass.

The most popular legend about the origin of Karaghiózis identifies him as a blacksmith in Turkey during the reign of Sultan Orhan (1326–59). While working on a mosque in Bursa, he and his friend, the mason Hadjiavat, had such humorous exchanges that all construction ceased as their co-workers listened. The enraged Sultan had them hanged but later was remorseful and missed them. To console him, one of his subjects manipulated likenesses of the two dead men on a screen and Karaghiózis theatre was born.

The early plays were passed along orally and the puppeteers memorised them but added their own improvisations or created new scripts. Many players adapt classical plots to include comments on politics and to satirize local personalities and events.

Although the Karaghiózis player has assistants, he is still a one-man wonder with an endless array of intonations to suit all roles of both sexes. He is judged by his mastery of mimicry of regional dialects and speech defects such as stuttering. Energy and skill are needed to coordinate the actions of the figures with the speech. Besides all this, in many performances the player recites poetry, sings, and plays an instrument such as the guitar for the musical themes often associated with particular characters.

Above all, Karaghiózis is a theatre of laughter. At the most basic level, this is achieved through crude jokes and slapstick; Karaghiózis and his three mischievous children are chased by a foe, which results in furniture and bodies being catapulted through the air. More subtly, repetition is used in gesture, movement and speech to parody character types such as the pompous dandy Morfónios from the Iónian Islands. Disguise and concealment are common; Karaghiózis masquerades as a bride which shocks the hapless bridegroom as he lifts the veil. Oddity of physical appearance and behaviour is exaggerated.

A typical story is *Days and Tricks of Karaghiózis*, written and performed by Frixos Gazepides, a spry septuagenarian who became infatuated with the shadow theatre as a young boy. Popular figures of Karaghiózis who are included in this vignette are Aglaía, Karaghiózis' nagging wife; Hadjiavátis, a well-educated, restrained philosopher who is Karaghiózis' best friend; Barbayiórgos (Uncle George), a tall rough-mannered shepherd from the mountains of Roúmeli; Mr Skordaliás (Mr Garlic Dip), a wealthy merchant from Naúplia who is an uncle of Aglaía, is a creation of Gazepides.

Days and Tricks of Karaghiózis involves Karaghiózis in a usual money-making scheme that backfires. Mr Skordaliás is preparing to leave for Switzerland for treatment of his extreme near-sightedness. Hadjiavátis meets him and tells him that Karaghiózis died that morning and left his family without a drachma. Aglaía is naturally distraught. Skordaliás believes him and goes to the house to pay his last respects.

He stoops to kiss the prone body but due to his myopia, kisses the backside rather than the face. The odour emanating convinces him that Karaghiózis is dead and he rushes to the bank to withdraw a large sum of money. On the way, he encounters Barbayiórgos, who has often been the victim of Karaghiózis' pranks and is sceptical about the news. They both go to Karaghiózis' house to investigate. Instead of finding the dead body and grieving widow, they witness the whole family prematurely celebrating their new wealth by eating, drinking and dancing. The play ends with Karaghiózis getting his inevitable thrashing from the angry Barbayórgios. As he lies bruised on the floor he proclaims, "I couldn't die before because I was hungry; but I would die happily now, because for once, I am full."

Before World War II, Mollas, a famous puppet-master commented: "A monster has come to us from America." He was referring to the cinema which had a technical sophistication that captured the general audience which had been attending the shadow theatre performances. With the emergence of television in Greece in the 1960s, the shadow plays which were once the entertainment highlight of many a neighbourhood, seemed to many old-fashioned and naïve.

Fewer than 10 older Karaghiózis players perform now in Greece with no young apprentices being recruited. Just one summer theatre and a weekly television programme are regularly devoted to shadow theatre. Yet it was apparent while watching an enthusiastic audience of all ages and nationalities during a recent request performance of Gazepides that this folk art has not lost its universal appeal. The cast of characters reflects the divergence of influences still evident in Greece today. Karaghiózis himself is the embodiment of the innate spirit of the Greek nation. He survives all adversity and starts every new adventure with renewed optimism and energy.

THEODORAKIS

Q: What was happening in music during the 1967–74 military junta?

A: Certain songs which in the ordinary way would have circulated freely went underground, while there was a general increase in the number of songs with hinted messages against the dictators; in fact, a kind of resistance activity and democratic communication went on through the medium of songs.

Q: Why do you think Theodorákis and the ballad writers of the Néo Kyma (New Wave) had enough success in the 1960s to ensure Greece a popular music unchallenged by disco and other Anglo-American imports?

A: The 1960s were a time of political unrest and saw the suppression of democratic institutions. Since the words "Greece" and "democracy" are inseparably linked, a tyrannical regime must always be foreign to Greece. In times of slavery all peoples go back to their roots, from which they derive the strength to survive as peoples. Nevertheless, this does not mean that the Greeks turned their backs on music from abroad during this period.

Q: Could you describe some of the differences between the calculated compositions of Theodorákis, Hadjidákis and the other Greek composers who have studied abroad and the more spontaneous rembétika and folk musics?

A: In certain of their songs (especially those written for the cinema), Theodorákis and Hadjidákis faithfully follow the spirit of the rembétika. But in their genuinely important songs they express themselves more personally, and in these one seldom finds striking similarities with the rembétika, even when these songs have a bouzoúki accompaniment. The public, of course, has its preferences, but it is not uncommon for the admirers of modern Greek "composer" songs to like rembétika too.

Q: Even if Greek popular music is not at all like classical, rock, disco or punk, could you still say that it is more influenced by the West than by the East?

A: What is noteworthy in Theodorákis and Hadjidákis, as in quite a number of their successors, is how well they blend the frequently contradictory Western and Eastern (Greco-Byzantine) compositional processes. Which source influences them most? In this matter, surely each composer chooses his own path.

Q: What is the extent of the collaboration that goes on between Greece's contemporary composers and poets?

A: I don't think we can talk about "collaboration" between composers and poets. The composers usually open anthologies of poetry and set those poems which they like, as they like; in fact, they often choose to set the work of poets who are no longer alive, such as Solomós, Kalvos, Sikelianós and Kavadias.

Q: Where do you think Greek music is going?

A: In the days before 1945, when the Greeks were writing waltzes and tangoes, could anyone have foreseen that in a few years Theodorákis and Hadjidákis would open a new epoch in the history of Greek song? I think not. Therefore I prefer to leave this question unanswered.

UNFINISHED BUILDINGS

There are many jokes about Greek bureaucracy and endless red tape. It's a well-known fact that in the Greek civil service there are five people to every one job. Although this diminishes unemployment it has its side-effects as well: it often takes five times longer to do anything, whether it's going through customs, paying road tax, changing money or registering for school.

For many outsiders it is unfathomable that such simple tasks could take so long. But you have only to take into consideration such practices as *hartósima* (the tax stamps) to realise that efficiency is not one of the main objectives. By law you are required to affix these tax stamps to most official documents; but, for some reason, state offices rarely have their own stock. So in the middle of filing an application you must run down to the nearest kiosk (see *Períptera*) to buy some.

Then after climbing four flights of stairs or surviving the ancient elevator crammed with people and coffee trays (see Coffee) you arrive only to find that the coffee you so

charitably balanced on your shoulder in the elevator on the way up was meant for the very civil servant who had been serving you and would therefore hold you up another half an hour. After his coffee break you find out that you also need three copies of one page and a photograph of yourself taken by a particular photographer on the other side of town... and so the story goes.

One of the main symptoms of this bureaucracy, or *graphiokratía* as the Greeks call it, is the multitude of unfinished buildings that dot the Greek cityscape. If paying road tax takes a day, just think how long a building project could take. It is impossible to foresee the many setbacks. Not only do the zoning laws change with every new government but cultural expectations shift as well. Fifteen years ago most parents felt it was their obligation to build their daughters houses as part of their dowry even if it was beyond their means. Now, though a young woman may receive an education rather than a house as "dowry", many of these building projects persist, gaining a wall or floor every summer, and, if the house is being built in a strictly zoned area, only at night. This is due to the peculiar law that zoning orders can only be enforced if the offender is caught in the act. Whole floors and extensions and fences go up in the dark.

But in all this shady business one law holds: covering over the iron supporting rods and putting on the roof come last, if ever. As long as a few iron supports stick out, no tax is levied. This, of course, is the main reason for so many unfinished buildings.

VENDETTA

Unlike brigandage, which was common throughout Greece, the vendetta tradition was found in only a few regions, where large families, a passionate sensitivity to personal honour and a love for fighting farmed an unholy trinity. Epirus was one such feud-ridden region, but the heartland of the Greek vendetta was the Máni. William Leake, visiting the Máni village of Vathiá in 1805, decided not to spend the night there after learning that a feud had been raging for the past 40 years, "in which time they reckon that about a hundred men have been killed".

Some observers, debunking the vendetta "myth", claimed that reports of casualties had been much exaggerated and that there was more shooting than bloodshed. But the 18th-century casebooks of Dr Papadákis, a Mániot surgeon with a flourishing practice, present a different picture of heads crushed by rocks, bullet-ridden limbs, stiletto and sword wounds commonplace.

But the turbulent Máni described by the doctor has subsided into a desolate silence. The main road built since the war transformed the old ways. Now the last signs of the vendetta visible to the traveller are the gaunt decaying stone towers in every village from which rival clans only a century ago attempted to exterminate one another.

WOMEN

Sit in a public place in Greece and the world – men, women and children – will pass you by. But watch more closely and you may begin to feel that this is not the women's world. They pass across this public stage bearing the signs of their errands – a tray of food for the baker's oven, or swollen shiny plastic bags of shopping, or with one or two well-dressed children in tow. Enter stage right, exit stage left. Their real drama is elsewhere. Even those who pause to chat lack the lordly confidence of the men whose every gesture reveals their certainty that they are running the show.

So where is the women's world? Are they kept in the wings, handing out the props and shifting furniture? Or are they performing in another arena? One where the crowds are not so big, perhaps, but where the rewards are enough to live on?

What it means to be a woman in Greece depends very much on which woman. Where does she live, is she married, how old is she, how well off is she? Above all, what choices can she make? Clearly the life choices for a woman of 80 have been very different from those confronted by her granddaughter. But different in which ways? And are there, along with new choices, new constraints?

The life-style of old: The old woman of 80 or 90, who spends the winter months curled on the corner of a striped divan near the stove and emerges in the summer to sit on a stool on balcony or doorstep, carries memories of a life punctuated by war and political turbulence. As she dandles her grandchildren and great-grandchildren, she is certain that the one thread that runs through all external events is family. But while she has a powerful sense of continuity which, no doubt, she tries to instil into the generations that follow after, she lives in a world where the very substance of life has been transformed.

If, as is likely, she started life in a small village (the cities and major towns all expanded during the course of this century), she will have seen the peasant's daily *aghóna* (struggle) in the fields transmuted into something more like a regular day's work. Women's labour in the fields is still a very significant part of the Greek economy (and it began, in the 1980s, to be recognised by the formation of farming-women's organisations with the encouragement of the PASOK government). But it is unlikely to be the intensively heavy work which broke down the health of women in the early part of the century and very often endangered their babies too. The coming of the *traktér*, the pride of the farming man, bedecked with necklaces like a favourite horse, has freed women's bodies for lighter labour.

Today's great-grandmother sees younger women able to spend more time in or near the house. In the traditional view a woman without a house is as incomplete as a house without a woman. Within the broader horizons of the modern woman a house may seem a paltry kingdom to inherit, especially if it is one box in a concrete block. But until the present day the link between the woman and the house has been a constant, varying according to economic and ideological constraints. Those wealthy merchants' houses of the 18th and 19th centuries which can still be seen in towns such as Kastoriá and Siátista were decorated inside with a painted profusion of flowers, fruit and friezes of wide rolling countryside. They were gilded cages for the women whose lives were passed within them.

It is commonplace that political repression is often replicated in relations between the sexes. While Greece was under Turkish rule (and in northern areas this period extended until 1912, well within living memory), Turks restricted Greeks and Greek men restricted Greek women. Christians and Muslims competed for the modesty of their women, that area of social relations which is often the most immediately available source of insult between alienated communities.

Notable incidents of Turkish oppression took the form of acts against women (many a female saint owed her martyrdom to a pasha whose attentions she resisted); but the constraints of modesty imposed on women were not simply measures to protect them against tyranny. Women represented, and still in many ways represent, the vulnerable interior of the family. Men's honour is at stake defending it.

The oldest women today often fret at the

immodest dress of young women, tapping their wrists with the side of a hand to show where sleeves should end and drawing a line halfway down their chests to show how far the excesses extend. Clothes are certainly strongly symbolic in Greece (of youth or age, social conformity or eccentricity, joy or mourning) but maybe in their reading of the messages of dress, the critics in the older generation disregard the less visible constraints which still have force for many young women – particularly the fact that an unmarried woman is, theoretically, answerable to her father if there is anything about her comportment of which he disapproves.

A woman's relationship to her house, to its physical fabric, affects her whole life. In many areas of Greece (broadly speaking, the south and the islands) there has traditionally been the expectation that the family of a woman who is about to be married will provide a house as well as some furniture and other goods or property. The dowry has strongly affected women's marriage chances and in addition the balance of male and female children in families has been critical for economic success or failure. Sons have sacrificed their inheritance to dispose of their sisters, women have been driven to the brink of suicide as their market value plummets in a family crisis.

Attempts are now being made to limit the power of these expectations, and the dowry is technically illegal. In northerly areas the normal pattern is the reverse: it is the man's family which expects to provide a house, or house room, for each new couple. Traditionally, families extended as the sons married and brought their wives to the parental house where they were subject to the often tyrannical rule of the *petherá* (mother-in-law) who had no doubt suffered at the hands of her own *petherá* when she was the new "bride". As families began to expect more comfort and privacy and, it is said, became less willing to "have patience" with each other, it became normal for only the latest married son to remain at home. Now it is the norm for a new house or flat to be made available for the new couple. But in these cases it is still most likely to be the mother-in-law who will keep a supervisory eye on the household management and child-rearing practices of her son's wife.

The house – a woman's show-case: Once a woman is established in her own house, she can exhibit her worth through the objects in it. As a visitor to a Greek house, you may be shown into the *salóni*, and the shutters may be thrown open in your honour so that every item in the room sucks up light like a sponge. The furniture gleams with a limpid varnish, the mirror-backed cabinet is filled with phalanxes of glasses of every category. There are glinting outposts of ornaments in every direction and, above, a formation of globes

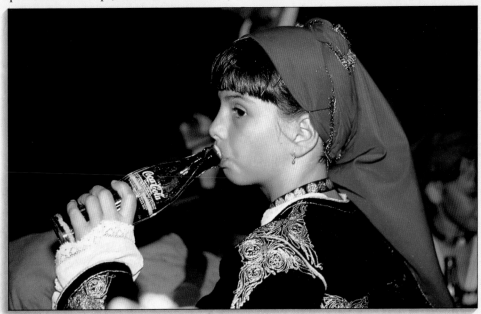

or crystal drops which defies both gravity and any creeping invasion of darkness at the room's edges.

The challenge to the housewife is clear; every speck of dust which is allowed to settle will be reflected back as two. But all is under her control. Her banner is raised victoriously on every side. Every item of furniture is dressed overall with a festive array of fabrics embroidered, crocheted, tasselled and trimmed. They are crisply ironed and draped just so, pressed so that their corners hang precisely at the midpoint of the table edges, or pushed into ripples by heavy vases.

The visitor who is left alone for a little longer, while the *Kyría* goes to make coffee in her back kitchen, may begin to dwell upon the stitches, the accumulated moments of women's hours and days – subtly toned flowers in blues and reds and gold, silky green leaves, intricately counted patterns of crosses involving many handfuls of colours from the haberdasher's glass topped drawer, encrusted edges, patient repetitions in the millions of tugged loops of a crocheted curtain. It is the crystallisation of many moments, calm moments, anxious moments, stitches drawn between sighs – of boredom, hope or resignation. Or more often, stitches shared with groups of neighbours, patterns borrowed from friends, hems and tassels wrought to the sound of laughter and gossip and never far from the clink of coffee cups.

Greek women's handiwork is no mere pastime. It is bound closely to the traditional sense of woman's role and destiny. A young girl learns to sew so that she will be marriageable. These skills symbolise, obscurely, all that she must be. The bride must show that she has the wherewithal to "dress" the house, all the ornamental and comfortable fabrics which will line the nest of marriage. The usually impressive accumulation of fabrics and furnishings is brought to the new house with some ceremony – in the past on the backs of a string of well-laden mules, now more often in a truck which creeps through village or neighbourhood with the horn sounding and shouts of merriment issuing from the back.

In viewing the goods, other women typically express admiration for the bride's "golden hands" and there is a strong sense that it is more than her skill that is being displayed. She has laid out her virtue before them. In the cities or wherever money is more available than time it has become customary for more and more items to be purchased. But handwoven fabrics were prized even when they were more common and today mothers and grandmothers hand on to their daughters items which probably lay in their own dowry chests, shrouded in the whiff of camphor, all their married lives.

Housework is, of course, a kind of display and in Greece the performance is almost always virtuoso. In both towns and villages many tasks are appropriately done in public view – hanging the washing, beating rugs. airing bedclothes, taking food to the bakeries to be cooked and shopping. A woman's work is manifested to the world. And, although the house is a private realm, it is opened to visitors; the worst would be assumed of a housewife who never opened her doors to her neighbours. A woman makes her command over the physical things of life apparent to all.

Seeing a woman washing a dusty public pavement, early in the morning, doubled over and using a tiny handmade broom, seeing her whitewashing the steps with the sole purpose, apparently, of enabling them to be made dirty so that they can again be cleaned, one might be inspired to ask, why does she enslave herself in this way? Older houses are not built or furnished for convenience and many tasks are performed with a frequency totally disproportionate to their labouriousness.

There is more than one answer and more than one demand for this symbolic tax from women. First, they are restoring order against the natural state of dirt and disorder that would otherwise take over. As each housewife sweeps the road in front of her house and whitens the trees and paving stones, she marks a territory where harmony is restored, where in religious terms that family has printed the stamp of redemption upon the fallen world. Correspondingly, grace is manifested in material things; if the bread rises well and the vegetables grow plump, the family seems (both to themselves and to others in the community) to be enjoying the protection of God and the saints.

Almost every house or flat has, somewhere, its saints who inhabit a quiet niche along with fragile dried leaves or flowers from a bygone festival, a phial of holy water from a place of pilgrimage, and the quickly faded wedding crowns of artificial twigs. It is part of the process of caring for the house to attend to the icons: icons need light. A small glass filled with water and olive oil with a floating wick provides a steady golden bud of flame. These ancient and simple lamps may be replaced by an electric bulb (do the saints blink at the lurid aquarium green?) for daily use. But at a time of crisis, and before a major festival, the woman of the house cleans and fills the little oil lamp, and fits a new pink wick, and maybe sets similar flames burning before the icons in a local church or roadside shrine. Women take responsibility for the family icons. They say the prayers and visit churches. "*Emeís plirónoume,*" they say. ("We women pay.")

On the other hand, the reverse, secular, side of this coin is marked with the same price. Given that, in Greek society, moral status is thought to be *visible*, every housewife, every individual, is vulnerable to the remarks of others. Even for those supported by a modern political ideology, it is difficult to stand against a norm set by peers and neighbours.

It is the bearing of children which brings a woman to her full status. It would be difficult to exaggerate the importance given to marriage in Greece. The feeling that there is no more appropriate mode of living for an adult of either sex is prevalent, and it is widely assumed that monks and nuns who explicitly reject it must have been disappointed in love. The fact that marriage is essential for a complete life is symbolised by the ritual in which a young adult who dies unmarried must be dressed in wedding clothes and, in a poignant ceremony, is "married" in the coffin with a single wedding crown.

Marriage and the woman's worth: The pressure for women to marry is intense. They are given less time to do so than men; an unmarried woman in her late twenties is a matter for concern to her relatives whereas a man can acceptably retain his "freedom" (unmarried people are always described as "free") until 40 or so. Women who choose not to marry have to confront the stubborn belief that they are single not through their own choice but of necessity. Circumstances have proved too much for them, runs the typical interpretation, so that that they have missed their chance of marriage.

Having married, a woman finds the pressure is relaxed – for a moment. The next anxiously awaited event is of course pregnancy. This anxiety may be forestalled if a bride is already pregnant. This has been common in some areas as much in the past as today, while elsewhere a woman's protest "My Dad will kill me!" has not always been an exaggeration. Pregnancy outside engagement has always been a serious matter in every part of Greece. Now that the concept of engagement is becoming less formal (the families may at first have a simple verbal understanding, rather than exchanging rings and gifts, or even less formally, the young people may come to an understanding by themselves) there is both greater flexibility in sexual matters and also greater scope for misunderstandings.

Although childbearing is their fulfilment, Greek mothers often talk of the suffering involved in having children. They don't just mean the pains of childbirth, either. They expect to suffer anxiety on the child's behalf from its first breath until it is safely married. They share this suffering with the *Panaghía*, the Virgin Mary, who is the model of womanhood explicitly offered by Greek Orthodoxy, and whose sufferings on behalf of her son are remembered during the course of the Church's year. Women are "Eves", caught in the trammels of human sexuality and only redeem themselves by bearing, as the Virgin Mary did, a child.

Motherhood means nurture. The mother gives substance to her child while she is pregnant and the process does not stop there. Mothers tend to feed their children with great anxiety (a reason sometimes given for preferring bottle-feeding is that "at least you can see what it has eaten"). Unfortunately many a Greek child is aware of this and exploits the mother's sensitivity on this matter. The degree of a mother's love for her family can be represented by the effort she puts into preparing food. If she produces boiled macaroni day after day she will be aware that she is skimping. The favourite dishes – *dolmáthes*, *pastítsio*, and *pítta,* for example – take hours to prepare and involve a number of different processes. A *hortópitta* even requires that the cook should wander the fields in search of the right kinds of greens.

While the ideal of motherhood is nurturing, ideally a mother should train her family to fast – that is to control the types of food they eat at certain times in order to achieve religious purity. Fasting is regarded quite flexibly these days in many households, with the consequence that women often casually enquire what other families are eating – so that their standards are neither higher nor lower than the average. Strict fasting means abstention from meat, all animal products and oil. Special dishes (*latherá*) are made with oil and vegetables as a kind of intermediary level of restraint. There are women, mostly old, whose races light up as they say, during a fast period, "Not a drop of oil have I eaten, not a drop…", who take their gift of abstention to the Vespers every evening and appear to enjoy a peaceful detachment from physical needs. These women may be viewed with suspicion by the less devout and the irreligious, lest they start to use their piety as a ground for judging others. For families there is a balance of opposing values to be maintained for to make children fast more than is generally thought to be necessary is a denial of mother love.

A woman's care of the other members of the family extends to everyone in it but is concentrated especially on those who are most helpless, children and the dead. Care for the dead also, paradoxically, involves the preparation of food. But it is, in fact, a kind of reversal of the nurturing process. During life a person needs to build up the body for life and health. After death it becomes necessary to let the body "melt", unburdening the soul and purifying the person ready for ultimate resurrection. By giving food away to other families a woman helps the dead person she is caring for to lose, symbolically, unwanted flesh.

On the five "Soul Saturdays" in the year black-clothed women can be seen in cemeteries all over Greece. They busy themselves with candles, or polishing the marble plaques around the graves; but most importantly, they take foil-wrapped bundles of food and, like children on a picnic, they swop with their neighbours – a piece of cake for a piece of *loukoúmi* (Turkish Delight) and the special kind of wheat porridge known as *kóllyva* for a long-ribbed biscuit. Such food is accepted with the words "May God forgive". It is an orgy of giving, each woman going away with a package as big as the one she brought. If for any reason a woman is unable to fulfil her duties towards the dead, she is quite likely to see the person in dreams. When she ceases to experience such dreams the dead person no longer needs her care.

Changed values: The pattern of expectations and fulfilment with regard to women's lives has changed little over most of the 20th century. Until very recently, what had changed was the nature of the materials with which a woman expressed her commitment to the family and its continuity. Clothes are now shop-bought, foods are richer, household furnishings often have an electrical plug attached. Today both old and new values coexist – the importance of being a wife and mother with the importance of being able to earn a good income. And it might be added that provision for the combination of the two roles is not worse than in many other European countries, especially given the usually reliable support of a young woman's mother in the background.

What was and has remained important has been the need for a woman to know that she has value. Where a woman's dowry has been external to herself she has been able to feel, once she is married, a solidity and security in relation to her husband. Where her value has been symbolised by the trivia of household furnishing she has still had a means of display and self-presentation. Now more substantial, though less visible, qualities are being appreciated: education, competence out in the world, the quality of being a *drastiria*, a "woman of action". But these new values do not necessarily mean freedom, and certain visible indicators of a woman's character – the way she dances, what she drinks, whether she smokes – are still given weight. Most of all, a woman is still expected to be linked to a family.

This is the most shocking thing about foreign women in Greece. Women travelling in Greece are often a little unnerved by the separation of men's and women's worlds. Add to this the rather obvious attentions from men which foreign women attract in areas accustomed to tourism and the female traveller is left wondering how she is viewed by local people.

"Pseudo-men": Because Greek fathers and brothers have traditionally been the guardians of female sexuality (the assumption being that individuals of either sex are not all that good at saying "no" on their own account), women who evidently have freedom of movement and economic independence are thought likely to be unconstrained in other ways. In this, they resemble men. Foreign women are often given small chances to be "pseudo-men", offered cigarettes or strong drink (offers which women from small and traditional villages would take as a joke or an insult but which Greek city women take in their stride) and even a seat in a *kafeneío*. Acceptance of such "privileges" simply makes overt the peculiar position that a foreign woman is necessarily in.

Women are likely to respond to the visiting anomaly with a barrage of questions: "*Mamá, babá, zoúneh?*" ("Mom, Dad, are they alive?"); "*Athélfia?*" ("Brothers and sisters?"); and, pointing to the ring finger of the right hand, "*Andras?*" ("Don't you have a husband?"). These are not routine polite enquiries but attempts to clarify what is, for them, the most important thing about a person – the link with family responsibilities.

The traveller can conduct herself as she wishes. She can allow herself to be placed in the sexually free category or emphasise that she's a nice family girl. But, powerful as these stereotypes are, there is no need to be pushed into either. There is such a strong sense of "how *we* do things" that there is a corresponding streak of open-mindedness in most Greeks, ready to accept that in your country you do things differently.

This acceptance of other values is having to be exercised more and more within the Greek family, between generations. The family's sphere of interests was once visibly contained within its own four walls and its fields. Now it is interpenetrated by the world, by television, by education, by its members' movements throughout Greece and further afield. But it represents, still, the front line of contact with the real moral issues of human weakness, human needs and mortality. This is where women are at work.

XENOMANIA

As a small country, Greece has always had to contend with the *xénos*, the foreigner. Whether as invader or just as visitor, the *xénos* has had a big impact on the Greek conception of self. A *xénos* isn't simply a non-Greek, he or she might be a Greek from another town. In the past when a woman married a man from over the mountain she married a *xénos*. The songs sung at her wedding were often laments wishing her well in the "after-life". Departure for another village and departure for another world were equated.

The *xénos* who carried her off was viewed with as much suspicion as any foreigner. Even today in many places the Athenian is almost as much a *xénos* as the punk rocker on his package tour from England. But whereas 50 years ago xenophobia (*xenofovía*) was the predominant sentiment, today its flip side, *xenomanía*, is by far more prevalent.

Tourism has been on the rise since the early 1960s. During the dictatorship (1967–74) foreigners were encouraged to buy property tax-free. By the end of the 1980s tourism was bringing in almost as much money as all other industries combined – from olive oil to scuba masks to large-scale machinery.

But *xenomanía* is not without its problems; in many ways Greece was not prepared for such expansion in the tourist industry. A baker and his wife on Amorgós who can earn three times their salary by renting out rooms to foreigners during the summer may not think too much about the aesthetics of the port or the influx of less traditional *mores* when they decide to add some guest rooms to the family house.

And although the wife may complain when her husband starts running after blonde Swedes (see *Kamáki*) or when her kids start demanding products she has never heard of like Coppertone tanning lotion, the casual relationship between a fast expanding tourist industry and her family's whims may not be deeply explored. And even if she does blame the tourists she depends on them for her family's livelihood. *Xénos* has clearly become a much more ambivalent term now that it pivots freely between "phobia" and "mania". One moment the tourist is the one to thank for the new road and the relative high standard of living and the next the tourist is the one to blame for sex and drugs and rock and roll.

What is particularly interesting about Greek tourism is the way it attends to the foreigner's particular material needs but still obstinately refuses to accommodate the foreigner's different pace of life. A trendy hotel on Hydra may serve all the right cocktails in its bar but the owner will absolutely refuse to get up before 10 a.m. to fix breakfast. According to him, no one who is anyone gets up that early. He hasn't thought that a trendy German may not have the same sleeping habits as a trendy Greek.

The speed with which Greece has become the vacation paradise for all of Europe means that until recently it was more equipped for backpackers than the clientèle of luxury liners. But this is slowly changing as Greeks realise that it needs to attract this latter group in order to profit from tourism. Tourists can look forward to more and more varied services – and also, perhaps, to a less manic reception, neither xenophobia nor *xenomanía* but *xenophilía*.

YOGHURT

Most visitors to Greece rave about the yoghurt. Rich, thick and creamy in its commercial form or tart and slippery in the *spitikó* (home-made) version, it is a much more substantial food than the watery yoghurt you find in other countries. For this reason, the American habit of "drinking" a yoghurt for lunch is completely unfathomable to a Greek.

Yoghurt is neither a beverage nor a meal. It has its own peculiar culinary function. Like parentheses, it separates the meal from the rest of daily activities. It cleans the palate. Meals often start with a plate of *tsatzíki* (a delicious thick spread of yoghurt, cucumber and garlic) or finish with a bowl of yoghurt smothered in the region's honey and walnuts. Whether as a preface or a finale to a meal, the yoghurt's smooth consistency helps digestion.

In general, yoghurt is regarded as soothing. In fact, in Greece when the sea is calm they say it is "'like yoghurt". In recent years England has begun importing Greek yoghurt to sell to holidaymakers when they return to dreary Britain after two weeks of Mediterranean sun and sea. Once upon a time tourists brought back pockets full of pebbles and shards as mementos of their trip; now they can forego the fuss – a quick trip to the corner deli provides all the ingredients for real Greek *tsatzíki*. Although the Delta and Fagé yoghurt available barely resembles its tangy, crusty *spitikó* counterpart, a good imagination can still conjure up the smell of thyme and oregano and the distant bells of sheep and goats scampering across a mountainside.

ZORBA

Nobody has done more for the image of the earthy, passionate, impulsive Hellenic hedonist than Hollywood's ethnic chameleon, Anthony Quinn. Níkos Kazantzákis may have invented Zórba but only Quinn could have danced that lusty rogue of a peasant into the hearts of millions. Kudos must go, too, to director Elia Kazan, who captured in stark black-and-white the austerity (of social morés no less than of mountains and architecture) of a highland Cretan village.

Though most foreigners know him as "Zorba the Greek", the original novel is titled *Aléxis Zorbás* – Kazantzákis would have found "the Greek" quite superfluous. Readers of the Greek novel know he couldn't be anything else. In fact, it's clear that Zórba was a real person, hailing (some say) from a small town on the Macedónian peninsula of Chalcidice, whom the author met when Zórba came to work on Crete.

He may have been mortal once, but Zórba has acquired mythic qualities. He's a modern stereotype, perhaps, but with a long lineage. European elites long regarded peasants as "noble savages" close to home, and romantic literature and travellers' accounts abound with rustic peasants dancing their troubles away. In Greece, there's a special twist; the peasants' "wild" dances and "discordant" music get likened to ancient Dionysian revels.

Yet, however trivialised they have become, Zórba and his predecessors represent quite sober explorations of a very old philosophical problem in Greece: the power of passion and the limits of reason. It's a prob-

NIKOS
KAZANTZAKHS

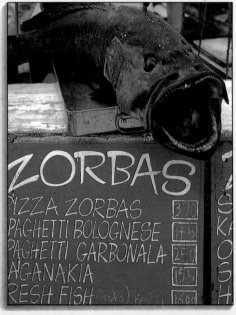

ZORBAS

PIZZA ZORBAS
PAGHETTI BOLOGNESE
PAGHETTI GARBONALA
AGANAKIA
RESH FISH

lem not confined to the ancients, nor to European philosophers grounded in that classical tradition. It has also been a core issue of Orthodoxy, whose rational, worldly power has always coexisted with the most mystical of theologies. This abstract, otherworldly faith flourished in the sensuous landscape of Kazantzákis' native Crete.

Kazantzákis was preoccupied with spiritual questions all his life. Though he eventually left the Orthodox Church, there is no doubt that his own personal conflicts over sex as well as his literary themes, come from early religious experiences. His novel about Zórba explores the problem of body and soul which always obsessed him. "The Boss" – who many say was really Kazantzákis himself – is an intellectual trapped in a world of words. He keeps himself from sin by repressing all feelings of desire for forbidden things. But he is totally unable to act. The Boss's paralysis finds its antithesis in Zórba, who confronts his desires – for food, for wine, for the charms of women – naturally, even defiantly. Kazantzákis may be forgiven his hint of Romanticism, for the rude peasant here is not just noble but wise. It's the scholar who needs to be taught by Zórba, the unlettered labourer who "knows himself".

It's somehow apt that for most of us today, Zórba is a celluloid, not a literary, figure. Words are not Zórba's *forte*. For all his pearls of earthy wisdom (laced with Quinn's exclamations in superbly accented Greek) Zórba knows the limits of words. When something profound happens – as when his daughter dies – Zórba must dance! Be it ecstasy or sorrow, Zórba seems to say, the body is better at translating the ineffable. Much the same message emerges in the film *Never on Sunday*, as Melina Mercoúri, playing the whore-with-a-heart-of-gold, dances joyously at quay-side with eager young sailors. How else can she get that stuffed-shirt scholar, Hómer, a Greek-American estranged from his own roots, to understand what life's about?

Zórba, Melína, Dionysios, the dancing Greek reincarnated under tourism in fanciful, distorted guises which sell everything from package holidays to tape cassettes still express something about what it means to be Greek: about dramatic self-assertion before a sceptical public, about the pleasures and tensions of sociability, about passion and control.

If foreigners barely understand what dancing, feasting, even smashing plates, mean to Greeks, we nonetheless find the exuberance we see there irresistible. For in Zórba and the rest we discern a spontaneity and collective *bonhomie* lost in the anonymity of our own more industrialised societies. Greeks and foreigners alike keep Zórba alive, because Zórba is "good to think with" – not just about Greeks, but about ourselves.

TRAVEL TIPS

Getting There

BY AIR

Greece has good air connections with all five continents and is serviced by numerous international airlines. There are ways of flying in at a much lower cost than the standard airline fares (APEX, stand-by, last-minute seats or "bucket shops", and you may want to familiarise yourself with the different possibilities, and their related advantages and disadvantages, before buying a ticket.

The great majority of airline passengers travelling to Greece make **Athens Hellenikon Airport** their point of entry. If you are flying with Olympic Airways you will arrive at the **West Air Terminal**. All other airlines service the **East Air Terminal**. Connecting the two terminals are taxi services and buses which depart every 20 minutes.

Between central Athens and Hellenikon there are various connecting services. A **taxi** ride from the West Terminal to Athens (Syntagma/Omonia) should cost approximately 550 drs. and will take roughly 30 minutes. From the East Airport, it should cost approximately 650 drs. and will take slightly longer. There's a fee of 15 drs. per bag as well.

Bus service is much cheaper and works well if you're not in a rush. Between the West Terminal and Syntagma, the Olympic Airways bus runs every half-hour for approximately 150 drs. and the blue city bus, which is considerably slower, for 50 drs. Between the East Terminal and Syntagma the yellow Express Bus runs every 20 minutes for approximately 100 drs.

Between Piraeus and the East-West Terminals, a yellow Express Bus runs to Akti Tzelepi, directly to the port centre. The same journey by taxi will cost between 500 and 1,000 drs.

BY SEA

By far, the majority of visitors entering Greece by sea do so from the west, that is from Italy. You can catch a boat to Greece from Venice, Ancona, Bari and Otranto, but the most regular service is from Brindisi. Daily ferry lines (somewhat less frequent in the low-season) connect Brindisi with the three main western Greek ports: Corfú, Igoumenítsa and Pátras. Corfú is a 9-hour trip; Igoumenítsa 11 hours; and Pátras 16 to 18 hours, depending on whether you take a direct boat or one that makes stops in Corfú and Igoumenítsa.

Igoumenítsa is the ideal port of call for those setting off to see central-western Greece. Pátras is best if you want to head directly to Athens or into the Peloponnése. Regular buses and trains connect Pátras and Athens (4 hours by bus). If you plan to take your car with you on the boat, you should definitely make reservations well in advance. Otherwise, arriving a few hours before the departure time should suffice, except during peak seasons when booking in advance is essential.

Italy and the west, however, are by no means the only provenance for Greece-bound sea travellers. Southward, boats connect Alexandria and Piraéus once every 10 to 15 days; eastward, boats run weekly between Haifa, Limassol and Piraéus, and once every five days between Vólos, Cyprus and Syria, not to mention the numerous crossing-points between the East Aegéan Islands and the Turkish coast; northward, frequent boats connect Piraéus and Istanbul, and in the summer boats run twice a month between Odessa (USSR) and Piraéus.

OVERLAND

From Europe via Yugoslavia: The overland route from northwestern Europe to Greece is a long one – some 1,900 miles from London to Athens. It is a rather arduous and impractical travel option if you're just trying to get to Greece for a brief vacation, but it can be an interesting trip if you make the journey a part of your vacation. By car there is a route that runs through the interior of Yugoslavia, entering Greece just above Thessaloníki.

There are also inexpensive bus services, like the famous Magic Bus, which connect Athens and Thessaloníki with many European cities – a three and a half day trip from London. The various trains you can take from northwest Europe will take about as long as the bus, cost considerably more, but may get you to Greece feeling more intact. Hitching to Greece is also a possibility, though hitching through Yugoslavia is reported to be difficult, if not dangerous, especially in Montenegro.

From Asia via Turkey: If you are travelling to Greece from Asia you'll pass through Istanbul and cross into Greece at the Evros River. The recommended route is by car or bus. The road is good and the journey from Istanbul to Thessaloníki takes approximately 15 hours; various bus companies run the route.

The train has the mythic appeal of following the route of the old Orient Express, but unless you're a great train fan, the travel time may be prohibitive: some 25 hours from Thessaloníki to Istanbul. The Thessaloníki–Istanbul trip crosses the fascinating region of Thrace: a fine adventure if you have the time and the spirit to hitchhike through it.

Travel Essentials

VISAS & PASSPORTS

With a valid passport, citizens of the European Community, the United States, Canada, Australia and New Zealand can enter Greece and stay in the country for up to three months. No visa is necessary. To stay longer than three months, you must obtain a permit from the Aliens' Bureau in Athens (9 Halkondili St., tel. 770-5711). Citizens of other countries should contact the nearest Greek embassy or consulate with regard to visa requirements.

MONEY MATTERS

An unlimited amount of foreign currency and travellers' checks may be brought into Greece, as long as amounts over US$1,000 are declared. However, if you plan to leave the country with more than $500 (or an equivalent in other currency) in bank notes, you must declare that sum upon entry into Greece. Each traveller is permitted to import and export no more than 10,000 drachmas.

All banks and most hotels are authorised to buy foreign currency at the official rate of exchange fixed by the Bank of Greece. Though it's safer to carry most of your currency in travellers' checks, it is also convenient to carry a limited sum in US dollars. On those occasions when you can't find a place to cash checks, you'll usually find a Greek who is interested in changing drachmas for dollars.

CREDIT CARDS

Many of the better established hotels, restaurants and shops accept major credit cards. The average pension or *tavérna* does not, however. Be sure to enquire before making your purchase.

TIPPING

Most restaurants and *tavérnes* add a 15 percent service charge to the bill, so a tip is discretionary. When service has been particularly good, it is customary to leave around 100 drachmas at a *tavérna*, more at an *estiatório*, for the waiter.

Just as important as any such gratuity, however, is your appreciation of the food you eat. Greek waiters and restaurant owners are proud when you tell them you like a particular dish.

HEALTH

Greece has few serious diseases apart from those that you can contract in the United States or the rest of Europe. Citizens of the United States, Canada and United Kingdom do not need any health immunizations to enter the country.

Observe caution in rural areas, and thoroughly wash greens or vegetables: echinococcus is a hazard on unwashed lettuce. Also, in the islands, pit vipers are a problem in spring and summer. Be extra cautious, keep an eye out for snakes if you hike across country to distant beaches.

The drinking water in Greece is safe.

WHAT TO WEAR

If you visit Greece during the summer months, you'll want to bring lightweight, casual clothing. Add a sweater or jacket to this and you'll be prepared for the occasional cool night breezes. Lightweight shoes and sandals are ideal for Greece in the summer, but you'll also want to bring a pair of comfortable, already broken-in walking shoes. If you plan to do any hiking in the mountains or on the islands, bring lightweight hiking shoes. A hat or scarf is also highly recommended for protection from the intense mid-day sun.

In general, both Greeks and tourists dine in casual dress. You'll only need formal dress if you plan to go to fancy establishments, casinos, formal affairs, etc. If you visit Greece during the winter months, bring the same kind of clothes you would wear during spring in the northern part of the United States or central Europe: that is, be ready for rainy, windy days and temperatures ranging between 40°F and 60°F (3°C–16°C).

While in Greece be aware of the social significance of the way you dress, and of how the Greeks perceive it. Greece, like any other country, has a set of codes, both stated and implicit, which define the socially acceptable range of attire. The Greeks will not expect you as a tourist to dress as they do. In certain places and regions, however, you will encounter requirements or conventions concerning the way you dress. To enter a church, men must wear long pants, and women, sleeved dresses. Often these will be provided for you at the church entrance if you do not have them. Not complying with this code will be taken as insulting irreverence on your part. Nude bathing is another activity which merits discretion. Nude bathing is legally sanctioned on very few Greek beaches, though socially acceptable on many. The main rule-of-thumb is this: if it is a secluded beach and/or a beach that has become a commonly accepted locale for nude bathing, you probably won't be bothered by, nor offend, anyone.

Lastly, you may need to conform to the socially acceptable dress code depending on the region you are in. On Mykonos, for example, male and female tourists alike will shock no one by wearing shorts or a swim-suit in most public places. But this same apparel will be severely alienating if worn in a mountain village in Epirus or Crete or in any other area which is less accustomed to tourists. The best approach is to observe what people around you are wearing and to dress accordingly.

CUSTOMS

According to Greek Customs you are allowed to bring into the country duty-free: all used personal belongings (clothes, camping gear, etc.); foodstuffs and beverages up to 10 kilos; 300 cigarettes or a comparable amount of tobacco; 1.5 litres of distilled spirits or 2 litres of still wine; and two packs of playing cards. Cards, like matches, are a Greek State monopoly.

You may also bring one of each of the following: a camera and film; a movie camera and film; a projector; a pair of binoculars; a portable musical instrument; a portable radio, phonograph or tape recorder; a bicycle; and sports gear (such as skis, tennis rackets, etc.).

You may bring $150 worth of new articles duty-free (excluding electronic devices), provided they are intended for your personal use or as gifts, but not for resale.

It is prohibited to import narcotics, medicine (except limited quantities prescribed by a licensed physician which is for your own use), explosives, weapons and (yes, that's right) windsurfers – unless a Greek national residing in Greece guarantees they will be re-exported.

For other specific restrictions regarding the import and export of such things as animals, plants, shotguns, pleasure craft and antiquities, contact the nearest Greek embassy, consulate or Tourist Organisation.

GETTING ACQUAINTED

TIME ZONES

Greek time is two hours ahead of Greenwich Mean Time. So, when it is noon in Greece it is 10 a.m. in London, 5 a.m. in New York and 8 p.m. in Sydney.

As in the rest of the European Community, the clock is advanced one hour during summer to give extended daylight hours.

CLIMATE

The Greece seen in tourist posters is a forever warm and sunny place. And it is, by European standards, warm and sunny. But this picture does not do justice to Greece's considerable climatic variety. The north and inland regions have a "modified continental" climate, meaning that the winters are quite cold and summers very hot. In Ioánnina and Thessaloníki, for example, snow and freezing temperatures are not uncommon.

In the mountain regions, winters are even more inclement. The southern islands, most of the Peloponnése and the Attic Peninsula conform more to the traditional Mediterranean image: a long season of sun and warmth extending roughly from mid-April to mid-October. But here too, the winters are cool and rainy.

In general, late spring (April–June) and fall (September–October) are the best times to visit. During these periods, you'll find mild to warm temperatures, sunny days and fewer tourists. In July and August you'll find Greece at its sultriest and most crowded. Still, millions of tourists seem to prefer the heat and the company, choosing this period for their vacation in Greece.

Seasonal averages in Centigrade (and Fahrenheit):

	Jan–Mar	Apr–June
Minimum	6 (43)	11 (52)
Maximum	16 (61)	29 (84)
	July–Sept	Oct–Dec
Minimum	19 (66)	8 (46)
Maximum	32 (90)	23 (73)

ELECTRICITY

220 AC is the standard household electric current throughout Greece. This means that appliances from the United States require converters, which are not available in Greece. Greek outlets and plugs are different from both American and most European types, so you'll probably need an adapter as well. It's best to purchase these items before your departure.

BUSINESS HOURS

All banks are open to the public from 8 a.m. to at least 1 p.m. Monday through Friday. Some banks close half an hour earlier on Fridays. In heavily visited areas, however, you may find banks open additional hours and on the weekends for currency exchange.

The schedule for business and shop hours is somewhat more complicated. Business hours vary according to the type of business and the day of the week. The main thing to remember is that businesses generally open at 8 a.m. and close on Mondays, Wednesdays and Saturdays at 2.30 p.m. On Tuesdays, Thursdays and Fridays **most** businesses close at

1.30 p.m. and reopen in the afternoon from 5 p.m. to 8.30 p.m.

You'll soon learn that schedules are flexible in Greece (both in business and personal affairs). To avoid disappointment, allow yourself ample time when shopping and doing business. That way, you may also enter into the Greek spirit of doing business, in which a good chat can become as important as the matter of business itself.

HOLIDAYS

New Year's Day – January 1
Epiphany – January 6
Shrove Monday, First Day of Lent – moveable
Feast of the Annunciation/Independence Day – March 25
Labour Day and Flower Festival – May 1
Good Friday – moveable
Orthodox Easter – moveable
Pentecost – June 19
Assumption of the Holy Virgin – August 15
"Ohi Day," National Holiday – October 28
Christmas Day – December 25
Boxing Day – December 26

FESTIVALS

Below is a partial listing.

January 1
Feast of St. Basil: celebrated all over Greece.

January 6
Epiphany – Blessing of the waters: all over Greece.

January 8
"Gynaecocracy" – men and women switch roles: villages in the areas around Komotiní, Xánthi, Kilkis and Sérres (village of Monoklissia).

February–March
(the three weeks before Lent) Carnival season: all over Greece. Some villages with celebrations of special interest are: Náoüssa, Véria, Kozáni, Zánte, Skyros, Xánthi, Chíos (Mésta, Olimbi), Galaxídi, Thebes, Poligiros, Thimiana, Lamia, Cephaloniá, Messini, Sohos, Sérres, Agiassos (Lésvos), Kárpathos, Irákleion, Amfissa, Efxinoupolis (Vólos), Aghía Anna (Euboea), Réthymnon, Pátras.

Shrove Monday
Beginning of Lenten fast. Picnics in the countryside. Kite flying: all over Greece.

March 25
Independence Day – anniversary of the day Bishop Germános raised the standard of revolt against the Turks at Kalávrita in 1821: military parades in all main towns.

Easter Cycle
Good Friday, Holy Saturday and Easter Sunday are celebrated throughout the whole of Greece.

April 23
Feast of St. George: celebrated especially in Kaliopi (Lémnos), Aráhova, Assi Gonia (near Haniá) and Pili (Kos).

May 1
Labour Day/Flower Festival – picnics in the countryside: all over Greece.

Mid/late-May
Anastenárides: fire-walking ritual at Aghía Eléni (near Sérres) and at Langada (near Thessaloníki).

August 15
Assumption of the Virgin: festivals all over Greece. Major pilgrimage to island of Tínos.

September
Cricket on Corfú.

October 28
"Ohi (No) Day" – anniversary of Greek defeat of invading Italian army in 1940 and Metaxás' response to the Italian ultimatum: "No". Military parades held in all the major cities.

Christmas season
All over Greece. Little children sing carols door-to-door for a small gratuity.

December 31
New Year's Eve. More carols. Most of Greece plays cards on this occasion. Special celebration in the town of Chíos.

SEASONAL EVENTS

April–October
Sound and Light. Performances in Athens at the Pnyx; on Corfú at Old Venetian Castle; Rhodes, at Grand Master's.

May
Folklore Festival at Eléfsis.
Flower Festival at Gastouni in the Peloponnése.

May–September
Folk Dancing by the Dora Stratou Group at the Filopáppou Theatre.

May–October
Rhodes. Theatre, concerts, dance, etc.

June
Réthymnon Wine Festival.

June–August

Iráklion, concerts, theatre, opera, etc.

Lycabéttus Festival. Theatre performances at the Lycabéttus Hill Theatre.

Pátras Festival at the ancient theatre in the Peloponnése.

June–September

Athens Festival. Ancient drama, opera, music and ballet at the Herod Atticus Odeon.

July–August

Alexandroúpolis Wine Festival.

Crete International Festival. Performances organised by the Folk Art Museum on Crete.

Philippi and Thássos Festival. Ancient drama performances in the ancient theatres at Philippi and on Thássos.

Sun and Stone Festival. Greek folk dances at Nea Karvali in Kavála.

July–September

Epídaurus Festival. Performances of ancient drama in the open-air Epídaurus Theatre.

Daphne Wine Festival (near Athens).

Mid-July

Dafnes Wine Festival (near Iráklion).

Late-July

Music Festival. On the island of Ithaca.

August

Dodóna Festival. Ancient drama performances in ancient theatre at Dodóna.

Epirotika Festival – Ioánnina. Epirot cultural and artistic events.

Hippokrateia Festival – Kos. Various cultural events.

Olympus Festival – near Kateríni. Various cultural events in village of Litohoro and in the Platamona Castle.

Raisin Festival – Krestena, near Olympía. Colourful celebration.

Réthymnon. Various cultural activities at the Venetian Fort.

Early-September

Thessaloníki Trade Fair.

October

Thessaloníki Dimitria Festival. Theatre, music, ballet, etc.

Information and tickets for many of the above events can be obtained from the **G.N.T.O. (E.O.T.) Festival Office**, 2 Spirou Miliou Arcade, (entrance from 4 Stadíou St.), tel: 322-1459 or 322-3222, ext. 240.

COMMUNICATIONS

MEDIA

The Press in English: The many kiosks throughout the city generally receive British newspapers either late the same night (in Omonia Square) or, more usually the next day. There are two home grown newspapers: the daily *Athens News* is of little use except for its classified ads and comic relief due to its fractured use of the English language; *Greek News Weekly* is published on Saturday night and is generally far more interesting and informative, with a regular "What's On" section, a more intelligible prose style and photographs.

The Athenian: Greece's English Language Monthly, is just that, with features covering Greek politics, topics of interest and the arts. *Greece's Weekly* concentrates on business and finance and is sound in both areas. A mini-magazine, *Week in Athens,* has been published for 41 years by the National Tourist Organisation of Greece, and is available at NTOG offices.

For those with more literary interests there is *The Southeastern Review: A Quarterly Review of the Humanities in the Southeastern Mediterranean,* available at Eleftheroudakis and Reymondos bookstores downtown as well as from *periptera* throughout the city.

RADIO & TELEVISION

ERT 1 and **ERT 2** are the two Greek State radio channels. ERT 1 is divided into three different "programmes". First (728 KHz) and Second (1385 KHz) both have a lot of Greek popular music and news, some foreign pop and occasional jazz and blues. Third Programme (665 KHz) plays a lot of classical music. ERT 2 (98 KHz) is much like the first two programmes.

News can be heard in English, French, German and Arabic on the First Programme at 7.40 a.m. every day of the week; in English twice a day on ERT 2 at 2 p.m. and 9 p.m. The BBC World Service offers news on the hour (plus other interesting programmes and features). The best short wave (MHz) frequencies on which to pick up the BBC in Athens are: 3–7.30 a.m. GMT–9.41 (31 m.), 6.05 (49 m.), 15.07 (19 m.); 7.30 a.m.–6 p.m. GMT–15.07 (19 m.); 6.30 p.m.–11.15 p.m. GMT–9.41 (31 m.), 6.05 (49 m.), U.S. Armed Forces Radio (AFRS) operates 24 hours at 1594 KHz and 1484 KHz with news on the hour.

There are two state-owned and operated television channels in Greece – **ERT 1** and **ERT 2**. These channels often transmit American and English movies and programmes which, conveniently for the English-speaking viewer, are not dubbed, but rather carry Greek subtitles.

POSTAL SERVICES

Greek post offices are officially open Monday to Friday from 7.30 a.m. to 7.30 p.m. and on Saturday until 1 p.m. In practise, however, the hours are much more restricted. Certain sections within the post office, such as Registered Letters and Parcel Collection, may close as early as 1.30 p.m. on weekdays. Some regional post offices are closed by mid-afternoon. So, if you want to get something done at the post office, it is advisable to do it in the morning.

Postal rates are subject to fairly frequent change, so you'll do best to inquire at the post office. Stamps are available at the post office, and from many kiosks (*periptera*) and hotels for a slight surcharge. If you want to send a parcel from Greece, remember **not** to wrap it until a post office clerk has inspected it. Some post offices will then provide you, for a fee, the necessary materials to wrap it up. Otherwise you'll have to bring your own wrapping paper, string, scissors etc. If you're sending home bought goods, get the store to do it for you. Sending a package from Greece can be an exasperating experience.

Letters can be sent Post Restante to any post office. Bring your passport when you go to pick up mail.

TELEPHONE & TELEGRAM

Most kiosks have phones, and this is the most convenient way to make a local phone call. A call costs 10 drs. There are also coin phones, usually red, that may be found in coffee shops, hotels, restaurants and kiosks as well. And in certain places you'll also find phone booths – the blue ones for local calls, the orange for long distance.

You can also make long distance calls from any one of the many kiosks which have metered phones. However, a call from a kiosk will cost somewhat more than from the state phone company, OTE. Still, sometimes getting to the local OTE is such a hassle that you'll find the 15–20 percent additional charge worth it. Many hotels also have these metered phones.

Telegrams can be sent from the OTE. There are at least four different types of cables that you can send: the regular cable; the urgent cable which costs twice as much; the greetings telegram, again twice as much; and the letter telegram.

Most sizeable Greek towns and cities have an OTE office where you can make long distance calls and send telegrams. Some in the larger cities are open 24 hours, others from 7.30 a.m. to 11.30 p.m.

For a listing of the area codes of major Greek cities, see the "Emergencies" section.

EMERGENCIES

MEDICAL SERVICES

PHARMACIES

In Greece there are certain pharmacies which are open outside normal shop hours and which work on a rotating basis. If you need a pharmacy after hours or on weekends, you can find out which ones are open either by looking at the card posted in any pharmacy's window (which gives details on 24-hour pharmacies) or by consulting a local newspaper.

HOSPITALS

In case of a medical emergency requiring hospital treatment in Athens, call 166. If for some reason this fails, call the local Tourist Police (*see listing below*). They should speak English and will have information as to which hospitals have emergency facilities.

The Greek health system will be bewildering to the tourist who needs to make use of it, particularly in an emergency. Perhaps most important in emergencies is to find a competent speaker of both Greek and English who can make the necessary maneuverings for the patient's safety and inform you of what is going on. If entirely helpless, try calling your embassy. US citizens can call the "**emergency**" number 721-2951 in Athens.

GREEK TOURIST POLICE
TELEPHONE NUMBERS

(with the area codes of main Greek cities)

Athens	(01) 171 & 8221-721
Aégina	(0297) 22-391
Agrínion	(0641) 23-381
Alexandroúpolis	(0551) 28-424
Argostóli (Cephaloniá)	(0671) 22-200
Arta	(0681) 27-580
Aghios Nikólaos	(0841) 28-156
Délphi	(0265) 82-200
Edessa	(0381) 23-355
Halkis (Halkída)	(0221) 24-662
Haniá	(0821) 24-477
Hios (Chíos)	(0271) 26-555

Hydra	(0298) 52-205
Igoumenítsa	(0665) 22-302
Ikaría	(0275) 22-222
Ioánnina	(0651) 25-673
Irákleion	(081) 283-190
Itéa	(0265) 32-222
Kalamáta	(0721) 23-187
Kalambáka	(0432) 22-813
Kaména Voúrla	(0235) 22-425
Kassándra	(0374) 22-204
Kastoriá	(0467) 22-696
Kateríni	(0351) 23-440
Kavála	(051) 222-905
Kéa	(0288) 21-200
Kerkyra (Corfú)	(0661) 30-669
	& 30-265
Kíthnos	(0281) 31-201
Kórinthos (Corinth)	(0741) 23-282
Kos	(0242) 28-227
Lamía	(0231) 23-281
Lárissa	(041) 227-900
Lefkas (Lefkáda)	(0645) 92-389
Loutra Edipsoú	(0226) 22-456
Loutra Kaiafa	(0625) 31-706
Loutra Kilínis	(0623) 96-267
Loutra Smokovu	(0443) 61-204
Loutráki	(0741) 42-258
Missolóngi	(0631) 22-555
Methana	(0298) 92-463
Mytilíni	(025) 22-776
Mykonos	(0289) 22-482
Náfplion	(0752) 27-776
Nea Moudania	(0373) 22-100
Olympía	(0624) 22-550
Párga	(0684) 31-222
Páros	(0284) 21-673
Pátras	(061) 220-902
Piraéus	(01) 4523-670
Pírgos	(0621) 23-685
Póros	(0298) 22-462
Préveza	(0682) 22-225
Réthymnon	(0831) 28-156
Ródos (Rhodes)	(0241) 27-423
Sámos	(0273) 27-404
Sérres	(0321) 22-001
Sitaía (Crete)	(0843) 24-200
Spárta	(0731) 28-701
Spétsai	(0298) 73-100
Spilaia Dirou (Máni)	(0733) 522-000
Thássos	(0593) 22-500
Thessaloníki	(031) 522-589
Tínos (Andros)	(0283) 22-255
Trípolis	(071) 223-039
Vólos	(0421) 27-094
Vouliagméni	(01) 8946-555
Xylókastro	(0743) 22-331
Zákynthos	(0695) 22-550

GETTING AROUND

DOMESTIC TRAVEL

BY AIR

Olympic Airlines is the exclusive operator of domestic air routes in Greece. Most areas of the country are well-connected by air routes to and from Athens. A few routes run directly out of Thessaloníki and Irákleion as well. As travelling across the land and sea is half the fun of being in Greece, you'll probably choose to fly as an expedient because you want to cross an unusually great distance in a rush (Thessaloníki and Rhodes or Irákleion, for example).

Flying is considerably more expensive than travelling by boat, bus or train (two and a half times more on the average), though still cheap when compared to the price of domestic flights in other countries. The flight between Thessaloníki and Athens costs less than $50. You can book tickets at any Olympic office. Fare information and timetables are available at most NTOG offices and many hotels. For information and reservations by phone, call: 9616161.

BY ROAD

A vast network of bus routes spreads across Greece, called KTEL. This is a privately-run syndicate of bus companies whose buses are cheap, generally punctual and will take you to almost any destination that can be reached on wheels. Among Greeks it's the most popular way of travelling, so you'll have good company. KTEL buses often have a distinct "personal touch". Many drivers also own the bus (or have some other "familial" stake in it), decorating and treating the bus with great care. They're proud of the bus and of the way they drive it.

The most important thing to note about KTEL is that in larger cities there will be different bus stations for different destinations. Travelling from Thessaloníki to Halkidikí, for example, you'll leave from one station, and to Ioánnina, from another.

An additional bus service is that of **OSE**, the state railway organisation. This is a limited service and runs only the major routes.

BY RAIL

The best thing about rail travel in Greece is the price: it is even less expensive than taking the bus. Otherwise, the Greek rail service, known as **OSE**, is quite limited, both in the areas it reaches and frequency of departures. Greek trains are also quite slow and, unless you are doing the Athens–Thessaloníki run overnight in a couchette, you'll probably find the bus more convenient.

You can speed things up by taking an express train for a small surcharge. If you're on a tight budget you can really cut costs by taking the train round-trip, in which case there's a 20 percent reduction.

WATER TRANSPORT

It's hard to imagine a trip to Greece without a boat trip. Nearly every island in the Greek seas can be reached by one kind of boat or another, be it a large car ferry, small passenger boat or fisherman's *caïque*.

FERRIES

Piraéus is the nerve centre of the Greek ferry network, and chances are you'll pass through it at least once.

In general, you can get information on ferries at the port police (in Piraéus and most other ports), known as the *limenarhío* in Greek, at most NTOG offices and at certain travel agents. The *limenarhío* has the most complete and up-to-date information. The NTOG bureau in Syntagma Square in Athens offers a weekly schedule which should be checked for accuracy. And when you inquire at a travel agent, be aware that they sometimes will inform you only of the ferry lines with which they are affiliated. In the high season the routes are numerous and it's worthwhile looking around before purchasing your ticket. It's also advisable not to purchase your ticket too far in advance of the boat's scheduled departure: very rarely do tickets for the boat ride actually sell out; more frequently there will be changes in schedules and you're left trying to get a refund. It's also possible to buy tickets on board and though it is sometimes more expensive, it's a last-minute alternative.

When you board your vessel in Piraéus, be sure you're on the right boat. With the number of last-minute changes, delays etc., it's possible to get on a boat headed to some other destination, or one not stopping at your chosen island.

All the above invokes this suggestion: be flexible when travelling the Greek seas. Apart from schedule-changes, a bad stretch of weather can keep you island-bound for as long as the wind blows. Strikes, too, occasionally are called during the summer, usually lasting a few days. However, when they do occur, there's usually advance notice given in the news media.

If you're travelling by car, especially during the high season, you'll have to plan somewhat further ahead because during the peak season, some lines are booked for many weeks in advance. Also if you want to book a room for an overnight trip during the high-season, it's wise to book ahead. Otherwise *gamma* class – also known as deck, tourist, or third – is the classic, cheap way to voyage the Greek seas. There's always a space of one sort or another – in community with an international multitude, singing with a guitar, passing a bottle around under the stars. And if the weather turns bad you can always go inside to the lounge, the snack bar or some quiet hallway corner.

FISHING BOATS

Apart from the major network of ferries there is also a whole informal sub-network of fishing boats that can get you to smaller, more remote islands. Sometimes, these boats cater to tourists, advertising their services in the harbour. Other times, if your destination is especially obscure, you'll have to ask around.

HYDROFOIL

At the other end of the naval spectrum, you'll find scheduled hydrofoil service to certain islands on the *Flying Dolphins*. These connect Piraéus with most of the Argo-Sarónic region (Aégina, Póros and many other ports, as far as Monemvasia), as well as Vólos with the Northern Spórades (Alónissos, Skiáthos, Skópelos etc.).

This is the executive way to island hop: the hydrofoils are more than twice as fast as normal ferries and twice as expensive. You'll get there quickly but unless you get one of the few available spaces aft, you'll have to weather the somewhat bumpy ride in a seat inside.

CRUISES

If you'd like to leave the planning and sailing and cooking in someone else's hands, then a cruise may be just the thing you want. A score of different Aegéan Sea cruises are available, some limited to Greek territory, other ranging as far as Venice and Port Said. Their length also varies considerably, from a one-day jaunt in the Argosaronic Gulf to a 14-day tour of the eastern Mediterranean. The names of cruise companies offering Mediterranean and Greek Island cruises are listed below. For more information see a travel agent.

Cruise Companies: Chandris Cruise; Cycladic Cruises; Epirotiki Lines; K Lines-Hellenic Cruises; Hellenic Mediterranean Lines; Intercruise LTD.; Mediterranean Sun Lines; Sun Line Cruises; Viking Yacht Cruises.

YACHT CHARTER

Chartering a yacht is one of the more exotic ways of island-hopping in Greece. It is by no means cheap, although renting a boat with a group of friends may not far exceed the price of renting rooms every night for the same number of people.

Depending on your nautical skills and your taste for autonomy, you can either take the helm yourself or let a hired crew do so for you. There are over 1,000 yachts available for charter in Greece, all of which are registered and inspected by the Ministry of the Merchant Marine. For more information about chartering a yacht in Greece contact:

The Greek Bareboat Yacht Owners Association, 56 Vas. Pavlou St., Kastélla-Piraéus (tel. 452-5465).
The Hellenic Professional Yacht Owners Association, 43 Freattydos St., Zéa Marina, Piraéus (tel. 452-6335).
The Greek Yacht Brokers and Consultants Association, 36 Alkyonis St., P. Pháliron, Athens (tel. 981-6582).

PUBLIC TRANSPORT

What follows is information on available forms of public transport and a few pointers on utilising them.

CITY BUSES

Travelling by the regular Athens blue buses is a fairly miserable way of getting around the city. They are crowded and hot, and the routes are a mystery even to long-time residents. However, they are reasonable, at 50 drachmas per ticket. Tickets, good for trolleys as well, are sold in books of 10, from specific news kiosks and special booths at bus and metro stations, and at various non-strategic points around the city. Most bus services run until midnight.

Separate services run to air and sea ports, and these can be useful. The Express service of distinctive blue and yellow double-decker buses runs from Syntagma Square (on Amalias Avenue) to both airports at regular intervals: buy your tickets (100 drs) at the kiosk by the stop. The Green bus 040 runs from Filellinon Street (near Syntagma Square) to Piraeus 24 hours a day, every 20 minutes (every hour after 1 a.m.). The Orange bus runs from 14 Mavromateon St., Areos Park, and takes approximately 90 minutes.

TROLLEY BUSES

Though marginally more comfortable than the regular bus service, the yellow trolleys are not recommended for short stay visitors as their routes are a mystery best left to the locals.

METRO

Due to extensive relics buried beneath the modern city, Athens does not have a comprehensive underground rail service. However, the one that exists runs between Piraéus and Kifissiá, is clean, reliable, and connects Piraéus with Monastiráki and Omonia. City centre stops are at Thisseíon, Monastiráki, and Omónia. Tickets are the same as those used on buses and trolleys, and are available at the stations.

TAXIS

On entry, ensure that the meter is switched on and registering "1" rather than "2", which is the rate between 1 a.m. and 5 a.m. Don't be worried if you find yourself joined, en route, by a large cross-section of Athenian society going roughly your way. It is perfectly legal for drivers to pick up as many people as is comfortably possible, and charge them all individually. The tariff regulations are:

Minimum fare – 240 drs
Flag down – 30 drs
Night hours: 1 a.m. to 5 a.m. – Roughly double the daytime rate.

There is a surcharge from airports, seaports, railway stations and bus terminals; passengers may also be charged a small fee for luggage.

Private Taxi Transfer Service: Affable Athenian cabbies are few and far between, and the inconvenience and sheer aggravation of finding a taxi in the city have given rise to private taxi services. One of the best may be contacted through Julie Hardenberg and Sylvia Rill, at tel: 323-2870 or 325-1176. This fleet of roomy, air-conditioned Mercedes and Volvos is available 24 hours to transport visitors to the airports, Rafina, Piraéus...anywhere at all. Private guided tours of Athens' sites, daytrips, *bouzoúki* evenings, and shopping jaunts may all be arranged by phoning in advance. Drivers will even carry your luggage in to the check-out counter at the airport.

PRIVATE TRANSPORT

Having a car in Greece enables you to get to a lot of otherwise inaccessible corners of the country. As a tourist you will be able to drive for up to four months without having to pay Greek road taxes. When you enter the country with your car it will be "written into" your passport. This entry will state that you are not allowed to leave the country without your car. If for some reason you want to leave without your car, you are obliged to have it "sealed" and withdrawn from circulation before your departure.

Warning: this process can be very complicated and time-consuming, and a real problem if you have to leave in a rush.

It is recommended that visiting foreign motorists

possess an international driver's license. These licenses are available through the auto club in your home country, or in Greece from **ELPA**, the Greek Automobile Touring Club.

Greek traffic control and signals are basically the same as in the rest of continental Europe. However, the actual practice of Greek driving has little in common with driving in Frankfurt or Oslo. Translate Zorba on wheels, if you will. A red light is often considered not so much an obligation as a suggestion. Greece has the highest accident rate in Europe after Portugal, so – drive defensively! Also, Greece now has a mandatory seat belt law. If you don't wear it you risk getting tagged with a considerable fine.

RENTALS

Cars: Renting a car in Greece is relatively expensive in comparison with other European countries. Prices vary according to the type of car, season, and length of rental and do not include local taxes and duties which can add to about 18 percent of the bill. Payment can generally be made with major credit cards. An International Driver's Licence (*see above*) is required and you must be at least 21 years old.

A few recommended firms in Athens are: **Hertz** (tel. 922-0102/03/04); **Avis** (tel. 923-8822 or 922-3760); **Hellascars** (tel. 323-3487). You can also make reservations through the **Association of Car Rental Enterprises** in Athens, 314 Syngrou Av., Kallithea (tel. 951-01). If you're a member of your home country's automobile club, chances are you're automatically granted full services from ELPA. For information call: 779-1615 (in Athens).

Motorcycles, Bicycles, Scooters: On most Greek islands and in many mainland tourist areas, you'll find agencies that rent small motorcycles, bicycles and various types of scooters. On the islands these are certainly the way to go. For a reasonable price, they give you the freedom to wander where you will. For longer periods, rates are cheaper. Before you set off, make sure the "bike" of whichever sort actually works.

Ask to take it for a test spin down the street. Otherwise you may get stuck with a lemon or, worse, they may hold you responsible for its malfunctioning when you return it. Above all, be extremely careful. More than one vacation in Greece has been ruined by the bumps, scratches and bruises of a moped accident.

WHERE TO STAY

The most widespread type of accommodation in Greece is the pension or cheap hotels, where you can still find a decent room at reasonable rates. Besides these, there is also a wide range of other possibilities, from the deluxe hotels to pension rooftops. Listed are a sampling of different categories of hotels in Athens and Thessaloníki. The abbreviations referred to are – single bed: sglb; double bed: dblb; suites: stes; and renovated: ren.

On the islands and in many parts of the mainland, another kind of cheap lodging is renting private rooms (*domátia*). These are rented out by local residents at prices controlled by the tourist police. In general, when looking for any kind of accommodation, the Tourist Police can be of considerable help. If you're in a fix, you can inquire at their office. If you'd like to make a reservation or arrangement in advance, call them and they'll often be able to help you out (*see listing in the "Emergencies" section*).

HOTELS

ATHENS

CATEGORY DE LUXE

Acropole Palace, 51, Patission St., 104 33 Athens (tel. 5223851-7, tlx. 21-5909). Built 1930, Ren 1981. Number of rooms: Sglb 40, Dblb 47, Stes 18. Air-conditioned throughout, has 2 bars, restaurant, roof garden, night club, convention facilities, transfer service also available from several points in Athens.

Amalia, 10, Amalias Ave., 105 57 Athens (tel. 3237301-9, tlx. 21-5161). Built 1961. Number of rooms: Sglb 6, Dblb 92, Stes 1. Air-conditioned throughout, central heating, bar, restaurant.

Astir Palace, Vass. Sophias & El. Venizelou corner, 106 71 Athens, Syntagma Sq. (tel. 36443112 [8 lines], tlx. 22-2380, Cbl. Astirathen). Built 1983. Number of rooms: Sglb 10, Dblb 38, Stes 28, VIP Stes 2. Fully air-conditioned, 4 channel audio system in all rooms and public areas, Apokalypsis gourmet restaurant, Asteria coffee shop, Athos bar, all rooms with TV and video, news-stand, sauna, health care, beauty parlor, conference and banquet facilities.

Athenaeum Inter-Continental, 89-93, Syngrou Ave., 117 45 Athens (tel. 9023666, tlx. 22-1554). Built 1982. Number of rooms: Dblb 630. Air-conditioned throughout, central heating, 2 bars, 3 restaurants, swimming pool, convention facilities with simultaneous translation in 4 languages and closed circuit TV, automatic dialling, colour TV in all rooms with in-house movies, secretarial service, valets, health studio, bank facilities.

Athens Chandris Hotel. 385, Syngrou Ave., 175 64 P. Phaleron (tel. 9414824-6, tlx. 21-8112, Cbl. Chandrotel-Athens). Built 1977. Number of rooms: Sglb 50, Dblb 300, Stes 22. Air-conditioned throughout, central heating, 2 bars, 2 restaurants, Four Seasons Restaurant, a-la-carte also for non-residents, coffee shop, room service, conference rooms, ballroom, swimming pool snack bar restaurant, parking facilities, free shuttle service between Hotel-Syntagma Sq.

Athens Hilton, 46, Vass. Sofias Ave., 106 76 Athens (tel. 7220201-9, tlx. 21-5808, Cbl. Hiltels). Built 1963, Ren 1974. Number of rooms: Dblb 480, Stes 24. Air-conditioned throughout, 3 bars, 5 restaurants, swimming pool, convention facilities, secretarial service, auto dress cleaning.

Athens Holiday Inn, 50, Michalakopoulou St., 115 28 Athens, (tel. 7248322-29, tlx. 21-8870). Built 1979. Number of rooms: Dblb 200. Air-conditioned throughout, central heating, American bar, restaurant, coffee shop, discotheque, bowling, meeting and banqueting facilities up to 500 persons, parking, Bistro Greek.

Caravel, 2, Vass. Alexandrou Ave., 161 21 Kessariani (tel. 7290721-29, 7290731, tlx. 21-4401). Built 1975. Number of rooms: Sglb 100, Dblb 316, Stes 55. 3 bars, 3 restaurants, roof garden, indoor & outdoor swimming pools, room service, 24-hour coffee shop, all hotel operations fully computerised, conference facilities, conventions and other professional group events, near business and sightseeing center.

Grande Bretagne, Syntagma (Constitution) Sq., 105 63 Athens (tel. 3230251-9, 3250701-9 [72 lines], tlx. 21-9615, 21-5346, Cbl. Hotbritan). Built 1862, Ren 1962, Refurbished 1981. Number of rooms: 450 rooms, plus 25 suites from Junior to Presidential. Air-conditioned throughout, central heating, 2 bars, 3 restaurants, 24-hour room service, convention & function facilities.

Ledra Marriott Hotel-Athens, 115, Syngrou Ave., 117 45 Athens (tel. 9525211, tlx. 22-1833, Res. direct line 9324642). Built 1983. Number of rooms: 258, Stes 25. All rooms with individual climate control, air-conditioning, radio, colour TV, in-room movies, minibar, 24-hour room service, direct dial telephone with message light, rooftop swimming pool, hydrotherapy pool, bar, coffee shop, cocktail and lobby lounge, poolside bar, 3 restaurants, conference rooms, ballroom, pre-function space outside ballroom, audiovisual equipment.

Park, 10, Alexandras Ave., 106 82 Athens (tel. 8832711-19, tlx. 21-4748, Cbl. Parxente). Built 1976. Number of rooms: Sglb 15, Dblb 111, Stes 20. Air-conditioned thoughout, central heating, coffee shop, pizzaria, roof garden, swimming pool, congress hall, room service gift shop, beauty parlor, garage.

N.J.V. Meridien Athens, Vass, Georgiou A' & Stadiou sts., 105 64 Athens, Syntagma Sq., (tel. 3255301 [9 lines], tlx. 21-0568, 21-0569). Built 1980. Number of rooms: Sglb 30, Dblb 124, Stes 28. Air-conditioned throughout, central heating, bar, restaurant, room service, all rooms with mini bar, colour TV & video.

Royal Olympic, 28, Diakou St., 117 43 Athens (tel. 9226411-13, 9220185, tlx. 21-5753, Cbl. Roytel). Built 1968. Number of rooms: Sglb 35, Dblb 262, Stes 8. Air-conditioned throughout, central heating, bar, restaurant, room service, convention facilities, transfer service is also available.

St. Geroge Lycabettus 2, Kleomenous St., Dexameni, Kolonaki, 106 75 Athens (tel. 7290711-19, tlx. 21-4253, Cbl. Mantzotel). Built 1973. Number of rooms: Sglb 21, Dblb 128, Stes 5. Air-conditioned throughout, central heating, bar, restaurant, room service, swimming pool, bank and convention facilities, roof garden, hairdressing, grill room with panoramic view to Acropolis.

CATEGORY A

Astor, 16, Kar. Servias St., 105 62 Athens (tel. 3255555, 3255111, tlx. 21-4018, Cbl Hotelastor). Built 1964, Ren 1983. Number of rooms: Sglb 32, Dblb 98, Stes 3. Air-conditioned throughout, central heating, bar, restaurant, room service.

Attica Palace, 6, Kar. Servias St., 105 62 Athens (tel. 3223006-8, Res 3237905, tlx. 21-5909). Built 1962. Number of rooms: Sglb 9, Dblb 69. Air-conditioned throughout, central heating, bar, restaurant, room service, snack bar.

Divani-Zafolia Palace, 19-23, Parthenonos St., 117 42 Athens (tel. 9229650-9, 9229151-5, tlx. 21-8306, Cbl Dizafotel). Built 1977. Number of rooms: Sglb 27, Dblb 159, Stes 7. Air-conditioned throughout, central heating, bar, restaurant, tavérna, swimming pool, convention facilities.

Electra Palace, 18, Nikodimou St., 105 57 Athens (tel. 3241401-7, tlx. 21-6896). Built 1973. Number of rooms: Sglb 20, Dblb 100. Air-conditioned throughout, central heating, bar, restaurant, room service, swimming pool.

Golden Age, 57, Michalakopoulou St., 115 28 Athens (tel. 7240861 [9 lines], tlx. 21-9292, Cbl Goldenage). Built 1975. Number of rooms: Sglb 18, Dblb 96, Stes 8. Air-conditioned throughout, central heating, bar, restaurant, cafeteria, tavérna, room service.

King Minos, 1, Pireos St., 105 52 Athens (tel. 5231111-18, tlx. 21-5339). Built 1964, Ren 1980. Number of rooms: Sglb 56, Dblb 122. Fully air-conditioned, central heating, bar, restaurant, room service, convention facilities, transfer service available.

Olympic Palace, 16, Filellinon St., 105 57 Athens (tel. 3237611, tlx. 21-5178, Cbl Olpallas). Built

1960, Ren 1965. Number of rooms: Sglb 26, Dblb 70. Air-conditioned throughout, central heating, bar, restaurant, room service, convention facilities.

CATEGORY B

Acadimos, 58, Akademias St., 106 79 Athens (tel. 3629220-9). Built 1962, Ren 1975. Number of rooms: Sglb 19, Dblb 104. Central heating, bar, restaurant, room service.

Acropolis View, 10, Galli & Webster sts., 117 42 Athens (tel. 9217303-5, tlx. 21-9936). Built 1971. Number of rooms: Sglb 3, Dblb 20. Air-conditioned throughout, central heating, bar restaurant, roof garden.

Adrian, 74, Adrianou St., 105 56 Athens (tel. 3250454, 3221553, 3250461). Built 1962, Ren 1976. Number of rooms: Sglb 22. Air-conditioned throughout, central heating, bar, roof garden.

Alfa, 17, Chalkokondyli St., 104 32 Athens (tel. 5243584-7). Built 1960, Ren 1984. Number of rooms: Sglb 9, Dblb 79. Central heating, bar, restaurant, room service.

Arethusa, Metropoleos & Nikis sts., 105 63 Athens (tel. 3229431-9, tlx. 21-6882). Built 1971. Number of rooms: Sglb 16, Dblb 72. Air-conditioned throughout, central heating, bar, roof garden, restaurant, room service.

Athens Center Hotel, 26, Sofokleous & Klisthenous sts., 105 52 Athens (tel. 5226110-19, tlx. 21-4488, Cbl Centerotel). Built 1976. Number of rooms: Sglb 13, Dblb 123. Air-conditioned throughout, central heating, bar, restaurant, roof garden, room service, parking facilities.

Athens City, 232 Patission St., 112 56 Athens (tel. 8629115-6). Built. 1985. Number of rooms: Sglb 6, Dblb 31, Stes 3. 40 bedrooms & stes. with 2 channel music, also rooms with TV & video, bar, air-conditioned, snack bar, 24 hours room service.

Athinais, 99, Vass. Sophias Ave., 115 21 Athens (tel. 6431133, 6441815, 6461682, 6431240, tlx. 21-9336, Cbl Athinotel). Built 1976. Air-conditioned throughout, central heating, bar, snack bar, restaurant, roof garden, room service.

Atlantic, 60, Solomou St., 104 32 Athens (tel. 5235361-6, tlx. 21-5723). Built 1960, Ren 1972. Number of rooms: Sglb 41, Dblb 117. Air-conditioned only in double rooms, central heating, bar restaurant, room service.

Balascas, Liossion & Epirou sts., 104 39 Athens (tel. 8835211-5, tlx. 21-0618). Built 1978. Number of rooms: Sglb 14, Dblb 69. Air-conditioned throughout, bar, restaurant.

Christina, 15, Petmeza & Kallirois sts., 117 43 Athens (tel. 9215353-7, 9215342-4, tlx. 21-9304). Built 1975. Number of rooms: Sglb 13, Dblb 80. Air-conditioned throughout, has central heating, 2 bars, snack bar, restaurant.

Dorian Inn, 15-17, Pireos St., 105 52 Athens (tel. 5239782, 5231753-7, tlx. 21-4779, Cbl Hoteldorian). Built 1974. Number of rooms: Sglb 5, Dblb 112,

Stes 29. Air-conditioned throughout, central heating, 2 bars, restaurant, room service, swimming pool, convention facilities, roof garden, direct dial telephone system.

El Greco 65, Athinas St., 105 52 Athens (tel. 3244553-7, tlx. 21-9682, Cbls Grecotel, Apriltd). Built 1958, Ren 1980. Number of rooms: Sglb 17, Dblb 75. Several rooms air-conditioned, central heating, bar, restaurant, room service, snack bar, cafeteria.

Eretria, 12, Chalkokondyli St., 106 77 Athens, Kaningos Sq., (tel. 3635311 [10 lines], tlx. 21-5474). Built 1966 Ren 1980. Number of rooms: Sglb 7, Dblb 49, Stes 7. Air-conditioned throughout, central heating, bar, restaurant, room service, cafeteria.

Grand, 19, Patission St., 104 32 Athens (tel. 5243156-9). Built 1975. Number of rooms: Sglb 8, Dblb 91. Air-conditioned throughout, central heating, bar, restaurant, room service, convention facilities.

Ilissos, 72, Kallirrois Ave., 117 41 Athens (tel. 9215371, 9223523-9, tlx. 21-0537). Built 1980. Number of rooms: Sglb 16, Dblb 80. Air-conditoned throughout, central heating, bar, restaurant, cafeteria, room service, convention facilities.

Ionis Hotel, 41, Chalkokondyli St., 104 32 Athens, (tel. 5232311 [4 lines], 5230413 [4 lines], tlx. 21-8425, Cbl Ionishotel). Built 1977. Number of rooms: Sglb 10, Dblb 92. Air-conditioned throughout, central heating, 2 channel music in the rooms, bar, restaurant.

Palladion, 54, El. Venizelou Ave., 106 78 Athens (tel. 3623291-5). Built 1907, Ren 1974. Number of rooms: Sglb 1, Dblb 57. Rooms air-conditioned, central heating, bar, room service.

Pan, 11, Metropoleos St., 105 57 Athens (tel. 3237817, tlx. 22-1911, Cbl Panhotel). Built 1960, Ren 1984. Number of rooms: Sglb 6, Dblb 46, Stes 8. Public rooms and most of rooms air-conditioned, central heating, snack bar, room service.

Plaka, 7, Kapnikareas St., 105 56 Athens (tel. 3222096-8, tlx. 22-1020. Cbl Plakotel Athens). Built 1960. Number of rooms: Sglb 11, Dblb 56. Air-conditioned throughout, has central heating, bar, restaurant, room service.

Titania, 52, El. Venizelou Ave., 106 78 Athens (tel. 3609611-9, tlx. 21-4673, Cbl Titanotel). Built 1976. Number of rooms: Sglb 42, Dblb 333, Stes 21. Rooms fully air-conditioned with private baths, radio music, TV sets on request, restaurant with Greek specialities and international dishes, snack bar, piano cocktail lounge "Taboo" in the roof garden, convention facilities, garage for 400 cars, shopping center.

Xenophon, 340, Acharnon St. 111 45 Athens (tel. 2020310-24, tlx. 21-5294). Built 1970. Number of rooms: Sglb 22, Dblb 164. Air-conditioned throughout, central heating, bar restaurant, room service, convention facilities, garage, parking facilities, transfer service available.

CATEGORY C

Achilleus, 21, Lekka St., 105 62 Athens (tel. 3233197, 3225826).

Achillion, 32, Ag. Konstantinou St., 104 37 Athens (tel. 5225618).

Albyon, 20, Akominatou St., 104 37 Athens (tel. 5231137, 5223058).

Alma, 5, Dorou St., 104 31 Athens (tel. 5240858-9).

Ami, 10, Iras St., 117 43 Athens (tel. 9220820).

Apollon, 14, Deligiorgi St., 104 37 Athens (tel. 5245211, 5245214).

Arias, 20, Karolou St., 104 37 Athens (tel. 5228527-9).

Aristidis, 50, Sokratous St., 104 31 Athens (tel. 5223881, 5223923).

Artemission, 20, Veranzerou St., 104 32 Athens (tel. 5230524, 5230036, 5234959).

Astra, 46, Deligianni St., 104 39 Athens (tel. 8213772).

Athinea, 9, Vilara St., 104 37 Athens (tel. 5243884-5, 5245737).

Attalos, 20, Athinas St., 105 54 Athens (tel. 3212801-3).

Capri, 6, Psaromilingou St., 105 53 Athens Koumoundourou Sq. (tel. 3252085, 3252091).

Crystal, 68, Kolonou & Achilleos sts., 104 37 Athens (tel. 5231083).

Delph, 21, Ag. Konstantinou Sq., 104 37 Athens (tel. 5222751, 5226549).

Economy, 5, Klisthenous St., 105 52 Athens (tel. 5220520-2).

Elite, 23, Pireos St., 105 52 Athens (tel. 5221523, 5223610).

Epidavros, 14, Koumoundourou St., 104 37 Athens (tel. 5230421).

Evropa, 7, Satovriandou St., 104 31 Athens (tel. 5223081).

Fivos, 12, Petta St., 105 58 Athens (tel. 3220142-3).

Florida, 25, Menandrou St., 105 53 Athens (tel. 5223214, 5239712).

Helicon, 3, Dorou St., 104 31 Athens (tel. 5221695, 5228428).

Hera, 9, Falirou St., 117 42 Athens, Makriyanni area (tel. 9235618, 9236682).

Jason, 3, Nikiforou St., 104 37 Athens (tel. 5248031-3).

Imperial, 46, Metropoleos St., 105 63 Athens (tel. 3227617-8).

Kalypso, 34, Epikourou St., 105 53 Athens (tel. 3251451-2).

Keramikos, 30, Keramikou & Iassonos Streets, 104 36 Athens (tel. 5247631, 5247443).

Kissos, 6, Mezonos St., 104 38 Athens (tel. 5243011-3).

Kronos, 18, Ag. Dimitriou St., 105 54 Athens (tel. 3211601-3).

Lido, 2, Nikiforou & Zinonos sts., 104 37 Athens (tel. 5248211-4).

Marina, 13, Voulgari St., 104 37, Athens (tel. 5224769, 5229109).

Medoussa, 4, Evripidou St., 176 74 Kallithea (tel. 9426216).

Minion, 3, Mezonos St., 104 38 Athens (tel. 5234222-3).

Morfeus, 3, Aristotelous St., 104 32 Athens (tel. 5234601).

Museum, 16, Bouboulinas St., 106 82 Athens (tel. 3605611-3).

Nafsika, 21, Karolou St., 104 37 Athens (tel. 5239381-3).

Nefeli, 16, Hyperidou St., 105 58 Athens (tel. 3228044-5).

Neon Kronos, 12, Assomaton St., 105 53 Athens (tel. 3251106-8).

Nestorion, 8, Pentelis St., 174 64 Amphithea (tel. 9425010, 9420272, tlx. 22-1427).

Niki, 27, Nikis St., 105 57 Athens (tel. 3220913-5, 3220886).

Olympia, 25, Pireos St., 105 52 Athens (tel. 5222429).

Omega, 15, Aristogitonos St., 105 52 Athens (tel. 3212421-3).

Orpheus, 58, Chalkokondyli St., 104 32 Athens (tel. 5224996).

Parnon, Tritis Septemvriou & Chalkokondyli sts., 104 32 Athens (tel. 5230013-14, 5235196).

Phedias, 39, Apostolou Pavlou St., 118 51 Athens (tel. 3459511-5).

Pringhipikon, 27, Veranzerou St., 104 32 Athens (tel. 5232376).

Rivoli, 10, Achilleos St., 104 36 Athens (tel. 5239714-6).

Roosvelt, 5, Favierou St., 104 38 Athens (tel. 5223413).

Sans Rival, 2, C. Paleologou & Liossion sts., 104 38 Athens (tel. 5248675, 5223431).

Stalis, 10, Akominatou St., 104 37 Athens (tel. 5241411-2).

Theoxenia, 6, Gladstonos St., 105 77 Athens (tel. 3600250).

Troikon, 20, Troias St., 112 57 Athens (tel. 8816695, 8217319).

Vienna, 20, Pireos St., 104 31 Athens (tel. 5225605-7).

Zinon, 3, Keramikou St., 104 37 Athens (tel. 5228811-13).

THESSALONÍKI

CATEGORY DE LUXE

Makedonia Palace, Meg. Alexandrou St., 546 40 Thessaloníki (tel. 837520-9, 837620-9, tlx. 41-2162, 41-2164 Cbl Macepal). Built 1972. Number of rooms: Sglb 44, Dblb 228, Stes 15. Air-conditioned throughout, bar, restaurant, room service, congress facilities.

CATEGORY A

Capitol, 8, Monastiriou St., 546 29 Thessaloníki (tel. 516221, tlx. 41-2272). Built 1967. Number of rooms: Sglb 35, Dblb 152, Stes 7. Air-conditioned throughout, central heating, bar, restaurant, room service, convention facilities.
Electra Palace, 5a, Aristotelous Sq., 546 24 Thessaloníki (tel. 232221, tlx. 41-2590). Athens office: 5, Ermou St., (tel. 3232104). Built 1972. Number of rooms: Sglb 32, Dblb 93 Stes 6. Fully air-conditioned, central heating, bar, restaurant, grill room, room service, convention facilities.
Nepheli, 1, Komninon St., 552 36 Panorama (tel. 942002, 042024, 942068, 942080, tlx. 41-0357). Built 1967. Number of rooms: Sglb 10, Dblb 55, Stes 5. Partially air-conditioned, central heating, bar, restaurant, room service, roof garden, night club, convention facilities, parking.
Panorama, 14, Analipseos St., 552 36 Panorama (tel 941123, 941266, 941229). Built 1969. Number of rooms: Sglb 12, Dblb 35 Stes 3. Central heating, bar, restaurant, room service, cafeteria.

CATEGORY B

Astor, 20, Tsimiski St., 546 24 Thessaloníki (tel. 527121-5, tlx. 41-2655). Built 1973. Number of rooms: Sglb 12 Dblb 72, Stes 6. Air-conditioned throughout, central heating, bar restaurant, parking facilities.
Capsis, 18, Monastiriou St., 546 29 Thessaloníki (tel. 521321-9, 521421-9, tlx. 41-2206, Cbl Capsotel). Built 1970. Number of rooms: Sglb 33, Dblb 395. Air-condition optional, central heating, bar, restaurant, room service, swimming pool, convention facilities, discotheque, hairdressing, sauna, dress cleaning.
City Hotel, 11, Komninon St., 546 29 Thessaloníki (tel. 269421-30, tlx. 41-2208). Built 1972. Number of rooms: 210 beds. Air-conditioned throughout, central heating, all rooms with telephone & verandah, bar, cafeteria, TV lounge.
El Greco, 23, Egnatias St., 546 30 Thessaloníki (tel. 520620-30). Built 1970. Number of rooms: Sglb 18, Dblb 72. Air-conditioned throughout, central heating, bar, restuarant, parking, automatic telephone service.
Metropolitan, Vass. Olgas & Fleming sts., 546 42 Thessaloníki (tel. 824221 [8 lines], tlx. 41-2380). Built 1979. Number of rooms: Sglb 12, Dblb 99, Stes 8. Stes air-conditioned, central heating, bar, restaurant, room service, olympic airways bus stop in front of the hotel, TV room, automatic outside telephone connection, parking facilities.
Olympia, Venizelou & 65, Olympou sts., 546 31 Thessaloníki, 12 km from the airport (tel. 235421 [5 lines], 263201 [5 lines], tlx. 41-8532, Cbl Olympotel). Ren 1980. Number of rooms: Sglb 15, Dblb 100. Air-conditioned throughout, central heating, bar, restaurant, cafeteria, fireplace, colour TV lounge, special halls for business or social events, car parking facilities.

Olympic, 25, Egnatias St., 546 30 Thessaloníki (tel. 522131-3). Built 1969, Ren 1975. Number of rooms: Sglb 13, Dblb 39. Central heating bar.
Palace, 12, Tsimiski St., 546 24 Thessaloníki (tel. 270505, 270855, 238838, 225368). Ren 1968. No. of rooms: Sglb 33, Dblb 25. Central heating, bar, restaurant, room service.
Philippion, Kedrinos Lofos, 5 km from the city centre (tel. 203320-22, tlx. 41-0210). Ren 1979. Number of rooms: Sglb 18, Dblb 70, Stes 2. Central heating, bar, restaurant, coffee-shop, mini golf, pizzaria, swimming pool, night club, disco.
Queen Olga, 44, Vass. Olgas Ave., 546 41 Thessaloníki (tel. 824621 [10 lines]). Built 1969. Number of rooms: Sglb 35, Dblb 113. Air-conditioned throughout, central heating, bar, restaurant, room service, parking facilities available.
Rotonda, 97, Monastiriou St., 546 27 Thessaloníki (tel. 517121-3, tlx. 41-2322, Cbl Hotel Rotonda). Built 1966. Number of rooms: Sglb 16, Dblb 63. Air-conditioned throughout, central heating, bar, restaurant, room service.
Victoria, 13, Lagada St., 546 29 Thessaloníki (tel. 522421-5, tlx. 41-2145). Built 1965. Number of rooms: Sglb 9, Dblb 58. Partially air-conditioned, central heating, bar, restaurant, room service.

CATEGORY C

ABC Hotel, 41, Agelaki St., Sidrivani Sq., 546 21 Thessaloníki (tel. 265421 [5 lines], 221761, 279765 tlx. 41-0056). Built 1968. Number of rooms: Sglb 15, Dblb 87, Stes 5. Partially air-conditioned, central heating, bar, cafeteria & breakfast room with fireplace and airconditioning, suites with air-conditioning, colour TV, mini bar, balcony.
Aegeon, 19, Egnatias Ave., 546 30 Thessaloníki (tel. 522921-3).
Amalia, 33, Hermou St., 546 24 Thessaloníki (tel. 268321).
Anessis, 20, 26th October St., 546 27 Thessaloníki (tel. 515505-6).
Ariston, 5, Diikitiriou St., 546 30 Thessaloníki (tel. 519630).
Continental, 5, Komninon St., 546 24 Thessaloníki (tel. 277553).
Delta, 13, Egnatias St., 546 30 Thessaloníki (tel. 516321-7).
Emborikon, 14, Syngrou St., 546 30 Thessaloníki (tel. 525560).
Park, 81, Ionos Dragoumi St., 546 30 Thessaloníki (tel. 524121-4).
Pefka, Panorama (tel. 941153, 941282).
Pella, 65, Ionos Dragoumi St., 546 30 Thessaloníki (tel. 524221).
Rea, 6, Komninon St., 546 24 Thessaloníki (tel. 278449).
Rex, 39, Monastiriou St., 546 27 Thessaloníki (tel. 517051, 517052).

Teleioni, 16, Ag. Dimitriou St., 546 30 Thessaloníki (tel. 527825-6).
Thessalikon, 60, Egnatias Ave., 546 27 Thessaloníki (tel. 277722, 223805).
Vergina, 19, Monastiriou, St., 546 27 Thessaloníki (tel. 527400-8).

FURNISHED APARTMENTS

ATHENS

CATEGORY A

Ariane, 22, Tim. Vassou St., 115 21 Athens (tel. 6466361-2, 6437302-4).
Ava, 9, Lyssikratous St., 105 58 Athens (tel. 3236618).
Delice, 3, Vass. Alexandrou St., 115 28 Athens (tel. 7238311-13).
Embassy, 15, Timoleontos Vassou St., 115 21 Athens (tel. 6421152-4).
Kolonaki, 7b, Kapsali St., 106 74 Athens (tel. 7213759, 7228412).
Lion, 7, Evzonon St., 115 21 Athens (tel. 7248722-4).
Perli, 4, Arnis St., 115 28 Athens (tel. 7248794-8, tlx. 21-5444).

CATEGORY B

Egnatia, 64, Tritis Septemvriou St., 104 33 Athens (tel. 8227807).
Iokastis, HOUSE 65, Aristotelous St., 104 34 Athens (tel. 8226647).

PENSIONS

ATHENS

CATEGORY A

Blue House, 19, Voukourestiou St., 106 71 Athens (tel. 3620341).

CATEGORY B

Acropolis House, 6, Kodrou St., 105 58 Athens (tel. 3222344, 3244143).
Adam's, 6, Herefontos & Thalou sts., 105 58 Athens (tel. 3246582, 3225381).
Adonis, Voulis & 3, Kodrou sts., 105 58 Athens (tel. 3249737, 3249738).
Akron, 16, Theras St., 112 57 Athens (tel. 8626220, 8626228).
Angela, 38, Stournara St., 104 33 Athens (tel. 5220216-7).
Antoniou, 232, Patission St., 112 56 Athens (tel. 8629841-2).
Apostolopoulos, 284, Patission & 5, Mistriotou sts., 112 55 Athens (tel. 2236375).

Aristofanis, 38, Aristophanous St., 105 54 Athens (tel. 3250872).
Athenian Inn, 22, Haritos St., 106 75 Athens (tel. 7238097, 7239552).
Athens House, 4, Aristotelous St., 104 32 Athens (tel. 5240539).
Byron, 9, Vironos St., 105 58, Athens (tel. 3230327).
Dryades, 4, Dryadon St., 114 73 Athens (tel. 3602961, 3622881).
Elisabeth, 46, Arkadias St., 115 27 Athens (tel. 7775448).
Elli, 29, Heyden St., 104 34 Athens (tel. 8823487).
Feron, 43, Feron St., 104 40 Athens (tel. 3632831-9, tlx. 21-5077).
George, 46, Nikis St., 105 58 Athens (tel. 3229569).
Heliki, 4, Enianos St., 104 34 Athens (tel. 8822560, 8810627).
Iokasti's House, 65, Aristotelous St., 104 34 Athens (tel. 8226647).
Iris, 8, Sorovits St., 112 52 Athens (tel. 8647442, 8653222, 8654229).
Kirki, 40, Kefalinias St., 112 57 Athens (tel. 8235733).
Kypseli, 7, Skyrou St., 113 61 Athens (tel. 8216232, 8213116, 8219898).
Lydia, 121, Liossion St., 104 45 Athens (tel. 8219980, 8237952, tlx. 21-9786).
Myrtc, 40, Nikis St., 105 58 Athens (tel. 3227237, 3234560).
Nora, 38, Antiochias St., 112 51 Athens (tel. 8628876).
Odysseus, 39, Kimothois St., 172 36 Athens (tel. 9700571).
Oniro, 57, S. Trikoupi St., 106 83 Athens (tel. 8832731-3).
Patissia, 221, Patission St., 112 53 Athens (tel. 8627511, 8627512).
Pnyx, 51, Apostolou Pavlou St., 118 51 Athens (tel. 3468859).
Remvi, 284, Patission & 3, Mystriotou sts., 112 55 Athens (tel. 2024124, 2231405).
Roy, 15, Rodou St., 112 52 Athens (tel. 8615765, 8618763, 8610843).
Soudan, 47, Mavromichali St., 106 80 Athens (tel. 2605037).
Steyer, 123, Char. Trikoupi St., 114 73 Athens (tel. 3615731).
Volcan, 10a, Ithakis St., 113 61 Athens (tel. 8815385).
Zorbas, 10, Gylfordou St., 104 34 Athens (tel. 8232543).

CATEGORY C

Amazon, 7, Pendelis St., 105 57 Athens (tel. 3234002-6).
Annabel, 28, Koumoundourou & Satovriandou sts., 104 37 Athens (tel. 5243454).
Argo, 25, V. Hugo St., 104 37 Athens (tel. 5225939).
Art Galery, 5, Erechthiou St., 117 42 Athens (tel. 9238376).

Athens Connections, 20, Ioulianou St., 106 82
Athens (tel. 8213940).
Christ, 11, Apollonos St., 105 57 Athens
(tel. 3220177, 3234581).
Diana, 3, Kotsika St., 104 34 Athens (tel. 8223179).
Dioskouros, 6, Pittakou St., 105 58 Athens
(tel. 3248165).
Greca, 48, Syngrou Ave., 117 42 Athens
(tel. 9215626).
Inn Student, 16, Kydathineon St., 105 58 Athens
(tel. 3244808).
John's Place, 5, Patroou St., 105 57 Athens
(tel. 3229719).
Kouros, 11, Kodrou St., 105 58 Athens
(tel. 3227431).
Marble House, 35, An. Zini St., 117 41 Athens
(tel. 9234058).
Milton, 4, Kotsika St., 104 34 Athens (tel. 8216806).
Paradise, 28, Mezonos St., 104 38 Athens
(tel. 5220084).
Pella Inn, 104, Ermou St., 105 54 Athens
(tel. 3250598).
Peter's, 32, Nikis St., 105 57 Athens (tel. 3222697).
San Remo, 8, Nissirou St., 104 38 Athens
(tel. 5243454).
Thesseus, 10, Thisseos St., 105 62 Athens
(tel. 3245960).
Tony's, 26, Zacharitsa St., 117 41 Athens
(tel. 9236370).

THESSALONÍKI

CATEGORY B

Athos, 20, Dagli St. (tel. 266990).
Elizabeth Motel, 293, Monastiriou St., 546 28
Thessaloníki (tel. 515712-3).
Haris Motel, Micra (tel. 417335).
Esperia, 58, Olympou St., 546 31 Thessaloníki
(tel. 269321-5).
Haris, Oreokastron (tel. 696174, 696198).
Grande Bretagne, 46, Egnatias Ave., 546 25
Thessaloníki (tel. 530735).
Madrino, 2, Antigonidon St., 546 30 Thessaloníki
(tel. 526321-5).
Minerva, 19, Syngrou Ave., 546 30 Thessaloníki
(tel. 530844).
Oceanis, 35, Nik. Plastira St., Aretsou (tel. 418870).

CAMP-SITES

Large numbers of tourists to Greece usually "rough
it" in one form or another. Those who want to camp
at organised camp-sites with facilities will find
hundreds of them all over Greece, some run by the
NTOG, some by the Greek Touring Club, and many
privately.

The most beautiful camp-sites in Greece, however,
are usually the ones you find on your own. While in
most places it is officially illegal just to lay out your
sleeping bag or pitch a tent, if you're discreet you'll

rarely be bothered. That means, asking permission
if you seem to be on private property, avoiding
"unofficial" camp-sites set up in popular tourist
areas, and, *always* leaving the place looking better
than when you came.

YOUTH HOSTELS

Greece has a number of youth hostels for which you
need a youth hostel card. However, you can often
buy one on the spot or just pay an additional charge.
There are youth hostels in: Athens, Mycénae,
Náfplion, Olympía, Pátras, Délphi, Litochoro,
Thessaloníki, Corfú, Santoríni, and on Crete at
Aghios Nikólaos, Haniá, Irákleion, St. Basil
(Réthymnon) and Sitía. There are also accommoda-
tions at the YMCA and YWCA in both Athens and
Thessaloníki.

MONASTERIES & CONVENTS

Monasteries and convents can often provide lodging
as well for travellers. Mt. Athos of course has a long
tradition of this hospitality (for men). Certain other
monasteries in Greece also welcome overnight visitors on a more informal basis. If you've found a
monastery that does accept overnight guests, realise
that you'll have to dress (no shorts) and behave
accordingly. The doors may close as early as sunset
and some kind of donation may be expected.

OTHER LODGINGS

There are two other special kinds of accommodations
in Greece worth mentioning: mountain refuges run
by the various Greek mountaineering clubs and
traditional settlements run by the NTOG.

MOUNTAIN REFUGES

Mountain refuges can range from a small 12-bed ski
hut where you need to bring your own food and
supplies to 100-bed lodges where all meals are
provided (*see listing in "Sports" section*).

TRADITIONAL SETTLEMENTS

The traditional settlements are villages recognised by
the Greek government as forming an important part
of the national heritage. Buildings in these villages
have been restored and set up by the NTOG for
tourist use. At the moment, there are eight such
villages with others to be restored and developed in
the future. These houses and villages are, in their
different ways, strikingly beautiful, and highly
recommended for a week or month retreat in rural
Greece. The NTOG traditional settlements are:

Oía (Santoríni), Paradosiakós Ikismós Oías, Oía,
Santoríni, Greece, tel. (0286) 71234.
Makrinítsa (on Pélion Mountain), Xenia Hotel,

Portaria Village, tel. (0421) 25922.
Vizitsa (on Pélion Mountain), tel. (0423) 86373.
Mesta (on Chíos Island), Paradosiakós Ikismós, Mesta, Chíos, Greece.
Psará Island, tel. (0251) 27908.
Fiskárdo (on Cephaloniá Island), Paradosiakós Ikismós Fiskárdou, Fiskárdo, Cephaloniá, Greece, tel. (0674) 51398.
Kapetanákos Tower (Areópolis, Máni), tel. (0733) 51233.
Papingo, Zagorohória (Epirus), tel. (0653) 25087/ (0651) 25087.

Reservations can be made either through the above addresses or by writing directly to: **Greek National Tourist Organisation**, EOT Dieftynisi Ekmetalefseos, 2 Amerikis Street, Athens 10564, Greece.

FOOD DIGEST

WHAT TO EAT

Eating out in Greece is above all a social affair. Whether it be with your family or your *paréä,* that sacred circle of friends, a meal out is an occasion to celebrate, a time for *kéfi.*

This may have something to do with the fact that eating out in Greece continues to be affordable and popular, not something restricted to those who have American Express cards. And the predominance of the *tavérna,* that bastion of Greek cuisine, reflects this popularity. These casual eating establishments have more or less the same style and set-up throughout Greece, and the menu too is more or less similar. Which is to say no frills, no packaging which tries to convince the "consumer" that this *tavérna* is different from the others – special, distinct. The place, and your being there, is somehow taken for granted: you eat the good food at Yannis's or Yorgos', you enjoy yourself, and you don't pay an arm and a leg for it.

This is the general background for eating out in Greece against which we find, of course, considerable variation. The *tavérna* is by no means the only kind of eating establishment. You'll also encounter: the *éstiatório,* the restaurant as we usually think of it – fancier and more polished than the *tavérna,* with linen table-cloths and higher prices; the *psistariá,* a barbecue-style restaurant which specialises in lamb, pork or chicken on a spit; the *psaro-tavérna* which specialises in fish; the *ouzerí* which is mainly an establishment for drinking, but which also serves *mezédes,* snacks of various types; the *gyros* stand with gyro sandwiches and the *souvlatzíthiko,* sometimes a sit-down place with salads.

There's also considerable regional variety in Greek cuisine and you should keep an eye out for those specialities of the house which you haven't seen before. Another thing you'll quickly learn in Greece is how strikingly different the same dish can be when it is prepared well or prepared badly, for example, a *melitsanosaláta* or stuffed tomatoes. It's therefore worthwhile shopping around for your *tavérna* (especially in heavily visited areas), asking the locals what they suggest, walking into the kitchen to look at the food (a customary practise), instead of getting stuck with the tourist trap which spoils your appetite for *moussaká for* the rest of the trip.

Here are few notes about Greek eating habits. In Greece, the main meal is eaten at midday, between 1.30 p.m. and 2.30 p.m. and is usually followed by a *siesta* break lasting until 6 p.m. The evening meal can either be another full meal, or an assortment of *mezéthes.* This is usually eaten sometime between 9 p.m. and 11 p.m. Breakfast in Greece is rather meagre, usually consisting of bread, butter, jam and coffee.

Some *tavérnes* you'll find do not have menus, or have menus without prices. It's a good idea to inquire with the restaurateur how much things cost before you eat them. And, as mentioned above, you can always find out what dishes they serve by walking into the kitchen.

The list below is a partial listing of some of the more popular foods you'll find on your travels.

STARTERS (MEZÉTHES)

Hors d'oeuvres **and dips – usually eaten as appetisers with** *psomí* **(bread):**
Kolokithákia – deep-fried courgettes (zucchini)
melitsánosálata – eggplant dip
rossikisaláta – cold potato salad, lots of mayonnaise
táramasaláta – fish roe pate/dip
tzazíki – yoghurt/cucumber dip, heavily garlicked

VEGETABLES (LAHANIKÁ)

angináres – artichokes
arakádes – peas
bámies – okra
dolmáthes – stuffed grape leaves
fasolákia – snap beans
horiátiki saláta – olive, feta cheese, onion, cucumber and tomato salad
hórta – steamed wild greens
koukiá – horse beans
maróuli – lettuce
patzária – beets
yemistés – stuffed tomatoes or peppers
yígantes – large haricot beans

VARIOUS MEATS (KRÉATA)

Note the following terms:
psitó – roasted; *sti soúvla* – barbecued on the spit;
tiganitó – fried; *sto foúrno* – baked; *skáras* – grilled;
vrastó – boiled; *kapnistó* – smoked.

arní – lamb
biftéki – "beefsteak," ground beef patty
brizóla – pork or beef chop (*hirinó* or *mosxhári* respectively)
keftédes – meatballs
kokorétsi – stuffed innards roasted on the spit
kotópoulo – chicken
loukániko – sausages
mialó – brain
païdákia – lamb chops
sikóti – grilled liver
souvláki – chunks of pork or lamb roasted on the spit or fried.

DISHES, SOUPS & SPECIALITIES

avgolémono – chicken stock thickened with egg and lemon
fasoláda – bean soup
moussaká – eggplant and ground lamb casserole with bechemel sauce
pastítsio – macaroni casserole
patsás – tripe stew, sold at special *patsás* stands
salingária – snails in oil and herbs
stifádo – spicey stewed meat, often rabbit
souzoukákia – baked meat rolls
yiorvoulákia – meat-and-rice balls

SEAFOOD

astakós – lobster
bakaliáros – cod
galéos – shark "steak"
garídes – shrimps
glóssa – sole, flounder
gópes – small, fried fish
kalamária – squid
ksifías – swordfish
ktapódi – octopus
péstrofa – trout
marídes – whitebait
sinagrída – red snapper
soupiés – cuttlefish

DESSERTS (GLIKÁ)

Rarely will you find dessert served where you eat dinner. You'll find sweets instead at *zacharoplastía* and some *galaktopolía* (dairy stores). One sweet you'll sometimes be served at *tavérnes* is *halvá*.

baklavá – streudel pastry, honey, nuts
bougátsa – sweet custard pie
galaktoboúriko – a heftier custard pie, less common

kataífi – chopped nuts wrapped in shredded wheat with honey
kréma – plain custard
loukoúmi – Turkish Delight
moustalevriá – grape pudding, usually in fall
rizógalo – rice pudding

OTHER SNACKS

kalambóki – roast corn on the cob, sold on the street
kástana – roast chestnuts, sold on the street
kouloúria – sesame-sprinkled "pretzels"
kreatópita – meat pie
spanakópita – spinach pie
tirópita – cheese pie
tost – toasted sandwiches sold at "tost" stands

OTHER USEFUL WORDS

aláti – salt & *pipéri* (pepper)
bokáli – bottle
potíri – glass
piroúni – fork
koutáli – spoon
mahéri – knife
katálogo/lista – menu
to logariasmó – the bill

WHERE TO EAT

ATHENS

Kafeneia (coffee shops)

Zonar's, 9 Panepistimiou St. (tel. 323-0336). A grand boulevard café. Breakfast, lunch and dinner are also available here, but Zonar's is best for coffee and sweets like their Black Venus.
Metropol, 1 Pandrossou & Mitropoleos Square (tel. 321-1980, 324-3862). On the trafficless square by the Cathedral, this is a pleasant oasis, summer and winter.

Chic little bars and (not very Greek) restaurants

Apenanti, 27 Haritos St., in Kolonaki (tel. 723-9400). A chic, Greek Yuppie watering hole whose name means "across the street". A good place to start the evening, or end it: this is less a place to dine than to see what young Kolonaki aristos are wearing, and drinking. Closed in summer.
Montparnasse, or **Ratka,** 30–32 Haritos St., in Kolonaki (tel. 729-0746). This split-level bar is one of the most fashionable district's most fashionable spots. (It's also the reason Apenanti is named as it is: it's across the street from Ratka's.) Reserve space for a late dinner – the food's definitely not Greek. This is a hot spot, packed after 10 p.m. Closed in summer.
Mets, 14 Markou Mousourou St., in Mets (tel. 922-9454). Another haunt of the young, trendy and

thirsty, this lively little place is conveniently located on the same street as the excellent *tavérnas,* Manesis and Myrtia (*see below under Tavérnes*).

Mezodopoleia

Apotsos, 10 Panepistimiou, in the arcade (tel. 363-7046). Since 1910, this has been a legendary nibbling and drinking spot for artists, politicians – and important Athenians in general. Try *taramasaláta* (fish roe spread), grilled liver, *yígandes* (giant broad beans) and *saganaki* (fried cheese) with your *oúzo.*
Kafeneio, 26 Loukianou St., in Kolonaki (tel. 722-9056). One of four places to book for dinner if you have only a day or so in the city. This 19th-century lookalike features some 40 starters on the superb menu. Order four or five plates, and get a true feeling for the country's cuisine. The restaurant is refined, intimate, downright sexy, and the service a pleasant surprise. (The other three "musts" are Gerofinikas, Vasilenas and Rodia: *see below.*)
Kafeneio, 1 Epiharmou, in Plaka (tel. 324-6916). A less pricey version of the above, with a more limited menu, but warmhearted Plaka atmosphere. A cozy place till the wee hours, especially in winter. Try the *saganáki* and *keftethákia* meatballs.
O Kouklis, 14 Tripodon, in Plaka (tel. 324-7605). Another bargain-basement of *mezéthes,* including herring or Greek sausage flambé, this starters-only spot is best in summer, when the tables spill out onto the pavement.
Perix, 14 Glikonos St., across from Dexamini Sq. (tel. 723-6917). A pleasant, reasonable place for starters and Perix *oúzo,* as well as dinner, if you like. Perix spills out into the square in summer.

Tavernas

• IN KOLONAKI

Vlassis, 16 Argiroupoleos St. (tel. 642-5337). This *tavérna,* just down the street from Ileana Tounta's art gallery cum bar, is noted for its fish. Reservations a must.
Rodia, 44 Aristipou St. (tel. 722-9883). One of the author's favourites, this is the haunt of foreign archaeologists. In summer or winter, the barrel wine's good. Order veal in lemon or oregano sauce, *bourekákia* (cheese croquettes), *dolmáthes* (stuffed vine leaves), and a *horiatiki* (Greek salad).
Rouga, 7 Kapsali St. (tel. 722-7934). A locals-only bistro, this *tavérna* has good *retsina* and grilled meats at reasonable prices.
To Kotopoulo, 3 Kolonaki Square. Between Citibank and Skoufa Street is a little hole in the wall with a few tables wobbling out front where, at lunch or dinner time, you can eat heavenly grilled chicken, *souvlakia* in *pítta* rolls, French fries, salad and beer. Too good to miss.
Ongo, 20 Haritos St., next to the Athenian Inn (tel. 722-4731). Do reserve space at this small, swanky

restaurant where fish and fillets are the order of the day. Open for lunch as well.

• IN AND NEAR METS

Manesis, 3 Markou Mousourou St. (tel. 922-7684). Dry red barrel wine from Lefkada is featured here, along with a wide array of *mezéthes, stifádo* (sweet beef or rabbit stew with lots of spice), and *kokorétsi* (grilled lamb intestines and organs – please forget you read this, and try it).
Myrtia, 35 Markou Mousourou St. (tel. 701-2276, 751-1686). The garden makes this a lovely place to dine in summer. Order *gardoúmba* (lamb entrail roll), suckling pig, shrimp, mussels. And enjoy the live music.
Karavitis, 4 Pafsaniou St., across from the statue of Truman (tel. 721-5155, 721-1610). An old friend of Athenians for 50 years, Mr. Linardos' garden is open May till October. Order grilled meats and *retsina,* all accompanied by guitar music.

• IN PLAKA

Bakalarakia, also known as *O Damigos,* after the owner, 41 Kidathineon St. (tel. 322-5084, 322-0395). The author's favourite winter *tavérna,* this basement is supported by a truly ancient marble column and has a reputation for phenomenal *retsina,* fried cod with garlic sauce, radishes, herring and *loukaniko* (spicy Greek sausage). Closed late May through September.
Xynos, 4 Aggelou Geronta St. (tel. 322-1065). Founded in 1936, this restaurant with its genuine old-Athens ambience, lamb fricassé, barrel wine, and three strolling guitarists is closed in July.
Platanos, 4 Diogenous St., near the Tower of the Winds (tel. 322-0666). *Stifado* and grilled meats are the specialities here. (Avoid other *tavérnas* in this area. They don't hold a candle to Platanos.)
Socrates' Prison, 20 Mitseon St. (tel. 922-3434). After Athens Festival performances, have the grilled chicken or lamb with your Pikermi wine.
Kalokerinos Tavern, 10 Kekropos St. (tel. 323-2054, 322-1679). This is an after-nine *tavérna* featuring traditional Greek fare, a *bouzouki* band (and Rumanian violinist!) plus a floor show of Greek dancing. Reservations are required.

Restaurants

Gerofinikas, 10 Pindarou St. (tel. 363-6710, 362-2719). Another favourite of the author's, this is the place to use your plastic. Reservations are a must. Order *Imam Baïldí* (Oriental eggplant starter), squab (baby chicken) with currant and pine nut pilaf, and finish with chocolate soufflé.
Ta Nissia, at The Athens Hilton (tel. 722-0201). Try the dinner buffet here, a vast array of Greek and Turkish *mezéthes.* The wine list is impressive: try a hearty Nemean, red or white.

Kuyu-Kaplanis, 23 Nafarhou Votsi St., at Mikrolimano in Piraeus (tel. 411-1623). Choose from 25 *mezéthes* at your table by the harbour, and go on to shrimp and lobster.

Vasilenas, 72 Etolikou St., in Piraeus (tel. 461-2457). Reserve a table (tell Mr. George that Elizabeth sent you), starve for at least a day, and then arrange for a taxi to pick you up afterwards: the table d'hote consists of some 16 courses. Since Winston Churchill and Tyrone Power signed the guestbook, this unpretentious, underpriced beauty of a restaurant has been drawing gastronomes from the world over. Allow several hours to savour your meal, and try to go with a group of mellow friends.

Not at all Greek

Kona Kai, the Ledra Marriott Hotel, 115 Syngrou Avenue (tel. 934-7711). Reserve ahead for authentic Polynesian cuisine.

Mitsiko, 27 Kidathineon St., in Plaka (tel. 322-0980). Sushi and saki in old Athens.

Pane E Vino, 8 Spefsippou St., in Kolonaki (tel. 722-5084). One of the two best, and most expensive, Italian restaurants in town.

Boschetto Ristorante-Bar, in the Evangelismos Park (tel. 721-0893, 722-7324). Alone in a green park, this is a pricey gem – Athens' other best Italian restaurant; reserve ahead.

Eden, 3 Flessa St., in Plaka (tel. 324-8858). Athens' only vegetarian restaurant. Peek in the kitchen before heading upstairs: the Spinach Special and lasagna are worthy choices.

Bakeries and Street Food

As you make your way around Athens on foot, you'll pass a neighbourhood bakery about every ten minutes. Stop in. This is where Athenians buy and eat breakfast, generally standing up. An uptown bakery that features most of the goodies Greece has to offer is Mr. Papayeorgiou's shop at 14 Skoufa St. in Kolonaki. Try the *karidópitta* (walnut muffin) or grape-must flavoured biscuits, *moustoukoúloura,* or the old standbys, the *tirópitta,* cheese pie, *spanakópitta,* spinach pie and the *milópitta,* Greece's version of apple pie. Busy shoppers on Ermou Street should stop in at the Ariston, at 10 Voulis St., where morning queues trailing out the door advertise this shop's excellent cheese pies. On the street corners are other goodies – *kouloúria,* the chewy, sesame-seed crusted "bracelets" commuters wear to work to eat with their coffee; roasted chestnuts, which scent the air downtown in fall and winter; nuts and coconut sticks; roast corn – stop and nibble.

Zacharoplasteia or Pâtisseries

Athens is a mecca for the visitor with an advanced case of sweet tooth. The place to indulge is the *zacharoplasteíon,* or confectioner's shop. Down-

town, the old fashioned **Zonar's,** at 9 Panepistimiou Ave., is hard to beat. The elegant tables facing the street are a fine vantage point from which to watch the passing parade while consuming enormous numbers of calories. **Floca's,** at 118 Kifissias Ave. in Ambelokipi is another oasis for sugar addicts. For Greek pastries with a Middle Eastern flavor, **Farouk Hanbali,** at 4 Messinias St., also in Ambelokipi, has *baklavá* and other *fílo* (streudel leaves) and nut delicacies, for sale by the kilo. But the best confections in the city are probably Evangelos Vlachakis' versions of traditional Oriental sweets. The **Lalaggis** shop, at Spefsippou 23 in Kolonaki features chocolate *baklavá,* among other things. Take a box home with you to make friends' mouths water.

Breakfast

Kolonaki Square is a great place to have breakfast and people-watch. The Ellinikon café, at the corner of the square and Koumbari Street, has elegant tables, outdoors in season, great coffee, and Western breakfasts. Another nice place to start your day, especially if you're heading into the Flea Market, is the Hermion Restaurant, at 15 Pandrossou St. in Plaka. For early risers and late-night owls, the Bretania, on Omonia Square, serves delicious yogurt, heavy cream topped with Attic honey, full breakfasts, hot milk – well, don't miss this place. You'll find yourself among deadbeats, theatre personalities, lawyers and other professionals etc., etc., all with one thing in common: they know the best milk-bar in the city.

THESSALONÍKI

Olympos-Naoussa, 5 Vas. Konstantinou St. (tel. 275715).
Elvetikon, 42 Ayios Sofias St. (tel. 275521).
Stratis, 19 Vas. Konstantinou St. (tel. 234782).
Tiffany's, 3 Iktinou St. (tel. 274022).

Luxury Restaurants

Dionysius, Panorama (tel. 941813).
Ted's House, 7 Mihalakopoulou St.–Aretsou (tel. 427334).

Tavernas

Liopesi, Platia Navarinou.
Iordanis, 1 Venizelou St.–Panorama (tel. 941138).
Klimataria, 34 P. Mela St. (tel. 277854).
Ta Nisia, 13 Koromila St. (tel. 285991).
I Folia Ton Filon Tou Falakra, 5 K. Melekinou (tel. 210905).

Ouzeries

Anapiros, 20 P. Nikolaou St. (tel. 238269).

Achileas, 17 Filikis Etairias St.
Corfu, 1 Stratigou Kazari St. (tel. 269109).

Patisseries

Agapitos, 57 Tsimiski St. (tel. 279107).
Ellinikon, 209 Vas. Olgas St. (tel. 411133).
Hatzifotiou, 37 P. Mela St. (tel. 232166).

DRINKING NOTES

BEER & WINE

Greeks never simply "go out drinking". Even if an evening involves heavy drinking of *retsína* or *oúzo*, these will always be accompanied by food – an inveterate habit which minimises the effects (and after-effects) of the alcohol. When it comes to ordering your wine, check to see if they serve wine from the barrel (ask for *hima*). This is the inexpensive local stuff which varies from town to town. Otherwise you can choose among the various bottled wines, some of the better Greek labels being: Rotonda, Cambas, Boutari, Calliga. *Aspro* is white, *mávro* is red, and *kokkinélli* is rose.

bíra – beer
kokkinélli – rosé wine
krasí – wine
mávro – red
me to kiló, or *hima* – wine by the kilo, local
neró – water
retsína – resin-flavoured wine
oúzo – anise-flavoured liqueur
rakí – grape-crush brandy
tsípouro – basically like *rakí*

COFFEE & TEA

Greeks generally drink their coffee and tea with lots of sugar. An essential phrase for those who like their hot drinks without sugar is – *horís záhari*, literally, "without sugar". Tag this phrase at the end of whatever drink you are ordering: for example, nescafé *horís záhari*. You can also ask for your drink *skétos* which means the same thing in a slightly less emphatic way. If you like some sugar ask for *métrio*. If you love sugar say nothing and they'll probably dump a few teaspoons into whatever you're drinking. *Me gála* means "with milk".

nescafé – freeze-dried coffee. In warmer weather, you may want *frapé* – cold nescafé mixed in a shaker.
elenikó café – Greek coffee, boiled and served with the grounds in the cup. If you want a large cup of it ask for *diplós*. *Elenikó café* is also known as *turkikó café* but this sometimes provokes patriotic objections.
tsaïï – tea either with milk or with lemon, *me lemóni*
kamomíli – camomille tea
tsaï tou vounóu – mountain tea. Tea made with any

one of various mountain herbs such as sage. Not easy to find.

CULTURE PLUS

The main question here is surely *which* museums, sites and churches to visit. Greece has such an abundance of them that in any one trip you'll just be able to see a fraction of what's available.

Below are listed most of the museums and archaeological sites and a few of the interesting churches and monasteries. Numerous aspects of Greece's cultural heritage have been necessarily excluded from this listing (fortresses, most churches, arches, mosques etc.). However, with patience and an inquisitive eye, you'll gradually discover them.

MUSEUMS & SITES

Guide to visiting hours: The archaeological sites and museums listed below are closed on 1st January, 25th March, Good Friday, Easter Sunday, 1st May and 25th December.

Museums will open from 8.30 a.m. to 12.30 p.m. on 2nd January, last Saturday of the Carnival, Good Thursday, Easter Tuesday, Christmas Eve and New Year's Eve.

• **ATHENS**

Acropolis Archaeological Site, (tel. 3210219). Open: Daily 8.30 a.m.–5 p.m. Entrance fee: 600 drs. (including fee to the Museum).
Acropolis Museum, on the Acropolis, (tel. 3236665). Open: Daily 8 a.m.–5 p.m. Closed on Tues. Entrance fee: 600 drs. (including fee to the archaeological site).
Ancient Agora Museum in the **Stoa Of Attalos**, Entrance from Thisseíon Sq., & 24, Andrianoú St. (tel. 3210185). Open: Daily 8.30 a.m.–3 p.m. Closed on Mon. Entrance fee: 400 drs. (including fee to the archaeological site).
Athens City Museum, 7, Paparigopoulou St. (tel. 3230168). Open: Mon., Wed. & Fri. 9 a.m.–1.30 p.m. Entrance fee: 200 drs.
Benaki Museum, 1 Koumbari Street and Vass. Sophias Av. (tel. 3611617). Open: Daily 8.30 a.m.– 2 p.m. Closed on Tues. Entrance fee: 200 drs.
Byzantine Museum, 22, Vass. Sophias Av. (tel. 7211027). Open: Daily 8 a.m.–3 p.m. Closed on Mon. Entrance fee: 300 drs.

Daphni Monastery, (tel. 5811558). Open: Daily 8.30 a.m.–3 p.m. Closed on Mon. Entrance fee: 200 drs.

Epigraphical Collection, 1, Tossitsa St. (tel. 8217637). Open: Daily 8.30 a.m.–3 p.m. Closed on Mon. Admission free.

Jewish Museum of Greece, 36 Amalias Av. (tel. 3231577). Open: Daily 9 a.m.–1 p.m. Closed on Sat. Admission free.

Museum of Cycladic and Ancient Greek Art, 4, Neofytou Douka St. (tel. 7249706). Open: Daily 10 a.m.–4 p.m. Closed: Tues. and Sun.

Greek Folk Art Museum, 17 Kydathineon St., Plaka (tel. 3213018). Open: Daily 10 a.m.–2 p.m. Closed on Mon. Entrance fee: 200 drs.

Historical And Ethnological Museum, Stadiou St. (tel. 3237617). Open: Tues. to Fri. 9 a.m.–2 p.m., Sat. & Sun. 9 a.m.–1 p.m. Closed on Mon. Entrance fee: 100 drs. Admission free on Thurs.

Kaissariani Monastery, (tel. 7236619). Open: Daily 8.45 a.m.–3 p.m., Sun. & Holidays 9.30 a.m.–2.30 p.m. Admission free.

Kanellopoulos Museum, Theorias & Panos Sts., Plaka (tel. 3212313). Open: Daily 8.30 a.m.–3 p.m. Closed on Mon. Entrance fee: 200 drs.

Keramikos Museum, 148, Ermou St. (tel. 3463552). Open: Daily 8.45 a.m.–3 p.m., Sun. & Holidays 9.30 a.m.–2.30 p.m. Closed on Tues. Entrance fee: 100 drs. (including fee to the archaeological site).

Keramikos Archaeological Site, Ermou & Pireos corner (tel. 3463552). Open: Daily 8.45 a.m.–3 p.m., Sun. & Holidays 9.30 a.m.–2.30 p.m. Entrance fee: 100 drs. (including fee to the Museum).

National Archaeological Museum, 1, Tossitsa St. (tel. 8217717). Open: Daily 8 a.m.–5 p.m. Closed on Tues. Entrance fee: 250 drs. (including fee to the exhibits from Thira & the Numismatic Museum).

National Gallery And Alexandros Soutsos Museum, 46, Vass. Sophias Av. (tel. 7211010). Open: Daily 9 a.m.–3 p.m. Closed on Mon. Admission fee.

Natural History, 13, Levidou St., Kifissia (tel. 8086405). Open: Daily 9 a.m.–2.30 p.m. Closed on Fri. Entrance fee: 30 drs.

Numismatic Collection, 1, Tossitsa St. (tel. 821779). Open: Daily 8.30 a.m.–3 p.m. Closed on Mon. Admission free.

Roman Agora, End of Eolou St. (tel. 3210185). Open: Daily 8.45 a.m.–3 p.m., Sun. & Holidays 9.30 a.m.–2.30 p.m. Entrance fee: 100 drs.

Temple of Hephaistos And Ancient Agora, (tel. 3210185). Open: Daily 8 a.m.–5 p.m. Entrance fee: 150 drs.

Temple of Olympian Zeus, Olgas & Amalias Av. (tel. 9226330). Open: Daily 8.45 a.m.–3 p.m., Sun. & Holidays 9.30 a.m.–2.30 p.m. Entrance fee: 100 drs.

Theatre of Dionysios, D. Areopagitou Av. (tel. 3236665). Open: Daily 8.45 a.m.–3 p.m., Sun. & Holidays 9.30 a.m.–2.30 p.m. Entrance fee: 100 drs.

War Museum of Greece, Vass. Sophias Av. (tel. 7290543-4). Open: Daily 9 a.m.–2 p.m. Closed on Mon. LIBRARY Open: Tues. to Sat. 9 a.m.–2 p.m. Admission free.

• **AMPHIPOLIS**

Archaeological Site, (tel. 051-224717). Open: Daily 8.45 a.m.–3 p.m., Sun. & Holidays 9.30 a.m.–2.30 p.m. Admission free.

• **ANDROS**

Archaeological Museum, (tel. 0282-23664). Open: Daily 8.45 a.m.–3 p.m., Sun. & Holidays 9.30 a.m.–2.30 p.m. Closed on Tues. Entrance fee: 100 drs.

Basil & Elise Goulandris Museum (Modern Art), (tel. 0282-22650). Open: Daily 10 a.m.–1 p.m., 5 p.m.–8 p.m. Closed on Tues. Admission free.

• **CHAIRONIA**

Museum, (tel. 0261-95270). Open: Daily 8.45 a.m.–3 p.m., Sun. & Holidays 9.30 a.m.–2.30 p.m. Closed on Tues. Admission free.

• **CORINTH**

Acrocorinth Archaeological Site, (tel. 0741-31443). Open: Daily 8.45 a.m.–3 p.m., Sun. & Holidays 9.30 a.m.–2.30 p.m. Entrance fee: 150 drs. (including fee to the Museum).

Museum, (tel. 0741-31207). Open: Daily 8.45 a.m.–3 p.m., Sun. & Holidays 9.30 a.m.–2.30 p.m. Closed on Tues. Entrance fee: 200 drs. (including fee to archaeological site).

• **CRETE**

Aghios Nikolaos Museum, (tel. 0841-22462). Open: Daily 8.45 a.m.–3 p.m., Sun. & Holidays 9.30 a.m.–2.30 p.m. Closed on Tues. Entrance fee: 100 drs.

Chania Museum, (tel. 0821-20334, 24418). Open: Daily 8.45 a.m.–3 p.m., Sun. & Holidays 9.30 a.m.–2.30 p.m. Closed on Tues. Entrance fee: 100 drs.

Heraklion (Irákleion) Archaeological Museum, (tel. 081-226092). Open: Daily 8 a.m.–5 p.m. Closed on Mon. Entrance fee: 200 drs.

Réthymnon Museum, (tel. 0831-29975). Open: Daily 8.45 a.m.–3 p.m., Sun. & Holidays 9.30 a.m.–2.30 p.m. Closed on Tues. Entrance fee: 100 drs.

Aghia Trias Archaeological Site, (tel. 081-226092). Open: Daily 8.45 a.m.–3 p.m., Sun. & Holidays 9.30 a.m.–2.30 p.m. Closed on Fri. Entrance fee: 100 drs.

Knossós Archaeological Site, (tel. 081-231940). Open: Daily 8 a.m.–5 p.m. Entrance fee: 200 drs.

Phaestós Archaeological Site, (tel. 0892-22615). Open: Daily 8 a.m.–5 p.m. Entrance fee: 150 drs.

Gortyn Archaeological Site, (tel. 081-226092). Open: Daily 8.45 a.m.–3 p.m., Sun. & Holidays 9.30 a.m.–2.30 p.m. Entrance fee: 100 drs.

Mallia Archaeological Site, (tel. 081-226092). Open: Daily 8.45 a.m.–3 p.m., Sun. & Holidays 9.30 a.m.–2.30 p.m. Entrance fee: 100 drs.

Tylissos Archaeological Site, (tel. 081-226092). Open: Daily 8.45 a.m.–3 p.m., Sun. & Holidays 9.30

a.m.–2.30 p.m. Closed on Mon. Entrance fee: 100 drs.
Other Archaeological Sites, (tel. 081-226092).
Saint Titus, Gournia, Open: Daily 8.45 a.m.–3 p.m.,
Sun. & Holidays 9.30 a.m.–2.30 p.m. Admission free.
Heraklion (Irákleion) Harbour Fortress (Koules),
(tel. 081-286228). Open: Daily 8.45 a.m.–3 p.m.,
Sun. & Holidays 9.30 a.m.–2.30 p.m. Entrance fee:
100 drs.

• Délos

Archaeological Site, (tel. 0289-22259). Open: Daily
8.45 a.m.–3 p.m., Sun. & Holidays 9.30 a.m.–3 p.m.
Entrance fee: 200 drs. (including fee to the Museum).

• Délphi

Archaeological Site, (tel. 0741-31207). Open: Daily
8.45 a.m.–3 p.m., Sun. & Holidays 9.30 a.m.–2.30
p.m. Entrance fee: 150 drs. (including fee to Museum).
Museum, (tel. 0265-82313). Open: Daily 8 a.m.–5
p.m. Closed on Tues. Entrance fee: 200 drs.

• Díon-Pieria

Archaeological Site, (tel. 0351-53206). Open: Daily
8.45 a.m.–3 p.m., Sun. & Holidays 9.30 a.m.–2.30
p.m. Entrance fee: 100 drs. (including fee to the
Museum).
Museum, (tel. 0351-53206). Open: Daily 8.45 a.m.–
3 p.m. Closed on Tues. Entrance fee: 100 drs.
(including fee to the archaeological site).

• Aégina

Temple Of Aphaía, (tel. 0297-32398). Open: Daily
8.45 a.m.–3 p.m., Sun. & Holidays 9.30 a.m.–2.30
p.m. Entrance fee: 100 drs.
Museum, (tel. 0297-22637). Open: Daily 8.45 a.m.–
3 p.m., Sun. & Holidays 9.30 a.m.–2.30 p.m. Closed
on Tues. Entrance fee: 100 drs. (including fee to the
temple of Apollo).

• Eléfis

Museum, (tel. 5546019). Open: Daily 8.45 a.m.–3
p.m., Sun. & Holidays 9.30 a.m.–2.30 p.m. Closed
on Tues. Entrance fee: 100 drs. (including fee to the
archaeological site).

• Epídavros

Archaeological Site & Museum, (tel. 0753-22009).
Open: Daily 8 a.m.–5 p.m. Closed on Tues. Entrance
fee: 200 drs.

• Eretria (Euboea)

Archaeological Site & Museum, (tel. 0221-62206).
Open: Daily 8.45 a.m.–3 p.m., Sun. & Holidays 9.30
a.m.–2.30 p.m. Closed on Tues. Entrance fee: 100 drs.

• Philippi

Archaeological Site, (tel. 051-516470). Open: Daily
9 a.m.–5 p.m., Sun. & Holidays 10 a.m.–5 p.m.
Entrance fee: 150 drs.
Museum, (tel. 05-516261). Open: Daily from 8.45
a.m.–3 p.m., Sun. & Holidays 9.30 a.m.–2.30 p.m.
Closed on Tues. Entrance fee: 100 drs.

• Corfu

Archaeological Museum, (tel. 0661-30680). Open:
Daily 8.45 a.m.–3 p.m., Sun. & Holidays 9.30 a.m.–
2.30 p.m. Closed on Tues. Entrance fee: 100 drs.
Museum Of Asiatic Art, (tel. 0661-23124). Open:
Daily 8.45 a.m.–3 p.m., Sun. & Holidays 9.30 a.m.–
2.30 p.m. Closed on Tues. Entrance fee: 100 drs.

• Kos

Museum, (tel. 0242-28326). Open: Daily from 8.45
a.m.–3 p.m., Sun. & Holidays 9.30 a.m.–2.30 p.m.
Closed on Tues. Entrance fee: 100 drs.
Castle, (tel. 0242-28326). Open: Daily 8.45 a.m.–
3 p.m., Sun. & Holidays 9.30 a.m.–2.30 p.m. Closed
on Tues. Entrance fee: 100 drs.
Restored Ancient Dwelling, (tel. 0242-28326).
Open: Daily 8.45 a.m.–3 p.m., Sun. & Holidays 9.30
a.m.–2.30 p.m. Entrance fee: 100 drs.
Asclepieion And Other Archaeological Sites, (tel.
0242-28763). Open: Daily from 8.45 a.m.–3 p.m.,
on Sun. & Holidays 9.30 a.m.–2.30 p.m. Entrance
fee: 100 drs.

• Lésvos

Eressós Archaeological Museum, (tel. 0251-22087).
Open: Daily 8.45 a.m.–3 p.m., Sun. & Holidays 9.30
a.m.–2.30 p.m. Closed on Tues. Admission free.
Mytilíni Archaeological Museum, (tel. 0251-22087).
Open: Daily 8.45 a.m.–3 p.m., Sun. & Holidays 9.30
a.m.–2.30 p.m. Closed on Tues. Entrance fee: 100 drs.

• Mílos

Archaeological Site & Museum, (tel. 0287-21620).
Open: Daily 8.45 a.m.–3 p.m., Sun. & Holidays 9.30
a.m.–2.30 p.m. Closed on Tues. Entrance fee: 100 drs.
Catacombs, (tel. 0287-21620). Open: Daily 8.45
a.m.–2.30 p.m., Sun. & Holidays 9.30 a.m.–2.30
p.m. Entrance fee: 50 drs.

• Mycénae

Archaeological Site, (tel. 0725-27502). Open: Daily
from 8 a.m.–5 p.m. Entrance fee: 200 drs.

• Mistrás

Archaeological Site, (tel. 0731-25363). Open: Daily
8.45 a.m.–3 p.m., Sun. & Holidays 9.30 a.m.–2.30

p.m. Entrance fee: 200 drs. (including fee to Museum).
Museum, (tel. 0731-25363). Open: Daily from 8.45
a.m.–3 p.m., Sun. & Holidays 9.30 a.m.–2.30 p.m.
Closed on Tues. Entrance fee: 150 drs. (including fee
to the archaeological site).

• **NÁFPLION**

Museum, (tel. 0752-27502). Open: Daily from 8.45
a.m.–3 p.m., Sun. & Holidays 9.30 a.m.–2.30 p.m.
Closed on Tues. Entrance fee: 100 drs.
Palamidi Fortress, (tel, 0752-28036). Open: Daily
10 a.m.–4.30 p.m., Sun. & Holidays 10 a.m.–3 p.m.
Remains open on March 25. Entrance fee: 100 drs.
Popular Art Museum, (tel. 0752-28379). Open:
Daily 9 a.m.–1 p.m. & 5 p.m.–7 p.m. Closed on
Tues. Admission free.

• **NEMÉA**

Museum, (tel. 0746-22739). Open: Daily from 8.45
a.m.–3 p.m., Sun. & Holidays 9.30 a.m.–2.30 p.m.
Closed on Tues. Entrance fee: 100 drs.

• **OLYMPIA**

Archaeological Site, (tel. 0624-22517). Open: Daily
from 8.45 a.m.–3 p.m., Sun. & Holidays 9.30 a.m.–
2.30 p.m. Entrance fee: 200 drs.
Museum, (tel. 0624-21529, 22742). Open: Daily
8.45 a.m.–3 p.m., Sun. & Holidays 9.30 a.m.–2.30
p.m. Closed on Tues. Entrance fee: 200 drs.
Historical Museum of Olympic Games, (tel. 0624-
25572, 22596). Open: Daily 8.45 a.m.–3 p.m., Sun.
& Holidays 9.30 a.m.–2.30 p.m. Closed on Tues.
Entrance fee: 100 drs.

• **OLYNTHOS (CHALKIDIKÍ)**

Archaeological Site, (tel. 0373-21862). Open: Daily
8.45 a.m.–3 p.m., Sun. & Holidays 9.30 a.m.–2.30
p.m. Admission free.

• **OROPÓS**

Amphiaraion Museum, (tel. 0295-62144). Open:
Daily 8.45 a.m.–3 p.m., Sun. & Holidays 9.30 a.m.–
2.30 p.m. Closed on Tues. Entrance fee: 100 drs.
(including fee to the archaeological site).

• **OSSIOS LOUKAS**

Byzantine Monastery, (tel. 3213571). Open: Daily
from 8.45 a.m.–3 p.m., Sun. & Holidays 9.30 a.m.–
2 .30 p.m. Entrance fee: 100 drs.

• **PÁTMOS**

Monastery Of St. John-Vestry-Library, (tel. 0241-
21954). Open: Daily 8.45 a.m.–3 p.m., Sun. &
Holidays 9.30 a.m.–2.30 p.m. Admission free.

• **PELLA**

Archaeological Site, (tel. 0382-31160, 31278):
Open: Daily 8.45 a.m.–3 p.m., Sun. & Holidays 9.30
a.m.–2.30 p.m. Entrance fee: 100 drs.
Museum, (tel. 0382-31160, 31278). Open: Daily
8.45 a.m.–3 p.m., Sun. & Holidays 9.30 a.m.–2.30
p.m. Closed on Tues. Entrance fee: 100 drs.

• **PIRAÉUS**

Maritime Museum of Piraeus, Akti Themistokleous
(tel. 4516822). Open: Daily 9 a.m.–12.30 p.m., Sun.
& Holidays 10 a.m.–8 p.m. Closed on Mon., Tues.
& Fri. Entrance fee: 100 drs.
Piraeus Archaeological Museum, 31, Char. Trikoupi
St. (tel. 4521598, 4518388). Open: Daily 8.45
a.m.–3 p.m., Sun. & Holidays 9.30 a.m.–2.30 p.m.
Closed on Tues. Entrance fee: 100 drs.

• **PYLOS**

Museum, (tel. 0723-22448). Open: Daily from 8.45
a.m.–3 p.m., Sun. & Holidays 9.30 a.m.–2.30 p.m.
Closed on Tues. Entrance fee: 100 drs.
Nestor's Palace, near Pylos (tel. 0723-31358).
Open: Daily 8.45 a.m.–3 p.m., Sun & Holidays 9.30
a.m.–2.30 p.m. Entrance fee: 100 drs.

• **RHAMNOIS**

Archaeological Site, (tel. 0294-93477). Open: Daily
8.45 a.m.–3 p.m., Sun. & Holidays 9.30 a.m.–2.30
p.m. Admission free.

• **RHODES**

Acropolis-Theatre-Stadium, (tel. 0241-27674). Open:
Daily 8.45 a.m.–3 p.m., Sun. & Holidays 9.30 a.m.–
2.30 p.m. Admission is free.
Museum, (tel. 0241-27674). Open: Daily from 8.45
a.m.–3 p.m., Sun. & Holidays 9.30 a.m.–2.30 p.m.
Closed on Tues. Entrance fee: 200 drs.
Palace Of The Knights, (tel. 0241-27674). Open:
Daily 8.45 a.m.–3 p.m., Sun. & Holidays 9.30 a.m.–
2.30 p.m. Closed on Tues. Entrance fee: 200 drs.
Perimeter Of The Medieval Walls, (tel. 0241-
27674). Open to visitors accompanied by a guide on
Mon. and Sat. afternoons. Visitors should gather in
the courtyard of the Palace of the Knights. Open: 3
p.m.–5 p.m. Admission free.
Camiros Excavations, (tel. 0241-27674). Open:
Daily 8.45 a.m.–3 p.m., Sun. & Holidays 9.30 a.m.–
2.30 p.m. Entrance fee: 100 drs.
Acropolis Of Ialyssos, (tel. 0241-27674). Open:
Daily 8.45 a.m.–3 p.m., Sun. & Holidays 9.30 a.m.–
2.30 p.m. Entrance fee: 200 drs.
Acropolis of Líndos, (tel. 0241-27674). Open: Daily
8.45 a.m.–3 p.m., Sun. & Holidays 9.30 a.m.–2.30
p.m. Entrance fee: 100 drs.
Decorative Collections, (tel. 0241-27674). Open to

the public on Mon., Wed. and Fri. from 9 a.m.–1 p.m. Entrance fee: 100 drs.

• SÁMOS

Hera Temple-Archaeological Site, (tel. 0273-61177). Open: Daily 8.45 a.m.–3 p.m., Sun. & Holidays 9.30 a.m.–2.30 p.m. Entrance fee: 100 drs.
Pythagorion Museum, (tel. 0273-61400). Open: Daily 8.45 a.m.–3 p.m., Sun. & Holidays 9.30 a.m.–2.30 p.m. Closed on Tues. Admission free.
Efpalinion Orygma, (tel. 0273-61400). Open: Mon., Thurs. & Sat. 10 a.m.–12 p.m. Admission free.

• SAMOTHRACE

Archaeological Site, (tel. 0551-41474). Dorion: *Doric* marble temple dated 260 B.C. *Arsrnoeion* circular construction dating 288–281 B.C. Open: Daily 8.45 a.m.–3 p.m., Sun. & Holidays 9.30 a.m.–2.30 p.m. Entrance fee: 100 drs.
Museum, (tel. 0551-41474). Open: Daily from 8.45 a.m.–3 p.m., Sun. & Holidays 9.30 a.m.–2.30 p.m. Closed on Tues. Entrance fee: 100 drs.

• SANTORÍNI (THÍRA)

Museum, (tel. 0286-22217). Open: Daily from 8.45 a.m.–3 p.m., Sun. & Holidays 9.30 a.m.–2.30 p.m. Closed on Tues. Entrance fee: 100 drs.
Archaeological Site, (tel. 0286-22217). Well preserved ruins of the ancient town (theatre, agora, temple, site of athletics, government-house, fortifications, private house, tombs of archaic and classical periods, early Christian relics). Open: Daily 8.45 a.m.–3 p.m., Sun. & Holidays 9.30 a.m.–2.30 p.m. Admission free.
Akrotirion Thiras Archaeological Site, (tel. 0286-81366). Open: Daily 8.45 a.m.–3 p.m., Sun. & Holidays 9.30 a.m.–2.30 p.m. Entrance fee: 150 drs.

• SIKYON

Archaeological Site, (tel. 0742-28900). Ruins of the town's walls, the Stadium, the Gymnasium, the Sacred Spring, the Bouleuterion, the temple of Artemis and the theatre are well preserved. Open: Daily 8.45 a.m.–3 p.m., Sun. & Holidays 9.30 a.m.–2.30 p.m. Admission free.
Museum, (tel. 0742-28900). Open: Daily 8.45 a.m.–3 p.m., Sun. & Holidays 9.30 a.m.–2.30 p.m. Closed on Tues. Admission free.

• SOÍNION

Archaeological Site, (tel. 0292-39363). Open: Daily from 9 a.m. till sunset, Sun. & Holidays 10 a.m. till sunset. Entrance fee: 150 drs.

• SPÁRTA

Museum, (tel. 0731-25363). Open: Daily from 8.45 a.m.–3 p.m., Sun. & Holidays 9.30 a.m.–2.30 p.m. Closed on Tues. Entrance fee: 100 drs.

• THESSALONÍKI

Archaeological Museum and Treasures Of Ancient Macedonia (Vergina Findings), (tel. 031-830538). Open: Daily 8.45 a.m.–3 p.m., Sun. & Holidays 9.30 a.m.–2.30 p.m. Closed on Tues. Entrance fee: 200 drs (both Museum & Vergina findings).
Folklore Museum, 68, Vass. Olgas St., (tel. 031-830591). Open: Daily 9 a.m.–2 p.m. Closed on Tues. Admission free.
Crypt Of Saint Dimitrios, (tel. 031-270008). Open: Daily from 8.45 a.m.–3 p.m., Sun. & Holidays 9.30 a.m.–2.30 p.m. Admission free.
The White Tower-Byzantine Museum, Vass. Konstantinou St. Open: Daily 9 a.m.–2 p.m. Closed Tues.

• THEBES

Museum, (tel. 0262-27913). Open: Daily 8.45 a.m.–3 p.m., Sun. & Holidays 9.30 a.m.–2.30 p.m. Closed on Tues. Entrance fee: 100 drs.

• TIRYNS

Archaeological Site, (tel. 0752-27502). Open: Daily from 8.45 a.m.–3 p.m., Sun. & Holidays 9.30 a.m.–2.30 p.m. Entrance fee: 100 drs.

• VERGINA

Archaeological Site, (tel. 031-830538). Open: Daily from 8.45 a.m.–3 p.m., Sun. & Holidays 9.30 a.m.–2.30 p.m. Entrance fee: 100 drs.

• VÓLOS (NEA ANCHIALOS)

Archaeological Site, (tel. 0421-25285). Open: Daily from 8.45 a.m.–3 p.m., Sun. & Holidays 9.30 a.m.–2.30 p.m. Entrance fee: 100 drs.

• VRAVRONA

Museum, (tel. 0294-71020). Open: Daily 8.45 a.m.–3 p.m., Sun. & Holidays 9.30 a.m.–2.30 p.m. Closed on Sun. Entrance fee: 100 drs (including fee to the archaeological site).
Archaeological Site, (tel. 0294-71020). Open: Daily 8.45 a.m.–3 p.m., Sun. & Holidays 9.30 a.m.–2.30 p.m. Entrance fee: 100 drs (including fee to the Museum).

THEATRES

Athens has an active theatre life. As most productions are in Greek, however, there are limited options for the English-speaking tourist. Most productions in English take place during the various festivals (*see "Seasonal Events"*). You'll do best to check the English-language publications for up-to-date information.

One recent cultural initiative has provided some excellent productions of both modern and ancient drama in English at one of Greece's most striking open-air theatres – the **"Stone Theatre"** (Pétra Theatre) in Petroúpolis in the suburbs of Athens. During the summer, plays are produced under the auspices of the "Stones and Rocks Festival".

MUSIC & DANCE

A considerable part of the good music and dance performances takes place during the various festivals (*see "Seasonal Events"*). Besides these performances, however, there are still numerous events worth attending in both Athens and Thessaloníki.

In Athens, outstanding Greek and foreign musicians often perform at the **Lycabettus Theatre** on Mount Lycabettus, not to mention the larger concerts that take place in the soccer stadiums. Opera can be seen at the **Olympia Theatre** performed by the Lyriki Skini (the National Opera Company). In Thessaloníki, performances of music, opera, dance and theatre take place at the **State Theatre** of Northern Greece. In both Athens and Thessaloníki, the cultural institutes (Goethe, British Council, French) sometimes sponsor interesting events.

Athens has an active dance scene with ballet, folk, modern, jazz and experimental dance troupes. The various troupes are: The Athens Ballet; The Contemporary Dance Group of Haris Mandafounis; The Small Dance Theatre of Lia Meletopoulou; The Ilanga Dance Theatre; Bouri; the Hellenic Chorodrama; The Young Dancers and Choreographers of Katerina Rodiou; The Dance Theatre of Nafsika; The Hellenic Ballet of Rene Kabaladou; the Dora Stratou Group.

GREEK MUSIC

Greece has incredible music, or rather, musics, ranging from folk to "light popular", *rembétika* to Byzantine chanting, Theodorakis and Hadzidakis to Dionisios Savopoulos. In the folk area, keep your ear tuned to the great regional variety which still exists today. Crete has one of the richest traditions, characterised by the *lyra* (fiddle), *laoúto* (lute) and *santoúri* (hammer dulcimer). Epirus is also notable, characterised by the extensive use of the *klaríno* (clarinet) and an extraordinary, disappearing tradition of polyphonic singing. *Nisiótika* is the general name for "island music" which has its own sound, style and instruments, varying from island group to island group (the Iónian, Cycládic, Dodecanése etc.).

If you want to explore the world of *rembétika*, listen for these greats: Vassilis Tsitsanis, Markos Vamvakaris, Sotiria Bellou, Kazantzides, Papazoglou, Papaioanou, and Tsaousakis. The best single introduction to *rembétika*, however, still remains the six-volume collection "The History of Rembetika" from EMI.

Little introduction is required for Mikis Theodorakis and Manolis Hadzidakis. You'll hear their songs on every bus, boat and plane in Greece. In a very different vein is the folk-rock hero Dionisios Savopulos. Dipping into the Greek well of Byzantine and Asia Minor melodies, he draws out a unique style of contemporary folk-rock music. Another recent group which, working out of the Greek folk tradition, produces a distinctly contemporary music, is Himeriní Kolimvités (with an album by the same name from Lyra Records in Greece).

MOVIES

Going to the movies in Greece during the summer-time is a special pleasure and not to be missed. Nearly all the movie theatres that run in the summer (the others shut down) are open-air – sometimes tucked among apartment buildings whose tenants watch the film from their balconies, while in other areas, perched on a seaside promontory under rustling palm trees, stars and the moon (on Aégina, for instance). The tickets are cheap and sound-tracks are in the original language. It's also a great way to beat the dog-day heat of high-summer in Greece.

LIBRARIES & CULTURAL CENTRES

In Athens there are two main cultural centres for those who speak English, the **British Council** and the **Hellenic American Union**.

The British Council in Kolonáki Square (tel. 363-3211) has a library with a wide range of books, periodicals and newspapers. It also sponsors occasional lectures, exhibitions and performances. It is open Mon.–Fri. 9.30 a.m. to 1.30 p.m. The Hellenic American Union, Massalias 22, 4th Floor (tel. 363-7740) similarly has a library and sponsors various cultural events. It also runs several courses in Greek dance, film, language, literature etc. for foreign visitors. Open Mon.–Fri. 9.30 a.m. to 2 p.m.; Mon.–Thurs. 5.30 to 8.30 p.m.

In Thessaloníki there are also two main cultural centres for those who speak English, the **British Council**, on the corner of Egnatias and Vas. Sofias streets (tel. 235236) and the **American Centre**, in Mitropoleos St. just off Aristotelous Square (tel. 276347). Though somewhat more limited in scope, their activities are similar to those of the centres in Athens.

ENGLISH LANGUAGE BOOKSTORES

Athens has numerous bookstores which carry books in English:

Compendium, Nikis 33, located just behind Syntagma Sq. (tel. 322-6931).
Eleftheroudakis, Nikis 4, Syntagma (tel. 322-9388).
Kakoulides – The Book Nest, Panepistimiou 25–29, Stoa Megarou Athinon (tel. 322-5209).
Pantelides, Amerikis 11 (tel. 362-3673).
Lexis Bookshop, Emm. Benaki and Academias Sts 72.

NIGHTLIFE

Metropolitan "nightlife" in Greece, which is to say in Athens and Thessaloníki, can be roughly divided into four categories: bars; live music clubs with jazz and rocks; discotheques; and *boites*, *tavérnes* and clubs with live Greek music.

It should be noted first, however, that for most Greeks, the *tavérna* remains the most popular site for a night out; where you pass an evening eating, drinking and, sometimes, singing with your *paréä* (*see* "*Language*"). In fact, locales with live Greek music are almost always *tavérnes* with an additional set-up for music. In general, younger Greeks frequent the bars, music clubs and discotheques, while the locales for popular Greek music are more favourable among the older generations.

In Athens, the weekly *Athenórama* (in Greek) has an extensive listing of all the various locales and events. If you really want to find out what's going on in the city, ask a Greek friend to help you check out the listings. For information on the local music scene you can also inquire at the Pop 11 record shop, Skoufa 15, Kolonáki. However, do take note that during the late summer (July–August) many of these locales close down.

SPORTS

Greece offers a wide variety of possibilities for sports and recreation. The following is a partial listing of these activities.

WATER SKIING

You'll find facilities for water skiing at: Vouliagméni (on the coast south-east of Athens); Agrínio (Lake Trihonida); Vólos; Edessa (Lake Vegoritida); Ioánnina; Thessaloníki; numerous locations on Corfú; Haniá, Crete; Eloúnda, Crete; Kíthera; Mytilíni; Pórto-Héli; Póros; Rhodes; Skiáthos; Gerakina, Halkidikí; Kalithéa, Halkidikí; Halkída; Chíos.

SAILING

Numerous locations in Greece have sailboats for rent. There are sailing schools, housed in the naval clubs of the following cities: Athens (Paleo Fáliro); Thessaloníki; Corfú; Vólos; Syros; Kalamáta; Alexandroúpolis. Further information can be obtained from the **Sailing Federation**, 15A Xenofondos Street, Athens (tel. 323-5560, 323-6813).

WINDSURFING

You' ll find windsurf boards for rental at many popular Greek beaches, and at all the beaches run by the G.N.T.O. For information contact the **Hellenic Windsurfing Association**, 7 Filellinon Street, Athens (tel. 323-0068, 323-0330).

FISHING

Where can't you catch a fish in Greece? In the villages of most islands you will find boats and fishing tackle for hire. If you'd like some suggestions contact the **Amateur Anglers and Maritime Sports Club**, Akti Moutsopoulou in Piraeus, (tel. 451-5731) or the **Piraeus Central Harbourmaster's Office**, (tel. 451-1311).

DIVING

Greece is *not* the place to come to for scuba diving: submarine activity with diver's breathing apparatus is forbidden in all Greek waters (seas, lakes and rivers), with the aim of preserving the nation's cultural heritage of submerged antiquities. However, masks and snorkels are permitted and can add a whole other dimension to your swimming in Greek waters.

TENNIS

You'll find tennis facilities at the tennis clubs in the following cities: numerous athletic clubs and centres in Athens; Glyfáda; Kalamáki; Thessaloníki; Pátras; Corfú; Irákleion; Haniá; Lárissa; Ioánnina; Rhodes; Halkída; Vólos; Alexandroúpolis; Sérres; Agrínio; Kateríni; Véria; Kavála; Trίkala. Many hotels and resorts have tennis facilities as well.

GOLF

Greece is by no means a golfing country. Still, if you get the yen to tee-up try: The Glyfáda Golf Course and Club, tel. 894-6820 (18 holes); The Afandou Golf Club, Rhodes, tel. (0214) 51225/6 (18 holes); The Corfú Golf Club, in the Ropa Valley, tel. (0661) 94220/1 (18 holes); The Pórto Carrás Golf-course, near Neos Marmaras, Halkidikí, tel. (0375) 71381, 71221 (18 holes).

HEALTH SPAS

You'll find health spas with hydrotherapy in the following locations: Edipsós, Euboea; Eleftheron, Kavála; Kaiafa, Illia; Kaména Voúrla; Kyllini, Illia; Kíthnos, the Cycládes; Langada, Thessaloníki (also mud baths); Lefkáda, Ikaría; Loutráki, Corinth; Methana, Sarónic Gulf; Platistomo, Smokovo, Kardítsa; Therma, Ikaría; Thermopylae; Vouliagméni, Attica; Ipati.

SKIING

Most Greek mountains have good snow cover for skiing from December to March with some of the higher mountains (Olympos, Parnássus and the Píndus) skiable until May. The following mountains have ski-lifts and are almost exclusively devoted to down-hill skiing, though there are also cross-country ski rental: Mount Vermio, Náoüssa (chairlift); Métsovo (chair-lift); Mount Pélion (chair-lift); Mount Parnássus (chair-lift); Mount Vitsi, Vigla Pissoderiou; Mount Vrondou, near Sérres; Mount Dirfis, Liri; Mount Lefka Ori; Kallergi; Crete; Mount Mainalon, Ostrakina; Mount Olympus, Vrissopoules; Mount Pangeo, Kiladea Orfea; Mount Timfristos, Karpanísi; Mount Falakro.

For further information contact the **Greek Skiing and Alpine Federation**, 7 Karageorgis Street, Athens, (tel. 323-4555). Also refer to chart provided.

CAVE EXPLORATION

Greece is honey-combed with caves. Usually the local tourist police has information on where local caves are and how you go about visiting them. The following caves have facilities for public visitation: Koutoúki, Peaneía, Attica; Pérama, Ioánnina; Drongorati, Cephaloniá; Melissani, Andíparos, the Cycládes; Glyfáda and Aleopotripa at Diros, Laconía; Kokkines Petres, Halkidikí.

HIKING & MOUNTAINEERING

Greece is a paradise for hikers and mountain climbers, with extensive trails and trail systems, mountain refuges (*see chart on the following page*), and expanses of mountains and forests untouched by the tourist masses. For information on trails, maps, refuges and excursions contact the **Greek Alpine Club** in Athens at Eolou 68-70, (tel. 321-2429), with offices in most major towns in mountainous areas; the **Greek Skiing and Alpine Federation**, 7 Karageorgis Street, Athens (tel. 323-4555); the **Greek Touring Club**, 12 Politechníou St, Athens, (tel. 524-8601); and the **Federation of Excursion Clubs of Greece**, 4 Dragatsaniou St., Athens, (tel. 323-4107). Also refer to chart provided.

SPECTATOR

Greece has a limited range of spectator sports. Soccer is the main one with matches played nearly every Sunday afternoon during the season. Check the local papers for information or contact the **Soccer Federation**, 137 Syngrou, Athens, (tel. 933-6410).

Basketball is becoming the second most popular sport in Greece after soccer and the national league competition is followed keenly. Check the local papers or call the **Basketball Federation**, 11 N. Saripolou Street, Athens, (tel. 824-5125, 822-4131).

Horse racing takes place at the **Fáliron Racecourse** at the seaward end of Syngrou Avenue in Athens. There are races every Monday, Wednesday and Saturday at 6.30 p.m. For information call: 941-7761.

Mountain Refuges

The Greek Skiing and Alpine Federation has organized the following mountain refuge huts:

Mountain	Location	Altitude (Meters)	Capacity (Persons)	Information Telephone
CRETE				
Lefka Ori	Kalergi	1,680	40	(0821) 24647, Hania
Lefka Ori	Volikas	1,480	30	(0821) 24647, Hania
Psiloritis	Prinos	1,100	16	(081) 267110, Heraklion
PELOPONNESE				
Taigetos	Varvara	1,600	28	(0731) 22574 and 26444 Sparta
Parnonas	Arnomousga	1,450	35	As above
Panahaiko	Psarthi	1,500	50	(061) 273912 Patras
Panahaiko	Prassoudi	1,800	16	As above
Helmos	Pouliou Vrissi	2,100	16	323-4555 Athens
Ziria	Megali Vrissi	1,650	50	As above
Ziria	Portes	1,750	20	As above
Menalo	Ostrakina	1,540	24	(071) 21574 Tripolis
Menalo	(refuge)			(0756) 21227
CENTRAL GREECE				
Parnassus	Sarandari	1,900	20	323-4555 Athens
Parnes	Bafi	1,150	100	323-1867 Athens
Parnes	Varimbombi	600	12	246-9050 (refuge)
Iti	Trapeza	1,800	28	(0231) 26786 Lamia
Timfristos	Diavolotopos	1,840	40	(0237) 23102 Kaprenissi
Vardoussia	Pitimaliko	1,750	18	(0231) 26786 Lamia
Oxia	Karvounolaka	1,700	40	(0231) 26786 Lamia
Kitheronas	Petalo	1,000	50	554-6572 Eleusis
EUBOEA				
Dirfis	Liri	1,100	36	(0221) 25230 Halkida and (0228) 51285 (refuge)
THESSALY				
Pelion	Agriolefkes	1,350	80	(0421) 25696 Volos
Pelion	Zagora Hostel	1,600	16	As above
Ossa (Kissavos)	Kanalos	1,600	20	(0421) 220097 Larissa
Olympus	Spilios Agapitos	2,100	80	(0352) 21329 Litohoro and 21800 (refuge)
Olympus	Vrissopoules	1,900	50	323-4555 Athens
Olympus	Stavros	1,100	40	(031) 278288 Thessaloniki
Olympus	Profiti Elia	2,650	18	323-4555 Athens
MACEDONIA				
Pieria	Ano Milia	1,050	52	(0351) 23102 Katerini and 21284 (refuge)
Vermio	Seli	1,400	60	(031) 278288 Thessaloniki
Vermio	Seli	1,400	100	(0331) 26970 Veria
Vermio	Pigadia	1,450	60	(0332) 28567 Naoussa
Vermio	Vermio Hostel	1,400	18	As above
Vrondou	Lailias	1,500	60	(0321) 23724 Serres
Pangeo	Vlahika Klivia	1,500	25	(051) 23464 Kavala
Pangeo	Kilada Orfea	1,700	80	As above
Vitsi	Vigia Pissoderiou	1,650	60	(0385) 28008 Florina
Falakro	Bartiseva	1,150	20	(0521) 23054 (Drama) and 23049
Falakro	Kouri	1,400	16	(0521) 23054 (Drama)
Falakro	Horos	1,700	20	As above
EPIRUS				
Pindo Gamila	Diaselo Astrakas	2,639	28	(0651) 22138 Ioannina
Mitsikeli	Vrissi Paleohori	1,400	25	As above

LANGUAGE

in Modern Greek. When you learn a Greek word, learn where the stress falls at the same time. Each Greek word has a single stress (marked in the following list with an accent). Greek is an inflected language as well, and noun and adjective endings change according to gender, number and case. Case endings, the rules governing them, and the conjugation of Greek verbs, are beyond the scope of a guide. For visitors staying on for a long period, there are language classes at the Hellenic American Union and other teaching centres in metropolitan Athens.

SURVIVAL GREEK

"Survival Greek" is actually a misleading title for this section, for it is possible to "survive" in Greece just knowing English. Greeks have seen so many English-speaking tourists and have such strong connections with the English-speaking world (through emigration, the media, education) that you're always bound to find Greeks that can understand your basic utterances.

This section isn't so much about survival as it is about beginning to bridge the gap between you the alien tourist and the native Greek, about being perceived as a *ksénos*, a foreigner or guest, instead of a *tourísta*. Greeks put great stock in their language and are highly responsive to the efforts of foreigners who try to learn it. Precisely because Greeks so effusively appreciate your efforts, Greek can be one of the most gratifying European languages to learn. With a little study and practise on your part, you too may soon be met with the stock praise: *"Pos émathes tóso kalá ta eliniká?"* That is, "How did you learn Greek so well?"

The following crash course in Greek and listing of words and phrases will be useful to you. You'll also want to carry a pocket-sized English-Greek/Greek-English dictionary. For those who actually want to study Greek, a few textbooks and dictionaries are listed in the "Further Reading" section.

Greek is a phonetic language. There are some combinations of vowels and consonants which customarily stand for certain sounds, and some slight pronunciation changes determined by what letter follows but, generally, sounds are pronounced as they are written, without additions or omissions. Thus, learning the phonetic values of the Greek alphabet, and then reading, say, street sounds out loud, is a good beginning to getting the feel of the language.

Most Athenians have some knowledge of English, and most Greeks are delighted to find a visitor making stabs at speaking Greek. (Unlike Parisians, the Greeks do not ridicule you for making mistakes: they themselves have a hard time with Greek spelling and the complicated Greek grammar.) Whatever you can accomplish – guide book in hand – will be rewarded.

In addition to pronouncing each letter, you should remember that stress plays an important role

THE GREEK ALPHABET

Cap.	l.c.	Value	Name
A	a	a in father	alfa
B	b	v in visa	vita
G	g	gh before consonants and a, o and oo; y before e, as in year	ghama
D	d	th in then	thelta
E	e	e in let	epsilon
Z	z	z in zebra	zita
H	h	e in keep	ita
Q	q	th in theory	thita
I	i	e in keep	yota
K	k	k in king	kapa
L	l	l in million	lamda
M	m	m in mouse	mi
N	n	n in no	ni
X	x	ks in jacks	ksi
O	o	o in oh	omikron
P	p	p in pebble	pi
R	r	r in raisin	ro
S	s	s in sun	sigma
T	t	t in trireme	taf
E	e	è in keep	ipsilon
F	f	f in favour	fi
C	c	h in help	hi
Y	y	ps in copse	psi
W	w	o in oh	omega

DIPHTHONGS

Type	Value
ai	e in let
au	av or af in avert or after
ei	e in keep
eu	ev or ef
oi	e in keep
ou	oo in poor

DOUBLE CONSONANTS

mp	b at beginnings of words; mb in the middle of words
nt	d at beginnings of words; nd in the middle of words
tz	dz as in adze
gg, gk	gh at the beginnings of words; ng in the middle of words

BASIC EXPRESSIONS

yes	né	yesterday	kthes
no	óhi	now	tóra
okay	en dáksi	here/there	ethó/ekí
please	parakaló	near/far	kondá/makriá
thank you	efharistó	small/large	mikró/megálo
(very much)	pára polí	less/more	ligótero/perisótero
excuse me	signómi	quickly	grígora
it doesn't matter	then pirázi	slowly	argá, sigá
it's nothing	típota	good/bad	kaló, oréo/kakó
certainly	málista	warm/cold	zestó/krío
good day	káli méra	shower with hot water	douz me zestó neró
good evening	káli spéra	hotel	ksenothohío
good night	káli níkta	bed	kreváti
goodbye	adío	key	klithí
Greetings!/"health	yá sou, yá sas	room (with a window)	domátio (me paráthiro)
to you"	– plural or formal	entrance	ísothos
Greetings!/"rejoice"	hérete	exit	éksothos
bon voyage	kaló taksíthi	toilet	toualéta
welcome	kalós ílthateh	women's	yinekón
good luck	kalí tíhi	men's	ándron
How are you?	ti kánis, ti káneth	store	magazí
	– plural or formal	kiosk	períptero
fine, well (in response)	kalá	open/shut	aniktós/klistós
so so (in response)	étsi kétsi	What time does it	ti óra anígi/klíni?
pleased to meet you	hárika (polí)	open/close?	
(very much)		post office	takithromío
I also, me too	kai egó	stamp	grammatósima
Have you...?	éheteh..?	letter	grámma
Is there...?	éhi...?	envelope	fákelos
How much does it cost?	póso káni?	postcard	kárta
It's (too) expensive	íneh (polí) akrivó	telephone	tiléfono
How much?	póso?	bank	trápeza
How many?	pósa?	bakery	foúrnos
Do you have	éheteh éna	embassy	presvía
a room?	domátio?	consulate	prokseníon
Can I...?	boró na...?	marketplace	agorá
When?	póteh...?	pharmacy	farmakío
Where is...?	pou íneh..?	doctor	yatrós
From where...?	ápo póu...?	hospital	nosokomío
Where are you from?	ápo póu ísteh?	police	astinomía
	– sing./formal	station	stathmós
What is your name?	pos seh/sas léneh?	stop (on a bus)	stási
	– sing./formal	bus/train	leoforío/tréno
Do you speak English?	milás/miláteh angliká?	automobile	aftokínito
	–(sing./plural-formal)	boat	karávi, vapóri
Do you understand?	katálaves?	petrol station	venzináthiko
What time is it?	tí óra íneh?	bike/moped	pothílato/móto-pothílato
What time will it leave?	ti óra tha fígi?	on foot	me ta póthia
I don't...	then + verb	ticket	isitírio
I want	thélo	road/street	thrómos/othós
I have	ého	beach	paralía
I am/we are	ímeh/ímasteh	church	eklisía
I understand	katalavéno, katalávo	ancient ruins	arhéa
I pay	pliróno	centre	kéntro
I go	pigéno, páo	square	platía
it must/I must	prépi na	sea	thálassa
I need a –	kriázomeh éna/mía –	village	horió
today	símera	spring	pigí
tomorrow	ávrio		

348

NUMBERS

1	*éna/mía*
2	*thío*
3	*tría/tris*
4	*tésera*
5	*péndeh*
6	*éksi*
7	*eptá*
8	*októ*
9	*enéa*
10	*théka*
11	*éntheka*
12	*thótheka*
13	*thekatría*
14	*thekatésera*
20	*íkosi*
21	*íkosi éna*
30	*triánda*
40	*saránda*
50	*penínda*
60	*eksínda*
70	*evthomínda*
80	*ogthónda*
90	*enenínda*
100	*ekató*
150	*ekatopenínda*
200	*thiakósia*
300	*triakósia*
400	*tetrakósia*
1000	*hília*

DAYS OF THE WEEK

Monday	*theftéra*
Tuesday	*tríti*
Wednesday	*tetárti*
Thursday	*pémpti*
Friday	*paraskeví*
Saturday	*sávato*
Sunday	*kiriakí*

UNTRANSLATABLE WORDS

kéfi – high spirits, a good time with your *paréä*

paréä – your group of close friends, your "gang"

kaïmós – is in a sense the opposite of *kéfi*, one's life-suffering, sadness

palikári – a good fellow (honourable, brave, intelligent etc.); a rough synonym is *levéndis*

filótimo – adjective meaning literally "love of honour"

mángas – a street tough, a "cool dude"

re – short for *moré*, baby, kid, dummy; a word thrown in when addressing another person, a buddy in that typically male Greek rough-affectionate manner

malákas – literally "masturbator", often combined with *re* (*re malákas*); can be directed to friends affectionately or to others more antagonistically

pethiá – "the boys", fellows, guys

alítis – a bum, roughly the opposite of *palikári*

lipón – well, so, now then

élla! – Come! Come on!

oríste(?) – Can I help you?

po po po! – Well well! What have we here!

ópa! – Look out!; also, at a music *tavérna* for example, "way to go!" "all right!" etc.

THE LANGUAGE OF GESTURES

Greek is a gestural language; you don't speak it with your hands in your pockets or with your head still. The body and its movements are signs which form an integral part of the communicative process. You can learn this aspect of Greek only through close observation. Two of the most common of these gestures are those indicating "yes" and "no". "No" is often communicated by jerking the head and chin up and back sharply. This is often a very slight movement. Sometimes, in fact, only the eyebrows or eyes make this upward gesture. The gesture indicating "yes" is a rather gentler one, a slow downward angling of the head.

FURTHER READING

ANCIENT HISTORY & CULTURE

Bowra, Maurice. *The Greek Experience*. London: Weidenfeld and Nicolson, 1957.

Burn, A.R. *The Pelican History of Greece*. Harmondsworth: Penguin, 1966.

Dodds, E.R. *The Greeks and the Irrational*. Berkeley and Los Angeles: U. of California Press, 1951.

Finley, M.I. *The Ancient Greeks*. Harmondsworth: Penguin, 1963.

Finley, M.I. *The World of Odysseus*. New York:

Viking Press, 1954.

Graves, Robert. *The Greek Myths*. Harmondsworth: Penguin Books, 1986.

Hammond, N.G.L. *A History of Greece to 322 B.C.* Oxford University Press, 1965.

Kerenyi, K. *The Gods of the Greeks*. London: Thames and Hudson, 1951.

Kerenyi, K. *The Heroes of the Greeks*. London: Thames and Hudson, 1951.

Kitto, H.D.F. *The Greeks*. Harmondsworth: Penguin, 1951.

Pollitt, J.J. *Art and Experience in Classical Greece*. Cambridge: CUP, 1972.

Renfrew, Colin. *The Emergence of Civilization: The Cyclades and the Aegean in the Third Millennium B.C.* New York: Simon and Schuster, 1970.

Thompson, George. *Aeschylus and Athens*. London: Lawrence and Wishart, 1980.

Vernant, J.P. *Myth and Thought*. London: Routledge & Kegan Paul, 1983.

BYZANTINE HISTORY & CULTURE

The Alexiad of Anna Comnena. Trans. By E.R.A. Sewter Harmondsworth: Penguin, 1969.

Michael Psellu. *Fourteen Byzantine Rulers*. Harmondsworth: Penguin, 1966.

Runciman, Steven. *Byzantine Style and Civilization*. Harmondsworth: Penguin, 1975.

Sherrard, Philip. *Byzantium*. New York: Time-Life Books, 1966.

Talbot Rice, David. *The Art of the Byzantine Era*. London: Thames and Hudson, 1963.

Talbot Rice, David. *The Byzantines*. London: Thames and Hudson, 1962.

MODERN HISTORY & CULTURE

Alexiou, Margaret. *The Ritual Lament in Greek Tradition*. Cambridge: Cambridge U. Press, 1974.

Beaton, Roderick. *Folk Poetry of Modern Greece*. Cambridge: Cambridge U. Press, 1980.

Campbell, John. *Honor, family and patronage: A study of institutions and moral values in a Greek mountain community*. Oxford: Oxford University Press, 1964.

Clogg, Richard. *A Short History of Greece*. Cambridge: Cambridge, 1979.

Danforth, Loring H. and Tsiaras, Alexander. *The Death Rituals of Rural Greece*. Princeton: PUP, 1982.

Du Boulay, Juliet. *Portrait of a Greek Mountain Village*. Oxford: Clarendon Press, 1974.

Eudes, Domenique. *The Kapetanios: Partisans and Civil War in Greece, 1943–1949*. NY and London: Monthly Review Press, 1972.

Fourtouni, Eleni. *Greek Women in Resistance*. New Haven: Thelphini Press, 1986.

Friedl, Ernestine. *Vasilika: A Village in Modern Greece*. New York: Holt, Rinehart and Winston, 1962.

Herzfeld, Michael. *Ours Once More: Folklore, Ideology and the Making of Modern Greece*. Austin: University of Texas Press, 1982.

Mackridge, Peter. *The Modern Greek Language*. Oxford: Oxford U. Press. 1985.

Matthews, Kevin. *Memoirs of a Mountain War, Greece: 1944–1949*. London: Longman, 1972.

McNeill, William. *Metamorphisis of Greece Since World War II*. Oxford: Blackwell, 1982.

Mouzelis, Nicos P. *Modern Greece: Facets of Underdevelopment*. London: MacMillan Press, 1978.

Papandreou, Andreas. *Democracy at Gun-point*. Harmondsworth: Penguin, 1972.

Sarafis, Marion. *Greece: From Resistance to Civil War*. Nottingham: Spokesman, 1980.

Tsoucalas, Constantine. *The Greek Tragedy*. Harmondsworth: Penguin, 1969.

Woodhouse, C.M. *Modern Greece: A Short History*. London: Faber and Faber, 1984.

ANCIENT GREEK LITERATURE

Aeschylus. *The Oresteia*. Trans. by Robert Fagles. New York: Viking Press, 1975.

Aesop. *Fables of Aesop*. Trans. by S.A. Hanford. Harmondsworth: Penguin, 1954.

Aristophanes. *Lysistrata/ The Acharnians/ The Clouds*. Trans. by A.H. Sommerstein. Harmondsworth: Penguin, 1973.

Aristotle. *The Nicomachean Ethics*. Trans. by Martin Ostwald. Indianapolis: Bobbs-Merrill, 1962.

Grene, David and Lattimore. *Greek Tragedies*. (3 vols.). Chicago: U. of Chicago Press, 1968.

Hesiod. *Theogony*. Trans. by Norman Brown. Indianapolis: Bobbys-Merrill, 1955.

Herodotus. *The Histories*. Trans. by A.R. Burn. Harmondsworth: Penguin, 1972.

Homer. *The Iliad*. Trans. by Robert Fitzgerald. New York: Anchor Books, 1975.

Homer. *The Odyssey*. Trans. by Robert Fitzgerald. New York: Anchor Books, 1963.

Plato. *The Republic*. Trans. by H.D.P. Lee. Harmondsworth: Penguin, 1955.

Plato. *The Symposium*. Trans. by Walter Hamilton. Harmondsworth: Penguin, 1951.

Sappho. Trans. by Mary Barnard. Los Angeles: U. of California Press, 1958.

Thucydides. *The Peloponnesian Wars*. Trans by Crawley. New York: Modern Library, 1951.

Trypanis, Constantine. *The Penguin Book of Greek Verse*. Harmondsworth: Penguin Books, 1971.

MODERN LITERATURE BY GREEKS

Barnstone, Willis (ed.). *Eighteen Texts: writings by contemporary Greek authors*. Cambridge: Harvard UP, 1972.

Cavafy, C.P. *Collected Poems*. Trans. by Edmund Keeley and Philip Sherrard. Princeton: Princeton U. Press, 1975.

Dalven, Rae (trans.). *Modern Greek Poetry*. (Anthology). New York: Russell and Russell, 1971.

Elytis, Odysseus. *The Axion Esti*. Pittsburgh: U. of Pittsburgh Press, 1974.

Elytis. *Selected Poems*. Trans. by Edmund Keeley and Philip Sherrard. London and NY: Viking Penguin, 1981.

Frair, Kimon (trans.). *Modern Greek Poetry*. (Anthology.) New York: Simon and Shuster, 1973.

Karapanou, Margarita. *Kassandra and the Wolf*. Trans. by N.C. Germanacos. New York: HBJ, 1976.

Kazantzakis, Nikos. *Zorba the Greek*. New York: Simon and Schuster/Touchstone, 1971.

Kazantzakis, Nikos. *Christ Recrucified (The Greek Passion)*. New York: Simon and Schuster/ Touchstone, 1981.

Haviaris, Stratis. *When the Tree Sings*. New York: Simon and Schuster, 1979.

Haviaris, Stratis. *The Heroic Age*. New York: Penguin, 1985.

Makriyannis, Yannis. *The Memoirs of General Makriyannis, 1797–1964*. London: OUP, 1966.

Myrivilis, Stratis. *The Schoolmistress with the Golden Eyes*. London: Hutchinson, 1964.

Ritsos, Yannis. *Ritsos in Parentheses*. Trans. by Edmund Keeley. Princeton: Princeton U. Press, 1979.

Ritsos, Yannis. *Yannis Ritsos: Selected Poems*. Trans. by Nikos Stangos: Penguin, 1974.

Papadiamantis, Alexandros. *The Murderess*. Trans. by Peter Levi, London: Writers and Readers, 1983.

Politis, Linos. *A History of Modern Greek Literature*. Oxford: Clarendon Press, 1973.

Seferis, George. *Collected Poems*. Trans. by Edmund Keeley. Princeton: PUP. 1981.

Sikelianos, Angelos. *Selected Poems*. Princeton: PUP, 1979.

Siotis, Dino (ed.). *Ten Women Poets of Greece*. San Francisco: Wire Press, 1982.

Taktsis, Costas. *The Third Wedding Wreath*. Trans. by John Choiles. Athens: Hermes Publishers, 1985.

Tsirkas, Stratis. *Drifting Cities*. Trans. by Kay Cicellis. New York: Alfred Knopf, 1974.

Vassilikos, Vassilis. *Z*. New York: Farrar, Strauss and Giroux, 1968.

FOREIGN WRITERS ON GREECE

Andrews, Kevin. *Athens Alive*. Athens: Hermes Press.

Andrews, Kevin. *The Flight of Ikaros*. Harmondsworth: Penguin, 1984.

Boleman-Herring, Elizabeth. *Greek Unorthodox*. Foundation Publishing, 1990.

Durrell, Lawrence. *Prospero's Cell*. London: Faber and Faber, 1945.

Durrell, Lawrence. *Reflections on a Marine Venus*. London: Faber and Faber, 1953.

Durrell, Lawrence. *Bitter Lemons*. London: Faber and Faber, 1978.

Fowles, Jophn. *The Magus*. London: Cape, 1977.

Gage, Nicholas. *Eleni*. London: Collins, 1983.

Greenhalgh, Peter and Edward Eliopoulos. *Deep into Mani*. London: Faber and Faber, 1985.

Levi, Peter. *Hill of Kronos*. New York: Penguin, 1984.

Miller, Henry. *The Colossus of Maroussi*. New York: New Directions, 1958.

Renault, Mary. *The Last of the Wine*. London: Sceptre, 1986.

TRAVEL BOOKS & GUIDES

Constantine, David. *Early Greek Travellers and the Hellenic Idea*. Cambridge: CUP, 1984.

Dubin, Marc. *Greece on Foot*. Leicester/London: Cordee, 1986.

Durrell, Lawrence. *The Greek Islands*. New York: Viking Press, 1978.

Durrell, Lawrence. *Mani: Travels in Southern Greece*. Harmondsworth: Penguin, 1984.

Holst, Gail. *Road to Rembetika*. Athens: Denise Harvey, 1975.

Holst, Gail. *Theodorakis: Myth and Politics in Modern Greek Music*. Amsterdam: Adolf Hakkert, 1980.

Hauxley and Taylor. *Flowers of Greece and the Aegean*. Chatto and Windus, 1971.

Leigh Fermor, Patrick. *Roumeli: Travels in Northern Greece*. Harmondswroth: Penguin, 1984.

Melas, Evi. *The Greek Islands*. Exeter: Webb and Bower, 1985.

Melas, Evi. *Temples and Sanctuaries of Ancient Greece: A Companion Guide*. London: Thames and Hudson.

Millard, Anne. *Usburne Pocket Guide to Ancient Greece: Everyday Life in Greek Times*. London: Usburne, 1981.

Pausanias. *Description of Greece*. 2 vols. Trans. by Peter Levi. Harmondsworth: Penguin, 1979.

Petrides, Ted. *Greek Dances*. Athens: Lycabettus Press, 1975.

Sfikas, George. *The Mountains of Greece*. Athens: Efstiadis, 1979.

Sfikas, George. *Trees and Shrubs of Greece*. Athens: Efstiadis, 1978.

Sfikas, George. *Wild Flowers of Greece*. Athens: Efstiadis, 1976.

Spencer, Terence. *Fair Greece Sad Relic*. London: 1974.

Stoneman, Richard (ed.). *A Literary Companion to Travel in Greece*. Harmondsworth: Penguin, 1984.

Stubbs, Joyce. *The Home Book of Greek Cookery*. London: Faber and Faber, 1963.

Stavroulakis. *Cookbook of the Jews of Greece*: Athens: Lycabettus, 1985.

Tsigakou, Fani-Maria. *The Rediscovery of Greece*. London: Thames and Hudson, 1981.

Zenfell, Martha Ellen (ed.). *Insight Cityguide: Athens*. Apa Publications, 1990.

Zenfell, Martha Ellen (ed.), *Insight Guide: Greek Islands*. Apa Publications, 1989.

TEXTS FOR LEARNING GREEK

Farmakidhes, Anne. *A Manual of Modern Greek*. New Haven: Yale Univ. Press, 1983, 2nd ed.

Rassias, John, and Peter and Chrysanthi Bien. *Demotic Greek*. Hanover, NH and London: University Press of New England, 1983.

Sofroniou, S.A. *Modern Greek*. New York: David McKay and London: Hodder & Stoughton, 1983.

Stone, Tom. *Greek Handbook*. Athens: Lycabettus Press, 1982. (A handy emergency phrase book.)

USEFUL ADDRESSES

TOURIST INFORMATION

If you would like tourist information about Greece before or during your trip, write, call or visit the nearest **Greek National Tourist Organisation** known as the GNTO, or EOT in Greece. There are 15 regional GNTO offices located across the country. The most complete GNTO is centrally located in Syntagma Square in Athens at this address:

EOT, Information Desk, National Bank of Greece, Syntagma Sq., 2 Karageorgis Servias St., (tel: [01] 322-2545, 323-4130).

The Greek Tourist Police, located in most large cities, can also be helpful in providing you with information about hotels and other services. They can also help you address a wide variety of travel-related questions and problems (*see* "*Emergencies*").

For information and assistance related to motoring contact **ELPA**, the Greek Automobile Association, which grants the same help to members of home-country auto clubs as it does to its own members:

ELPA, 2–4 Messogeíon St., Athens Tower B (tel. 779-1615) and 6 Amerikís St., near Syntagma (tel. 363-8632).

GREEK NATIONAL TOURIST ORGANISATION OFFICES

The Greek National Tourist Organisation has offices in the following countries:

• USA & Canada

Head Office, Olympic Tower, 645 Fifth Ave., 5th Floor, New York, New York 10022 (tel. [212] 421-5777, tlx. 640125).

168 North Michigan Ave., Chicago, Illinois 60601 (tel. [312] 782-1084, tlx. 283468).

National Bank of Greece Building, 31 State Street, Boston, Massachusetts 02109 (tel. [617] 227-7366, tlx. 940493).

611 West Sixth Street, Suite 1998 Los Angeles, California 90017 (tel. [213] 626-6696, tlx. 686441).

1233 Rue De La Montagne Montreal, Quebec H3G 1Z2, Canada (tel. [514] 871-1535, tlx. 05560021).

80 Bloor Street, Suite 406 Toronto, Ontario M5S 2V1 Canada (tel. [416] 968-2220, tlx. 06218845).

• Offices Abroad

Australia & New Zealand: Greek National Tourist Organisation, 51-57 Pitt St., Sydney N.S.W. 2000 (tel. 241-1663/4).

Austria: Griechische Zentrale fur, Fremdenverkehr, Karntner Ring 5, 1015 Vienna (tel. 525317/8, tlx. 111816).

Belgium: Office National Hellenique de Tourisme, 62-66 Boulevard de L'Imperatrice, 1000 Brussels (tel. 513-0206, 513-2712, tlx. 24044).

Denmark: Det Graeske Turistbureau, Vester Fartmagsgade 3, DK 1606 Copenhagen (tel. 123063).

Finland: Kreikan Valtion Matkailutoimisto, Stora Robertsgatan 3-5 C38, 00120 Helsingfors, Helsinki 12 (tel. 607552, 607113).

France: Office National Hellenique de Tourisme, 3 Avenue de L'Opera, Paris 75001 (tel. 260-6534, tlx. 680345).

Germany: Frankfurt, Griechische Zentrale fur, Fremdenverkehr, Neue Mainzer Str. 22, 6 Frankfurt/Main 1 (tel. 236-561/2/3, tlx. 412034).

Hamburg: Griechische Zentrale fur, Fremdenverkehr, 2000 Hamburg 36, Never Wall 35 (tel. 366910, 366973).

Munich: Griechische Zentrale fur, Fremdenverkehr, Pacelli Str. 2, 8000 Munich 2 (tel. 222035/6, tlx. 528126).

Italy: Rome, Ente Nazionale Ellenico per il Turismo, Via L. Bissolati 78-80, 00187 Roma (tel. 474-4249, 474-4301, tlx. 611331).

Milan: Ente Nazional Elenico per il Turismo, Paizza Diaz 1, (Ang. Via Rastrelli), Milan (tel. 860-470, 860-477, tlx. 62331).

Japan: Greek National Tourist Organisation, No. 11 Mori Building, 2-6-4 Toranomon, Minato-Ku, Tokyo 105 (tel. 503-5001/2, tlx. 2225529).

Netherlands: Griekse Nationale Organizatie Voor,

Toerisme, Leidsestraat 13, NS Amsterdam (tel. 254-212/3, tlx. 15465).
Norway: Den Greske Stats Turistbyra, Ovre Slottsgatan 15 B, 0157 Oslo 1 (tel. 426501/2, tlx. 74025).
Saudi Arabia: Embassy of Greece/Office of Tourism and Information, Madina Road, City Centre, P.O. Box 13262/Code No. 21493, Jeddah (tel. 667-6280).
Spain: Oficina Nacional Helenica de Turismo, Alberto Aguilera 17, Madrid 15 (tel. 248-4889/90, tlx. 45796).
Sweden: Grekiska Statens Turistbyra, Birger Jarlsgaten 8 IV, 2 P.O. Box 5298, 10246 Stockholm 5 (tel. 210930, tlx. 10443).
Switzerland: Griechische Zentrale fur, Fremdenverkehr, Gottfried Keller Strasse 7, 8001 Zurich (tel. 251-8487/8/9, tlx. 57720).
United Kingdom and Ireland: Greek National Tourist Organisation, 195-197 Regent St., London WIR 8DR (tel. 734-5997, tlx. 21122).

For all offices listed above, the cable address is "GRECTOUR" followed by the name of the city concerned.

In Mexico and South America the Greek National Tourist Organisation is represented by the following governmental agencies:

Argentina: Embajada de Grecia, Avenida Pte. Rocke Saenz, Pena 547, Buenos Aires, R.Argentina.
Brazil: Embaixada da Grecia/Escritorio de Imprensa, Caixa Postal 12.2604, SHI-SULQ1 11 Conj. 01 Casa 11, Brasilia D-F.
Mexico: Embajada de Grecia, Paseo de las Palmas 2060, Colonia Lamas Reforma, Mexico, D.F. 11020.
Venezuela: Embajada de Grecia/Press Office, Avenida San Gabriel 60, Alta Florida, Caracas, Venezuela.

BANKS

GREEK BANKS

National Bank of Greece, 2 Karageorgi Servias St. (tel. 321-0411).
Commercial Bank of Greece, 11 Sophokleous St. (tel. 321-0911).
Ionian and Popular Bank, 45 Panepistimiou Ave. (tel. 322-5501).
Bank of Attica, 19 Panepistimiou Ave. (tel. 324-7415).
Bank of Greece, 21 Panepistimiou Ave. (tel. 320-1111).
Credit Bank, 40 Stadiou St. (tel. 324-5111).

OVERSEAS BANKS

Algemene Bank, 3 Paparigopoulou St. (tel. 324-3973).
American Express Bank, 31 Panepistimiou Ave. (tel. 323-5401).
Arab Bank, 10 Stadiou St. (tel. 325-0823).

Arab-Hellenic Bank, 43 Panepistimiou Ave. (tel. 325-0823).
Bank of America, 39 Panepistimiou Ave. (tel. 325-1901).
Bank of Novia Scotia, 37 Panepistimiou Ave. (tel. 324-3891).
Bank Saderat, 25 Panepistimiou Ave. (tel. 324-9531).
Bankers Trust, 3 Stadiou St. (tel. 322-9835).
Banque Franco-Hellenique de Commerce Internationale et Maritime, 12 Amalias Ave. (tel. 323-9701).
Banque Nationale de Paris, 5 Koumbari St. (tel. 364-3713).
Barclays Bank, 15 Voukourestiou St. (tel. 364-4311).
Chase Manhattan, 3 Korai St. (tel. 323-7711).
Citibank, 8 Othonos St. (tel. 322-7471); Kolonaki Sq. (tel. 361-8619); 47–49 Akti Miaouli Ave., Piraeus. (tel. 452-3511).
Credit Banque Commercial de France, 20 Amalias Ave. (tel. 324-1831).
Grindlays Bank, 7 Merlin St. (tel. 362-4601); 15 Akti Miaouli Ave., Piraeus (tel. 411-1753).
Midland Bank, Kolonaki Square (British Council building) (tel. 364-7410); 93 Akti Miaouli Ave., Piraeus (tel. 413-6403).
Morgan Grenfell, 19–20 Kolonaki Sq. (tel. 360-6456).
National Westminster Bank, 24 Stadiou St. (tel. 325-0924); 7 Merarhias St., Piraeus (tel. 411-7415).
Royal Bank of Scotland, 61 Akti Miaouli Ave., Piraeus (tel. 452-7483).
Société General, 23 Ippokratous St. (tel. 364-2010).

AIRLINE OFFICES

Aeroflot, 14 Xenofondos St. (tel. 322-0986).
Aerolineas Argentinas, 5 Mitropoleos St. (tel. 324-0233).
Air Canada, 10d Othonos St. (tel. 322-3206).
Air France, 4 Karageorgi Servias St. (tel. 355-5095–7).
Air India, 15 Omirou St. (tel. 360-3584).
Air Lanka, 31–33 Voulis St. (tel. 324-9098).
Air Zimbabwe, 39 Panepistimiou Ave. (tel. 323-9101–2).
Alitalia, 10 Nikis St. (tel. 324-4383–8).
Austrian Airlines, 8 Othonos St. (tel. 323-0844–6).
Balkan-Bulgarian Airlines, 23 Nikis St. (tel. 323-7547).
Biman-Airlines of Bangladesh, 15 Panepistimiou Ave. (tel. 324-1116).
British Airways, 10 Othonos St. (tel. 322-2521–5).
Canadian Pacific, 4 Karageorgi Servias St. (tel. 323-0344–7).
China Airlines, 5 Mitropoleos St. (tel. 322-6686).
CSA, 15 Panepistimiou Ave. (tel. 323-0174).
Cyprus Airways, 10 Filellinon St. (tel. 324-7801–3).
Egyptair, 10 Othonos St. (tel. 323-3575–7).
El Al, 8 Othonos St. (tel. 323-0116–8).
Ethiopian Airlines, 17 Filellinon St. (tel. 322-4551/3).

Finnair, 16 Nikis St. (tel. 325-5234–5).
Gulf Air, 23 Nikis St. (tel. 322-6684).
Iberia, 8 Xenofondos St. (tel. 324-5514–5).
Icelandair, 5 Syngrou Ave. (tel. 922-8263).
Interflug, 20 Panepistimiou Ave. (tel. 362-4808–9).
Iranair, 16 Panepistimiou Ave. (tel. 360-7611).
Japan Airlines, 4 Amalias Ave. (tel. 324-8211–5).
JAT, 4 Voukourestiou St. (tel. 323-6429).
Kenya Airways, 5 Stadiou St. (tel. 324-7000).
KLM, 2 Karageorgi Servias St. (tel. 325-5041).
Korean Air, 6 Psylla St. (tel. 324-7511).
LOT, 4 Amalias Ave. (tel. 322-1121).
Lufthansa, 11 Vasilissis Sophias Ave. (tel. 369-2511).
Malev, 15 Panepistimiou Ave. (tel. 324-1116).
Middle East Airlines, 10 Filellinon St.
(tel. 322 6911–5).
Olympic Airways, 96 Syngrou Ave. (tel. 961-6161).
Pakistan International Airlines, 15 Panepistimiou
Ave. (tel. 323-1931).
Pan Am, 4 Othonos St. (tel. 323-5242).
Philippine Airlines, 15 Panepistimiou Ave.
(tel. 324-1116).
Royal Air Maroc, 5 Mitropoleos St.
(tel. 324-4302–4).
Sabena, 8 Othonos St. (tel. 323-6821).
SAS, 6 Sina St. (tel. 363-4447–9).
Saudia, 30 Amalias Ave. (tel. 322-8211).
Singapore Airlines, 9 Xenofondos St.
(tel. 323-9111–5).
South African Airways, 12–14 Karageorgi Servias
St. (tel. 322-9007).
Sudan Airways, 44 Amalias Ave. (tel. 324-4716–7).
Swissair, 4 Othonos St. (tel. 323-1871).
Syrianair, 39 Panepistimiou Ave. (tel. 323-8711–2).
TAP, 31–33 Voulis St. (tel. 325-1711).
Thai International, 3–5 Lekka St. (tel. 324-3241–3).
Tunis Air, 14 Xenofondos St. (tel. 322-0104–5).
Turkish Airlines, 19 Filellinon St. (tel. 322-0561).
TWA, 8 Xenofondos St. (tel. 324-4764).
UTA, 31–33 Voulis St. (tel. 324-9300).
Varig, 10 Othonos St. (tel. 322-6743).
VIASA, 5 Mitropoleos St. (tel. 324-0233).
Virgin Atlantic Airways, 12–14 Mitropoleos St.
(tel. 323-0434).
Yemenia, 9 Patission St. (tel. 524-5912).
Zambia Airways, 15 Panepistimiou Ave.
(tel. 413-3244–5).

EMBASSIES & CONSULATES

All embassies are open from Monday through
Friday, usually from 8 a.m. until 2 p.m.

Algeria: 14 Vasiliou Constantinou St. (tel. 751-3560).
Argentina: 59 Vasilissis Sophias Ave. (tel. 722-4753).
Australia: 37 Dimitris Soutsou St. (tel. 644-7303).
Austria: 26 Alexandras Ave. (tel. 821-1036).
Belgium: 3 Sekeri St. (tel. 361-7886).
Brazil: 14 Kolonaki Sq. (tel. 721-3039).
Bulgaria: 33 Stratigou Kallari St. (tel. 647-8105).
Canada: 4 Gennadiou St. (tel. 723-9511).

China: 2a Krinon St. (tel. 672-3282).
Columbia: 91 Marathonodromo St. (tel. 647-4457).
Cyprus: 16 Herodotou St. (tel. 723-7883).
Czechoslovakia: 6 George Seferis St. (tel. 671-3755).
Denmark: 11 Vasilissis Sophias Ave. (tel. 360-8315).
Egypt: 2 Vasilissis Sophias Ave. (tel. 361-8612).
European Community: 2 Vasilissis Sophias Ave.
(tel. 751-9795).
Finland: 1 Eratosthenous St. (tel. 701-2122).
France: 7 Vasilissis Sophias Ave. (tel. 361-1665).
Germany: 10 Vasilissis Sophias St., Maroussi.
(tel. 369-4111).
Hungary: 16 Kalvou St. (tel. 671-4889).
Iceland: 5 Paraschou St. (tel. 672-6154).
India: 4 Meleagrou St. (tel. 721-6227).
Iran: 16 Stratigou Kallari St. (tel. 647-1436).
Ireland: 7 Vasiliou Constantinou St. (tel. 723-2771).
Israel: 1 Marathonodromou St. (tel. 671-9530).
Italy: 2 Sekeri St. (tel. 361-1722).
Japan: 2 Mesogeion Ave. (tel. 775-8101).
Jordan: 30 Pan Zervou St. (tel. 647-4161).
Korea: 1 Erotasthenous St. (tel. 701-2122).
Lebanon: 26 Kifissias Ave. (tel. 778-5158).
Liberia: 2 Efplias St., Piraeus. (tel. 453-1046).
Luxembourg: 12 Platanos St., Piraeus.
(tel. 417-9515).
Mexico: 5–7 Vasiliou Constantinou St.
(tel. 723-0754).
Morocco: 14 Mousson St. (tel. 647-4209).
Netherlands: 7 Vasiliou Constantinou St.
(tel. 723-9701).
New Zealand: 15 An. Tsoha St. (tel. 641-0311).
Norway: 7 Vasiliou Constantinou St.
(tel. 724-6173).
Pakistan: 6 Loukianou St. (tel. 729-0214).
Panama: 21 Vasilissis Sophias Ave. (tel. 360-2992).
Paraguay: 2 Alopekis St. (tel. 724-9511).
Peru: 105–107 Vasilissis Sophias Ave.
(tel. 641-1221).
Philippines: 9 Xenofondos St. (tel. 324-1615).
Poland: 22 Chrissanthemon St. (tel. 671-6917).
Portugal: 19 Loukianou St. (tel. 729-0096).
Rumania: 7 Emmanuel Benaki St. (tel. 671-8020).
Saudi Arabia: 71 Marathonodromou St.
(tel. 671-6911).
South Africa: 124 Kifissias Ave. (tel. 692-2125).
Spain: 29 Vasilissis Sophias Ave. (tel. 721-4885).
Sweden: 7 Vasiliou Constantinou St. (tel. 729-0421).
Switzerland: 2 Iassiou St. (tel. 723-0364).
Syria: 79 Marathonodromou St. (tel. 671-1604).
Thailand: 23 Tiagetou St. (tel. 671-7969).
Turkey: 8 Vasiliou Georgiou St. (tel. 724-5915).
United Kingdom: 1 Ploutarchou St. (tel. 723-6211).
United States of America: 91 Vasilissis Sophias Ave.
(tel. 721-2951).
USSR: 28 Nikiforou Lytra St. (tel. 672-5235).
Uruguay: 1c Lykavittou St. (tel. 360-2635).
Yugoslavia: 106 Vasilissis Sophias Ave.
(tel. 777-4344).

ART/PHOTO CREDITS

Photography by

INDEX

R

S

T